U.S. Court Cases

Revised Edition

U.S. COURT CASES

Revised Edition

Volume 1

Law and the Courts

Court Cases:

Abington School District v. Schempp —
Genesee Chief v. Fitzhugh

Edited by
Thomas Tandy Lewis
St. Cloud State University

SALEM PRESS
Pasadena, California   Hackensack, New Jersey

∞ The paper used in these volumes conforms to the American National Standard for Permanence of Paper for Printed Library Materials, Z39.48-1992 (R1997).

Some of the essays in this work originally appeared in the following Salem Press sets: *Criminal Justice* (2006), *Encyclopedia of the U.S. Supreme Court* (2001), *Great Events from History: The Nineteenth Century* (2007), *Great Events from History: The Twentieth Century* (2008), *U.S. Court Cases* (1999), and *U.S. Supreme Court* (2007). New material has been added.

Library of Congress Cataloging-in-Publication Data
U.S. court cases / editor, Thomas Tandy Lewis. — Rev. ed.
    p. cm. — (Magill's choice)
    Includes bibliographical references and index.
    ISBN 978-1-58765-672-9 (set : alk. paper)
    ISBN 978-1-58765-673-6 (vol. 1 : alk. paper)
    ISBN 978-1-58765-674-3 (vol. 2 : alk. paper)
    ISBN 978-1-58765-675-0 (vol. 3 : alk. paper)
    1. Law—United States—Cases. 2. Courts—United States. I. Lewis, Thomas
T. (Thomas Tandy) II. Title: US court cases. III. Title: United States court cases.
    KF385.A4U15 2010
    347.73'1—dc22
                                                                    2010019782

CONTENTS

Law and the Courts

Court Cases

CONTENTS

CONTENTS

PUBLISHER'S NOTE

U.S. Court Cases, Revised constitutes such a massive revision of the set's 1999 edition that it might justly be considered a wholly new work. Its 674 essays covering 700 individual cases more than triple the 211 essays on cases of the original edition, making it almost certainly the largest collection of articles on individual court cases available in any compact reference work. Moreover, more than 25 percent of the original essays have been replaced by longer essays. In addition to 11 overview essays placing the cases in broader historical and legal perspectives, the set also has 5 appendixes including 3 new to this set: a Glossary, a Time Line of Cases, and a Categorized List of Entries.

U.S. Courts

The least understood branches of American government may be the judiciary branches at the state and federal levels. Actions undertaken by officials and members of the various state and federal executive and legislative branches tend to be more visible than what judges and justices do. It is not because American courts work in secret; they do not. The difference is due to the fact that top executive and legislative offices are elected by citizens who want to know what their political leaders do after they are elected. By contrast, most high-level state judges and all federal judges and Supreme Court justices are appointed. Judges tend to labor away from the public eye, and only their most dramatic decisions generally attract public attention. Some court rulings—particularly those of the U.S. Supreme Court—do attract a great deal of attention, but these are in the minority. As the essays in these volumes demonstrate, however, there have been a great many less well-known cases that have had profound impacts on American law.

Despite their comparative anonymity, American courts play a role in interpreting, applying, and, occasionally, modifying laws that is comparable in importance to that of the legislative bodies that create the laws and the executive branches charged with enforcing them. Under the common-law tradition and the practices that have evolved along with the U.S. Constitution, decisions passed down by the courts become part of American law. For this reason alone they merit attention. Moreover, the processes by which cases reach the courts and contribute to the ever-changing U.S. legal system are themselves of great interest. The stories of individual court cases offer often poignant insights into American history and the development of the legal system, and many are filled with human drama.

The U.S. judicial system has separate federal and state court systems, but because the U.S. Supreme Court is the final arbiter of all judicial disputes left unresolved by the lower federal and state courts, the overwhelming bulk of rulings having wide legal ramifications are made in that Court. Not surprisingly, therefore, all but a handful of the decisions covered in essays in these volumes were handed down by the Supreme Court.

Content of the Set

U.S. Court Cases, Revised serves several purposes. The most obvious is to make clear information on individual court cases readily available to students, teachers, and general readers. The 700 cases covered within the set's pages clearly fulfill that first purpose. The set also shows how decisions of the U.S. Supreme Court and other federal and state courts have affected American history. The set achieves that goal in its hundreds of detailed analyses of individual cases and in the overview essays that help put the cases in broader perspectives.

Reviewers of the first edition of *U.S. Court Cases* noted that the fact that the set drew its essays from a large number of different Salem reference sets gave it a special value. Since that edition appeared in 1999, Salem has published *Encyclopedia of the U.S. Supreme Court* (2001), *Criminal Justice* (2006), *U.S. Supreme Court* (2007), and revised editions of its *Great Events from History* series. These publications account for more than 500 of the essays in *U.S. Court Cases, Revised*. Other essays come from Salem's decades sets and from the recent *Encyclopedia of American Immigration* (2010), and 13 essays are entirely new.

Organization

As in its first edition, *U.S. Court Cases, Revised* opens with a section titled "Law and the Courts" containing a series of overview essays explaining the historical and legal contexts in which American courts operate. These overviews cover the Anglo-American Legal Systems, Law, Jurisprudence, The U.S. Constitution, The Bill of Rights, Constitutional Law, The U.S. Judicial System, State and Local Courts, The U.S. Supreme Court, Judicial Review, and Due Process of Law.

The second and much longer section of the set, "Court Cases," contains 674 articles on court cases, arranged alphabetically under the names by which the cases are best known, such as *Brown v. Board of Education*, *Plessy v. Ferguson*, and *Roe v. Wade*. Fifteen of these essays cover groups of cases that are commonly discussed together, such as the *Cherokee Cases* (1831), *Chinese Exclusion Cases* (1884-1893), *Civil Rights Cases* (1883), and *Head Money Cases* (1885). The top matter in the articles identifies the courts in which the cases were decided, the cases' official citation numbers (see explanatory note on page xxi), dates of the rulings, categories of relevant issues, and brief summaries of the cases' significance. All the overview articles and more than 100 essays on cases are followed by Further Reading notes, and all articles end with lists of cross-references to other articles on related cases.

The third section of the set contains five appendixes: a table summarizing the careers of all U.S. Supreme Court justices through mid-2010, when Justice John Paul Stevens retired, an annotated general bibliography, a glossary, a time line of the cases, and a categorized list of entries. The glossary and time line are new to this edition. Also new is the Categorized List of Entries. The appendixes are followed by a photo index and a detailed general subject index.

Acknowledgments

As is the case with all Salem Press's reference works, these volumes would not be possible without the contributions of a large team of scholars. We therefore wish to thank, once again, the 122 scholars who wrote the articles appearing in *U.S. Court Cases*. Their names are listed immediately after this note. We particularly wish to thank the set's Editor, Professor Thomas Tandy Lewis, who lent his expertise not only to the set's organization and updating but also to the writing of many of the set's essays, including all those new to this edition.

CONTRIBUTORS

J. Stewart Alverson
University of Tennessee

Mary Welek Atwell
Radford University

Charles Bahmueller
Center for Civic Education

Ann Marie B. Bahr
South Dakota State University

Thomas E. Baker
University of Scranton

Paul Albert Bateman
Southwestern University

Bruce Andre Beaubouef
University of Houston

Patricia A. Behlar
Pittsburg State University

Alberto Bernabe-Riefkohl
John Marshall Law School

Joseph M. Bessette
Claremont McKenna College

R. Matthew Beverlin
Rockhurst University

Denis Binder
Western New England College

Heidi Jo Blair-Esteves
Wayne State College

Steve D. Boilard
Sacramento, California

James J. Bolner
Louisiana State University

Michael R. Bradley
Matlaw College

John Braeman
University of Nebraska, Lincoln

Alan E. Brownstein
University of California, Davis

Johnny C. Burris
Nova Southeastern University

David Carleton
Middle Tennessee State University

Brian J. Carroll
California Baptist College

Jack Carter
University of New Orleans

Gilbert T. Cave
Lakeland Community College

Maxwell O. Chibundu
University of Maryland School of Law

Drew Christie
University of New Hampshire

John G. Clark
University of Kansas

Douglas Clouatre
Kennesaw State University

Susan Coleman
West Texas A&M University

William H. Coogan
University of Southern Maine

Mark S. Coyne
University of Southern Maine

Randall Coyne
University of Oklahoma

David A. Crain
South Dakota State University

Jennifer Davis
Independent Scholar

Fredrick J. Dobney
St. Louis University

Davison M. Douglas
William & Mary School of Law

Jennifer Eastman
Clark University

Cecil L. Eubanks
Louisiana State University

John W. Fiero
University of Southwestern Louisiana

Brian L. Fife
Ball State University

Phyllis B. Gerstenfeld
California State University, Stanislaus

Richard A. Glenn
Millersville University

William Crawford Green
Morehead State University

Michael Haas
University of Hawaii

Timothy L. Hall
Austin Peay State University

Louise A. Halper
Washington & Lee University

William Haltom
University of Puget Sound

Robert M. Hardaway
University of Denver College of Law

Roger D. Hardaway
*Northwestern Oklahoma State
University*

Katy Jean Harriger
Wake Forest University

Mary A. Hendrickson
Wilson College

David G. Hicks
Pollak & Hicks, P.C.

Samuel B. Hoff
Delaware State University

Robert Jacobs
Central Washington University

Robert J. Janosik
Occidental College

CONTRIBUTORS

Shakuntala Jayaswal
West Haven Connecticut

Carl Jensen
Sonoma State University

K. Sue Jewell
Ohio State University

David M. Jones
University of Wisconsin, Oshkosh

Charles L. Kammer
College of Wooster

Theodore P. Kovaleff
New York, New York

Barbara G. Kramer
Santa Fe Community College

Sumner J. La Croix
University of Hawaii

Robert W. Langran
Villanova University

Jim Lee
Fort Hays State University

Ann M. Legreid
University of Central Missouri

Thomas Tandy Lewis
St. Cloud State University

Ronald W. Long
*West Virginia University Institute
of Technology*

William C. Lowe
Mount St. Clare College

Joseph M. McCarthy
Suffolk University

Marie McKendall
Grand Valley State University

Bill Manikas
Gaston College

Barry Mann
Atlanta, Georgia

Dyan E. Mazurana
University of Wyoming

Steve J. Mazurana
University of Northern Colorado

Laurence W. Mazzeno
Alvernia College

Joseph A. Melusky
St. Francis College

Scott Allen Merriman
Troy University, Montgomery

Diane P. Michelfelder
California Polytechnic State University

Thomas J. Mortillaro
Nicholls State University

John F. O'Connell
College of the Holy Cross

David E. Paas
Hillsdale College

Lisa Paddock
Cape May Court House, New Jersey

Richard A. Parker
Northern Arizona University

Darryl Paulson
University of South Florida

Marilyn Elizabeth Perry
Prospect Heights, Illinois

Jessie Bishop Powell
American Public University System

Janice G. Rienerth
Appalachian State University

Stephen F. Rohde
Los Angeles, California

Michelle R. Royle
Northern Arizona University

Joseph R. Rudolph, Jr.
Towson University

Richard H. Sander
Northwestern University School of Law

Gustav L. Seligman
North Texas State University

Elizabeth Algren Shaw
Cleveland, Ohio

Donald C. Simmons, Jr.
Mississippi Humanites Council

Donna Addkison Simmons
Jackson, Mississippi

Kevin F. Sims
Cedarville College

Christopher E. Smith
Michigan State University

Glenn Ellen Starr
Appalachian State University

David L. Sterling
University of Cincinnati

Geralyn Strecker
Ball State University

Timothy E. Sullivan
University of Michigan

Susan M. Taylor
Indiana University, South Bend

Jonathan L. Thorndike
Belmont University

Glen E. Thurow
University of Dallas

Victoria M. Time
Old Dominion University

Leslie V. Tischauser
Prairie State College

Paul B. Trescott
Southern Illinois University

William M. Tuttle
University of Kansas

Elizabeth Van Schaack
Yale Law School

Theodore M. Vestal
Oklahoma State University

Mary E. Virginia
Venice, Florida

Thomas J. Edward Walker
Pennsylvania College of Technology

Harvey Wallace
California State University, Fresno

Donald V. Weatherman
Lyon College

Shanda Wedlock
Fresno, California

Marcia J. Weiss
Point Park College

Scott A. White
University of Wisconsin, Platteville

LaVerne McQuiller Williams
Rochester Institute of Technology

Richard L. Wilson
University of Tennessee, Chattanooga

Thomas Winter
University of Cincinnati

Thomas Aaron Wyrick
University of Tennessee, Chattanooga

Cynthia Gwynne Yaudes
Indiana University

Clifton K. Yearley
State University of New York, Buffalo

U.S. Supreme Court
Citation Numbers

Since the year 1876, official versions of U.S. Supreme Court decisions and opinions have appeared in volumes titled *United States Reports*, published by the federal government. Each standard citation listed in these volumes usually includes this information:

- names of the parties involved in the case, in italics
- volume number of *United States Reports* containing the case
- abbreviation "U.S."
- page number on which the case begins
- page number of quoted passage (where relevant)
- year in which the decision was made, in parentheses

This is a typical example: "*Brown v. Board of Education of Topeka*, 349 U.S. 294, at 342 (1954)."

For Supreme Court rulings earlier than 1876, each official government volume was published under the last name of the Court reporter who supervised its editing and publication. Standard citations to pre-1876 cases include the names of the reporters preceded by the numbers of the volumes within the series the reporters edited. The citations then give the volume numbers used by *United States Reports* in parentheses. This is a typical example: "*Marbury v. Madison*, 1 Cranch (5 U.S.) 137, at 146 (1803)."

Through 1875, the volumes were edited by seven different Court reporters whose names (Dallas, Cranch, Wheaton, Peters, Howard, Black, and Wallace) appear in citations. Howard (abbreviated How.) supervised the publication of the most volumes (twenty-four); Black the fewest (two).

The names given to U.S. Supreme Court decisions sometimes are different from the standard forms discussed above. For example, petitions for habeas corpus frequently do not include two parties; names of such cases typically include the Latin expression *Ex parte*, which means "in behalf of" or "for one party," as in "*Ex parte Milligan*, 71 U.S. 2 (1866)." Also, the Latin expression *In re*, which means "concerning" or "in the matter of" is frequently employed in judicial proceedings when there are no adversarial parties, as in "*In Re Gault*, 387 U.S. 1 (1967)."

After the Supreme Court hands down a ruling, its official version is generally not published until one or two years later. Consequently, until the decision is officially published, its page number in *United States Reports* cannot be known. Early publications of such cases are known as "slip opinions," and their citations utilize an underscore line to substitute for the volume number, as in "*Ricci v. DeStefano*, 555 U.S. ____ (2009)."

Although the vast majority of lawyers and legal writers refer to the federal government's official publications, some prefer to utilize one of the privately published and unofficial compilations, such as *Supreme Court Reporter* or *United States Supreme Court Reports, Lawyers' Edition*. Until the Court's official opinions are published in *United States Reports*, many writers cite numbers from these unofficial compilations. This is an example of a citation from the former publication: "*Reno v. American Civil Liberties Union*, 117 S.Ct. 2329 (1997)." In *United States Reports*, the same case is cited as "*Reno v. American Civil Liberties Union*, 521 U.S. 824 (1997)."

For more detailed information on citing court cases, one of the best resources is *The Bluebook: A Uniform System of Citation* (19 ed., 2010), an annually updated publication of the *Harvard Law Review*. Another useful publication is *ALWD Citation Manual: A Professional System of Citation* (2005) by Darby Dickerson and the Association of Legal Writing Directors.

COMPLETE LIST OF CONTENTS

Volume 1

Law and the Courts

Court Cases

Volume 2

Volume 3

Contents. lxxxv

Appendixes

U.S. COURT CASES
Revised Edition

Law and
the Courts

ANGLO-AMERICAN LEGAL SYSTEMS

- Both the United States and Canada use a legal system based on principles derived from colonial experience under Great Britain. The three legal systems have diverged over the years, but the general outline of Anglo-American legal principles has remained recognizable and distinguishable from other legal systems.

In the popular mind, the Anglo-American legal system depends on statutes passed by a legislature, whether Parliament or Congress. The U.S. system is a common law rather than a statutory law system typical of continental Europe; it is derived from the Anglo-Saxon common law tradition rather than a rival Roman law tradition. Although the two systems have some distinct differences, the common law and Roman law traditions both can be compatible with a broader concept known as the rule of law. A basic distinction has to do with the source of the law, that is, whether the law comes principally from judges or from legislatures. Although both traditions are mixed in practice, the common law legal tradition follows the notion that judges "discover" what the law is that "naturally" ought to be accepted by all citizens. In theory, judges are not lawmakers, but as a practical matter much of this "discovery" is actually the making of new law.

The Concept of Common Law

The fact that realistically judges do make law should not detract from the common law's ideal notion that judges should be merely "discoverers" of what the law is. To depart from this ideal of the judge as a neutral, impartial discoverer of the law is to open the legal system to politicization. If judges openly become lawmakers, then they increasingly face pressure to be treated as legislators who must be directly controlled by an electorate. Making judges more dependent on the electorate threatens the independent judiciary, one principle of the rule of law.

The common law arose out of the desire of English kings following William the Conqueror to create a common system of courts and thereby a common law throughout the country. The word "common" in this case does not mean "ordinary," but rather that the law is "common" or uniform throughout the country. Uniformity evolved over at least a few hundred years. To further this goal, courts of appeal were created so that an individual judgment in a local court could be reviewed by a higher court with a broader perspective.

Uniformity was important not only across the country but also over time, leading to the important practice of courts following the precedents set in earlier cases. This rule of precedent is also known as the concept of *stare decisis*, a Latin phrase that means generally that a decision should be followed in all like cases. The practice of establishing precedents continues in American, British, and Canadian courts. The notion that a judge discovers the law by finding precedents in similar cases is important if the system is to maintain its uniformity.

The concept of *stare decisis* is strongly related to predictability, valued in the rule of law. Predictability applied to legislatures as sources of law requires that legislatures enact clear statutes. The same principle applies to judge-discovered (or judge-made) law, in that judges should discover the uniform principles behind current and previous decisions. Ordinary citizens can then be educated as to what the law requires because they can know the precedents.

Roman Law Tradition

These important principles of the common law are not followed in the Roman law tradition. In the Roman legal tradition, the critical source of law is the body of statutes passed by the legislature or provided by a lawgiver. In earlier times, this tradition included the notion that legislatures also "discovered" natural laws, but that idea was less important to the Roman tradition and gradually declined. The common law tradition has judges discovering "natural" laws that may be in a sense higher than ordinary law passed by a legislature. The Roman law tradition has no such notion. Legislatures became paramount sources of law, and judges tended to restrict themselves to deciding facts rather than acting as referees in an adversarial proceeding in which juries decided facts.

Judges still interpreted the law to a degree, but unlike common law judges, they were bound more by context than by precedent. Roman law judges took over this fact-deciding role because they had a much more limited role in interpreting what the law was. In contrast, the common law system has jurors or panels of ordinary citizens (called peers) to act as the neutral deciders of fact. The judge in the common law system is to act as a referee between two sides in an adversarial legal system. The adversarial tradition expects that the truth will emerge from the conflict between two sides presenting their positions before a neutral jury, with the judge acting as a referee to make sure neither side misleads the jury with false information. This role as referee means that the common law judge must be extremely well informed as to previous decisions on the law. The common law judge also has a large role in deciding what the law is or should be.

Judges in the Roman law tradition decide facts rather than discover the law; the law has already been provided in detailed codes. Accordingly, in the Roman law tradition the judge always applies a statute to the facts of the case rather than relying on a prior decision. The judge's role is to decide the facts, select an appropriate statute, and apply it.

Because the Roman law system has the judge so involved in deciding the facts, there is far less need for an adversarial system to discover facts. The Roman law system does not depend on juries relying on an investigative arm of the government to assist the judge in the search for truth. The defense attorney's role is much more limited and tends to be reduced to pleading for mercy for the accused. There is a greater presumption of guilt: The police and procurator (government investigator) presumably are committed to never convicting an innocent person. The accused then would not be brought to trial in the Roman law system unless the police have determined the accused to be the perpetrator of some crime recognized by statute.

Common and Roman Law Traditions

The common law and Roman law traditions coexist in Western thought. Neither can be said to be superior in principle. Both systems have advantages and disadvantages from the point of view of the rule of law. The common law system has a disadvantage from the rule of law perspective in that it may tend to create uncertainty when new cases arise and judges must discover what the law should be after a particular event has occurred. The judge-made or judge-determined law then becomes somewhat retroactive in its effects. On the other hand, Roman law can have a disadvantage from the point of view of the rule of law in that the need for detailed codes may lead to a legal fabric so complex that it cannot easily be understood by citizens. Thus, it may work against the goal of predictability.

The common law system obviously cannot solve all problems. Common law systems need a corresponding, alternative form of law known as equity law, or a law based on fairness. Fairness becomes particularly important when a citizen is faced with the threat of future damage. Equity legal systems usually include the possibility of an injunction to prevent an action. Both equity law and injunctions are infrequently used in the Roman law tradition because presumably statutes have taken account of all possible situations, so that an illegal future action would prompt certain punishment. Under common law, injunctions delay actions while judges decide if they are legal.

The common law tradition has never prohibited the passage of statutes. In a common law system, statutory law replaces common law as decisions are codified into laws. Common law systems have converged with Roman law systems as statutes increasingly replaced the common law as a source of prevailing law. In twentieth century Canada, Britain, and the United States, statutory law has become increasingly important. The notion of the courts as interpreters of statutes, however, continues to follow the common law tradition, and precedent remains important.

Importance of Precedent

One indication of the importance of precedent in the Anglo-American legal systems is the nature of law schools and legal libraries. American, Canadian, and British law libraries use codes, but a more prominent place is given to various "reporters" of decisions in cases. These reporters are important sources of the prior decisions or precedents that have such value under the concept of *stare decisis*. Law libraries in the Roman law tradition focus on the detailed codes of law.

Both these legal traditions may produce constitutions as a form of higher statutory law. The constitution as statute in the Roman law tradition does not necessarily include the concept of judicial review, which rests somewhat uncomfortably with the Roman law tradition. In those Roman law countries allowing judicial review, the notion of precedent has become more important; this has tended to move Roman law closer to the common law. In the common law tradition, a constitution is a discovery of the most important higher (or natural) law principle that exists. Constitutions then can include the notion of judicial review, as in the United States.

Differences Among the Anglo-American Nations

Although the United States, Canada, and Britain all follow the same basic legal principles, there are some clear differences. The United States has used a written constitution since 1789, and Canada has done so since its independence in 1867, but Britain has never done so. The British have no single document from which one can date the British legal or "constitutional" regime. It is frequently said that British parliamentary practice has been reasonably uniform at least since the Reform Act of 1867. After that act, mass political parties developed, as American political parties had. From the mid-1800's on, both the United States and Britain had democratic systems with mass political parties and reasonably modern governments. Both generally accept basic principles of the common law.

Within that common law tradition, Britain and the United States diverged after the American Revolution and the ratification of the U.S. Constitution. The United States came to rely more on statutory law than on common law.

The most obvious example is the Constitution, which set a standard against which statutes could be measured. Statutory textualism was also implied by the concept of judicial review, which allows courts to strike down laws as being unconstitutional. The U.S. Constitution stands above all three branches of the government, but the branches are equal to each other. The British maintain that Parliament is supreme, so no constitution is higher and no institution exists to declare laws unconstitutional.

To say that British courts cannot declare a law unconstitutional is not to say that courts are powerless, for they have the common law power to interpret parliamentary statutes. Although they cannot declare parliamentary enactments unconstitutional, their interpretation is broad enough to include limits on Parliament they derive from the "traditional" constitution included in the common law. Judicial review is growing now that British courts have an obligation to interpret the European Community Charter as it bears on acts of Parliament.

At the top of the U.S. court system is the nine-member Supreme Court. The British "court of last resort" consists of eleven Law Lords. The Law Lords are distinguished judges appointed by the prime minister to be "life peers" in the House of Lords. These specifically designated Law Lords sit on cases in panels of three to five judges. Although appointed by the prime minister, they are not narrow partisans. Customary practice requires them to be distinguished in the law. Less distinguished judges have probably been appointed to the U.S. Supreme Court than as Law Lords in Britain.

The rights of the accused are not as carefully protected in Britain as they are in the United States. For example, the U.S. Constitution provides the guarantee of a writ of habeas corpus; no such overriding guarantee exists in Britain. The accused are not normally incarcerated for long periods without trial, but occasionally people have been held for long periods without being charged.

The Rule of Law

All legal systems can be evaluated as to how closely they correspond to the rule of law. Within that concept, there are two grand traditions: the common law and Roman law. The common law is more dependent on judge-made or determined law, and the Roman legal tradition is more dependent on statutes. Both traditions use both statutes and judge-made law to various degrees. The common law developed in England after the Norman Conquest of 1066 and was used in all British colonies, including the United States and Canada. Although the United States and Canada are still recognizable as common law countries, both diverged from the British experience. Most notably, Canada and the United States have written constitutions, but Britain does not.

Common law countries rely on juries to determine facts as they emerge from an adversarial proceeding. A judge acts as a referee between the contending parties. The judge acts as an authority on the law bearing on the case, finding the law by consulting precedents, or prior cases of similar nature. To provide uniformity, an appeals process allows for higher courts to unify judgments. The United States uses juries to a far greater degree than do either Canada or Britain.

Roman law countries rely on judges to determine facts and apply relevant law. Roman law judges are expected to rely on the words of the statutes and are less dependent on precedents. Roman law countries use a procurator system in which the state is expected to determine that an accused is in fact guilty before a trial is held. The defense attorney has a much more limited role in the Roman law system. Over time, the common law and Roman law systems have tended to converge, although real differences still exist.

Richard L. Wilson

Further Reading

Blackstone, Sir William. *Commentaries on the Laws of England.* 9th ed. 4 vols. Edited and introduced by Wayne Morrison. London: Cavendish, 2001.

Cosgrove, Richard A. *Scholars of the Law: English Jurisprudence from Blackstone to Hart.* New York: New York University Press, 1996.

Dragnich, Alex N., Jorgen S. Rasmussen, and Joel C. Moses. *Major European Governments.* 8th ed. Pacific Grove, Calif.: Brooks/Cole, 1991.

Finnis, John. *Natural Law and Natural Rights.* Oxford, England: Clarendon Press, 1992.

Glendon, Mary Ann, Michael Wallace Gordon, and Christopher Osakwe. *Comparative Legal Traditions in a Nutshell.* St. Paul, Minn.: West, 1982.

Harman, Charles E. *The Men Who Made the Law: During the Time of Justinian's Compilation and Blackstone's "Commentaries."* Brookings, Oreg.: Old Court Press, 2002.

Raz, Joseph. *The Authority of Law.* Oxford, England: Clarendon Press, 1979.

Walker, Geoffrey De Q. *The Rule of Law.* Carlton, Vic.: Melbourne University Press, 1988.

LAW

• Law is among the principal tools a civilized society uses to create order. In a modern constitutional democracy, law maintains a free society by restricting governmental power and forming boundaries within which citizens are free to act as they please. In Western societies law is seen as a body of rules based on statutes, judicial decisions, and customs which are enacted by a politically organized society and backed by its sanctions.

There is no single agreed-upon definition of law. It was once thought that law could be defined as "the commands of a sovereign backed by a force," but some people found this definition to be inadequate because some laws are permissions rather than commands. It is generally agreed, however, that laws are kinds of rules and that a legal system is a body of rules. Like other rules, law is intended to govern some aspect of human conduct. Rules in every arena of life are intended to mark out approved courses of conduct, from table manners and etiquette to the requirements of employers to the rules parents make for children. These rules do not have the force of law. Only those rules that are made in required ways by legitimate authority receive the sanction of society as a whole and are called laws. The rules that make up the legal system may be divided into four categories.

One is laws that regulate conduct. These laws make up the great bulk of what is ordinarily thought of as law. Some laws forbid some conduct, such as force or fraud; other laws command conduct, such as the performance of a public service—for example, military service or jury duty. These laws are generally enforced by courts and are backed by the state's coercive power.

Another category is fundamental (constitutional) law, which determines what valid law is. Some laws govern which institutions (such as Congress) are recognized by the legal system as authorized to make law. They are therefore more fundamental than other laws and are called "constitutional law." Constitutional law serves as a body of rules for determining what will count as valid law. Thus, while the people in a constitutional democracy are said to be sovereign, the rules of the constitution define the ways the people exercise their sovereignty.

A third category, rules for changing laws (usually called rules of legislation) specify how and by whom existing law may be changed or new law added. They are the rules that govern legislative procedure. Only laws that pass through a prescribed legislative process are recognized as valid by the legal system.

A final category is rules for interpreting law. Laws can seldom, if ever, be applied without being interpreted. Rules for interpreting law specify who is authorized to interpret law and what procedures must be used for interpretation. The process of authoritatively interpreting law is generally undertaken by courts. The last three of these categories of rules restrain authorities, setting limits to legitimate action in the eyes of the law—and in the eyes of knowledgeable citizens.

Purposes and Functions of Law

Law attempts to further central purposes of society and performs key functions. The overall purpose of law may be said to be a search for justice. Justice is usually taken, in general terms, to mean fairness. There is often disagreement, however, about what is and is not just or fair. Thus law is perennially subject to criticism regarding its fairness.

One of the functions of law is to serve as an instrument for reforming society and setting its future course. Thus a legislative program for a city or town, a state, or a nation as a whole can form the substance of social reform, whether it be a new departure for society or a return to the nation's original principles. Law protects people and property. Law restrains behavior, forbidding certain actions. The purpose of this restraint is the protection of people from harm arising from sources such as force, fraud, and negligence. A further function is resolving conflicts—keeping peace.

Modern legal systems attempt to establish systems of courts whose procedures and decisions will be widely believed to be fair and just. If successful, legal systems remove demands for justice from the street to the courtroom. In criminal cases, legal systems attempt to substitute public justice for private vengeance. Similarly, in civil (noncriminal) disputes, the legal system moves grievances and disputes from the realm of private quarrel to public adjudication, in accordance with recognized principles of justice. The legal system is never entirely successful in fulfilling these purposes; to the extent that it is, however, society is civilized. Since the legal system cannot work without taxation, U.S. Supreme Court Justice Oliver Wendell Holmes, Jr., once remarked, "Taxes are the price we pay for civilization."

A further function is the creation of special legal facilities. Modern legal systems create facilities such as special courts and officials so that citizens may transfer property to their heirs through wills, establish trusts, register patents, and in other ways use or protect their property as they wish.

A most important purpose of modern legal systems can be summarized as "security of expectations." Law attempts to secure expectations by protecting citizens and their property from harm and abuse. Citizens can plan their lives with the expectation that if they act within the boundaries of the law, legal authorities will not interfere with them.

The idea of the "rule of law, not of men" has long been a fundamental principle of Western democracies, especially the United States. The rule of law can be understood in contrast to rule by the arbitrary whims of rulers and government officials—or, indeed, the whims of anyone in society. Criminals subject their victims to their arbitrary whims. Anyone exercising power in society, whether a public official, an employer, or anyone else, may act arbitrarily. Bullies are everywhere. Aspects of everyday life, such as driving automobiles, if left unregulated by law, would subject some to the whims of others, creating danger and arousing fear.

In modern legal systems, the rule of law is intended to overcome all these problems, but it refers in particular to controlling public officials. Two ideas are central. First, the powers of officials to set and enforce rules are overseen by impartial tribunals that ensure that powers are exercised fairly, within legal limits. Second, everyone subject to legal authority must be liable to follow only preestablished laws and be given clear guidance about rights and duties under the law, and must not be subject to punishment without being able to follow the law.

"Freedom under law" has likewise been central in European and American thinking since the seventeenth century. In the 1680's the English philosopher John Locke wrote, "Where law ends, tyranny begins." According to this concept, in a fair legal system, law, while placing restrictions on citizens' behavior, also enlarges and enhances their freedom. This is so, it is argued, because an effective legal system removes significant obstacles to the exercise of freedom. Thus when people are terrified because they are threatened by violence, they can hardly be said to be free; when they are protected by an effective and fair legal system, their freedom is enlarged.

Types of Law

Law may be divided into several categories. Constitutional law sets up governmental offices and institutions and distributes power among them. In the American tradition, constitutional law also acts as a "higher law" that binds the people themselves as well as their elected representatives unless and until the Constitution is changed. Constitutional law thus provides government restricted to specified purposes and limited in the means to pursue them.

A second type of law is statutory law, which is enacted by legislative bodies. In the American constitutional tradition, however, statutory law must not conflict with constitutional law. If it does, the practice of judicial review em-

The concept of natural law that most influences American law was that developed by political philosopher John Locke. (Library of Congress)

powers courts to declare such a law unconstitutional and therefore null and void.

A third type of law, common law (from the Latin *jus commune*), is created by judicial decisions, which act as the basis, or precedent, for future decisions. Courts in the Anglo-American tradition follow the idea of *stare decisis*, or "let the precedent stand." Decisions of courts accordingly become the basis for common law.

A fourth type of law, administrative law, governs the powers of administrative agencies to regulate areas such as food, drugs, the environment, industrial safety, and many others. The rules and regulations made by administrative agencies are also part of administrative law. Administrative law is overseen by the courts, which in the United States require administrative agencies to conform to administrative due process, such as the idea of fair hearing.

A fifth variety of law is international law. This law is the body of rule accepted as binding by independent countries or states. It is derived from both custom and explicit agreements and is created by the consent of sovereign states. International law addresses topics such as war and peace, human rights issues, the ratification of treaties, economic affairs, and environmental issues. Some deny that international law is law at all. There are many arguments regarding the extent to which international law is binding and the extent to which developments in international law erode national sovereignty.

Sources of American Law

Law in the United States is derived from several principal sources. One is statute law—that is, law passed by a legislative body such as Congress or a state legislature and approved by the executive, as constitutionally required. A variant of statute is the municipal ordinances passed by legislative bodies such as city councils. These laws are made under powers granted to cities by state government. A second source is the principles of the common law of England and the judicial decisions of American courts themselves. A third source is custom, although legal philosophers state that in the modern world custom is not an important source of law and is generally subordinate to other sources. Thus no American court would find that custom takes precedence over statute law in cases where they conflict.

The Place of Law in American Society

Since the beginning of the American republic, law has played an enormous role in U.S. society. One reason for this lies in the revolutionary origin of the new American state. Rather than evolving through many centuries, as occurred in much of modern Europe, certain basic rules of society had to be thought out and enacted "from scratch."

The United States was a new society in a "new world." One revolutionary said, "We have it in our power to start the world over again." Custom counted for less in America than in Europe, since it was less deeply ingrained. Indeed, customary ways of thinking, such as notions of the natural hierarchy of society and the deference resulting from it, were transformed by the new ideas of liberty and equality that swept the colonies prior to the outbreak of revolution.

Protecting the Innocent

One of the most significant aspects of law in modern constitutional states is its attempt to protect the innocent. A principal means of doing so is legal restraint of the actions of all members of society. Constitutional and statute law put special legal restraints on public officials. However, the innocent are protected only so long as public officials as well as ordinary citizens comply with the law. Thus, certain countries with written constitutions still fail to provide "constitutional" (limited) government, because in practice, constitutional and other law fails to restrain public officials. Similarly, laws that protect members of society from one another may not be enforced, either because government lacks the will or because social disorder makes enforcement impossible.

Assuming, however, that law is working as it should, how does it protect the individual? First, law prescribes the boundaries of behavior within which individuals are to act. By laying down rules specifying what may not be done or what must be done, law provides a framework for legitimate expectations. By enforcing law regarding property, for example, the legal system secures important individual expectations.

A principal way in which law and legal systems of modern constitutional democracies protect the freedom of law-abiding individuals is to ensure that public officials abide by legally prescribed procedures. Police cannot do as they please in dealing either with suspected criminals or with individuals caught *in flagrante delicto*, in the act of lawbreaking. In the United States, procedures enforced by courts ensure that police inform those arrested of their rights.

In Anglo-Saxon law, those arrested are accorded a "presumption of innocence" by courts and are protected by courtroom procedures, rules of evidence, provisions for legal representation, and other measures intended to ensure fair treatment at the hands of authority. Thus, in the United States, illegally obtained evidence may not be used to convict defendants. Police cannot go on unauthorized "fishing expeditions" for evidence of illegal activity in individuals' homes or stop them in public without probable cause to believe that they have committed a crime. If judges convict defendants in violation of the rules of evidence and other procedural rules, or if in other ways they behave capriciously, their rulings are reversed on appeal to higher courts.

Americans generally favor the protection of the innocent, but there is a price to pay. Protections of the rights of innocents increase the chances that the guilty will go free. Diminishing these rights could increase the chances of convicting the guilty. It can be argued that such convictions would increase the security of the innocent, since more malefactors would be behind bars. In reply, it may be said that although the latter idea may be true, the argument that the innocent would be more secure is at best questionable.

American and Foreign Concepts of Law

The Anglo-Saxon system of law upon which the American legal system is based is often contrasted with the civil law system of continental Europe. The civil law system is so called because it is based on the Roman civil law, codified by the Byzantine emperor Justinian in the sixth century. While Anglo-Saxon law grew up in a haphazard way, civil law is set out in logical, orderly codes. The purpose of civil law codes such as the "Code Civil" is the creation of a purely rational body of law (as opposed to possibly contradictory or uneven law resulting from the judicial decisions of a common law system), the equality of all citizens, separation of civil from ecclesiastical regulation, and the principles of the freedom of the person, freedom of contract, and the inviolability of private property.

Within these codes, there are national differences in civil law countries. The Netherlands, for example, uses Roman-Dutch law. The idea of law encompassed by civil law is not different from that of Anglo-Saxon, but the operation of civil law systems is different. First, judges are not bound by precedent, as they are in Anglo-Saxon systems. Second, while Anglo-Saxon systems are adversarial, civil law systems are "inquisitorial." That is, in criminal law cases, Anglo-Saxon systems pit prosecutors and defense attorneys in a contest. This is not so in civil law systems. Instead, there are three phases in criminal cases: an investigative phase, undertaken under the direction of a public prosecutor; an examining phase, which is not carried out in public and is primarily written; and then a trial. The trial phase differs from trials in adversarial systems, since the evidence has already been taken. The trial presents the case to a trial judge and jury, with cases made by prosecutor and defense counsel. The jury may not be required to reach a unanimous verdict.

An entirely different conception is found in various religious bodies of law. Islamic law, for example, does not apply to people by virtue of their citizenship or nationality but on account of religion. Islamic law is based upon a religious text, the Koran, and certain other Muslim religious texts. Further, this law is generally considered to be unchangeable. Only God can make law; God is the only lawgiver.

This kind of law differs from Western law in general, and American law in particular, in several significant ways. American law is obligatory only upon those who are in territory governed by the United States; it is secular law, since it is known to be human-made and not created by legislators by virtue of their religion or religiosity. American law is not made to conform to a religious text and is not considered unchangeable.

Charles Bahmueller

Further Reading

Abraham, Henry J., and Barbara A. Perry. *Freedom and the Court: Civil Rights and Liberties in the United States.* 8th ed. Lawrence: University Press of Kansas, 2003.

Barron, Jerome A., and C. Thomas Dienes. *Constitutional Law in a Nutshell.* 6th ed. St. Paul, Minn.: West, 2005.

Epstein, Lee, and Thomas Walker. *Constitutional Law for a Changing America.* 5th ed. Washington, D.C.: CQ Press, 2003.

Harman, Charles E. *The Men Who Made the Law: During the Time of Justinian's Compilation and Blackstone's "Commentaries."* Brookings, Oreg.: Old Court Press, 2002.

Hart, H. L. A. *The Concept of Law.* New York: Oxford University Press, 1961.

Raz, Joseph. *The Authority of Law.* Oxford, England: Clarendon Press, 1979.

Roberson, Cliff. *Constitutional Law and Criminal Justice.* New York: Taylor & Francis, 2009.

JURISPRUDENCE

- The broad philosophy of law, jurisprudence seeks to discover the nature and justification of law. It clarifies concepts used in law, exposes the law's presuppositions, and offers constructive criticism of legal doctrines. Jurisprudence thus seeks answers to fundamental questions about law and its function in society, questions that have been asked for many generations.

Written discussions of law go back to the ancient Greeks, but the subject of jurisprudence has received increasing attention since the nineteenth century. Not merely the domain of scholars, jurisprudence is an integral part of the practice of law. Judges, particularly in appeals courts, typically consider the implications of their decisions beyond the case immediately at hand. Among the central aspects of jurisprudence are defining law and weighing the differing philosophies of what law should be based on and what it should accomplish.

Defining Law

By definition, law can be distinguished from related concepts such as morality. Some legal philosophers, it should be noted, such as H. L. A. Hart, reject attempts at definition and instead analyze law as a group of interrelated ideas. Actual definitions have varied widely according to time and place. The ancient Greek philosophers Plato and Aristotle viewed law as practical reasoning aimed at the common good of citizens in a city-state. The purpose of law was to enhance virtue and create a just social order. During the first century B.C., the Roman statesman Cicero extended Greek concepts into an explicit natural law theory: Law is reason in agreement with nature, and such law is unchanging. All positive law is derived from natural law. The scholars of the middle ages, such as Thomas Aquinas, adapted natural law to Christianity and derived law from theological doctrines. One consequence of a belief in natural law is that any positive human law that is inconsistent with natural law is not really law and may be disobeyed. Natural law theories, after a period of disuse, regained acceptance in the twentieth century in the guise of fundamental freedoms that no law can override.

Opposed to natural law is positivism, which views law as a set of commands issued by a sovereign power and enforced by sanctions. Its representatives, such as John Austin and Hans Kelsen, denied that laws can be criticized or evaluated on nonlegal grounds such as morality.

Utilitarianism, identified with Jeremy Bentham and John Stuart Mill, equated a good law with rules that promote the happiness of the greatest number. Karl Marx, on the other hand, viewed law as an instrument of capitalism whose real purpose was to protect the ruling classes from the workers. Law, Marx theorized, would ultimately wither away along with capitalism. Legal realism in the twentieth century defined law in terms of what courts and officials do when deciding cases and not as a set of rules at all. Sociological jurisprudence, inspired by people such as Roscoe Pound, saw law as balancing the interests of various groups in society. It used a "social engineering" model to describe the function of law. Utilitarianism, legal realism, and sociological jurisprudence emphasized the operation of law in society. As a result, they spawned major law reform movements.

Law and Morality

Positivism saw no connection between law and morals. The tyrannies and atrocities of the twentieth century led to a revival of natural law, which sees a close connection. Minimalist versions of natural law, such as the version of Lon Fuller, based law on the needs of people who live in communities governed by rules. Legal realism and sociological jurisprudence granted the relevance of morality to law but grouped it with considerations such as social policy and economic efficiency. Even among philosophers who agree that morality is relevant to law, there is intense disagreement over how the connection is to function and the ultimate effect of morality on particular laws.

Positivism identified the obligation to obey law with the threat of a sanction or punishment. Natural law and utilitarianism found threats inadequate and saw a moral basis for such an obligation. The moral basis of law is a sufficient reason to obey it. Thomas Hobbes and John Locke found the obligation in the social contract. People in a "state of nature" may have had an absolute right to do as they wished with no external restraint, but they gave up such rights when entering society, where the right to act was transferred to a sovereign or government. The social contract was a voluntary creation of an obligation to obey law.

Law creates and enforces various rights and duties, such as the right of privacy and a duty to avoid inflicting unwarranted harm. The nature and sources of such rights and duties need some explanation. Legal rights and duties are sometimes reduced to nonlegal interests. Natural law theories easily identified legal rights and duties with moral rights and duties. Other concepts derived rights and duties from more basic wants and needs of individuals. For example, criminal laws against murder can be derived from the need for personal safety and security.

Besides identifying the sources of rights and duties, philosophers such as Wesley Hohfeld traced the relationships between fundamental legal conceptions. Rights and duties are correlative: For every right there is a duty. If an individual has a right of ownership in a piece of property, then others have a duty not to interfere with the property.

Justice in a Legal System

A fundamental purpose of law is the promotion of justice, if justice means equal treatment in similar cases. This notion was embodied in the equal protection clause of the Fourteenth Amendment to the U.S. Constitution. This general concept does not explain when people or situations are really alike, however, so jurisprudence seeks deeper meanings. Justice may be divided into the concepts of distributive and retributive justice. Distributive justice requires that benefits and burdens be divided equally, while retributive justice seeks to rectify denials of benefits by sanctions and punishments. The idea of justice as fairness, associated with John Rawls, argues for a minimal conception in terms of fair procedures used to allocate benefits and burdens. A distribution is just if the procedures used to accomplish it are viewed as fair, even if the final distribution is unequal. Such notions have obvious applications to a welfare state, where law allocates entitlements among a variety of recipients.

The standards to be used in passing a just law are also a matter for jurisprudence. Rawls insists on fair procedures. Utilitarians, on the other hand, base just laws on the happiness of the greatest number. Immanuel Kant advanced the principle that all persons are to be treated as ends in themselves and never merely as a means. Kant would reject slavery and discrimination as illegal because they treat victims as means, even if sometimes such treatment could result in overall happiness for most of society. The legal basis for U.S. laws forbidding race and sex discrimination can be seen as Kantian because they are based on a perception that people have inherent value.

Most philosophers recognize fundamental rights such as freedom of expression, privacy, and the right to pursue an individual plan of life. When can law restrict the pursuit of such rights? John Stuart Mill argued that law is justified in restricting rights only when the action of an individual will harm someone else and that paternalism, which amounts to protecting people from the effects of their own acts, is never justified. Other philosophers do not use a harm-to-others criterion as the sole basis for law. They appeal to morality, the common good, and the social contract in limiting rights and liberties. Arguments concerning liberty and paternalism have direct consequences in law. For example, laws requiring motorcycle riders to wear helmets seem paternalistic because they are designed to protect people from the consequences of their own choices.

Punishment and Responsibility

Law imposes sanctions on persons found violating legal duties. Criminal penalties such as imprisonment are an example, as are money damages imposed in civil cases for tort and breach of contract. Not every action which causes an injury will result in a sanction, however; law normally requires a showing of fault on the part of the perpetrator and causation flowing from the perpetrator to the injury. Fault is usually defined in terms of intentional or negligent action. Liability without some element of fault is rare. When it occurs, jurisprudence must justify it. For example, modern tort law imposes strict liability without fault on manufacturers of dangerous products that injure consumers. Jurisprudence seeks to justify such a legal rule in terms of social policy or social insurance.

Criminal punishment, particularly capital punishment, raises profound questions because it involves the intentional infliction of pain. A utilitarian would punish only when the balance of pleasure over pain to be gained by punishment is greater than the balance of pleasure over pain for any alternative system (such as psychological treatment for the criminal or not punishing at all). Other philosophies view punishment as a matter of just deserts, the criminal having committed acts that allow the legal system to impose sanctions as a matter of principled justice. Punishment may also serve the purposes of reforming the offender and deterring others. Utilitarians reject punishment simply as a matter of just deserts because it obviously inflicts pain with no resulting pleasure; they evaluate criminal justice systems by how well they either reform or deter. A Kantian, however, would reject both reformation and deterrence because they involve treating the offender as a mere means to the ends of others. The subject of punishment remains highly controversial.

Legal Reasoning

Legal rules, even those found in very detailed statutes that begin with lists of legal definitions, are often indeterminate or open-textured. The application of legal rules to particular cases can be controversial, as in cases of negligence, in which a jury is required to decide if a defendant acted as a reasonable, prudent person. The test in such cases is to decide whether the defendant acted like the "ordinary person in the street." This is certainly not an obvious or well-defined concept but is the only test that can determine what is meant by negligence. Jurisprudence attempts to discover the limits of discretion in applying such indeterminate legal rules and to find ways to make particular applications consistent.

While legislatures and courts carefully seek to avoid inconsistency, the massive detail of law can result in glaring inconsistencies that must then be resolved. For example, in the famous 1889 New York case of *Riggs v. Palmer*, a grandson murdered his grandfather to inherit a farm. The grandfather had left the farm to the grandson in a will, and under New York law the grandson clearly inherited it. Yet this situation was inconsistent with such equitable maxims as "no one shall profit by his own wrong." The court resolved the issue by examining the apparent intent of the legislature in passing the statute on wills and then attempted to fit this intention with other legal rules such as the equitable maxim. As a result, the grandson did not inherit the property in spite of what the clear words of the statute said.

David E. Paas

Further Reading

Arthur, John, and William H. Shaw, eds. *Readings in Philosophy of Law.* Englewood Cliffs, N.J.: Prentice-Hall, 1984.

Dworkin, R. M., ed. *The Philosophy of Law.* New York: Oxford University Press, 1977.

Dworkin, Ronald. *Taking Rights Seriously.* Cambridge, Mass.: Harvard University Press, 1977.

Feinberg, Joel, and Hyman Gross, eds. *Philosophy of Law.* 2d ed. Belmont, Calif.: Wadsworth Publishing, 1980.

Hart, H. L. A. *The Concept of Law.* New York: Oxford University Press, 1961.

Kautz, Steven, ed. *The Supreme Court and the Idea of Constitutionalism.* Philadelphia: University of Pennsylvania Press, 2009.

Postema, Gerald J. *Bentham: Moral, Political, and Legal Philosophy.* 2 vols. Burlington, Vt.: Ashgate/Dartmouth, 2002.

Rawls, John. *A Theory of Justice.* Cambridge, Mass.: Belknap Press of Harvard University Press, 1971.

THE U.S. CONSTITUTION

- The Constitution is the fundamental document establishing the national government of the United States of America. It describes the nature and limits of political power within the national government and how the different branches of government were to be structured. The Constitution is an extraordinary document, both theoretically and historically. Knowing how this document was developed is important to understanding both its purpose and its success.

The Constitution of the United States was not the first—and some would argue that it is not the most important—of the United States' founding documents. The Constitution was developed eleven years after the approval of the Declaration of Independence. After declaring and then winning independence from Great Britain, the new nation spent a number of years governed by the Articles of Confederation. The Articles created a loose federation of states which eventually proved too weak to serve the needs of the young nation. In 1787 delegates from twelve of the states (all but Rhode Island) met to discuss ways of revising the Articles of Confederation to create a more adequate government.

The Constitutional Convention of 1787 quickly decided that the basic premise behind the Articles of Confederation rendered them inadequate for governing the nation. The Convention began discussing a far more centralized form of government than was possible under the Articles of Confederation. James Madison and Edmund Randolph, two Virginia delegates who had anticipated this possibility, arrived at the Convention with the rough outlines of a totally new form of government. After considerable debate and numerous compromises, the Convention approved the Constitution of the United States and sent it to the states for their ratification. After further debate and much political maneuvering, the Constitution was eventually ratified by all thirteen states.

Basic Principles of the Constitution

One of the most unique aspects of the Constitution was that it was (and is) firmly based on a clear set of theoretical principles. To describe the Constitution as a document of the Enlightenment—an eighteenth century movement in European thought that celebrated the capacity of reason to solve human problems—would be to tell the truth but not necessarily the whole truth. Alexander Hamilton, a delegate to the Constitutional Convention from New York, claimed that the U.S. Constitution reflected what he described as a "new science of politics." According to Hamilton, this new science was based on principles either unknown to or not fully understood by previous generations. It is generally acknowledged that the most fundamental principles of the Constitution are separation of powers, federalism, and republicanism.

Each of these principles is critical to a clear understanding of the American system of government, but each was developed because of the founders' commitment to a prior principle—the principle of limited governmental power. A government founded on the principle of limited powers must develop safeguards to ensure that the people who wield the powers of government do not go beyond the limits. Within the American constitutional system this is accomplished by the three principles cited above.

Separation of Powers

Separation of powers was a political principle advocated by English philosopher John Locke and French philosopher Baron de Montesquieu. The Constitution of the United States was the first national political document to apply this concept of government. Distinct governmental powers had long been recognized, but the Constitution of the United States was the first to place these powers in separate branches of government. The first three articles of the Constitution describe the location and authority of the legislative, executive, and judicial powers of government.

Article I, section 1 of the Constitution begins by stating: "All legislative Powers herein granted shall be vested in a Congress of the United States, which shall consist of a Senate and House of Representatives." In addition to establishing the location of the legislative powers, this statement declares that those powers will be shared by two separate legislative chambers. Bicameralism (the term used to describe a two-chambered legislature) permits the two legislative chambers to provide internal checks on each other.

The notes taken at the Constitutional Convention reveal that disagreements over how the representatives to Congress would be apportioned and selected were the most difficult for the delegates to settle. At one point, delegates threatened to withdraw from the convention over this issue. The solution to this dispute produced one legislative chamber that represents states equally (the Senate) and another that represents states according to their population (the House of Representatives).

The Senate consists of two senators from each state in the Union. Senators are elected for six-year terms; the long term was intended to give them relative freedom from the passing whims of the electorate. One of the rationales for such long terms was that the Senate would be freer to speak to the long-term needs of the nation. The Constitution requires staggered terms for the senators so that a third of the Senate seats are up for election every two years. This requirement provides a degree of stability and continuity in the national government.

In contrast, the members of the House of Representatives hold two-year terms. These shorter terms keep House members in much closer contact with the American voters. By requiring that House members seek reelection every two years, the Constitution provides the voting public with regular access to national lawmakers.

Legislators who desire new laws or want to alter old ones must be able to persuade a majority of the lawmakers in both legislative chambers of Congress. By design, this process was not intended to be quick or easy. The legislature was meant to be a deliberative group that carefully examines all proposed laws. In a bicameral legislature, proposals that might be rushed through one chamber may be examined carefully in the second chamber. The Framers of the Constitution believed that it was more important that laws be carefully and thoughtfully examined than that they be approved quickly.

Article II, section 1 of the Constitution places the executive powers of the United States government in the hands of "a President." The Constitutional Convention had considerable difficulties developing the executive branch of government. In part, this was attributable to their basic suspicion of executive power. They also realized, however, that one of the greatest shortcomings of the Articles of Confederation was the absence of a clearly defined executive branch. The first question was whether the executive authority should be placed in a single executive or multiple executives. The second question, and one of the last to be settled at the Convention, concerned the method for selecting the executive.

After much debate, the Convention settled on a single executive. In the words of Alexander Hamilton, only a single executive would provide the "unity and dispatch" modern governments required. This sentiment prevailed, and the Convention then had to determine how "the President of the United States" would be selected. The electoral college was the method upon which they eventually settled. This system utilizes the states as electoral units and follows the representative principle devised for Congress to distribute the votes among the states.

The president's basic responsibilities are to see that national laws are faithfully executed, to serve as the commander in chief of the national armed forces, to appoint the executive officers of the different federal agencies, and to recommend judges to serve on the Supreme Court and the lesser courts established by Congress. In addition to these responsibilities, the president has a limited veto over the acts of Congress.

Article III of the Constitution describes the judicial branch of government. More specifically, it establishes the Supreme Court and any additional courts Congress may establish. One of the more unusual aspects of the Constitution is its establishment of an independent judiciary. Judges receive lifelong appointments, so they are as free from political influences as is humanly possible. The only qualification to this independence is that Congress has the power to impeach and remove judges if they behave in a manner that would warrant such removal. In this respect, judges are subjected to the same kind of scrutiny as are members of the executive branch of government.

One aspect of the separation of powers that is often given particular consideration is the concept of checks and balances. The Constitution provides that each of the three branches of government has certain "checks" on its power that are under the control of another branch. Congress, for example, controls the budget of the president and the judiciary. The president, on the other hand, can veto acts of Congress. Congress, in turn, can override a veto with a two-thirds vote in both houses. The president also appoints justices to the Supreme Court (with congressional approval). Finally, the Supreme Court can rule that the laws of Congress or the actions of the president are unconstitutional.

Federalism

This aspect of the Constitution is one of the more ingenious creations to grow out of the Constitutional Convention. Historically, national governments had been either unitary governments or confederal governments. Unitary governments place all power in the hands of a centralized authority. The British government is an example of such a system. In a confederal system, the ultimate power is decentralized among member states. Some responsibility may be given over to a centralized authority, but the real power remains with the decentralized units of government. This was the case under the Articles of Confederation. The federal system established by the Constitution was unique in that it created a governmental system in which the real powers of the political system were truly divided between the centralized and decentralized units of government.

The distribution of powers between the states and the national government has created considerable political tensions during the course of American history. It is important to realize that these tensions were largely intended by the founders. Federalism, like the separation of powers, was built into the constitutional system as a check on governmental powers. Article VI establishes the Constitution, acts of Congress, and treaties as the "supreme Law of the Land," but the Tenth Amendment to the Constitution declares the limits of that supremacy: The states and the people possess all powers not delegated to the United States by the Constitution.

Republicanism

Article IV of the Constitution guarantees that every state in the union will have a republican form of government. The Federalist Papers, a collection of essays written by Alexander Hamilton, James Madison, and John Jay in 1787 and 1788, explain why a republican system of government was considered preferable to a democratic system. The tenth essay of this collection provides a detailed comparison of these two popular systems of government. The first advantage of republicanism is that governmental authority is delegated to a small group of citizens. The second is that republican governments can cover a much larger geographical area than a direct democracy can.

When a smaller group has the responsibility of representing a larger group, each of the representatives must speak for a variety of interests. By learning the interests and needs of a diverse number of groups, representatives approach governmental decision making with a broader perspective than they would if they were simply advocating their own interests and needs. Public opinion is thereby filtered through a select group of representatives who must keep the many needs of their district in mind.

The advantage of a large geographical area is that it produces a great diversity of interests. This diversity decreases the likelihood that a single interest will constitute a majority on any given issue. For example, while chicken processors may hold a majority interest in Arkansas or oil producers may be a major political force in Texas, neither of these groups can dominate a large geographical area such as the entire United States. Together, these factors increase the likelihood that governmental decisions will serve the general interests of the nation instead of one or a few dominant groups.

The existence of these basic principles within the Constitution creates a significant barrier to government guided by passion as opposed to government guided by reason. The many checks within the system provide numerous obstacles to laws that are not in the interest of a fairly wide and diverse group of citizens. The system also places a substantial burden of proof on those who want to change existing laws or develop new laws. The cumbersome nature of the political process exposes any legislative initiative to a series of examinations before a number of different bodies.

Amendments

The Constitution has been a remarkably stable political document. The method described in Article V for amending the Constitution has not been utilized very often. By 1995 there were only twenty-seven amendments to the Constitution. The first ten amendments, known as the Bill of Rights, were passed within three years of the Constitution's ratification.

Three amendments (thirteen through fifteen) were passed at the end of the Civil War to make the institution of slavery unconstitutional and to extend certain citizenship rights to African Americans liberated by the Civil War. One of these, the Fourteenth Amendment, through its requirements of "due process" and "equal protection of the laws," has been instrumental in expanding basic civil rights to a number of other groups as well. The Seventeenth Amendment instituted the direct election of senators, the Twenty-second Amendment limited presidents to two terms, and the Twenty-fifth Amendment provided for the transfer of power in cases of presidential disability. A number of amendments (fifteen, nineteen, twenty-three, twenty-four, and twenty-six) have expanded the electorate.

One of the reasons often cited for the Constitution not having gathered more amendments through the years is the role the federal courts have played in determining questions of constitutionality. This process, known as judicial review, has permitted the courts to clarify and fine tune aspects of the Constitution. At times the courts have been accused of taking undue advantage of this authority. President Woodrow Wilson, for example, once referred to the Supreme Court as an ongoing constitutional convention.

The Constitution has proved to be one of the most durable political documents of all time. One of the key reasons for this durability is the document's brevity. The founders had a sense of what a constitution needed to specify and what it did not. Leaving many details unsettled, the founders recognized that statutory laws, administrative law, and precedents could handle the more specific and transient details of government.

Donald V. Weatherman

Further Reading
Beard, Charles Austin. *The Supreme Court and the Constitution.* Mineola, N.Y.: Dover, 2006.

Breyer, Stephen G. *Active Liberty: Interpreting Our Democratic Constitution.* New York: Alfred A. Knopf, 2005.

Carrithers, David W., Michael A. Mosher, and Paul A. Rahe, eds. *Montesquieu's Science of Politics: Essays on "The Spirit of the Laws."* Lanham, Md.: Rowman & Littlefield, 2001.

Fisher, Louis. *The Supreme Court and Congress: Rival Interpretations.* Washington, D.C.: CQ Press, 2009.

Kautz, Steven, ed. *The Supreme Court and the Idea of Constitutionalism.* Philadelphia: University of Pennsylvania Press, 2009.

Levy, Leonard, and Kenneth Karst, eds. *Encyclopedia of the American Constitution.* 2d ed. 6 vols. New York: Macmillan Reference, 2000.

Pollock, Earl E. *The Supreme Court and American Democracy: Case Studies on Judicial Review and Public Policy.* Westport, Conn.: Greenwood Press, 2009.

Savage, David G. *The Supreme Court and the Powers of the American Government.* 2d ed. Washington, D.C.: CQ Press, 2009.

Stephens, Otis H., and Richard A. Glenn. *Unreasonable Searches and Seizures: Rights and Liberties Under the Law.* Santa Barbara, Calif.: ABC-CLIO, 2006.

Whittington, Keith E. *Constitutional Interpretation: Textual Meaning, Original Intent, and Judicial Review.* Lawrence: University Press of Kansas, 2001.

THE BILL OF RIGHTS

- The first ten amendments to the U.S. Constitution, proposed in 1789 and ratified in 1791, constitute the U.S. Bill of of Rights, the Constitution's most concentrated statement of civil liberties. The first eight amendments provide specific prohibitions against government action, while the last two appear to be more explanatory.

British common law had evolved many rights that British citizens had in relation to their government, but these rights were not necessarily granted to American colonists; this was one of the grievances that led to the American Revolution. There was a direct relationship, in fact, between certain British actions and certain amendments in the Bill of Rights.

Not only grievances against the British but also fear of the potential power of the national government under the newly proposed Constitution led to the Bill of Rights. Some opponents of the proposed document seized on the lack of a list of citizens' rights as an argument against adopting the Constitution. The inclusion of a Bill of Rights was accepted by the Constitution's proponents as a means to sway undecided voters to vote for ratification. Still, not all proponents liked the idea. In one of the Federalist Papers, Alexander Hamilton argued that the entire Constitution was so limited as to be itself a "Bill of Rights," that no further list was needed, and that there might even be the danger that a narrow list of rights would be regarded as the only rights people had. To meet Hamilton's objection, the Ninth Amendment stated explicitly that the mere enumeration of these rights was not meant to preclude other rights belonging to Americans. The Ninth Amendment and the Tenth Amendment (which reserves power to the states and people, respectively) therefore are explanatory and do not have the same character as the first eight. The decision to promise inclusion of a Bill of Rights was a great strategic success for the Constitution's proponents and was a key feature in several wavering states' support for the new union.

Early in the First Congress under the new Constitution, James Madison led in suggesting the amendments that, after committee deliberation, became the text of the Bill of Rights. There were twelve amendments, but only ten were ratified initially. For all of the twentieth century celebration of the Bill of Rights, at their centennial in 1891 there was almost no mention of them. At that time they were understood to apply only to the federal government,

THE BILL OF RIGHTS

Amendment I

Congress shall make no law respecting an establishment of religion, or prohibiting the free exercise thereof; or abridging the freedom of speech, or of the press, or the right of the people peaceably to assemble, and to petition the Government for a redress of grievances.

Amendment II

A well regulated Militia, being necessary to the security of a free State, the right of the people to keep and bear Arms, shall not be infringed.

Amendment III

No Soldier shall, in time of peace be quartered in any house, without the consent of the Owner, nor in time of war, but in a manner to be prescribed by law.

Amendment IV

The right of the people to be secure in their persons, houses, papers, and effects, against unreasonable searches and seizures, shall not be violated, and no Warrants shall issue, but upon probable cause, supported by Oath or affirmation, and particularly describing the place to be searched, and the persons or things to be seized.

Amendment V

No person shall be held to answer for a capital, or otherwise infamous crime, unless on a presentment or indictment of a Grand Jury, except in cases arising in the land or naval forces, or in the Militia, when in actual service in time of War or public danger; nor shall any person be subject for the same offence to be twice put in jeopardy of life or limb, nor shall be compelled in any criminal case to be a witness against himself, nor be deprived of life, liberty, or property, without due process of law; nor shall private property be taken for public use without just compensation.

Amendment VI

In all criminal prosecutions, the accused shall enjoy the right to a speedy and public trial, by an impartial jury of the State and district wherein the crime shall have been committed; which district shall have been previously ascertained by law, and to be informed of the nature and cause of the accusation; to be confronted with the witnesses against him; to have compulsory process for obtaining witnesses in his favor, and to have the assistance of counsel for his defence.

Amendment VII
In Suits at common law, where the value in controversy shall exceed twenty dollars, the right of trial by jury shall be preserved, and no fact tried by a jury shall be otherwise re-examined in any Court of the United States, than according to the rules of the common law.

Amendment VIII
Excessive bail shall not be required, nor excessive fines imposed, nor cruel and unusual punishments inflicted.

Amendment IX
The enumeration in the Constitution, of certain rights, shall not be construed to deny or disparage others retained by the people.

Amendment X
The powers not delegated to the United States by the Constitution, nor prohibited by it to the States, are reserved to the States respectively, or to the people.

which was not significantly involved in regulating individual behavior. Even after the passage of the Fourteenth Amendment, which the Supreme Court later used to extend the Bill of Rights to the states, the actual incorporation of these rights for use of citizens against either level of government did not come until much later. In the twentieth century, the "selective incorporation" process has applied most essential provisions to the states under the "due process" clause of the Fourteenth Amendment.

The First Four Amendments and Their Current Significance
The First Amendment's promise that "Congress shall pass no law" establishing religion or blocking the free exercise of religious belief, speech, press, peaceful assembly, or petition is of core importance to the whole realm of free expression. Of all the sections of the Bill of Rights, the provisions of the First Amendment were the first to be incorporated under the due process clause of the Fourteenth Amendment and applied to the states. All of its sections have been the subject of considerable litigation.

Most scholars believe that the Second Amendment's language—"a well regulated militia, being necessary to the security of a free state, the right of the people to keep and bear arms, shall not be infringed"—is misunderstood by those who attempt to find in it a broad individual right to own unregulated firearms. Adopted because of the British attempt to disarm the colonial militias before the Revolution and the fear that the new U.S. national government might do the same, this amendment has never been interpreted by the Supreme Court to establish an absolute individual right to own guns or to bar regulation of them. It has not been applied to state regulation of firearms. The amendment was intended to prevent national disarmament of state militias, which is no longer a substantial concern. Clearly, Congress cannot regulate guns in such a way as to disarm state militias, but not much more is banned by this amendment. For example, *United States v. Miller* (1939) held that a ban on sales of sawed-off shotguns did not violate the amendment, since these guns would not be used by a militia.

The Third Amendment was written in response to British stationing of troops in the homes of civilian colonists without compensation for the service—purportedly to cut the cost of the army needed to defend against American Indians, but probably also as a device for controlling rebellious colonists. The Third Amendment bans such a practice: "No soldier shall, in time of peace, be quartered in any house, without the consent of the owner, nor in time of war, but in a manner to be described by law." The Supreme Court has not heard any cases contesting the Third Amendment because the language is so clear, the quartering of soldiers in civilian houses is impractical in modern times, and the amendment has not been applied to the states under the incorporation theory.

The Fourth Amendment's promise—"the right of the people to be secure in their persons, houses, papers, and effects, against unreasonable searches and seizures, shall not be violated, and no warrant shall be issued but upon probable cause, supported by oath or affirmation, and particularly in describing the place to be searched, and the persons or things to be seized"—arose out of British colonial practices. Although British citizens had gained some protection against unreasonable searches and seizures in England itself, the British government did not extend this protection to the colonists. To protect citizens from such abuses by the new national government, the requirement for a search warrant provided an important judicial control on search and seizure actions by the police.

Although the police may both search and seize, they must obtain court approval, which is to be granted only with probable cause. Any material seized through an unreasonable search and seizure may be found inadmissible as evidence in federal courts, under a legal doctrine known as the exclusionary rule, which was applied to the states as a result of incorporation in *Mapp v. Ohio* (1961). In the early history of the United States, searches and seizures were largely physical acts, but later, as of *Katz v. United States* (1967), the Court held that electronic eavesdropping and wiretapping also require a warrant from a judge based on probable cause.

The Fifth Amendment

The Fifth Amendment is so comprehensive that each section must be examined separately. The first section provides that "no person shall be held to answer for a capital, or otherwise infamous crime, unless on a presentment or indictment of a Grand Jury, except in cases arising in the land or naval forces, or in the Militia, when in actual service in time of War or public danger. . . ." While the grand jury (not the petit jury which sits at a trial) is one of the oldest institutions in Anglo-American law, its use has declined, and this right has not been incorporated and applied to the states. Many states do not use a grand jury and proceed to a trial with an indictment or presentment by the prosecutor.

The second section prohibits "double jeopardy": "Nor shall any person be subject for the same offense to twice be put in jeopardy of life or limb." The double jeopardy provision covers only criminal cases and was not applied to the states until the case *Benton v. Maryland* (1969). The double jeopardy provi-

James Madison, the principal author of the Bill of Rights. (Library of Congress)

sion is important as a safeguard against a government that seeks to try to retry a person until it finally gains a conviction, as the British did in colonial times. It is an important individual protection against the government, but the provision does not always prohibit a retrial if a mistrial has occurred or if the defendant appeals a conviction.

The third widely known provision of the Fifth Amendment protects against self-incrimination: "Nor shall [any person] be compelled in any criminal case to be a witness against himself." Churches' and monarchs' ancient practice of torturing people to force them to confess to crimes was gradually overcome in England in the sixteenth and seventeenth centuries, and it was natural for Americans to include protection against it. The Supreme Court did not consider this right so fundamental that it needed to be applied to the states until the case of *Malloy v. Hogan* (1964). Those who testify before some congressional committees are not protected by this section, although most congressional committees now voluntarily allow witnesses "to take the Fifth." With this exception, the U.S. legal system does provide a broad, significant protection against self-incrimination.

The fourth section states, "Nor [shall any person] be deprived of life, liberty, or property without due process of law." Identical words are used in the Fourteenth Amendment, and subsequent judicial interpretation has applied the due process clause of the Fourteenth Amendment to all the other protections included in the Fifth Amendment and many other protections as well. For most of U.S. history, the Supreme Court has treated the due process clause of the Fifth Amendment as if it were redundant (merely reincorporating the procedural due process guarantees listed elsewhere).

On some occasions, the due process clause has been interpreted as meaning that substantive due process issues (such as reasonableness or fairness) can also be examined under the Fifth Amendment. The Fifth Amendment was used in this way to strike down national economic legislation under a substantive due process concept early in the twentieth century, but more recently the Court has departed from this practice without completely abandoning the substantive due process notion. Specifically, the Supreme Court has allowed this section of the Fifth Amendment to be used to resolve substantive due process questions in the civil rights area.

This represents a substantial shift in the meaning of substantive due process. In *Bolling v. Sharpe* (1954), the Court included the legal equal protection concept of the Fourteenth Amendment under the due process portion of the Fifth Amendment. In this way, the notion of equal protection of the law was applied on the federal level, whereas previously it had applied only on the state level through the Fourteenth Amendment.

The last provision, "nor shall private property be taken for public use without just compensation," represented an attempt by the Framers to limit the power of eminent domain, or the government's power to reclaim private land for society's benefit. Clearly, in war property owners might need to yield their property for the good of all, or lose it to the enemy. Such situations make any limit on government difficult, so the U.S. drafters should be credited for trying. This restraint has been seriously weakened in the twentieth century. As the courts have stopped second-guessing legislatures on what constitutes a "public purpose," the phrase has become vague and meaningless.

The Supreme Court has even allowed the government to take land from one private party and sell it to another for a commercial use, so that all any owner can do is haggle over the sales price. Even this is difficult, because "just compensation" should match the "fair market value," which implies a willing seller. This was the first portion of the Bill of Rights to be incorporated under the due process clause of the Fourteenth Amendment—in *Chicago, Milwaukee and St. Paul Railway Co. v. Minnesota* (1890), and even more clearly so in a second case, *Chicago, Burlington and Quincy Railroad Co. v. Chicago* (1897).

The Sixth Amendment

The Sixth Amendment enumerates basic rights for those accused of committing crimes. First, "in all criminal prosecutions, the accused shall have the right to a speedy and public trial, by an impartial jury of the state and district wherein the crime shall have been committed, which district shall have previously been ascertained by law." These are virtually the same words used in Article III of the Constitution; clearly, the Framers were convinced that these rights were absolutely vital. These rights, which had evolved over time in Anglo-Saxon law, had not been extended to the American colonists by the British, and the Framers wanted to avoid the possibility of similar difficulties recurring. These provisions did not apply to the states until *Duncan v. Louisiana* (1968).

A second speedy, public trial section was applied to the states in *Klopfer v. North Carolina* (1967). Klopfer had been indicted by North Carolina for criminal trespass for taking part in a sit-in demonstration in a restaurant. At the trial, the jury failed to reach an agreement; the resulting mistrial allowed the state to retry Klopfer. The state elected to delay the trial indefinitely, but the U.S. Supreme Court ruled unanimously against North Carolina, stating that the resulting uncertainty and delay deprived Klopfer of his liberty without due process of law. "Public" trials have turned out to be an even more difficult issue for the courts because they readily bring the rights of the accused into conflict with the rights of the press under the First Amendment.

The Sixth Amendment's requirement of an impartial jury has been used on occasion to prevent racial discrimination in the selection of local juries as

> ## BILL OF RIGHTS PROTECTIONS NOT EXTENDED TO THE STATES
>
> - Second Amendment right to keep and bear arms
> - Third Amendment limit on quartering of soldiers in private homes
> - Fifth Amendment right to indictment by grand juries
> - Seventh Amendment right to jury trials in civil cases
> - Eighth Amendment right against excessive fines (scholars disagree about the status of the right against excessive bail)

well as discrimination based on sex, nationality, and religion. Prior to the American Revolution, the British had hauled American colonists across the Atlantic to stand trial in England. Not only was the expense prohibitive for the accused colonist, but also the chances of bringing witnesses in the accused's defense or of a fair trial were nonexistent. Thus the right to a "local" jury was included to prevent the federal government from doing the same to residents of various states. Other rights basic to the common-law tradition of the Anglo-Saxon judicial tradition, including the right to be informed of the nature and cause of an indictment, to be confronted by witnesses, to have compulsory process (subpoenas) for obtaining reluctant witnesses in one's behalf, and to have the assistance of counsel for defense, are also in the Sixth Amendment.

Notable among the Sixth Amendment guarantees applied to the states is the right to the assistance of counsel in the defense of criminal cases, as established in the case *Gideon v. Wainwright* (1963). Prior to this time, the right to counsel in capital cases had been granted to criminal defendants, but until 1963 it was not clear that all defendants in criminal proceedings should have counsel provided. Later, the more controversial *Escobedo v. Illinois* (1964) and *Miranda v. Arizona* (1966) cases provided for the assistance of counsel not only at the trial but also at the time an accused is arrested by the police.

Provisions of the Seventh and Eighth Amendments
The Seventh Amendment states, "In suits at common law, where the value in controversy shall exceed twenty dollars, the right of trial by jury shall be

preserved, and no fact tried by a jury, shall be otherwise reexamined in any court of the United States according to the rules of common law," providing guarantees in federal civil cases. Because civil cases are held to be less directly related to an individual's basic rights and civil liberties, and because the original limit of twenty dollars is unrealistically low, the Supreme Court has not applied the Seventh Amendment to the states.

The Eighth Amendment provides that "excessive bail shall not be required, nor excessive fines imposed, nor cruel or unusual punishment inflicted." The ban on excessive bail (not yet applied to states) means that bail should not be set higher than would be reasonable to ensure the presence of the defendant at the trial. It also allows the denial of bail when no bail could guarantee the presence of the accused at trial, as in capital cases or those where the accused might commit other crimes pending trial. The prohibition of excessive fines has been extended to states; it means that an indigent person does not have to pay a fine, since failure to pay a fine cannot result in imprisonment unless imprisonment is otherwise a penalty for the same crime.

Controversy has emerged over the Eighth Amendment's prohibition of cruel and unusual punishment, since opponents of capital punishment argue that it is "cruel and unusual." Throughout U.S. history, however, capital punishment has existed in most states, and the prevailing view is that capital punishment is not cruel and unusual. Former U.S. Supreme Court Justices Harry A. Blackmun, William J. Brennan, and William O. Douglas have maintained that public sensibilities have gradually changed and that capital punishment is now, by nature, "cruel and unusual." These justices did not persuade a court majority to this view, but in *Furman v. Georgia* (1972) a majority did rule that capital punishment as administered in the various states was cruel, unusual, and discriminatory in its impact because vastly more blacks were executed than whites. Subsequently, many states revised their capital punishment laws, and the revisions were upheld.

The Ninth and Tenth Amendments

The Ninth Amendment was added to try to overcome the objections of those who opposed adding a Bill of Rights for fear that such a list would lead people to conclude that only those rights would be protected. The Ninth Amendment states, "The enumeration in the Constitution, of certain rights, shall not be construed to deny or disparage others retained by the people." The Ninth Amendment has been used principally to include a broad range of rights under the general notion of privacy, which can be found in the Fourth, Fifth, and Sixth Amendments.

Technically, the Tenth Amendment adds nothing to the Constitution, because it simply makes explicit what everyone regarded as understood: that the power of the federal government consisted in certain delegated or enumerated powers which could not expand. The Framers considered it important, however, to make clear that certain rights were retained by the states or the people, so they added the words, "The powers not delegated to the United States by the Constitution, nor prohibited to the states, are reserved to the states respectively, or to the people."

Richard L. Wilson

Further Reading

Abraham, Henry J., and Barbara A. Perry. *Freedom and the Court: Civil Rights and Liberties in the United States.* 8th ed. Lawrence: University Press of Kansas, 2003.

Abrams, Floyd. *Speaking Freely: Trials of the First Amendment.* New York: Penguin Books, 2006.

Amar, Akhil Reed. *The Bill of Rights: Creation and Reconstruction.* New Haven, Conn.: Yale University Press, 2000.

Fisher, Louis. *The Supreme Court and Congress: Rival Interpretations.* Washington, D.C.: CQ Press, 2009.

Franklin, Paula. *The Fourth Amendment.* New York: Silver Burdett Press, 2001.

Garcia, Alfredo. *The Fifth Amendment: A Comprehensive Approach.* Westport, Conn.: Greenwood Press, 2002.

McInnis, Thomas. *The Evolution of the Fourth Amendment.* Lanham, Md.: Lexington Books, 2009.

Perry, Michael J. *We the People: The Fourteenth Amendment and the Supreme Court.* New ed. New York: Oxford University Press, 2002.

Savage, David. *The Supreme Court and Individual Rights.* Washington, D.C.: CQ Press, 2009.

Taylor, John B. *Right to Counsel and Privilege Against Self-Incrimination: Rights and Liberties Under the Law.* Santa Barbara, Calif.: ABC-CLIO, 2004.

Volokh, Eugene. *First Amendment: Law, Cases, Problems, and Policy Arguments.* New York: Foundation Press, 2001.

CONSTITUTIONAL LAW

- Constitutional law is a dynamic body of law that defines and limits the powers of government and sets out its organizational structure. As the fundamental law contained in the U.S. Constitution and in Supreme Court decisions interpreting that document, constitutional law blends legal decisions with elements of politics and political theory, history, economics, public policy, philosophy, and ethics.

A resilient document, the U.S. Constitution has endured with only twenty-seven amendments since its formulation in 1787. Its sweeping language and generalities allow change and interpretation in the face of altered circumstances, from the changing human condition to the changing composition of the Supreme Court. The Constitution contains few rules and is not self-explanatory. That lack of specificity was intentional. The Framers outlined their general intent to create the fundamentals of a national government, prescribing how it should operate and limiting its scope of power. The ongoing interpretative process engaged in by the Court allows the provisions of the Constitution to change and adapt over time. The Court refers to the original Constitution because by doing so, it can bring resolution of the new and often divisive issues of each generation. The genius of constitutionalism, therefore, lies in the opportunities provided in the document for change and continuity, the method of judicial interpretation, and the overall skill and sensitivity of the justices. The fact that the justices are lifetime appointees frees them from concerns about approval by political leaders and voters and permits concentration on the issues.

Constitutional Decision Making

Virtually all cases before the Court involve seeking review of a decision by a federal court of appeals or a state supreme court. As the final authority on federal matters and questions dealing with the Constitution and treaties, the Court exercises appellate jurisdiction (appeals) and functions as a trial court (original jurisdiction) only in certain limited situations involving ambassadors or where a state is a party. Most of the cases reach the Court for review by means of a writ of *certiorari*, or through the exercise of the Court's discretion. This means that the Court has almost complete control of its docket. Of the 7,000 petitions for review annually, only 2 percent are granted. The Court issues an average of 110 opinions per year, permitting a selected group of policy issues to be addressed.

The Court is shrouded in secrecy, assuming some of the awe and mystery of the document it interprets. Some have criticized the Court for remaining in an "ivory tower" far removed from the phrase "we the people" set out in the preamble to the Constitution. Decisions to grant or deny review are made in secret conferences attended only by the nine justices with no support staff. A traditional unwritten rule specifies that a case is accepted for review if four justices feel that it merits the Court's attention (rule of four) and that it would serve the interests of justice. The Court does not have to explain its refusal.

When the Court decides to hear a case, the clerk schedules oral argument during which the justices may interrupt and ask questions of the attorneys to clarify, debate, or explain the written briefs. Cases are discussed in secret conferences following oral argument. It takes a majority vote to decide a case.

Following the conference and ensuing discussion, an opinion or reasoned argument explaining the legal issues in the case and the precedents on which the opinion is based must be drafted. The manner in which a majority opinion is written can have a great impact on Americans. That impact depends in part on who writes the opinion and how it is written, and also on the extent of support or dissent by the remaining justices. A 5-4 plurality opinion does not demonstrate the firm conviction of the Court that is present in a unanimous or 8-1 decision.

Any justice can write a separate opinion. If justices agree with the majority's decision but disagree with its reasoning, they may write a concurring opinion. If they disagree with both the result and reasoning contained in the majority opinion, they may write a dissenting opinion or simply go on the record as dissenting without an opinion. More than one justice can join in a concurring or dissenting opinion.

Decision making or opinion writing is a painstaking and laborious process. The time involved varies from one justice to another depending on the complexity of the issues in the case. The actual reporting of decisions has changed from the days in which members of the Court read long opinions aloud, sometimes taking days to do so. When Charles Evans Hughes became chief justice in 1930, he encouraged the delivery of summaries of opinions. That practice has continued, and the justice writing the majority opinion delivers the summary. Dissenting justices deliver their own opinions. Computerization and Lexis and Westlaw legal databases have made newly decided opinions accessible to all within hours of their release.

The Highest Court

Decisions of the U.S. Supreme Court are final because there is no higher court to which to appeal. Its interpretation of statutes can be reversed only by congressional legislation, and its constitutional rulings overturned only by constitutional amendment. Absent these remedies, all courts are obliged to follow the Supreme Court in matters of federal law. In its decisions, the Court attempts to adhere to precedent, or *stare decisis*, and in that capacity serves as final authority in constitutional matters, thereby providing a uniform interpretation of the law, historical continuity, stability, and predictability. Just as the Court sets its own agenda and controls what it hears, accepting or rejecting cases according to individual and collective goals such as avoiding troublesome issues, resolving legal conflicts, and establishing policies favored by the justices, Court decisions are group products shaped by the law, the Court and the country's environment, and the personal value systems of and interactions among the justices.

The power to define the Constitution makes the Court unique among government institutions. Through the exercise of its constitutional role together with the rule of law, the Court has wielded far-reaching power. The proper functioning of federalism and the scope of the rights of the individual depend on the actions of the Court, whose words mark the boundaries of the branches and departments of government.

The justices function as "nine little law firms," autonomous but working as a collegial body to decide a case. In important cases, the opinions issued by the Court are often negotiated among the members, the result of a cooperative collaboration in which the end product is the joint work of all rather than the product of the named author alone.

Self-Imposed Limitations

The Supreme Court imposes certain limitations or barriers before accepting a case for review. It poses certain threshold questions to deal with tactical issues that must be resolved before the Court reaches the substance of the controversy. Referred to as "judicial restraint," if these elements are not overcome, the Court will not exercise jurisdiction over a case. Article III, section 2 of the Constitution requires that there exist an ongoing "case or controversy" at all stages of the proceedings, including appeal. As interpreted by the Court, these words limit the power of federal courts to resolving disputes between adversaries whose rights are truly in collision. Often called "justiciability," the requirement provides concreteness when a question is precisely framed. The case, therefore, must present a live dispute.

Precluded are advisory opinions, or giving advice on abstract or hypothetical situations, as the Court ruled in *Muskrat v. United States* (1911), and moot cases, or those that have already been resolved, settled, or feigned, or those in which circumstances or time have removed the dispute or conflict because there is nothing for a court to decide, as it ruled in *DeFunis v. Odegaard* (1974). Several narrow exceptions to the mootness rule exist where conduct is of short duration but capable of repetition such as election disputes or abortion cases such as *Roe v. Wade* and its companion case *Doe v. Bolton* (1973). In *Baker v. Carr* (1962), the Court determined that political questions or those matters more properly applicable to another branch of government will not be accepted, nor will friendly or collusive suits and test cases. Standing to sue requires that the litigants have a personal stake in the outcome of the case, having suffered an actual injury, in order to assure concrete adverseness. Ripeness requires the issues in the case to be clearly delineated and sharply outlined, not premature, in flux, or abstract. Moreover, the Court will not engage in speculation, contingencies, or predictions or issue extrajudicial advice.

Judicial Review

Courts participate in the development of constitutional law through judicial review. In the landmark case *Marbury v. Madison* (1803), considered to be the point at which constitutional law begins, the Court held that Article III empowers courts to review government actions and invalidate those found to be repugnant to the Constitution by declaring them unconstitutional. The supremacy clause of Article IV states that no provision of state law and no legislative enactment may conflict with the national Constitution, which is the supreme law of the land.

The Framers of the Constitution decentralized control through federalism, considered one of the most important contributions to government. Federalism is a dual system in which powers are divided between national and state authorities.

The Bill of Rights

Protecting the fundamental rights of individuals was considered of the utmost importance. The Framers believed that explicit enumeration of those rights would make the rights more secure. In order to achieve ratification of the main body of the Constitution, therefore, in 1791 the Framers appended to it a Bill of Rights, consisting of the first ten amendments of the present document. While the body of the main Constitution concerns government, the Bill of Rights represents the popular perception of constitutional guarantees.

Basic to American identity is the First Amendment and its central guarantees of freedom of speech, press, religion, assembly, and the right to petition for redress of grievances. Despite language to the contrary, the rights contained in the Bill of Rights are not absolute. In the speech area, for example, certain categories of expression can be regulated; others are not protected at all. "Pure" speech that creates no danger to the public is protected. However, if speech advocates an imminent lawless action that presents a "clear and present danger," the speech loses its protection, as the Court ruled in *Schenck v. United States* (1919). In *Texas v. Johnson* (1989), the Court found that symbolic speech or use of actions as a substitute for words is generally protected, such as flag burning as a controversial but valid expression of political views. Obscenity or pornography, defamatory communications (libel and slander), and "fighting words" that provoke an immediate breach of the peace do not receive First Amendment protection.

Some rights that Americans consider basic to their fundamental freedoms are not mentioned specifically in the Constitution. Among these are the right of personal privacy, which protects the individual from state interference. The Court struggled with the constitutional foundation of the right, suggesting various sources: the due process guarantee of the Fourteenth Amendment and the penumbras or emanations from the interests protected by the First, Third, Fourth, Fifth, and Ninth Amendments.

Marcia J. Weiss

Further Reading

Abraham, Henry J., and Barbara A. Perry. *Freedom and the Court: Civil Rights and Liberties in the United States.* 8th ed. Lawrence: University Press of Kansas, 2003.

Barron, Jerome A., and C. Thomas Dienes. *Constitutional Law in a Nutshell.* 6th ed. St. Paul, Minn.: West, 2005.

Baum, Lawrence. *The Supreme Court.* 10th ed. Washington, D.C.: CQ Press, 2010.

Beard, Charles Austin. *The Supreme Court and the Constitution.* Mineola, N.Y.: Dover, 2006.

Breyer, Stephen G. *Active Liberty: Interpreting Our Democratic Constitution.* New York: Alfred A. Knopf, 2005.

Epstein, Lee, and Thomas Walker. *Constitutional Law for a Changing America.* 5th ed. Washington, D.C.: CQ Press, 2003.

Hensley, Thomas, Christopher Smith, and Joyce Baugh. *The Changing Supreme Court: Constitutional Rights and Liberties.* 2d ed. Belmont: Thomson/Wadsworth, 2007.

Kahn, Ronald, and Ken I. Kersch, eds. *The Supreme Court and American Political Development.* Lawrence: University Press of Kansas, 2006.

Kautz, Steven, ed. *The Supreme Court and the Idea of Constitutionalism.* Philadelphia: University of Pennsylvania Press, 2009.

Maltzman, Forrest, et al. *Crafting Law on the Supreme Court: The Collegial Game.* New York: Cambridge University Press, 2000.

O'Brien, David M. *Constitutional Law and Politics.* 7th ed. New York: W. W. Norton, 2008.

Pollock, Earl E. *The Supreme Court and American Democracy: Case Studies on Judicial Review and Public Policy.* Westport, Conn.: Greenwood Press, 2009.

Roberson, Cliff. *Constitutional Law and Criminal Justice.* New York: Taylor & Francis, 2009.

Stephens, Otis H., Jr., and John M. Scheb. *American Constitutional Law.* 3d ed. Belmont, Calif.: Thomson/Wadsworth, 2003.

Tushnet, Mark, ed. *I Dissent: Great Opposing Opinions in Landmark Supreme Court Cases.* Boston: Beacon Press, 2008.

Urofsky, Melvin I., ed. *One Hundred Americans Making Constitutional History: A Biographical History.* Washington, D.C.: CQ Press, 2004.

Urofsky, Melvin I., and Paul Finkelman. *A March of Liberty: A Constitutional History of the United States.* 2d ed. 2 vols. New York: Oxford University Press, 2004.

Van Geel, T. R. *Understanding Supreme Court Opinions.* 6th ed. New York: Longman, 2008.

Vile, John. *The Essential Supreme Court Decisions: Summaries of Leading Cases in U.S. Constitutional Law.* 15th ed. Lanham, Md.: Rowman & Littlefield, 2010.

Whittington, Keith E. *Constitutional Interpretation: Textual Meaning, Original Intent, and Judicial Review.* Lawrence: University Press of Kansas, 2001.

The U.S. Judicial System

- The United States has a dual judicial system composed of federal and state courts that are organized as separate and independent systems; these systems are integrated and coordinated in subtle and complex accommodations of judicial federalism. What is called the U.S. judicial system encompasses the broad organization and interrelatedness of the courts of the federal government with the courts in the fifty states.

The basic duality of the U.S. judicial system, in which the federal judiciary coexists alongside the judiciaries of the fifty states, is a blueprint for conflicts. Although today this arrangement is taken for granted, the conceptual idea that two independent sovereigns could occupy the same territory and govern at the same time was a radical innovation of eighteenth century political philosophy. The Framers of the Constitution of 1787 were uncertain that such a federal system would work; they were certain that there would be conflicts between the federal and state governments, particularly between the federal courts and the state courts. Judicial federalism is the term used to describe the ongoing accommodation of these conflicts.

Historical Origins

The study of the U.S. judicial system begins with two eighteenth century events: ratification of Article III of the U.S. Constitution and passage of the Judiciary Act of 1789. Article III settled the issue of whether Congress should be given the power to create independent federal courts. The debate over Article III at the Constitutional Convention of 1787 was protracted and intense. An early draft of the Constitution had provided for a federal judicial branch. The delegates had second thoughts, however, and voted to strike the provision and make no mention of national courts other than the Supreme Court. Their rationale was that the existing state courts were equal to the judicial tasks of the nation; all that was needed was to provide for appeals from state courts to some supreme national court to preserve the uniformity and the supremacy of the national law. The state courts would have been the chief expositors of federal law had that position prevailed, and U.S. history would have developed far differently.

After further intense parliamentary wrangling, however, a compromise was reached, and the text of Article III was redrafted to read as it does today. It begins, "The judicial Power of the United States, shall be vested in one supreme Court, and in such inferior Courts as the Congress may from time to time ordain and establish." This language left the issue to Congress whether to create lower courts below the Supreme Court.

The delegates' compromise was the subject of controversy in the debates in the state ratifying conventions. The Federalist Papers (numbers 78 to 82, 1788) defended the wisdom of a separate and independent federal judiciary. Numerous amendments to Article III were proposed in the state ratifying conventions, and some of the provisions in the Bill of Rights, such as the Sixth Amendment right to a jury in a civil case, owe their origin to the controversy over Article III.

The anti-Federalists were mistrustful of the proposed Constitution. They campaigned against the document in most of its particulars and especially opposed the power to create a new federal judiciary. They feared that it would increase political power in the central government at the expense of the sovereign states. They wanted the state courts to remain supreme, and they nearly prevailed. The ratification outcome was in no measure certain, and the Federalists—who championed the Constitution—prevailed by the smallest of margins in several key states (the vote in Massachusetts was 187 to 168; Virginia, 89 to 79; and New York, 30 to 27). Thus, from the beginning, judicial federalism has been a theme in U.S. constitutional history.

Upon ratification, one of the transcendent achievements of the first Congress under the new Constitution was the passage of the Judiciary Act of 1789, also known as the First Judiciary Act. That statute established the tradition of a system of inferior federal courts. Today there are complex and detailed statutes in the U.S. Code and in the statutes of the fifty states describing the organization and jurisdictions of their judicial branches. The most controversial of these jurisdictions and procedures always have involved the interrelationship between the federal courts and the state courts.

Organization of Federal Courts

The structure of the federal judiciary is pyramidal. The Supreme Court, the courts of appeals, and the district courts form the three levels of federal courts.

At the apex is the Supreme Court of the United States, the only federal court created directly by the Constitution, which declares that there shall be "one supreme Court." The Supreme Court is the highest supervisory court within the federal judiciary. Therefore, it reviews the decisions of the lower federal courts, and it interprets the laws Congress enacts. The Supreme Court also has appellate authority over the state courts, but only for matters of federal law.

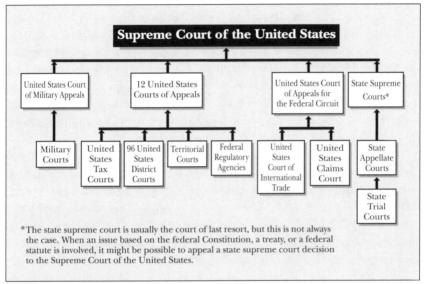

Source: Barbara A. Bardes et al. *American Government Politics Today: The Essentials* (St. Paul, MN: West Publishing, 1994).

The Court comprises nine justices, appointed by the president with the advice and consent of the Senate. Justices have lifetime tenure. Each justice is assigned to one of the courts of appeals for emergency matters, and the chief justice of the United States has additional administrative duties. The Supreme Court sits only *en banc*, with all of its members participating. Its annual term begins on the first Monday of October and continues usually through the end of June. Its annual docket consists of more than seven thousand cases. Most of its jurisdiction is discretionary, and the Court exercises great care in selecting cases for full review. Most cases are disposed of, without a decision on the merits of the case, by a brief order denying the petition for review or dismissing the appeal for want of a substantial question. Of the thousands of cases presented each term, the Supreme Court selects about 120 of the most important for full briefing, oral argument, and decision by written opinion.

At the level of intermediate federal courts, there are thirteen United States courts of appeals and the Court of Appeals for the Armed Forces. Twelve of the courts of appeals have jurisdiction over federal cases in certain geographical areas, each covering a number of contiguous states. The thirteenth, the federal circuit, has a national jurisdiction over specific types of cases, mostly involving patents, trademarks, international trade, and claims against the United States.

The number of judges appointed for each court of appeals varies from six to twenty-eight. These courts of appeals sit in panels of three judges, subject to rare full court rehearings before all the circuit judges sitting *en banc*. Appeals to the courts of appeals, for the most part, are appeals as of right: The party who lost in the trial court files a notice of appeal, and the matter must be heard and decided. Most matters appealed from the trial courts are affirmed by the courts of appeals; the reversal rate hovers between 10 and 20 percent. The courts of appeals have evolved into what could be called "junior varsity" supreme courts that determine the federal law for their geographical region, unless and until the Supreme Court overrules them.

The court with primary original or trial jurisdiction in the federal judiciary is the United States district court. Federal statutes divide the country and territories into ninety-four geographical districts. Districts do not extend beyond state boundary lines; each state constitutes at least one district, and many states are divided into one, two, three, or four districts. Districts are sometimes internally arranged into divisions for administrative purposes. There are more than six hundred district judges, and each district has a chief judge, designated on the basis of seniority, who has additional administrative responsibilities.

In a statistical year, the district courts decide more than two hundred thousand civil cases, including civil rights actions, personal injury or property damage actions, and prisoner petitions. There are nearly fifty thousand additional federal criminal cases, mostly felonies. Two additional federal judicial officers serve at the bottom of the federal court pyramid: U.S. magistrate judges and bankruptcy judges. Magistrate judges are appointed by the district judges and

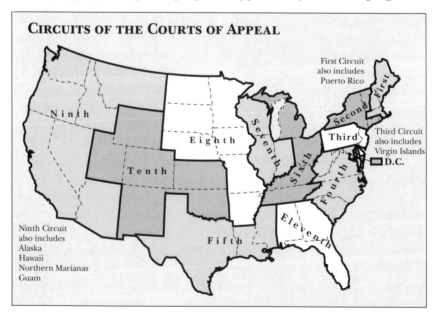

CIRCUITS OF THE COURTS OF APPEAL

First Circuit also includes Puerto Rico

Ninth

First

Second

Eighth

Seventh

Third

Third Circuit also includes Virgin Islands
D.C.

Tenth

Sixth

Fourth

Fifth

Eleventh

Ninth Circuit also includes
Alaska
Hawaii
Northern Marianas
Guam

perform as their adjuncts, handling miscellaneous judicial tasks specified by statute and holding civil trials with the consent of the parties. Bankruptcy judges are appointed by the courts of appeals and preside over the various categories of exclusive federal jurisdiction for individual and business reorganizations.

Organization of State Courts

Because state court structures vary widely from state to state, only broad generalizations are possible. All the states have some version of the pyramid-shaped structure of the federal judiciary, although the specific names of courts and their particular jurisdictions are highly state-specific.

Most state judges are elected, in contrast to the appointed judges in the federal system who serve "during good behavior" (effectively for life), although state judicial elections frequently are solely retention elections and often are nonpartisan. Unlike the federal judiciary, most state court structures have a bifurcated trial level. In a bifurcated system, trial courts of limited jurisdiction hear disputes on specified matters, generally involving small monetary matters or minor criminal offenses. Trial courts of general jurisdiction have jurisdiction over more important civil matters and more serious criminal offenses. The courts of general jurisdiction usually are courts of record—transcripts of their proceedings are required. Their procedure is more formal, and they sometimes hear appeals from the courts of limited jurisdiction, commonly by a trial *de novo*, which means that an entirely new proceeding is held.

A growing majority of states have established intermediate appellate courts, often as a response to caseload pressure on the highest court in the state. These intermediate appellate courts hear appeals from the trial courts of general jurisdiction and typically are arranged geographically within the state, usually hearing appeals from contiguous counties. It is not uncommon for state intermediate courts to have some reviewing authority of decisions issued by state administrative agencies.

Each state has a state supreme court, although jurisdictional provisions vary considerably. In some states, the appeal to the highest state court is discretionary, much like the U.S. Supreme Court, but in others such an appeal is a matter of statutory entitlement and the state supreme court is obliged to hear the appeal. The state supreme courts are the great common-law courts in the American judicial system. They have developed bodies of decisional law in torts and contracts, for example, that are comprehensive and highly sophisticated. The common law is developed by application of the principle of *stare decisis*, which basically obliges a court deciding an issue to follow the precedent established by an earlier court deciding the same issue unless there are compelling reasons to do otherwise.

When considered collectively, the fifty state judiciaries almost defy statistical measure. They dwarf the more elite federal courts. In 1992, there were nearly 28,000 state trial judges presiding over approximately 16,500 state trial courts of general and limited jurisdictions in the fifty states. That year there were more than 250,000 appeals filed; more than 60 percent were mandatory appeals to intermediate appellate courts, and the rest were appeals to state courts of last resort. Many state trial and appellate courts have experienced great difficulty keeping up with accelerating increases in caseload. More generally, budget problems in the states have resulted in funding crises for state courts.

Comparisons with Other Countries

The jurisdictions of the state and federal courts in the United States overlap to a large extent. There are some jurisdictions that are exclusively assigned to the federal courts, such as bankruptcy and patent cases, but those are the exceptions. Most of the jurisdiction of the federal courts is concurrent with the state courts. This means that the same lawsuit can be filed in either the U.S. district court or in a state court of general jurisdiction. Sometimes the parties actually file two separate lawsuits. When this happens, the first proceeding to reach a final judgment is then deemed controlling in the other court, state or federal. Questions of federal law decided in state trial or appellate courts are subject to review by the U.S. Supreme Court. Besides these vertical conflicts between the federal and state courts, it frequently happens that horizontal conflicts arise—when, for example, the state courts in one state must decide a question by applying the law of another state.

Thus the United States has a comparatively complex judicial system. Other Western democracies with federal systems use an entirely different model: The state/provincial courts perform the trial function, and the federal/national courts perform the appellate function. Australia and Canada, two federal systems that share the English common-law tradition with the United States, adhere to this alternative model, with some variations. In some federations, the federal authorities appoint all the judges, federal and state. In other federations, federal courts hear and decide only federal matters, and state courts hear and decide only state matters.

Conflicts Between State and Federal Courts

Issues of state court jurisdiction versus federal court jurisdiction are issues of constitutional power. Because federal courts are courts of limited jurisdiction, there is a presumption that the court lacks subject matter jurisdiction until it can be shown that the case falls within the appropriate constitutional and statutory authorizations. In contrast, a state court is not so limited. The presumption is that jurisdiction exists to hear and decide the matter and to afford appropriate relief. There are several points of regular conflict between state courts and federal courts.

The U.S. Supreme Court hears appeals from the highest courts of the states involving issues of federal law, interpretations of the U.S. Constitution, and federal statutes. State court judges are bound by their constitutional oath to follow the rulings of the U.S. Supreme Court, but the state court interpretations of state laws, including state constitutions, are binding on the U.S. Supreme Court so long as they are not inconsistent with federal law. Under the doctrine of the independent and adequate state ground, the Supreme Court will not hear a case if the decision of the state's highest court is supported by a state law rationale that is independent of federal law and adequate to sustain the result. The rationale is that it is better to decline to hear the case if a reversal of the state court's federal law ruling will not change the outcome of the case.

By federal statute, a person convicted for a state crime and serving a sentence in state custody may petition for a writ of habeas corpus in the U.S. district court. The petition must allege that the conviction and custody violate the U.S. Constitution. The U.S. district court can issue the writ and order the state authorities to release the prisoner unless a new trial is held. Appeals from the denial of the writ go to a U.S. court of appeals and then to the U.S. Supreme Court. This federal court jurisdiction is most controversial in cases in which the state prisoner has been sentenced to death and there are repeated federal appeals, often brought just before a scheduled execution.

Ever since the Judiciary Act of 1789, Congress has afforded federal courts jurisdiction in diversity cases, which are suits between citizens of different states or between a citizen of a state and an alien, when the amount in controversy exceeds a certain amount (set at $50,000 in 1988). When these requirements are satisfied, the plaintiff has a choice of filing in a U.S. district court or in a state court of general jurisdiction. Even if the plaintiff files in state court, the defendant may remove the case to the U.S. district court, under a federal statute. The policy behind this jurisdiction is a worry that a state court might be prejudiced against an out-of-state party. In theory, the federal judge hearing a diversity case must apply the law that a state judge would apply in state court. State judges, on the other hand, are not bound by the decisions of federal judges based on state law.

The principles of judicial federalism are not found in so many words in the U.S. Constitution, but nevertheless they are part of its deep structure. It would not simply be "bad form" for a federal court to entertain a case not within its jurisdiction; it would be an unconstitutional invasion of the powers reserved to the states. The intersovereign judicial interactions made possible by concurrent jurisdictions in such a complex court system cause problems that must be solved by complex statutes and sophisticated court doctrines.

Thomas E. Baker

Further Reading

Abraham, Henry J. *The Judicial Process: An Introductory Analysis of the Courts of the United States, England, and France.* 5th ed. New York: Oxford University Press, 1986.

Abraham, Henry J., and Barbara A. Perry. *Freedom and the Court: Civil Rights and Liberties in the United States.* 8th ed. Lawrence: University Press of Kansas, 2003.

Breyer, Stephen G. *Active Liberty: Interpreting Our Democratic Constitution.* New York: Alfred A. Knopf, 2005.

Fino, Susan P. *The Role of State Supreme Courts in the New Judicial Federalism.* New York: Greenwood, 1987.

Fisher, Louis. *The Supreme Court and Congress: Rival Interpretations.* Washington, D.C.: CQ Press, 2009.

Giddens-White, Bryon. *The Supreme Court and the Judicial Branch.* Chicago: Heinemann Library, 2006.

Glick, Henry Robert. *State Court Systems.* Englewood Cliffs, N.J.: Prentice-Hall, 1973.

Johnston, Richard E. *The Effect of Judicial Review on Federal-State Relations in Australia, Canada, and the United States.* Baton Rouge: Louisiana State University Press, 1969.

Meador, Daniel J. *American Courts.* St. Paul, Minn.: West, 1991.

Neubauer, David W. *America's Courts and the Criminal Justice System.* 8th ed. Belmont, Calif.: Wadsworth/Thomson Learning, 2005.

Pollock, Earl E. *The Supreme Court and American Democracy: Case Studies on Judicial Review and Public Policy.* Westport, Conn.: Greenwood Press, 2009.

Stuckey, G. B., Cliff Roberson, and H. Wallace. *Procedures in the Justice System.* 7th ed. Upper Saddle River, N.J.: Prentice-Hall, 2004.

Surrency, Erwin C. *History of the Federal Courts.* New York: Oceana, 1987.

Tarr, G. Alan, and Mary Cornelia Aldis Porter. *State Supreme Courts in State and Nation.* New Haven, Conn.: Yale University Press, 1988.

Wright, Charles Alan. *The Law of Federal Courts.* 5th ed. St. Paul, Minn.: West, 1994.

STATE AND LOCAL COURTS

- State and local court systems handle most civil and criminal cases in the United States. As the judicial branch of state governments, they issue decisions that control the acts of local authorities, state officials, and all the citizens within their jurisdictions.

While no two state or local court systems are identical, most share many common features, such as being separated into three distinct levels. Knowledge of these similarities is critical to understanding how state and local courts function. Each system normally comprises a three-step hierarchy, with courts of limited jurisdiction, courts of general jurisdiction, and courts of appellate jurisdiction. At each level, the specified court provides a service that is important to the functioning of the judicial system within the state. The nature and type of case determines which court will have jurisdiction.

Limited Jurisdiction Courts

Courts that can hear and decide only certain limited legal issues are known as courts of limited jurisdiction. Typically, these courts hear matters such as certain types of minor civil or criminal cases. For example, they handle traffic tickets, set bail for criminal defendants, resolve small claims matters, and issue rulings on lawsuits dealing with contracts, personal injuries, or other matters where the amounts of money involved are small.

In the United States, there are approximately thirteen thousand local courts, which include county, magistrate, justice, and municipal courts. Judges may be either appointed or elected to these courts. In many jurisdictions, these are part-time positions and the incumbents may have other jobs in addition to serving as judges. The fact that these courts handle minor civil and criminal matters does not mean their duties are not important. The only contact many citizens have with the judicial system occurs in such courts.

Courts of limited jurisdiction also may hear certain specialized matters such as probate of wills and estates, divorces, child custody matters, and juvenile hearings. In some states, these matters are heard in local courts; in others, there are courts of general jurisdiction that are designated by statute to hear and decide specific types of cases. For example, in California, a "superior court" is considered a court of general jurisdiction but certain of these courts are designated to hear only juvenile matters; they thus become courts of limited jurisdiction when they sit as juvenile courts.

General Jurisdiction Courts

Courts of general jurisdiction are granted authority to hear and decide all issues that are brought before them. They are known by a variety of names, such as superior courts, circuit courts, district courts, or courts of common pleas. These are the courts that normally hear major civil or criminal cases. As courts of general jurisdiction, they have authority to decide issues that occur anywhere within the state. Larger jurisdictions such as Los Angeles or New York City may have hundreds of courts of general jurisdiction within their city limits. Typically, these courts hear civil cases involving the same types of issues that courts of limited jurisdiction hear, but the amounts of damages are higher and may reach millions of dollars. These courts also hear the most serious criminal matters, including death penalty cases.

Courts of general jurisdiction traditionally have the power to issue injunctions prohibiting certain acts or requiring individuals or entities to perform certain functions or duties. This authority is derived from the equity power that resides in courts of general jurisdiction. Equity is the concept that justice is administered according to fairness, as contrasted with the strict rules of law. In early English common law, such separate courts of equity were known as Courts of Chancery. These early courts were not concerned with technical legal issues; they focused on rendering decisions or orders that were fair or equitable. In modern times, the power of those courts has been merged with courts of general jurisdiction, allowing them to rule on matters that require fairness as well as the strict application of the law.

Appellate Courts

Appellate jurisdiction is reserved for courts that hear appeals from both limited and general jurisdiction courts. These courts do not hold trials or hear evidence; they decide matters of law and issue formal written decisions or opinions. The two classes of appellate courts are intermediate and final.

Intermediate appellate courts are known as courts of appeals. Approximately half the states have designated intermediate appellate courts. These courts may be divided into judicial districts and hear all appeals within their district. They hear and decide all issues of law that are raised on appeal in both civil and criminal cases. These courts accept the facts as determined by the trial courts; since they deal strictly with legal or equitable issues, they do not use juries to decide factual disputes.

Intermediate appellate courts have the authority to reverse decisions of the lower courts and send the matters back with instructions to retry the cases in accordance with their opinion. Alternatively, they may uphold the decision of the lower court. In either situation, a party who loses the appeal at this level may file an appeal with the next higher appellate court.

Final appellate courts are the highest state appellate courts. They may be known as supreme courts or courts of last resort. Five, seven, or nine justices generally sit on these courts, depending on the state. Such courts have jurisdiction to hear and decide issues dealing with all matters decided by lower courts, including ruling on state constitutional or statutory issues. Their decisions are binding on all other courts within the state. Once such a court decides an issue, the only appeal left is to file in the federal court system.

Organization of Courts

State and local courts are traditionally characterized by an absence of supervision, specialization, and geographic organization. Each trait can cause problems within the judicial system.

Since local and state court judges are usually elected to their positions, they can and do claim that they answer only to the general public. Many state court systems have a presiding judge who is elected or appointed by the other judges. This judge may act as a supervisor and regulate the type and amount of cases assigned to all other judges, but can not censure or remove another judge for incompetence or wrongdoing. That function is normally left in the hands of the state supreme court, a state judicial panel, or the state legislature. Therefore, no one person or agency is responsible for the effective administration of the state's court system.

The dividing of courts into courts of limited and general jurisdiction results in specialization and fragmentation of duties. Within each state court system, courts may be further divided into areas of specialization, with one judge hearing all probate matters, another hearing all family matters, and another hearing all juvenile matters. While this system may allow judges to develop expertise in their special areas, it can result in uneven workloads. Many judges cooperate to reduce each other's workloads by accepting cases from colleagues who have heavier workloads, but statutes do not require it.

Geographic Organization

A third common characteristic of state and local courts is their geographic organization. Courts have established boundaries that have implications for the citizens that reside within their jurisdiction. These courts will reflect the different social values and attitudes of their citizens. For example, a court in a rural jurisdiction may view a certain type of crime as more serious than a court in an urban area.

Cases heard in state and local courts may be civil, criminal, or equitable matters. The civil justice system of state and local courts punishes private wrongs committed within the state, or wrongs that occurred outside the state that resulted in injuries to citizens living in the state. These wrongs may involve disputes with respect to contracts, personal injury, and statutory or constitutionally created rights. Private parties must litigate such claims, usually represented by attorneys, against their opponent in that dispute.

Generally, state and local court actions involving civil disputes request money damages, and the litigants have a right to a jury trial. In order to obtain a judgment against a civil defendant, the plaintiff has the burden of proof: He or she must prove the elements of the case by a preponderance of the evidence—that is, that it is more likely than not that the defendant was at fault. A civil defendant must disprove the evidence against him, or show that he had a justifiable defense, in order to avoid civil liability.

For example, a person might buy a defective appliance, which explodes while being used and causes severe injuries to the individual. She or he may file a civil action in state court alleging that the appliance was defective and that the defect caused injuries, and requesting money damages as compensation for these injuries. If it is shown by a preponderance of the evidence that the appliance failed to perform in a safe manner and the company is unable to refute the evidence against it, she or he may obtain a monetary award from the company.

Criminal Prosections

The state and local criminal justice system punishes those who violate state penal statutes, attempts to rehabilitate criminals, and strives to deter criminals and to educate the public. Representatives of the local or state government prosecute claims against those who are accused of violating state or local laws. These attorneys are usually known as district attorneys, county attorneys, or state attorneys general. Most crimes require proof that a physical act occurred, the person committing it had a certain mental state, and there was a concurrence of the act and the mental state. A person charged with a crime is presumed innocent until proven guilty. To obtain a conviction in a state or local court, the prosecutor must prove that the defendant committed the acts beyond a reasonable doubt. This standard does not require the state to prove the case against the defendant is 100 percent certain, only that there is no reasonable doubt as to his or her guilt.

In a murder case, for example, the prosecutor first presents the evidence of guilt. The defendant is then allowed, but not required, to refute that evidence. The accused may deny committing the crime, or contend that although guilty, he or she should not be held responsible for the act because, for example, the defendant acted in self-defense or was insane at the time of the offense. If the jury believes the prosecutor has proved the case beyond a reasonable doubt, it can convict the defendant of murder.

Injunction Powers of the Courts

Citizens may ask state or local courts to issue a mandatory injunction. This is a civil action where the legal remedy of money damages is inadequate. This remedy is an equitable remedy, as the court compels the defendant to perform in a certain way or face contempt of court. In equitable proceedings, the parties do not have a right to a jury trial and such cases are decided solely by the judge. To obtain an equitable remedy ordering the defendant to perform or to refrain from certain acts, a plaintiff must show that he or she has no other adequate remedy at law and faces irreparable injury without the remedy being enforced. Injunctions may be temporary, preliminary, or permanent in nature.

For example, people may sue the owners of factories that are dumping toxins onto their properties and seek injunctive relief to compel the factory owners to refrain from further dumpings. Then they will try to show that money damages are inadequate to compensate them, as it would be impossible to calculate the damages the toxins may inflict on their properties and their health. The plaintiffs may also contend that if the dumpings continue, their properties and health would suffer irreparable injuries. If the plaintiffs succeed, judges may compel the factory owners to cease dumping their toxins on the plaintiffs' properties.

State and local courts handle a variety of civil, criminal, and equitable cases every day. These cases affect personal safety, air quality, and many other aspects of daily life.

The state court judicial system is one of the three independent branches of all state governments. In many ways it mirrors the federal government, which also has three distinct branches of government. State courts interpret state constitutions, statutes, and other issues of concern to state citizens. State court decisions normally have a more direct impact on the lifestyle and quality of life of state citizens than do decisions issued by federal courts other than the U.S. Supreme Court.

Most of a state court's time is taken up with criminal cases. Not only are more crimes committed than civil wrongs, but other factors cause the state court system to prioritize criminal cases over civil cases. The Sixth Amendment to the U.S. Constitution requires that a criminal defendant receive a speedy trial, mandating that criminal cases take precedence over civil matters. As a result, it is not unusual for a civil case to languish for five years before it is tried.

Nonjudicial Methods of Resolving Civil Cases

Courts and judicial administrators have responded to this predicament by trying a variety of nonjudicial methods to handle civil cases. Some courts are limiting the amount of discovery or pretrial investigation that can occur. Other systems have instituted preprinted forms that all parties must use. Many court systems have encouraged or even mandated that certain civil matters be decided by arbitration or other alternate dispute mechanisms. Alternate methods of resolving civil disputes often are less costly than a court trial; more important, they are faster than waiting for the court to hear the matter. Despite attempts at modernization and use of alternate dispute mechanisms such as arbitration or mediation, the local and state court systems are overcrowded and respond very slowly to most issues.

Harvey Wallace and Shanda Wedlock

Further Reading

Abraham, Henry J. *The Judicial Process: An Introductory Analysis of the Courts of the United States, England, and France.* 5th ed. New York: Oxford University Press, 1986.

Black, Henry. *Black's Law Dictionary.* 6th ed. St. Paul, Minn.: West, 1990.

Fino, Susan P. *The Role of State Supreme Courts in the New Judicial Federalism.* New York: Greenwood, 1987.

Glick, Henry Robert. *State Court Systems.* Englewood Cliffs, N.J.: Prentice-Hall, 1973.

Meador, Daniel J. *American Courts.* St. Paul, Minn.: West, 1991.

Neubauer, David W. *America's Courts and the Criminal Justice System.* 8th ed. Belmont, Calif.: Wadsworth/Thomson Learning, 2005.

Roberson, Cliff. *Constitutional Law and Criminal Justice.* New York: Taylor & Francis, 2009.

Tarr, G. Alan, and Mary Cornelia Aldis Porter. *State Supreme Courts in State and Nation.* New Haven, Conn.: Yale University Press, 1988.

THE U.S. SUPREME COURT

• The highest court in the federal court system, the U.S. Supreme Court interprets the Constitution, sets limits to the scope and power of the legislative and executive branches of government, and establishes policies that affect the daily lives of Americans. Within the nation's dual system of state and federal courts, the Supreme Court wields enormous power.

Sitting at the top of the federal judiciary, the Supreme Court is the court of last resort in the federal court system and for the fifty state courts when a federal question is involved. From this position, the Court acts as the nation's conscience, determines the meaning of the Constitution, declares the acts of both Congress and the president unconstitutional when these acts do not conform with the Court's interpretation of constitutional principles, and protects the rights and liberties of minorities from the tyranny of hostile majorities.

Article III

Because of disagreements over how the federal courts should be organized and how much power they should have, the Framers left Article III of the Constitution, which established the judicial branch of government, short and vague. The only court required by the Constitution is the Supreme Court. The establishment of lower federal courts is left to Congress, as is the power to add to or subtract from the number of justices who sit on the Court. In the first century of its existence, the number of Supreme Court justices ranged from five to ten. In 1869, it was changed to nine. Justices are appointed by the president with the approval of the Senate.

The founding fathers clearly intended the courts to be independent of Congress and the executive branch. In order to immunize federal judges from retaliation for unpopular decisions, Article III provides them with lifetime appointments as well as the guarantee that their salaries will not be reduced while they hold office. The only constitutional mechanism for their removal is impeachment, a cumbersome and little-used procedure. As of 1995, no Supreme Court justice had ever been removed from the bench in this manner.

Article III also limits the Court's original jurisdiction, or authority to hear a

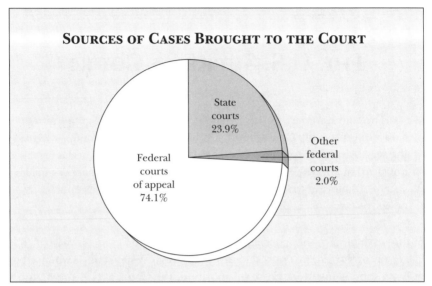

SOURCES OF CASES BROUGHT TO THE COURT

State
courts
23.9%

Other
federal
courts
2.0%

Federal
courts
of appeal
74.1%

Note: Figures, which do not include original jurisdiction cases, apply to cases in which the Court granted or denied hearings in October, 1996.
Source: Lawrence Baum, *The Supreme Court* (6th ed. Washington, D.C.: Congressional Quarterly, 1998), p. 13.

case first, to cases involving ambassadors, other public ministers and consuls, and certain cases in which a state is a party. Throughout the entire history of the Court, fewer than two hundred cases have arisen out of its original jurisdiction. Most of the cases that come before the Court each year are heard on appeal from U.S. courts of appeal and state courts of last resort. The Court's appellate jurisdiction, or authority to hear cases on appeal from lower courts, is left to Congress. Today, because of a combination of congressional acts and court decisions, the Supreme Court has control of its own agenda. It decides what cases it wants to hear and denies hearings to those it does not want to hear.

The Power of the Court

The Supreme Court got off to a slow and shaky start. In the first decade of its existence, it conducted little business and commanded little respect. When it convened for the first time on February 1, 1790, two justices did not even bother to attend, and both resigned before the end of the first term. At a later date, the first chief justice also resigned to become envoy to England because he was not convinced that the Court would ever acquire the dignity and respect that he believed it should be afforded.

From 1790 to 1803, little happened to dispel the concerns of the first chief justice. During this period, Congress did pass the Judiciary Act of 1789, which established the federal court system, but the role of the Supreme Court was still ambiguous, particularly in regard to the all-important power of judicial review—the power to declare the acts of Congress, the president, and the legislatures of the various states unconstitutional if they are judged to be in conflict with the Constitution. On this matter, the Constitution was silent. Without the power of judicial review, the Supreme Court could never realistically be considered a coequal branch of government. When Thomas Jefferson appointed John Marshall chief justice in 1801, however, the Court's fortune was destined to change.

Marshall devoted his thirty-four years as chief justice to enhancing the prestige and powers of the Court. His most famous decision came in the case of *Marbury v. Madison* (1803), when the Court, speaking through Marshall, declared section 13 of the Judiciary Act of 1789 unconstitutional because it conflicted with the specific limitations the Constitution places on the original jurisdiction of the Supreme Court. Section 13 was a relatively insignificant part of the act, but by striking down this minor provision of a law passed by Congress, the Court established its right to exercise judicial review over the legislative branch of government. Subsequent cases extended the power of judicial review to presidential acts and to the actions of state legislatures.

The impact of Supreme Court decisions often reaches far beyond the particulars of a given case and creates public policy as far-reaching as any produced by Congress or the president of the United States. For example, on May 17, 1954, when the Court ruled in *Brown v. Board of Education* against segregation in public schools, it signaled the end of legally created segregation of the races in the United States. The *Brown* case stands as testimony to the depth and breadth of the Court's policy-making power. Yet vast power is subject to vast abuse.

In *Plessy v. Ferguson* (1896), the same Court had upheld a Louisiana statute requiring the segregation of railroad cars and in so doing had reinforced the right of states to segregate the races for the use of drinking fountains, washrooms, restaurants, and other public facilities. Though the *Plessy* decision is now considered both immoral and ill conceived, from 1896 through 1954 the segregation of public facilities in the United States was constitutional. What is constitutional is what the Supreme Court says is constitutional, and what is unconstitutional is what the Supreme Court says is unconstitutional. Such is its awesome power.

The enormous power of the Supreme Court does not, however, go unchecked. In the first place, the justices have no police force or army at their disposal. They are dependent upon the executive branch for the enforcement of their decisions. Occasionally, this enforcement is not forthcoming. A classic example was President Andrew Jackson's refusal to return land that the state of Georgia had seized from the Cherokee Nation between 1827 and 1830. Jackson was able to get away with defying the Court's *Cherokee Nation v. Georgia* (1831) decision because public opinion weighed heavily in his favor and against the Native Americans.

The point here is that the Court cannot entirely ignore public opinion. The Court's powers are also restrained by the other branches of government and the states. The fact that justices are appointed by the president with the consent of the Senate ensures the other two branches of government a major role in determining the composition of the Court and, indirectly, the character of the Court's decisions. Finally, Congress and the states can undo a Court decision interpreting the Constitution of the United States by changing that document through the amendment process.

The Justices

Supreme Court justices are not representative of the general population. The typical justice is a white male Protestant from a relatively well-to-do family. As of 1995, only two African Americans (Thurgood Marshall and Clarence Thomas) and two women (Sandra Day O'Connor and Ruth Bader Ginsburg) had served on the Court. Most of its justices have previous judicial experience.

The criteria for selecting justices are highly political. As a general rule, presidents appoint individuals from their own political party. Approximately 90 percent of all nominees to the federal bench since the time of President Franklin D. Roosevelt have been members of the president's party who are believed to share the president's ideological views. Once justices are appointed to the Supreme Court, however, predictions about their future decisions often prove extremely unreliable, as President Dwight D. Eisenhower learned after his selection of Earl Warren as chief justice. Eisenhower's choice of Warren had been based to a large extent upon Warren's solid conservative record as governor of California, yet Chief Justice Warren led the way toward some of the most liberal decisions in the Court's history.

When a justice dies or steps down and a vacancy occurs, the president and his staff put together a list of possible nominees whose names are gathered from a wide variety of sources, including the attorney general, influential members of the legal community, party leaders, and interest groups. The Justice Department then helps the president screen potential nominees and subjects serious contenders to a background check by the Federal Bureau of Investigation. Since 1946, the Standing Committee on the Federal Judiciary of the American Bar Association, the largest organization of lawyers in the United States, ranks prospective nominees on a four-point scale ranging from "exceptionally well qualified" to "not qualified."

Once a nominee has been chosen, the president submits the nomination to the Senate, which must confirm the nomination by a majority vote. It is before the Senate Judiciary Committee that major battles over judicial confirmation, when they occur, usually take place. Nevertheless, the presumption is that presidents should be allowed considerable discretion in judicial appointments. As of 1995, the Senate had refused to confirm 29 of the 138 presidential nominees to the Supreme Court, and only 7 of these in the twentieth century.

The formal powers of the chief justice are relatively meager. The chief justice decides which petitions for a hearing are to be considered by the full Court, presides over the Court in oral argument and in conference, and assigns the writing of opinions whenever the chief justice is in the majority, which is most of the time. In those instances in which this is not the case, the senior justice in the majority assigns the opinion. These powers, by themselves, do not guarantee leadership as much as afford the opportunity to lead. Not surprisingly, then, the power of chief justices to provide intellectual leadership and policy direction for the Court has varied considerably with the personality and ability of the incumbents.

The Administration of Justice

Because the Supreme Court makes national policy that has such far-reaching impact on every American citizen, it is important to have an understanding of how justices decide which cases to hear and how they formulate and arrive at their decisions. In the later twentieth century, the caseload of the Supreme Court increased dramatically, from fewer than nine hundred in 1930

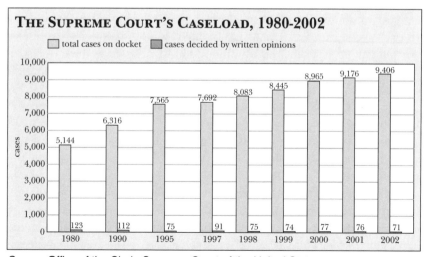

THE SUPREME COURT'S CASELOAD, 1980-2002

☐ total cases on docket ■ cases decided by written opinions

Year	total cases on docket	cases decided by written opinions
1980	5,144	123
1990	6,316	112
1995	7,565	75
1997	7,692	91
1998	8,083	75
1999	8,445	74
2000	8,965	77
2001	9,176	76
2002	9,406	71

Source: Office of the Clerk, Supreme Court of the United States.

to more than six thousand per year in the 1990's. Yet of the thousands of cases that find their way to the Court's calendar each year, fewer than two hundred are selected by the justices for consideration. For the vast majority that are denied review, the decisions of the lower courts are left standing. The method for deciding which cases warrant oral arguments and full consideration by the Court is the informal "rule of four." By tradition, when four or more justices agree that a case should be heard, the Court issues a writ of *certiorari*, or order to the lower court to prepare a record of the case and to send it up to the Supreme Court for review.

Not only are the odds against a case ever receiving full consideration by the Supreme Court, but the costs are also extremely high. Unlike litigants in most European countries, parties in the United States must pay their own way. This is referred to as the "American rule." The Court's filing fee is three hundred dollars; another one hundred dollars is added if a case is granted oral argument. While other fees may be encountered, the direct costs to a litigant are well under a thousand dollars. Nevertheless, before the case reaches the Supreme Court, the costs of bringing a case through the trial and appeal process can cost millions of dollars.

Not all litigants bear these expenses themselves. Interest groups often assume the costs for cases in which they have an interest. For indigent (without funds) defendants in criminal cases, the government provides an attorney without cost. Indigents in noncriminal cases can petition the Court *in forma pauperis* (in the manner of a pauper) for exemption from the usual fees.

Once the Court agrees to review a case, the lawyers for each side submit a brief that summarizes the lower court's opinion, presents their arguments, and discusses past cases on which the Court has ruled that are relevant to the legal issues in question. Sometimes other written briefs, called *amicus curiae* (friend of the court) briefs, may be submitted by individuals, organizations, or government agencies that have an interest in the case. After these briefs are circulated among the justices, a date is set for the attorneys to present their oral arguments. During oral arguments, the justices often interrupt to ask questions or to request additional information. At times, the justices may even try to help attorneys if they are having a difficult time.

After hearing oral arguments, the justices meet in a conference room where no outsiders are allowed. There, in complete secrecy, they debate the cases before them. The chief justice summarizes the facts and legal issues involved in each case and makes suggestions for their disposal. Then each justice, in order of seniority, presents his or her views or conclusions. Cases are decided on the basis of majority rule. In the event of a tie, the ruling of the lower court is left standing. (A tie is possible when one of the nine justices is absent.) Yet the conference vote is not binding. The justices are free to change their votes until the moment when the final opinion is read in open court.

After the conference vote, an opinion must be written. This is the most difficult and time-consuming task of a Supreme Court justice. Writing an opinion for a major case can take months. Once an opinion is drafted, it is circulated among the other justices for review and comment. Because these cases involve complex and difficult issues, it is often the case that the first draft is not acceptable to a majority. Frequently, an opinion has to be redrafted and recirculated several times before a majority can be reached.

The goal of the author is always to achieve the largest majority possible. This frequently entails considerable political negotiating and bargaining among the justices. Yet a decisive majority is important because the legal system of the United States is based upon the principle of *stare decisis* (let the decision stand) or precedent, which means that the principles of law established in earlier cases should be accepted as authoritative in similar cases. The greater the majority, the clearer the message. This is particularly true where the Supreme Court is concerned, for this court is expected to provide direction and guidance to the entire judicial system.

When in the majority, the chief justice decides who will write the opinion. On the other hand, when the chief justice is the minority, the senior justice in the majority makes the assignment. There are five kinds of opinions:

- *curiam* (brief and unsigned) opinions
- unanimous opinions, when all the justices agree
- majority opinions, when the Court is divided
- concurring opinions, when one or more of the justices agree with the ruling but for different reasons which they wish to state
- dissenting opinions, written by one or more of the justices on the losing side

Judicial Activism

The Supreme Court has always generated political controversy. Yet the more activist role of the Court in recent times has brought the issue of judicial power to the forefront of the political debate. Supporters of judicial activism argue that the Court corrects injustices that the White House, Congress, state legislatures, and city councils fail to address, such as racial discrimination in public facilities prior to *Brown v. Board of Education*. Such corrections, they argue, are vital for a democratic society. Critics of judicial activism advocate judicial restraint. From their perspective, no matter how desirable Court-declared rights and principles might be, when the justices depart from their proper roles as interpreters of the Constitution to undertake broad and sweeping policy initiatives, they become nonelected sover-

Under Chief Justice Earl Warren, the Supreme Court took on somewhat of an activist role. Members of the Warren Court were (counterclockwise from upper left) Abe Fortas, Potter Stewart, Byron R. White, Thurgood Marshall, William J. Brennan, Jr., William O. Douglas, Warren, Hugo L. Black, and John M. Harlan II. (Harris & Ewing/Collection of the Supreme Court of the United States)

eigns in black robes usurping the legitimate authority of Congress and state legislatures.

Other Court observers believe that both those who support judicial activism and those who advocate judicial restraint fail to grasp the complexity of the issues that come before the Court. According to this group, the Court should take an activist role whenever legislation restricts the democratic process by which decisions are made or whenever legislation interferes with the rights of minorities. In all other instances, they contend, established political process should be allowed to work without interference from the Court. Given the power of the Court in the American political system, it is little wonder that questions over its proper role fuel one of the perennial debates of American politics.

Thomas J. Mortillaro

Further Reading

Baum, Lawrence. *The Supreme Court.* 10th ed. Washington, D.C.: CQ Press, 2010.

Bloch, Susan Low, Vicki C. Jackson, and Thomas G Krattenmaker. *Inside the Supreme Court: The Institution and Its Procedures.* 2d ed. St. Paul, Minn.: Thomson/West, 2008.

Breyer, Stephen G. *Active Liberty: Interpreting Our Democratic Constitution.* New York: Alfred A. Knopf, 2005.

Hall, Kermit L., ed. *The Oxford Companion to the Supreme Court of the United States.* 2d ed. New York: Oxford University Press, 2005.

Hensley, Thomas, Christopher Smith, and Joyce Baugh. *The Changing Supreme Court: Constitutional Rights and Liberties.* 2d ed. Belmont: Thomson/Wadsworth, 2007.

Hoffer, Peter Charles. *The Supreme Court: An Essential History.* Lawrence: University Press of Kansas, 2007.

Jost, Kenneth. *The Supreme Court A to Z.* 4th ed. Washington, D.C.: CQ Press, 2007.

Lewis, Thomas T., and Richard L. Wilson, eds. *Encyclopedia of the U.S. Supreme Court.* 3 vols. Pasadena, Calif.: Salem Press, 2001.

O'Brien, David. *Storm Center: The Supreme Court in American Politics.* 7th ed. New York: W. W. Norton, 2005.

Parrish, Michael. *The Supreme Court and Capital Punishment.* Washington, D.C.: CQ Press, 2009.

Pollock, Earl E. *The Supreme Court and American Democracy: Case Studies on Judicial Review and Public Policy.* Westport, Conn.: Greenwood Press, 2009.

Savage, David. *Guide to the U.S. Supreme Court.* 4th ed. Washington, D.C.: CQ Press, 2004.

_____. *The Supreme Court and Individual Rights.* Washington, D.C.: CQ Press, 2009.

Spann, Girardeau. *Law of Affirmative Action: Twenty-five Years of Supreme Court Decisions on Race and Remedies.* New York: New York University Press, 2000.

Vile, John. *The Essential Supreme Court Decisions: Summaries of Leading Cases in U.S. Constitutional Law.* 15th ed. Lanham, Md.: Rowman & Littlefield, 2010.

Whittington, Keith E. *Constitutional Interpretation: Textual Meaning, Original Intent, and Judicial Review.* Lawrence: University Press of Kansas, 2001.

JUDICIAL REVIEW

- Judicial review is the power of a court to determine whether actions of government officials are in accord with the U.S. Constitution, when the matter is before the court in a proper case. Changing interpretations of the Constitution have enabled the eighteenth century document to respond to modern problems.

Under the Articles of Confederation, the first governing document of the United States, there was no national court system. When that document was replaced by the U.S. Constitution in 1789, Article 3 of the new Constitution provided that the new government would have a court system. It stated that the judicial power of the United States would be lodged in one Supreme Court and whatever lower courts Congress would create. Much of Article 3 is devoted to defining the jurisdiction of the Supreme Court. There is no statement in the judicial article that the Supreme Court was being given the power to review the constitutionality of the actions of Congress or the president.

Had U.S. political and legal development faithfully followed British tradition, U.S. courts would not have had the power of judicial review. Many other legal practices in the United States have their roots in the nation's British heritage, but not judicial review. In the largely unwritten British constitution, the legislative branch of government is supreme.

The United States, however, has a written Constitution that explicitly states that "This Constitution" is the "supreme Law of the Land." This is known as the supremacy clause. It further states that laws passed by Congress are the supreme law of the land, but only if they are pursuant to the Constitution. It does not say that all laws passed by Congress are supreme. If all laws are not supreme, then there must be a decision maker to decide which laws of the Congress are the supreme law of the land and which laws are unconstitutional.

That decision maker might also be called upon by persons who claimed that the president had exceeded the authority conferred on that office by the Constitution. Although the language of the Constitution appeared to have abandoned the British tradition of legislative supremacy, it did not identify any particular decision maker in the government as having the power to decide which laws were constitutional and which were not. The Supreme Court was not expressly given that power.

Judicial Review

The Supreme Court assumed the power of judicial review in 1803, in the case of *Marbury v. Madison*. In that case, steeped in the partisan politics of the period, the Supreme Court for the first time held congressional legislation unconstitutional. Since the Constitution did not explicitly confer on the Court the authority to do this, the task fell to Chief Justice John Marshall to write a judicial opinion justifying the Court's decision. Marshall observed that the Constitution is law and that it is the function of the justices to interpret and apply the law. When a law enacted by Congress conflicts with the law of the Constitution, the Supreme Court is obliged to apply the law of the Constitution rather than the law of Congress, because the Constitution is the supreme law of the land, and the justices of the Supreme Court swore to uphold the Constitution when they took their oaths of office. Thus, Chief Justice Marshall justified the Supreme Court's exercise of judicial review.

Although his opinion was well reasoned, it did not win universal acceptance. Critics of Marshall's opinion accurately observed that all public officials, not just Supreme Court justices, take an oath to support the Constitution. The doctrine of judicial review was opposed because it was believed that it would make the Supreme Court, whose members were appointed to office, superior to the president and Congress, both of which were elected to office. Marshall denied that judicial review meant judicial supremacy, contending that it merely implied the supremacy of the Constitution over all three branches of government. He contended that without judicial review, a written constitution would be meaningless.

During the remainder of Marshall's years as chief justice, the Supreme Court did not again hold congressional legislation unconstitutional. That does not mean, however, that the court did not exercise judicial review. In 1819, in the case of *McCulloch v. Maryland*, it used judicial review to uphold a congressional statute that created the Bank of the United States, when the constitutionality of that legislation was challenged by the state of Maryland. Although the creation of a bank was not among the enumerated powers of Congress, the Supreme Court found ample constitutional authority for the legislation in the necessary and proper clause of Article 1, section 8.

History of Judicial Review

Over the years, the Court has used its power of judicial review far more often to legitimize the actions of the elected branches of government than to hold them unconstitutional.

Even the legitimizing use of judicial review could result in controversy and rejection of the judiciary's special role as constitutional interpreter. Although Congress had seen fit to create a national bank, and the Supreme Court had exercised judicial review to uphold the power of Congress to do so, President Andrew Jackson vetoed similar legislation in 1832, when Congress rechartered the bank. Jackson contended that the legislation was unconstitutional and that he was not bound by the Court's contrary interpretation of congressional power. He too had taken an oath to support the Constitution and so had the right and the responsibility to interpret the document himself in the exercise of the powers of his office.

Judicial review had not yet won universal acceptance. That would not come until the post-Civil War period, when the Court aligned itself with the dominant political and economic forces of industrialization.

Whatever doubts remained concerning the Supreme Court's power in relation to Congress and the president, the two elected branches that were considered co-equal with the Court, there were few real doubts about the authority of the Supreme Court to review the constitutionality of state actions, when they were brought before the Court in a proper case. After the Constitution went into effect, the first Congress passed the Judiciary Act of 1789, the statute that set forth the structure of the national judicial system. Section 25 of the Judiciary Act gave the Supreme Court the power to review state legislation challenged as being inconsistent with the Constitution.

Even though the Court was clearly given the power of judicial review over state legislation at various times throughout American history, individual states have defied, or attempted to defy, the Court's authority when it held their legislation unconstitutional. Defiant states were rarely able to win the support of a significant number of states not directly involved in the controversy. Those not directly involved have tended to recognize the Supreme Court's power of judicial review over state legislation. They have recognized that such power is necessary, if the federal union is to be maintained.

Permanency of Court Decisions

Whether called upon to exercise judicial review of congressional actions, executive actions, or state actions, the constitutional decisions of the Supreme Court are relatively permanent. They may be reversed by constitutional amendment, but the amending process is difficult; it requires extraordinary majorities in Congress and the states. If a constitutional decision is to be changed, it is far more likely to be done by the Court itself. After the passage of time, the Court may overrule an earlier decision. An overruling decision is generally the result of new justices having been appointed to the Court who interpret the Constitution differently than earlier justices did.

In a few instances, however, decisions reached by a closely divided Court have been overruled when one or more members of the Court's majority changed their minds about how the Constitution should be interpreted. Since the Court's constitutional decisions are infrequently overturned by constitutional amendments or overruling decisions, the power of judicial review is an important power.

The Court and Civil Rights

Among the Supreme Court's more controversial exercises of judicial review have been those in the area of civil rights. At various times, the Court has reviewed actions of Congress and actions of state governments, sometimes legitimizing those actions and sometimes holding them unconstitutional.

In the aftermath of the Civil War, the Fourteenth Amendment was adopted to overturn the pre-Civil War Supreme Court decision *Scott v. Sandford* (1857). In the *Scott* decision, the Supreme Court said that slaves were not citizens of the United States, could not be citizens, and had no rights under the Constitution. The Fourteenth Amendment overturned the *Scott* decision by extending citizenship to all persons born or naturalized in the United States and under its authority.

The Fourteenth Amendment, however, did more than extend citizenship to the recently freed slaves; it prohibited the states from denying them "the equal protection of the laws." The amendment concluded with an authorization to Congress to enforce the amendment by appropriate legislation.

Relying upon that authorization, Congress passed the Civil Rights Act of 1875. The law prohibited persons who operated various kinds of businesses, such as hotels, restaurants, theaters, and coaches, from discriminating against potential customers on the basis of their race. Challenges to the constitutionality of the law came from business operators in various parts of the nation who denied service to blacks. They argued that in enacting this law, Congress had exceeded its constitutional authority.

The Supreme Court agreed. In the *Civil Rights Cases* of 1883, the Supreme Court exercised its power of judicial review to hold the Civil Rights Act of 1875 unconstitutional. The Court concluded that the Civil Rights Act was not appropriate legislation for enforcing the terms of the amendment because it was directed at the operators of private businesses, but the Fourteenth Amendment did not restrict the activity of private businesses, only that of states. In a dissenting opinion, Justice John Marshall Harlan criticized the Court's majority for its interpretation of the language of the Fourteenth Amendment, which he believed violated the spirit of the amendment.

Modern Civil Rights Legislation

Title II of the Civil Rights Act of 1964 represented a twentieth century attempt to accomplish what the Supreme Court had held unconstitutional in the *Civil Rights Cases* of 1883. It prohibited racial discrimination in public accommodations. In passing the 1964 statute, however, Congress did not rely upon the Fourteenth Amendment alone as the source of its authority to enact the legislation. Congress also asserted its authority under the commerce clause, which has been a major source of congressional power in the twentieth century.

Like the Civil Rights Act of 1875, the Civil Rights Act of 1964 was challenged as unconstitutional. In *Heart of Atlanta Motel v. United States* (1964), however, the Supreme Court handed down a decision that legitimized the use of the commerce power to prohibit racial discrimination in public accommodations. The Court examined the legislative history of the 1964 Civil Rights Act and found that there was considerable testimony at congressional hearings that discrimination continued to exist in all parts of the country and that this discrimination in public accommodations had a detrimental effect on interstate travel by African Americans. The Court held that Congress had acted within its legitimate commerce power when it passed the Civil Rights Act. Since the commerce clause provided ample support for this legislation, the Court did not find it necessary to reexamine the extent of congressional authority under the Fourteenth Amendment; thus, it did not overrule the *Civil Rights Cases* of 1883.

State Legislation

Judicial review of state legislation requiring segregation of the races followed a path somewhat similar to that of congressional legislation banning discrimination in public accommodations, in that the Court initially legitimized state segregation statutes but years later adopted a different interpretation of the Constitution. In *Plessy v. Ferguson* (1896), the Supreme Court upheld a Louisiana law requiring that black passengers and white passengers ride in separate railroad cars. Homer Adolph Plessy, legally considered black although racially mixed, had challenged the constitutionality of the state law, arguing that it denied him the equal protection of the laws which the Fourteenth Amendment guaranteed. He argued that this state-imposed segregation placed a badge of inferiority on black people.

The Supreme Court rejected Plessy's argument and legitimized state-imposed segregation of the races. The Court considered the Louisiana law to be a reasonable regulation that took into consideration the customs and traditions of the people. Out of this came the "separate but equal" doctrine, which came to be applied not just to railroad transportation but to virtually all areas of life in the southern states.

Dismantling of Segregation Laws

By 1954, the Supreme Court was using its power of judicial review to begin dismantling the segregated society that it had previously legitimized. In that

Chief Justice Earl Warren is regarded as second only to John Marshall in the impact on the Supreme Court that he had as chief justice. He led a major expansion of constitutional rights for defendants in state courts and the transformation of the meaning of the equal protection clause of the Fourteenth Amendment. (Supreme Court Historical Society)

year, it rendered a decision that state-imposed racial segregation violated the equal protection clause of the Fourteenth Amendment. In the landmark case of *Brown v. Board of Education*, the Supreme Court overruled *Plessy v. Ferguson*, insofar as it applied to public education. Writing for a unanimous Supreme Court, Chief Justice Earl Warren stated that it was impossible to determine how those who proposed and ratified the Fourteenth Amendment intended for its equal protection clause to apply to public education, for the simple reason that public education was virtually nonexistent then.

By the mid-twentieth century, however, public education was among the most important functions of state and local governments, as their own compulsory school attendance laws recognized. The Court concluded that in this modern context, legally imposed racial segregation could never provide equal education, even if all tangible elements were equal, because of the psychological damage done to black children. In the view of the Court, such segregation generated feelings of inferiority in black children, which had a detrimental effect on their motivation to learn. Thus, the Court rejected the "separate but equal" doctrine in public education.

Judicial Review in the Lower Courts

Judicial review is not a power that belongs solely to the Supreme Court of the United States. It may also be exercised by federal district courts and federal courts of appeals. The decisions of those courts, however, may be appealed to the Supreme Court. State courts may also exercise judicial review and determine whether challenged actions of their own state officials are in accord with the U.S. Constitution. The decisions of the highest court of a state on such matters may be appealed to the Supreme Court of the United States. Thus, the Supreme Court provides uniformity in constitutional interpretation.

The decisions of the Court have involved a multitude of constitutional issues, not just civil rights. The Supreme Court has defined the constitutional authority of the states and of the three branches of the national government. In the late twentieth century, for example, the Court held that the legislative veto—that is, the power of one house of Congress to pass a resolution negating a decision of administrative officials—was unconstitutional. Another decision legitimized congressional legislation creating the position of independent counsel.

Because the justices of the Supreme Court are politically appointed, the Court's exercise of judicial review has generally reflected the dominant values of U.S. society. As those values change over time, the Court's interpretation of the Constitution changes. The flexible language of the Constitution and the infusion of new ideas and values as new justices join the Court have enabled the U.S. Constitution, adopted by a young nation in the eighteenth century, to remain the basic governing document of the United States for over two hundred years. Judicial review has become as much a part of the constitutional system in the United States as those powers specifically written in the Constitution.

Patricia A. Behlar

Further Reading

Amar, Akhil Reed. *The Bill of Rights: Creation and Reconstruction.* New Haven, Conn.: Yale University Press, 2000.

Clinton, Robert Lowry. *Marbury v. Madison and Judicial Review.* Lawrence: University Press of Kansas, 1989.

Cox, Archibald. *The Court and the Constitution.* Boston: Houghton Mifflin, 1987.

Fisher, Louis. *The Supreme Court and Congress: Rival Interpretations.* Washington, D.C.: CQ Press, 2009.

Garraty, John A., ed. *Quarrels That Have Shaped the Constitution.* Rev. ed. New York: Perennial Library, 1987.

Johnston, Richard E. *The Effect of Judicial Review on Federal-State Relations in Australia, Canada, and the United States.* Baton Rouge: Louisiana State University Press, 1969.

Pollock, Earl E. *The Supreme Court and American Democracy: Case Studies on Judicial Review and Public Policy.* Westport, Conn.: Greenwood Press, 2009.

Sloan, Cliff, and David McKean. *The Great Decision: Jefferson, Adams, Marshall, and the Battle for the Supreme Court.* New York: PublicAffairs, 2009.

Warren, Charles. *The Making of the Constitution.* New York: Barnes & Noble, 1967.

Whittington, Keith E. *Constitutional Interpretation: Textual Meaning, Original Intent, and Judicial Review.* Lawrence: University Press of Kansas, 2001.

_____. *Political Foundations of Judicial Supremacy: The Presidency, the Supreme Court, and Constitutional Leadership in U.S. History.* Princeton, N.J.: Princeton University Press, 2009.

DUE PROCESS OF LAW

- The concept of due process of law pertains to a fundamental principle of fairness in all legal matters, both civil and criminal, especially in the courts. All legal procedures set by statute and court practice, including notice of rights, must be followed for each individual so that no prejudicial or unequal treatment will result. Due process of law is a safeguard of both private and public rights against unfairness.

The concept of due process originated in the Magna Carta siged by England's King John in 1215. English nobles used this document to limit the authority of the king. It required the king and his agents to respect the "legal judgment of his peers" and "the law of the land." Over time, the ideas of that charter of liberties protecting the public against the government's arbitrary and random acts came to be represented in the phrase "due process of the law."

Essentially, the Anglo-American tradition of due process requires a fair hearing for persons charged with an offense and a decent opportunity to defend themselves. This is one of the major foundations of the American tradition of personal liberty. It is most highly developed in the oldest form of public action, the criminal prosecution.

In the modern United States due process depends partially on written guarantees of the U.S. Constitution. The Fifth Amendment to the U.S. Constitution applies to the federal government and provides that "No person shall . . . be deprived of life, liberty, or property, without due process of law." The Fourteenth Amendment, with similar language, constrains the states. Many legal decisions determining both procedural and substantive rights—especially in criminal justice cases—arise from these two amendments. In criminal law, interests of "liberty" would include freedom from incarceration and a parolee's interest in staying on parole. Other constitutional amendments, from the Fourth through the Eighth, provide additional substance to due process.

Due process also depends on American values of fairness. The Constitution does not specify certain standards in criminal justice, such as the requirement that guilt be proved beyond a reasonable doubt, that the accused be presumed innocent until proved guilty, or that the burden of proof rest on the prosecution. Nevertheless, such standards are part of American custom dating back to the early years of the republic and are integral to the concept of due process. As Justice Louis Brandeis described it, procedural "fundamentals do not change; centuries of thought have established standards."

Obviously, due process cannot be fully defined in a neat catchall rule. Perhaps Judge Learned Hand expressed it best when he stated that it embodies the English sporting sense of fair play. In the language of Justice Oliver Wendell Holmes, Jr., state administration of criminal law offends due process "if it makes you vomit."

Historically, the U.S. Supreme Court has interpreted due process in two distinct categories: substantive and procedural. Substantive due process is concerned with limitations on the power or authority of government to abridge any person's life, liberty, or property interests. The body of the Constitution and the Bill of Rights contain numerous limitations on the power of government to interfere with individual rights. Substantive due process is used to invalidate government actions interfering with individual freedoms in such areas as abortion, marriage, procreation, and interstate travel when no more specific constitutional ground can be found.

Procedural Due Process

Procedural due process is concerned with fair procedure when the government is a party in a case where an individual has been deprived of a recognized liberty or property interest. The Supreme Court, as guardian of the criminal justice systems, has provided general guidelines rather than precise delineations of due process. In each case the Court asks whether the challenged practice or policy violates "a fundamental principle of liberty and justice which inheres in the very idea of a free government and is the inalienable right of a citizen of such government." The Court has held that, at a minimum, due process means that an accused must be given notice of a charge and adequate opportunity to appear and be heard in one's own defense. Criminal defendants have a right to a fair and public trial conducted in a competent manner and a right to an impartial jury. Laws must be written so that a reasonable person can understand what constitutes criminal behavior.

The Bill of Rights requires the federal government to observe explicit criminal procedure standards. The Fourth Amendment protects people from unreasonable searches and seizures and describes the requirements for a search warrant. In addition to protecting the right to "due process of the law," the Fifth Amendment requires indictment by grand jury and protects defendants from double jeopardy and from being required to testify against themselves. The Sixth Amendment provides the accused with the right to a speedy and fair trial by an impartial jury; the right to be confronted by the witnesses against them and the right to cross examine such witnesses; the right of compulsory processes for obtaining witnesses in their favor; and the right to counsel. The Eighth Amendment prohibits excessive bails and fines and protects the guilty from cruel and unusual punishments.

Although Bill of Rights protections were enforced against the federal government, state criminal law and procedures were traditionally afforded greater autonomy under the American system of federalism. With respect to the state courts, the Supreme Court's authority had historically been less extensive, as it had held in *Barron v. Baltimore* (1833) that the specific provisions of the Bill of Rights dealing with judicial procedure did not apply to the states. The adoption of the Fourteenth Amendment in 1868, however, required the Court to reconsider its position in *Barron*. In *Hurtado v. California* (1884), the Court rejected the claim that the due process clause incorporated the Fifth Amendment requirement of indictment by grand jury to apply to the states. What the Court did concede was that the due process clause was a general guarantee of fairness, prohibiting the states from interfering with fundamental principles of liberty and justice.

The Incorporation Doctrine

By the 1930's the Court had found that some provisions of the Bill of Rights had been made applicable to the states by the Fourteenth Amendment due process clause. In *Palko v. Connecticut* (1937), the Court held that the due process clause incorporated those parts of the Bill of Rights "so rooted in the traditions and conscience of our people as to be ranked fundamental" or which are "the very essence of a scheme of ordered liberty." For the Court, justice Benjamin Cardozo announced this "fundamental fairness doctrine" and found that double jeopardy protections did not meet its requirements. To require more than that would be to put a "straitjacket" on the states and their administration of criminal law according to proponents of the fundamental fairness theory.

During the 1940's, four justices of the Court—Hugo L. Black, William O. Douglas, Frank Murphy, and Wiley B. Rutledge—argued that the due process clause made every provision of the Bill of Rights applicable to the states. These proponents of "total incorporation" were never able to persuade a fifth justice to their view, so the Court continued to use the fundamental fairness approach in interpreting due process. As explained by justice Felix Frankfurter, the question of whether a state criminal procedure was consistent with the requirements of due process imposed upon the Court "an exercise of judgment" upon the whole course of the proceedings in order to ascertain whether they "offend those canons of decency and fairness which express the notions of justice of English-speaking peoples even toward those charged with the most heinous offenses."

During the 1960's, the Earl Warren court provided a third view of the ap-

SUPREME COURT DECISIONS ON SELECTIVE INCORPORATION IN CRIMINAL JUSTICE CASES

Date	Case	Constitutional provision	Amendment
1948	Cole v. Arkansas	Notice clause	Sixth
1948	In re Oliver	Public trial	Sixth
1949	Wolf v. Colorado	Search and seizure	Fourth
1961	Mapp v. Ohio	Exclusionary rule	Fourth
1962	Robinson v. California	Cruel and unusual punishment	Eighth
1963	Gideon v. Wainwright	Right to counsel in felony cases	Sixth
1964	Malloy v. Hogan	Self-incrimination	Fifth
1965	Pointer v. Texas	Confrontation clause	Sixth
1966	Parker v. Gladden	Impartial jury	Sixth
1967	Klopfer v. North Carolina	Speedy trial	Sixth
1967	Washington v. Texas	Compulsory process clause	Sixth
1968	Duncan v. Louisiana	Jury trial	Sixth
1969	Benton v. Maryland	Double jeopardy	Fifth
1971	Schilb v. Kuebel	Excessive bail	Eighth
1972	Argersinger v. Hamlin	Right to counsel in misdemeanor cases with possible jail terms	Sixth

propriate relationship between the Fourteenth Amendment and the Bill of Rights—"selective incorporation." In cases dealing with state criminal prosecutions, the Court used selective incorporation that combined aspects of both the fundamental rights and the total incorporation interpretations. The Court agreed with proponents of the fundamental fairness approach that the due process clause of the Fourteenth Amendment protects only those rights that are "fundamental to ordered liberty." Whereas justices following the fundamental fairness concept would incorporate only the particular part of a constitutional guarantee involved in the specific case at hand, proponents of selective incorporation look less to the particulars of the case and instead determine whether the guarantee as a whole should apply to the states—a view similar to that of the total incorporation theory.

Applying this selective incorporation analysis, the Court in the twenty-first century has held that practically all the criminal procedural guarantees of the Bill of Rights include limitations that are fundamental to state criminal justice systems and that the absence of a particular guarantee denies a defendant due process of law (only the Fifth Amendment requirement of indictment by grand jury and the Eighth Amendment prohibition of excessive fines have not been incorporated to apply to the states). In making these determinations, the Court struggled with the problems of accommodating competing

Hugo L. Black, who would later become a champion of the incorporation doctrine, facing a battery of news cameras on the steps of the Capitol Building shortly after his nomination to the Supreme Court in 1937. (Harris & Ewing Collection/Library of Congress)

interests—the most important of which was the concept of a minimum national standard of due process competing with the position and authority of the states in maintaining their systems of justice within the structure of federalism. However, the due process clause of the Fourteenth Amendment is not limited to the specific guarantees of the Bill of Rights but also contains protection against practices that may violate values of fundamental fairness without abrogating a specific provision of the Constitution.

Other Elements of Due Process

Among elements of due process enunciated by the Court are: the void-for-vagueness doctrine that requires detailed legislation providing ascertainable standards of guilt; statutory notice providing for definiteness in criminal statutes so that a person may know that something must not be done or, alternatively, that unless something is done criminal liability will result; the "entrapment" defense that protects people from punishment for illegal conduct induced or encouraged by police agents; the criminal identification process that regulates the conduct of police seeking to identify perpetrators of crimes by lineups or photographic displays; and indictment, which in the states may be by grand jury or information (a document issued by the prosecutor officially charging an individual with criminal violations) but must include adequate notice to defendants of the offenses charged against them and for which they are to be tried.

"Due process" is also used as a title of a social science model of the criminal justice system. The due process, or adversarial, model of criminal court operations emphasizes regularity of procedures, the elimination of mistakes, and prevention of official misconduct while maintaining that an individual accused of criminal conduct must be assumed innocent until proven guilty—even when doing so hinders the efficiency with which the criminal justice system operates. In contrast, the administrative, or crime control, model assumes that the accused is guilty and values efficient and cost-effective disposition of cases.

The large number of criminal due process cases that come before federal and state courts each year indicate the changing nature of the concept and its central position in American criminal justice.

Theodore M. Vestal

Further Reading

Acker, J. R., and D. C. Brody. *Criminal Procedure: A Contemporary Perspective.* 2d ed. Sudbury, Mass.: Jones and Bartlett, 2004.

Amar, Akhil Reed. *The Bill of Rights: Creation and Reconstruction.* New Haven, Conn.: Yale University Press, 2000.

Clancy, Thomas K. *The Fourth Amendment: Its History and Interpretation.* Durham, N.C.: Carolina Academic Press, 2008.

Garcia, Alfredo. *The Fifth Amendment: A Comprehensive Approach.* Westport, Conn.: Greenwood Press, 2002.

McInnis, Thomas. *The Evolution of the Fourth Amendment.* Lanham, Md.: Lexington Books, 2009.

Neubauer, David W. *America's Courts and the Criminal Justice System.* 8th ed. Belmont, Calif.: Wadsworth/Thomson Learning, 2005.

Orth, John V. *Due Process of Law: A Brief History.* Lawrence: University Press of Kansas, 2003.

Perry, Michael J. *We the People: The Fourteenth Amendment and the Supreme Court.* New ed. New York: Oxford University Press, 2002.

Roberson, Cliff. *Constitutional Law and Criminal Justice.* New York: Taylor & Francis, 2009.

Stevens, Richard. *Reason and History in Judicial Judgment: Felix Frankfurter and Due Process.* New Brunswick, N.J.: Transaction, 2008.

COURT CASES

ABINGTON SCHOOL DISTRICT V. SCHEMPP

Court: U.S. Supreme Court
Citation: 374 U.S. 203
Date: June 17, 1963
Issues: Education; Establishment of religion

- This landmark U.S. Supreme Court ruling prohibited public schools from conducting religious exercises, including Bible readings for religious (rather than literary) purposes.

Like the Progressive Era and the New Deal, the 1960's in the United States have assumed the stature of an important, almost classic, age of reform and liberalism. Civil rights legislation, the Great Society programs, and antiwar protests were all symptomatic of a general quest for greater justice. Unlike earlier episodes of reform, however, the changes of the 1960's often were introduced almost in defiance of popular opinion. Although liberal measures often resulted from, and received the support of, vocal and active groups, just as often they did not reflect the goals of the "average" citizen, nor was there the kind of massive endorsement of reform that Franklin Roosevelt had enjoyed in 1936. One of the prime examples of these unpopular reforms was the Supreme Court's ruling regarding prayer and Bible reading in the public schools.

The issue of Bible reading in public schools reached the Supreme Court in 1963, in two cases emanating from the adjoining states of Pennsylvania and Maryland. Pennsylvania law required that ten verses from the Bible be read without comment at the beginning of each public school day. Although participation in the exercises was voluntary, Edward and Sidney Schempp and their children, Roger and Donna, members of a Unitarian church, filed suit in the federal district court for the Eastern District of Pennsylvania to enjoin the state's superintendent of public instruction from continuing to conduct religious recitations in public schools. At Abington Senior High School, which Roger and Donna Schempp attended, the religious exercises were broadcast into classrooms through the intercommunication system and consisted of a student reading ten verses of the Bible of his or her choosing, followed by students standing in class and repeating the Lord's Prayer in unison.

The Maryland case originated in Baltimore, where, since 1905, religious exercises had been held in the public schools and included a reading from the Bible or the recitation of the Lord's Prayer. Madalyn Murray O'Hair and her son, William Murray, both professed atheists, filed suit to force the cancellation of the religious exercises in Baltimore schools.

The Majority Opinion

The majority opinion in *Abington School District v. Schempp* was written by Associate Justice Tom C. Clark and was handed down on June 17, 1963. One year earlier, the Supreme Court, in *Engel v. Vitale*, had struck down the New York Board of Regents' prayer ("Almighty God, we acknowledge our dependence upon Thee; we beg Thy blessings upon us, our parents, our teachers, and our country") as a violation of the establishment clause of the First Amendment, which had been made applicable to the states through the due process clause of the Fourteenth Amendment. Clark now did the same for the recitation of biblical passages and the Lord's Prayer.

In his opinion, Clark pointed out that the Court had firmly rejected the argument that the establishment clause prohibited only governmental preference of one religion over another. An examination of the precedents demonstrated conclusively that the First Amendment was designed to forbid all laws

Justice Tom C. Clark.
(Harris and Ewing/
Collection of
the Supreme Court
of the United States)

respecting the establishment of a religion. Justice Clark denied that the Court's decision would establish a religion of secularism. He noted that nothing in the opinion precluded the study of the Bible in the public schools in its literary or historical context.

Although the Court's 8-1 decision provoked widespread disappointment and anger, it was not unexpected. For nearly twenty years, a series of eight rulings by the Supreme Court had gradually removed the practice of religious activities from state-supported schools. After World War II, a growing number of freethinkers, Jews, and liberal Protestants had resisted the assumption of most local and school authorities that society was, or should be, based on the teachings of the New Testament. Most states permitted or encouraged a variety of religious exercises in the schools, ranging from Bible classes to the recitation of prayer. Increasingly, these practices were challenged in the courts.

In the New Jersey case of *Everson v. Board of Education* (1947), the Supreme Court had defended the use of state funds to bus children to parochial schools but warned that a wall of separation between church and state must be maintained. A year later, in *McCollum v. Board of Education* (1948) the Court banned a program of religious instruction from the schools of Champaign, Illinois. The justices' chief objection to the Champaign system was that religious teachers were actually brought into the schools, thus involving the state too closely with religion and pressuring dissenting students into conformity with the majority. In 1952, however, the Supreme Court approved a released-time program whereby students could apply to leave schools early in order to attend religious classes at their churches or synagogues.

Significance

While the Supreme Court's opposition to classroom instruction in religion enjoyed widespread support and sympathy, even among churches, the question of school prayers and Bible reading was more delicate. Most people agreed with Justice William O. Douglas's observations that Americans were a religious people; it seemed right and natural that the school day should begin with some recognition of the general belief in God. To prohibit any sort of observance in schools was tantamount, many argued, to state opposition to religion. There were widespread protests after the Court's ruling in *Engel v. Vitale*, and a hostile reaction to the Court's decision in Abington School District. Most people tended to agree with dissenting Justice Potter Stewart, who wrote that he could not see "how an official religion is established by letting those who want to say a prayer say it." At the same time, most religious and educational leaders expressed relief that the Court had finally laid down clear limitations for the schools to follow and had placed responsibility for religion firmly in the hands of families and churches.

Since 1963 and Abington School District, the Supreme Court's construction of the establishment clause has been erratic and, at times, confusing. The Court's record has reflected a profound philosophical division between those justices who favored an almost complete separation of church and state and those who advocated an accommodation with religion. In *Lemon v. Kurtzman* (1971), the Court, under Chief Justice Warren E. Burger, established a three-pronged test to determine the constitutionality of state laws providing various forms of support for religious schools. The test required that the statute must have a secular legislative purpose, its principal effect must be one that neither advances nor inhibits religion, and it must not foster an "excess government entanglement with religion."

Richard H. Sander and David L. Sterling

Further Reading

Boles, Donald E. *The Bible, Religion, and the Public Schools.* Ames: Iowa State University Press, 1965. Covers a wide array of material on the historical, legal, and cultural background of the Abington School District decision.

Bravin, Jess. "Court Hears Cases on Public Display of Commandments." *The Wall Street Journal*, March 3, 2005, p. A2. News story discussing issues arising from an incident in which the Bible's Ten Commandments were exhibited in a government building.

Duker, Sam. *The Public School and Religion: The Legal Context.* New York: Harper & Row, 1966. Discusses the major court rulings concerning religion in the schools, providing lengthy excerpts from court opinions.

Eastland, Terry, ed. *Religious Liberty in the Supreme Court: The Cases That Define the Debate over Church and State.* Washington, D.C.: Ethics and Public Policy Center, 1995. Includes the Court's decision in *Abington School District v. Schempp*, as well as three essays reflecting on the church and state debate in the United States. Bibliographic references and indexes.

Farish, Leah. *Lemon v. Kurtzman: The Religion and Public Funds Case.* Berkeley Heights, N.J.: Enslow, 2000. Designed for young-adult readers, this volume examines the issues leading up to *Lemon v. Kurtzman*, people involved in the case, the legal development of the case, and the historical impact of the ruling. Includes chapter notes, further reading list, and index.

Irons, Peter, ed. *May It Please the Court: The First Amendment—Transcripts of the Oral Arguments Made Before the Supreme Court in Sixteen Key First Amendment Cases.* New York: New Press, 1997. Includes the complete transcript of the oral arguments made in *Abington School District v. Schempp*. Includes audio cassettes and bibliographic references.

Levy, Leonard W. *The Establishment Clause: Religion and the First Amendment.*

New York: Macmillan, 1986. Analyzes the origins of the establishment clause and critiques the Supreme Court decisions pertaining to its construction.

Lytle, Clifford M. *The Warren Court and Its Critics.* Tucson: University of Arizona Press, 1968. Traces the reaction of Congress, interest groups, and the general public to the major rulings of the Warren Court; tries to explain the lasting hostility to the Court.

Sizer, Theodore R., ed. *Religion and Public Education.* Boston: Houghton Mifflin, 1967. Contains a wide selection of provocative essays; some are partisan, others are exclusively analytical.

Sullivan, Winnifred Fallers. *Paying the Words Extra: Religious Discourse in the Supreme Court of the United States.* Cambridge, Mass.: Harvard University Press, 1994. Examines the religious viewpoints of Justices Warren Burger, Sandra Day O'Connor, and William Brennan as illustrated in their opinions in the Christmas crèche case.

See also *Engel v. Vitale; Everson v. Board of Education of Ewing Township; Illinois ex rel. McCollum v. Board of Education; Lemon v. Kurtzman.*

ABLEMAN V. BOOTH

Court: U.S. Supreme Court
Citation: 21 How. (62 U.S.) 506
Date: March 7, 1859
Issues: Federal supremacy; Habeas corpus

• The U.S. Supreme Court held that the Fugitive Slave Law of 1850 was constitutional and ruled that a state court may not issue a writ of habeas corpus to release a person from federal custody.

Joshua Glover, a fugitive slave from Missouri, found work in a Wisconsin mill. Under the Fugitive Slave Law of 1850, the U.S. commissioner in Milwaukee issued an order for Glover's arrest. An angry group of about one hundred men broke into the Milwaukee jail and rescued Glover, who escaped to Canada. Sherman Booth, a dynamic speaker who edited an antislavery newspaper, was convicted in federal court for taking part in the rescue. Not long after, the Wisconsin Supreme Court declared the 1850 law invalid, and one

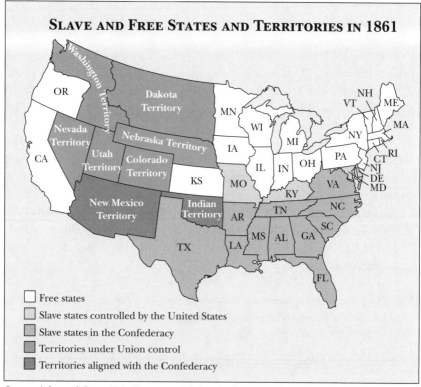

SLAVE AND FREE STATES AND TERRITORIES IN 1861

☐ Free states
☐ Slave states controlled by the United States
☐ Slave states in the Confederacy
☐ Territories under Union control
■ Territories aligned with the Confederacy

Source: Adapted from Eric Foner and John A. Garraty, eds., *The Reader's Companion to American History.* (Boston: Houghton Mifflin, 1991.)

judge of the court issued a writ of habeas corpus to have Booth released. The court's action was appealed to the U.S. Supreme Court.

Writing for a unanimous Court, Chief Justice Roger Brooke Taney reaffirmed the authority of the federal government to capture runaway slaves and ruled that a state court lacked jurisdiction over a person in federal custody. In response, Wisconsin's supreme court split evenly concerning whether to recognize federal supremacy in the matter. Taney's opinion on federal supremacy was upheld in *Tarble's Case* (1872), and that aspect of the decision remains good law.

Thomas Tandy Lewis

See also *Jones v. Van Zandt; Kansas v. Hendricks; McCleskey v. Zant; Printz v. United States; Stone v. Powell; Ware v. Hylton.*

ABRAMS V. UNITED STATES

Court: U.S. Supreme Court
Citation: 250 U.S. 616
Date: November 10, 1919
Issues: Freedom of speech

- The Abrams case involved questions of the meaning of free speech and the definition of the clear and present danger test, as defined by Judge Oliver Wendell Holmes, Jr.

In August of 1918, Jacob Abrams, Mollie Steimer, Hyman Lachowsky, Samuel Lipman, and Jacob Schwartz were arrested by New York police authorities for distributing leaflets opposing American intervention in the Soviet Union. They were charged with violating the 1918 Sedition Act, which made it a crime to willfully "utter, print, write, or publish any disloyal, profane, scurrilous, or abusive language" about the United States, its government and its officials.

The defendants were indicted on charges of conspiracy before the Southern District Court of New York by U.S. attorney Francis Gordon Caffey. Harry Weinberger took on the defense of Abrams and the others. Throughout the trial, judge Henry DeLamar Clayton, Jr., actively aided the prosecution's case. The defendants were convicted on October 22, 1919, and the sentence was issued on October 25. Abrams, Lipman, and Lachowsky received twenty years each and fines of up to one thousand dollars. Mollie Steimer was sentenced to fifteen years in the Missouri penitentiary and was fined five hundred dollars. Jacob Schwartz died of pneumonia, possibly exacerbated by the effects of police torturing, while awaiting his trial.

Weinberger appealed the ruling before the U.S. Supreme Court, which gave the case a first hearing on October 21, 1919. The Court upheld the sentence with a vote of seven to two on November 10, 1919, with Oliver Wendell Holmes, Jr., and Louis D. Brandeis dissenting. Free on ten thousand dollars bail each, Abrams, Steimer, and Lipman tried to escape but were captured. Weinberger negotiated with American and Russian authorities for their deportation, which was granted at the defendants' own expense in 1921.

The significance of the Abrams case lies in its importance for the meaning of free speech and its limitations under the clear and present danger test. In the *Schenck v. United States* (1919), *Frohwerk v. United States* (1919), and *Debs v. United States* (1919) rulings, Holmes had imposed limitations to the right to free speech by introducing the clear and present danger test: "The question in every case is whether the words used are used in such circumstances and are of such a nature as to create a clear and present danger that they will bring about the substantive evils that Congress has a right to prevent" (*Schenck*).

In his dissenting opinion in the Abrams case, Holmes modified the test significantly. He argued "that the best test of truth is the power of the thought to get itself accepted in the competition of the market." Only in extreme cases, Holmes said, should the law check the expression of opinions. Holmes's permissive redefinition of the clear and present danger test in his dissent in the Abrams case was invoked by justices into the 1960's to protect the right to freedom of expression.

Thomas Winter

See also *Brandenburg v. Ohio; Gitlow v. New York; Noto v. United States; Scott v. Harris.*

ADAIR V. UNITED STATES

Court: U.S. Supreme Court
Citation: 208 U.S. 161
Date: January 27, 1908
Issues: Bankruptcy law; Labor law

- In *Adair v. United States*, the U.S. Supreme Court declared unconstitutional a provision of the 1898 Erdman Act that prohibited "yellow-dog" labor contracts.

To understand the importance of the U.S. Supreme Court's decision in *Adair v. United States* for the evolution of labor relations, one must understand the nature of the employment relationship examined in that case. "Yellow-dog contracts" were agreements between employers and prospective employees that the employees did not belong to and would not join any labor union. Through such agreements, employers were able to make the promise not to join a union a condition of employment, effectively barring unions from the workplace. These contracts might be arrived at individually between a worker and an employer, or they might take the form of collective agreements between employers and groups of workers.

The earliest collective agreements, in the printing trades in 1795 and in the iron industry in 1866, were little more than wage scales, but over time the subject matter of agreements extended to cover other aspects of the employer-employee relationship, including provisions precluding union membership and union organizing activity. Yellow-dog contracts increased in frequency in response to the growing use of the strike by unions in the railroad industry, use that culminated in the Pullman Strike of 1894, one of the most violent strikes of the period. The Erdman Act of 1898 (named for its principal sponsor, Congressman Constantine Jacob Erdman of Pennsylvania) attempted to strengthen the ability of employers and employees to resolve conflicts between themselves, but it also provided for federal mediation and conciliation. It outlawed discrimination against employees based on union membership, in effect rendering yellow-dog contracts illegal. In addition, many states passed legislation making it illegal for an employer to force workers to agree not to join a union as a condition of employment.

The Court's Ruling

These issues came to the attention of the U.S. Supreme Court in October, 1907, when *Adair v. United States* was argued. William Adair was a supervisor for the Louisville and Nashville Railroad when O. B. Coppage, a member of the Order of Locomotive Firemen, was discharged. The only apparent reason for the discharge was Coppage's union membership. In a ruling issued on January 27, 1908, the Supreme Court affirmed the discharge of Coppage. The Court, in the majority opinion written by John Marshall Harlan, concluded that the prohibition of yellow-dog contracts was a violation of the property right of the employer to hire and fire, a right protected by the Fifth Amendment of the Constitution. Adair had a responsibility to prescribe conditions of employment that were in the best interests of his business. As long as those conditions were not injurious to the public interest, the Court ruled, legislation should not interfere with individual freedom.

The Court also made two additional points. First, there had been no stated or implied length of employment agreed to between the employer and the employee, so that the dismissal was not a breach of contract. In addition, although Congress had the right to regulate interstate commerce, that right extended only to those aspects of the employer-employee relationship that affected interstate commerce. Membership in a labor organization had nothing substantive to do with how commerce was conducted or with the ability of workers to perform their function. Congress did not have the right to prescribe conditions of union membership, as such a prescription did not fall within its constitutional powers to regulate commerce among the states. In the same way that a worker may choose whether to accept a job, an employer has a reciprocal right to specify the terms and conditions of employment.

The Court's decision was a significant blow against unions on two fronts. First, it made organizing workers more difficult, because the very fact of union membership might lead to dismissal. Second, it greatly diminished the bargaining power of the unions by lessening the effectiveness of strikes. Striking workers could be replaced with workers who would agree not to join the union. In workplaces that were unionized, the employer could, by precipitating a strike, effectively eliminate the union by replacing the striking union workers with nonunion workers.

Two justices wrote dissenting opinions in *Adair v. United States.* Joseph McKenna expressed the view that the intent of the Erdman Act was to resolve industrial conflict in the workplace. This end could be served better if the employer dealt with members of a labor organization rather than with separate individuals. The potential gains to society from the law thus overrode any losses of individual freedom to the employer. Oliver Wendell Holmes, Jr., presented the second dissenting opinion. He saw the outlawing of yellow-dog contracts as a means of protecting the worker, usually the weaker party in an employment contract, from the potentially discriminatory exercise of power by the employer. The rights of the employer are not without bound, and the interest of the public welfare takes precedence over that of the employer. Foreshadowing future events, Holmes concluded that even if the only outcome of the Erdman Act was to promote the growth of organized labor in railroads, that would be sufficient justification for passage. A strong union was in the best interests of the individual workers, the railroad industry, and society as a whole.

In 1915, the Court found illegal a state statute prohibiting yellow-dog contracts, in *Coppage v. Kansas.* In this case, the Court held that the state statute violated the due process clause of the Fourteenth Amendment. Although the individual had the right to join or not join a union, the employer was not obligated to hire or to continue to employ a union member. In the same way that the individual does not have the right to join the union without the consent of the union organization, the individual does not have the right to be employed without the consent of the employer.

Significance

During the early twentieth century, the United States faced a question that would shape the nation's political and social structure. The issue was whether workers should have the right to bargain collectively. In the laissez-faire world of the eighteenth and nineteenth centuries, employers bargained individually with workers. The rights of the employer were relatively unbounded, although workers did have access to the court system when they believed they had been wronged. The technological advances that accompanied the Industrial Revolution brought workers together in factories, where the same terms and conditions of employment affected many people. These common concerns inevitably led to collective mechanisms to resolve conflicts with employers.

Previously, if conditions in the workplace were unacceptable, an employee's main recourse was to quit; now there was the possibility of groups of employees having a voice. Unions offered the possibility of affecting the terms and conditions of employment, and the threat of the strike gave unions bargaining power. Social acceptance of the right of unions to bargain collectively implied a jurisprudence in the workplace separate from that in the courts. Although the right of the employer to bargain with individual employees over the preconditions of employment may be acceptable in the abstract, it may not hold universally. In other words, private contracting may not be in the public's best interest because it denies workers the right to a voice; it denies them democracy in the workplace. The yellow-dog contract might be in the interests of the employer and possibly even of the worker directly involved, but it is not in the best interests of society.

Legislative Changes

Adair v. United States set the stage for a dramatic change in legislation concerning unions. The yellow-dog contract served as an effective tool for employers to keep out unions and, in the event of a strike, to replace union workers with workers who promised not to join a union. The idea of "employment at the will of the employer," however, was being slowly circumscribed. The majority and dissenting opinions in this case, especially that of Holmes, highlight the complexity of the issue.

The right to bargain over the terms and conditions of employment was assured by the Fifth Amendment. In that context, yellow-dog contracts can be viewed in two quite different ways. On one hand, their prohibition by Congress ensured that employers, assumed to have the greater power in the bargaining context, would not be allowed to use that power to exploit an individual worker and indirectly all workers or the labor movement. Given that the prohibition of union membership was not essential to the performance of the job and did not alter the worker's productivity, it should not be permitted and in fact was discriminatory because it was unrelated to job performance. Yellow-dog contracts would be illegal because they were coercive on the part of the employer or because such subject matter was beyond the scope of legitimate contracts.

The alternative view was that Congress was interfering with the rights of individuals to engage in potentially mutually advantageous trades. The private property rights of the employer made union membership a legitimate matter for contracting, and the right of the prospective employee to refuse the job offer precluded coercion. This right of the employer was affirmed in the 1917 U.S. Supreme Court case of *Hitchman Coal and Coke Company v. Mitchell.* A yellow-dog contract was in effect when union agents attempted to organize the employees and become their exclusive bargaining agent. The Court determined that the employer could seek injunctive relief against the union. Justice Mahlon Pitney asserted that the right of the employer to make union membership a condition of employment is as sacrosanct as the right of the employee to join the union and that these rights derive from the constitutional rights of private property and individual freedom. In another 1917 case, *Eagle Glass & Manufacturing Company v. Rowe,* the Court ruled that the employer could enjoin the officers and members of the union from conspiring to induce employees to violate such a preemployment contract.

At the federal level, the change in public attitude toward unions is symbolized by the Railway Labor Act of 1926, which forbade the use of yellow-dog contracts by employers and rendered invalid any such existing contracts. The constitutionality of the act was affirmed in the 1930 Supreme Court case of *Texas & N.O.R. Company v. Brotherhood of Railway & Steamship Clerks.* The Court sustained a decision of a lower court that workers discharged because of union membership must be reinstated. The Court reconciled its decision in this case with those in *Adair v. United States* and related cases by making a subtle distinction. The employer's right to hire whom it wanted was not being interfered with. The employees, however, had a right to be represented by individuals of their own choosing. The law was not limiting the right of the employer; rather, it was ensuring the right of employees to choose their own representatives. The employer does not have a constitutional right to limit the right of workers to choose their representatives.

The Court's opinion in *Adair v. United States* stated that the worker and the employer were equal parties in the contracting process, that unions inhibited individual rights, and that unions were in some cases conspiracies in restraint of trade that could be enjoined. These legal ramifications were changed by the Norris-La Guardia Act (the Anti-Injunction Act) of 1932. The main focus of the act was to prevent employers from seeking injunctive relief against striking unions, but it also acknowledged the helplessness of individual workers in bargaining with employers. Section 3 of the Norris-La Guardia Act made yellow-dog contracts nonenforceable and not subject to injunctive relief. The prohibition of the use of the injunction was extended to railroads the next year.

In 1933, Congress amended the Bankruptcy Act to prevent railroad carriers in bankruptcy from using yellow-dog contracts to circumvent unions. This prohibition was extended and reinforced in the Emergency Railroad Transportation Act of 1933 and in the 1934 amendments to the Railway Labor Act. The change in the public's attitude toward unions from one of tolerance to one of encouragement culminated in the passage of the National Labor Relations Act (Wagner Act) in 1935.

The opinions articulated in *Adair v. United States* defined the terms in the debate concerning the role of organized labor in the American economy. The Court's decision represents one of the last times the Court has ruled that the rights of the employer to freedom and to private property dominate the rights of the worker. In *Adair v. United States*, the Court saw the role of the union as negatively affecting private rights without consideration of the public good. Implicit was the eighteenth century view that the private good is compatible with the social good. Holmes challenged this attitude of individual rights in his minority opinion, in which he stated that in the interest of the public good and the collective social well-being, the unilateral right of the employer must be limited. The unrestricted right of the employer limits the right of the employee and is not in the best interests of society. Once this view was accepted, the institution of unionism could no longer be seen as an obstructionist conspiracy contrary to the Constitution. Unions instead became recognized as vehicles to safeguard individual rights.

John F. O'Connell

Further Reading

Commerce Clearing House. *Labor Law Course.* 24th ed. New York: Author, 1976. A complete summary of the law governing labor relations. Both topic and legal case indexes are provided. Major legislation and court opinions are presented and cross-referenced.

Herman, E. Edward, and Gordon S. Skinner. *Labor Law: Cases, Text, and Legislation.* New York: Random House, 1972. An introduction to labor law. Each major topic is summarized. The principal legislation is presented, and the most important legal cases are excerpted.

Myers, A. Howard, and David P. Twomey. *Labor Law and Legislation.* 5th ed. Cincinnati: South-Western, 1975. Uses both essays and legal cases to trace the evolution of societal views on labor relations, beginning with British common law.

Taft, Phillip. *Organized Labor in American History.* New York: Harper & Row, 1964. One of the best descriptions of the role of unions in the United States prior to 1960. Analyzes the influence of yellow-dog contracts and labor legislation on union growth.

See also *Duplex Printing Co. v. Deering; Gompers v. Buck's Stove and Range Co.; Lochner v. New York.*

ADAMSON V. CALIFORNIA

Court: U.S. Supreme Court
Citation: 332 U.S. 46
Date: June 23, 1947
Issues: Due process of law; Right to privacy; Self-incrimination

- This case reaffirmed the "fundamental rights" interpretation of the due process clause of the Fourteenth Amendment; Justice Hugo Black wrote a widely noted dissent in which he argued that the clause should be read to incorporate all Bill of Rights guarantees against encroachment by state governments.

Admiral Dewey Adamson was convicted of murder in the first degree in California in 1946 and condemned to death. California's criminal procedure at that time authorized the judge and prosecutor to comment on the defendant's refusal to testify. Adamson had committed earlier offenses which would have been revealed to the jury on cross-examination had he testified in his own defense. The prosecutor pointed out to the jury Adamson's refusal to take the stand.

After his conviction, Adamson appealed on the ground that the due process clause of the Fourteenth Amendment protects his privilege against self-incrimination. Justice Stanley F. Reed, writing for a U.S. Supreme Court majority of five, held that the privilege against self-incrimination is not part of the right to a fair trial protected by the due process clause of the Fourteenth Amendment. Reed argued that "the purpose of due process is not to protect a defendant against a proper conviction but against an unfair conviction. When evidence is before a jury that threatens conviction, it does not seem unfair to require him to choose between leaving the adverse evidence unexplained and subjecting himself to impeachment through disclosure of former crimes." In short, California's procedure was not "fundamentally unfair."

Justice Felix Frankfurter concurred, arguing that the due process clause of the Fourteenth Amendment was not meant by its Framers to include the whole Bill of Rights: "It would be extraordinarily strange for a Constitution to convey such specific commands in such a roundabout and inexplicit way" as the due process clause.

Justice Hugo Black's dissenting opinion argued that inclusion of the entire Bill of Rights in the Fourteenth Amendment had been the intention of its

Framers. He attached to his opinion a long historical appendix citing many of the speeches of Congressman Jonathan Bingham and other influential members of Congress who had participated in the drafting and ratification of the Fourteenth Amendment. Black argued further that the "fundamental fairness" rule was too open-ended; it gives too much power to judges to include and exclude rights according to their personal wishes rather than on the basis of principled constitutional analysis.

Frankfurter's position prevailed in theory and Black's in practice. By 1970 nearly the entire Bill of Rights had been incorporated into the Fourteenth Amendment. The major exceptions are the Second Amendment's right to keep and bear arms and the Fifth Amendment's command that criminal defendants are entitled to indictment by grand jury. The Court's specific decision in *Adamson* was overruled in 1964 in *Malloy v. Hogan.*

The open-ended character of the due process clause of the Fourteenth Amendment permitted later courts to expand personal liberty and privacy rights. *Griswold v. Connecticut* (1965) and *Eisenstadt v. Baird* (1972) established constitutional rights to receive and use birth control devices and information; *Roe v. Wade* (1973) established a constitutional right to an abortion in the first trimester of pregnancy. Had the Supreme Court accepted Justice Black's interpretation of the Fourteenth Amendment, these expansions of individual autonomy would have been much more difficult to achieve.

Robert Jacobs

See also *Elfbrandt v. Russell; Griffin v. California; Grosjean v. American Press Co.; Mapp v. Ohio; Robinson v. California; Romer v. Evans.*

ADARAND CONSTRUCTORS V. PEÑA

Court: U.S. Supreme Court
Citation: 515 U.S. 200
Date: June 12, 1995
Issues: Affirmative action; Regulation of commerce

• In the case of *Adarand Constructors v. Peña*, the U.S. Supreme Court ruled that all racial preferences in government-financed programs were inherently suspect and must be assessed using the standard of "strict scrutiny," which meant that they were unconstitutional unless narrowly tailored to promote a compelling governmental interest.

The U.S. Supreme Court's landmark decision in the 1995 case of *Adarand Constructors v. Peña* is one in a long series of Court decisions relating to affirmative action—that is, policies designed to increase the participation of underrepresented minorities and women in business, employment, and education. Although the Civil Rights Act of 1964 explicitly disallowed the use of racial and ethnic preferences in hiring, the agencies of the federal government soon began to enforce the statute by requiring that employers and schools achieve particular statistical outcomes. In the Public Employment Act of 1977, the U.S. Congress for the first time utilized the quantitative approach, mandating that contracts for public works projects include, whenever feasible, a 10 percent "set-aside" for minority business enterprises (MBEs).

An angry group of nonminority contractors went to federal court to challenge the set-asides as a form of unconstitutional "reverse discrimination" against white males. Referring to the precedent of *Bolling v. Sharpe* (1954), the plaintiffs argued that the due process clause of the Fifth Amendment to the U.S. Constitution contains an implicit "equal protection component" that protects all persons equally. Their hopes were dashed, however, when the Supreme Court, in *Fullilove v. Klutznick* (1980), voted six to three to uphold MBE set-asides as a "reasonable necessary means of furthering the compelling governmental interest" in redressing the discrimination that had long affected minority contractors. This ruling encouraged substantial expansion of minority set-aside provisions by the federal government as well as at the state and local levels.

Randy Pech, the white owner of Adarand Constructors in Colorado Springs, Colorado, was one of many entrepreneurs who was disappointed by the *Fullilove* decision. Pech's company, which specialized in building guardrails on public highways and bridges, had been founded in 1976 by Pech and Tom Adams (the name Adarand was a combination of the founders' names). By the mid-1980's, Adarand Constructors had grown to become the most successful guardrail company in Colorado, but Pech was infuriated to observe that because of minority-owner preferences, his company was losing 10 to 15 percent of the jobs for which it was the low bidder. Testifying at hearings, Pech emerged as a vociferous opponent of racial preferences. He even considered transferring ownership of Adarand to his wife, Val Pech, so that the company would qualify as a disadvantaged enterprise, but he eventually concluded that such a maneuver, even if commonly practiced, would be fraudulent.

Because of the conservative judicial appointments of President Ronald Reagan, the Supreme Court was gradually taking a more skeptical view of government requirements for remedial preferences. In the case of *Richmond v. J. A. Croson Co.* (1989), a 5-4 majority of the Court overturned a city council's plan mandating that at least 30 percent of the value of city contracts be awarded to MBEs. Justice Sandra Day O'Connor, the swing vote in the case, wrote in the majority opinion that set-aside plans by state and local governments must be based on a showing of past discrimination, not simply reliance on general societal discrimination, and she insisted that they be assessed by the demanding standard of "strict scrutiny." The *Croson* ruling, however, applied only to state and local programs under the Fourteenth Amendment, and thus it was uncertain whether the Court would evaluate the constitutionality of federal programs by the same standards.

In 1989, Adarand Constructors submitted the lowest bid to subcontract the guardrail work for a large project in the San Juan National Forest—a project sponsored by the Federal Highway Administration, which was part of the Department of Transportation (DOT). Instead of accepting the low bid, the prime contractor selected a minority-owned company, the Gonzales Construction Company. In federal court, Pech sued the DOT and its head, Federico Peña, arguing that the *Croson* principles should apply to the federal government under the Fifth Amendment. As the case was being argued in lower federal courts, however, the Supreme Court decided the similar case of *Metro Broadcasting v. F.C.C.* (1990), with the justices voting five to four to uphold federal preferences designed to increase black ownership of broadcast licenses. The ruling appeared to endow Congress with almost unlimited discretion to authorize race-based preferences. Applying this precedent, two lower federal courts ruled against Pech.

The Court's Ruling

When the case reached the Supreme Court, however, in *Adarand Constructors v. Peña*, the justices decided, in a 5-4 vote, that federally financed set-asides were in the same constitutional category as state and local mandates, thereby overturning the *Metro Broadcasting* ruling. The impact of this decision was to apply the demanding test of strict scrutiny to federal programs that disadvantaged nonminority applicants because of race. This meant, according to Justice O'Connor's opinion for the Court, that all governmental race-conscious classifications must be "subjected to detailed judicial inquiry to ensure that the personal right to equal protection of the laws has not been infringed." The two most conservative justices, Antonin Scalia and Clarence Thomas, wrote concurring opinions that condemned all race preferences as unconstitutional. Scalia declared: "In the eyes of the government we are just one race here. It is American." Thomas argued that set-asides and other preferences are patronizing and reinforce the perception that blacks are incapable of success based on the principle of equal opportunity.

The four dissenters, led by Justices John Paul Stevens and Ruth Bader Ginsburg, argued that the history of racial discrimination in the United States provided a constitutional rationale for the federal government to take remedial action. Stevens argued that when Congress authorizes benign race-conscious measures, the appropriate test of review is the less demanding "important governmental objective test." Similarly, Ginsburg argued that the DOT program was carefully designed to achieve a valid objective and was therefore consistent with the equal protection clause of the Fourteenth Amendment. Noting that the Court's conservative justices claimed to be opposed to judicial activism, she chided the majority for failing to allow legislatures appropriate discretion in deciding how to apply the amendment.

Significance

The Supreme Court's ruling in *Adarand Constructors v. Peña* did not automatically overturn the DOT program challenged by Pech. Instead, the ruling sent the case back to the lower courts for a decision concerning whether the program was unconstitutional according to the strict scrutiny standard, which required that the program be justified by a compelling reason and be narrowly tailored to eliminate discrimination that could be proven (not just generalized bias). At the time of the ruling, nevertheless, the courts had struck down almost all policies that had been evaluated according to the rigorous test, to the extent that most law books characterized it as "strict in theory but fatal in practice." As expected, the lower courts soon determined that the program violated the constitutional rights of nonminority contractors such as Adarand.

Eight years later, however, in the case of *Grutter v. Bollinger* (2003), the Supreme Court for the first time approved a less demanding application of the strict scrutiny test. The case involved the admissions policy of the University of Michigan Law School, which included preferences for members of underrepresented groups in order to enhance the "diversity" of the school's student body. Although claiming to utilize the strict scrutiny test, the Court ruled that the admissions policy was constitutional. Writing for the 5-4 majority, Justice O'Connor argued that diversity was a compelling goal and that the policy, which guaranteed individualized consideration, was narrowly tailored. Although the *Grutter* decision did not directly affect public works contracts, it did suggest that the Court would likely approve of preferential programs that are not inflexible or grossly discriminatory.

Thomas Tandy Lewis

Further Reading

Anderson, Terry H. *The Pursuit of Fairness: A History of Affirmative Action.* New York: Oxford University Press, 2004. Presents an excellent and balanced historical account of affirmative action from the beginning of racial and gender preferences to the early twenty-first century.

Bean, Jonathan J. *Big Government and Affirmative Action: The Scandalous History of the Small Business Administration.* Lexington: University Press of Kentucky, 2001. Critical evaluation of the Small Business Administration argues that many of its scandals have resulted from the agency's use of gender and racial preferences, to the detriment of meritocracy.

Eastman, Terry. *Ending Affirmative Action: The Case for Colorblind Justice.* New York: Basic Books, 1996. Provides a historical summary of affirmative action and presents a case for ending all preferences based on race or gender, arguing for a policy of equal opportunity.

Kranz, Rachel. *Affirmative Action.* New York: Facts On File, 2002. Introductory research guide for students summarizes the political debate and includes a historical overview as well as a summary of important legal cases.

Leiter, Samuel. *Affirmative Action in Antidiscrimination Law and Policy: An Overview and Synthesis.* Albany: State University of New York Press, 2002. Examines various affirmative action programs, including their origins, growth, impacts, and future prospects.

Spann, Girardeau. *Law of Affirmative Action: Twenty-five Years of Supreme Court Decisions on Race and Remedies.* New York: New York University Press, 2000. Comprehensive work chronicles the Court's rulings from *DeFunis v. Odegaard* (1974) to the end of the twentieth century.

Wise, Tim J. *Affirmative Action: Racial Preference in Black and White.* New York: Routledge, 2005. Presents a one-sided defense of racial preferences as necessary remedies for historical discrimination against minorities.

See also *Bolling v. Sharpe; Booth v. Maryland; Fullilove v. Klutznick; Gratz v. Bollinger/Grutter v. Bollinger; Metro Broadcasting v. Federal Communications Commission; Roberts v. United States Jaycees; Texas v. Hopwood.*

Adderley v. Florida

Court: U.S. Supreme Court
Citation: 385 U.S. 39
Date: November 14, 1966
Issues: Civil rights and liberties; Freedom of assembly and association

- U.S. Supreme Court Justice Hugo L. Black underscored a distinction between speech and action in upholding the conviction of civil rights demonstrators.

Justice Hugo L. Black, writing for a five-member majority, upheld the conviction of civil rights protesters who demonstrated directly on the grounds of a county jail in Tallahassee, Florida, where demonstrations had never been permitted. Reading the First Amendment literally, Black found that it allowed a government to protect jails and courthouses from demonstrations if it did so consistently. Assembly, he argued, is not an absolute right but conditioned by the inclusion of the word "peaceably" in the First Amendment.

Although often regarded as a civil libertarian, Black disappointed many liberals with his opinion in this case. His critics failed to perceive that his so-called "absolute standard" was logically compatible with a distinction between speech, which was absolutely protected, and assembly, which was limited by the Constitution's use of the word "peaceably" and could never be so absolutely protected. Justice William O. Douglas, Black's frequent partner in dissent, disagreed with him in this case and was joined by Chief Justice Earl Warren and Justices William J. Brennan, Jr., and Abe Fortas.

Richard L. Wilson

See also *Adkins v. Children's Hospital; Branzburg v. Hayes; Cox v. Louisiana; Hall v. DeCuir; Muller v. Oregon; Stromberg v. California; United States v. O'Brien.*

ADKINS V. CHILDREN'S HOSPITAL

Court: U.S. Supreme Court
Citation: 261 U.S. 525
Date: April 9, 1923
Issues: Freedom of contract; Labor law

• By ruling that minimum wage legislation was unconstitutional, the U.S. Supreme Court declared its support of laissez-faire policy and upheld the doctrine of freedom of contract.

On April 9, 1923, the U.S. Supreme Court ruled five to three in the case of *Adkins v. Children's Hospital* that minimum wage laws violated the freedom of contract between employers and workers as well as the due process clause of the Fifth Amendment to the U.S. Constitution. The Court's decision, surprising to many, was consistent with established laissez-faire economic policies of the time as well as the Court's own doctrine of freedom of contract, which it had been developing since the late 1890's but would eventually repudiate in its 1937 decision in *West Coast Hotel Company v. Parrish*. This doctrine held that private parties to a contract were to be free from state intervention except in those limited cases in which public health, welfare, or the morals of the community were involved.

Massachusetts had adopted a minimum wage law in 1912, which was quickly followed by similar laws in several other states. The Adkins case stemmed from a 1918 federal law that created the Minimum Wage Board within the District of Columbia. The board's function was to inspect working conditions and then establish a legal minimum wage after negotiating with representatives of employers and employees. Moreover, the board was given the power to enforce its standards of minimum wages in order to protect female and teenage workers within the District of Columbia from economic conditions detrimental to their "health and morals." Failure of an employer to abide by the act was classified as a misdemeanor and carried a possible fine and imprisonment.

In 1920, the Minimum Wage Board determined that the cost of the "necessaries of life" had risen to a minimum of $16.50 a week and that many of the women working in the district's hotels, restaurants, and hospitals were being paid less, often much less, than the estimated living wage. The Children's Hospital, which employed a large proportion of women, refused to pay the wage set by the board. The hospital, along with others, brought suit to challenge the authority of the board to set wages.

The case was argued before the Court by Harvard Law School professor Felix Frankfurter in collaboration with the National Consumers League (Frankfurter would later take a seat on the Court as an associate justice in 1939). In his argument, Frankfurter stressed that the law had not harmed local industry or reduced the level of employment and in fact had improved the welfare of the district's women and children. He and his supporters submitted a large volume of documentary evidence in support of their arguments, but they ultimately failed to convince the Court that minimum wage legislation was valid. The opponents of the legislation held to a basic conservative argument of the need to protect private property and stressed the importance of freedom of contract.

The Court's Ruling

Writing for the majority, Associate Justice George Sutherland held that the 1918 law not only disrupted the right of a private contract but also violated the right of property protected by the due process clause of the Fifth Amendment. He asserted that the right of private contracts could be restrained only in exceptional cases and that in the view of the Court, at least for the time being, labor relations were largely beyond the police powers and regulatory powers of the states, Congress, and the courts.

Because in earlier rulings the Court had given mixed signals about when and where it was appropriate to set maximum work hours, the opinion in Adkins drew a sharp distinction between minimum wage laws and maximum hour laws. In Adkins, the Court held that contractual wages are appropriately set by the value of labor in the free market and that any attempt to fix wages places a burden on private employers concerning what in fact is a social issue. In the 1908 case of *Muller v. Oregon*, the Court had ruled that because of the state's interest in women's health it could, because of gender, legitimately set maximum hours. Because the decision in Adkins was handed down after the adoption of the Nineteenth Amendment in August of 1920, the Court's opinion also held that gender differences did not constitute a valid reason to ignore freedom of contract.

Chief Justice William Howard Taft, normally fairly conservative, issued a rare written dissent to the Court's decision in Adkins. Taft contended that laws could, in certain situations, be enacted to limit freedom of contract. It was, for example, within the police powers of the states, or Congress, to set maximum hours as well as to establish minimum wages. His dissent questioned the majority's distinction between wages and hours as a test of the liberty of contract, noting that one was as important as the other. Taft went on to note that although the adoption of the Nineteenth Amendment provided women with some political power, it did nothing to alter the physical distinctions between women and men. Constitutional issues therefore did not need to be recast simply because of its adoption.

Also dissenting in the Adkins decision was Associate Justice Oliver Wendell Holmes, Jr., who accepted the notion that Congress had the power to establish minimum wage rates for women in the District of Columbia but then questioned the constitutionality of liberty of contract. As Holmes noted, laws exist to forbid people from doing things they want to do. He questioned why labor contracts should be singled out for exemption, and he listed several cases in which liberty of contract had been limited by statute with validation by the Court. Holmes's attempt to get the Court to abandon its doctrine of liberty of contract would not be accepted by a majority of the Court for some years, but in his dissent he expressed the differences in approach among the justices concerning economic issues and labor relations. In Holmes's view, an appointed board could be held to reasonably determine a standard for a living minimum wage. Such a standard need not come from the operations of a free market.

William Howard Taft served as president of the United States from 1909 to 1913, but his greatest ambition was to be chief justice of the United States. (Deane Keller/Collection of the Supreme Court of the United States)

Significance

The Court's decision in Adkins demonstrates the impact that laissez-faire policies had on judicial temperaments, the economy, and the citizens of the United States in the 1920's and 1930's. The decision reflected popular, although not universal, attitudes toward labor relations in the late nineteenth and early twentieth centuries. A direct impact of the Adkins decision was its use throughout the 1920's and early 1930's to overturn several states' minimum wage laws and other early New Deal legislation. The times and opinions were changing, however, and the Court's earnest endorsement of freedom of contract in Adkins would be overturned in 1937.

Initial reactions to the Court's ruling in Adkins were mixed. Those who favored a free and open market hailed it as an important and necessary endorsement of private property and the protection of freedom of contract under the due process clause. Those who favored direct regulation of economic and social conditions attacked it as a shameful example of inhumanity. The New Republic, for example, ran an editorial stating that the Court had in effect endorsed the legal right to starve.

Regardless of whether one agrees with the Court's ruling in Adkins, the case makes it clear that wages and prices are central to the operation of an economy. For that reason, various groups followed the case very closely. Groups opposed to minimum wage legislation had long stressed that such laws were potentially harmful not only to industry but also to labor itself, as unemployment would rise in response to higher legislated wages. Rising labor costs would be imposed on business and passed along to consumers, and labor groups themselves would have diminished ability to bargain. Those in favor of minimum wage legislation attempted to refute these claims. They argued that such laws protect the weak, raise standards of living, improve the general health and welfare, improve workers' bargaining power, and provide benefits to employers by increasing morale and worker efficiency.

Others debated the significance of an absolute power to fix wages. Did, for example, the right to set a minimum wage then also imply the ability to set a maximum wage? Was it feasible to determine and then fix a workable wage or a living wage? How would work performed at home be legislated? How would the enforcement of a minimum wage be handled?

Because of the importance it placed on freedom of contract, the Court's decision in Adkins was a major setback to the progressive labor movement. During the early decades of the twentieth century, progressive groups sought legislative remedies for many of the inequities and other problems they believed existed in labor relations. The gains made by these groups were, at least for the time being, stalled by this ruling. The Court had ruled in essence that the free marketplace and not mandated regulation would guide the decisions of society. Because minimum wage legislation was seen as a means to regulate as well as to prohibit certain labor practices, progressive groups had hoped that the Court would rule to uphold the minimum wage as a means of protecting the health and welfare of women and children. Conservatives saw minimum wage legislation simply as an unconstitutional intrusion into private affairs between employers and employees.

The Court's ruling in this case, among others, provides a good deal of insight into the role of women and children in the American economy during the early years of the twentieth century. Minimum wage legislation often specified that the health and welfare of women and children were to be protected by a minimum living wage. This emphasis can be explained by the fact that gender- and age-specific legislation was more likely to be accepted, or, alternatively, that women and children were employed in less productive industries, had lower wages, and had less bargaining power in the market, thus legislation on their behalf was necessary.

By ruling minimum wage legislation unconstitutional, the Court demonstrated a belief in the merits of a marketplace free from government intervention. The decision in Adkins affirmed the Court's belief that the freedom of contract doctrine remained, at least for the time, paramount to the operation of the free market. Moreover, if the freedom of contract doctrine were broadly applied, the nation, the economy, and labor relations would remain dominated by laissez-faire policies. The significance of this was made obvious in the *West Coast Hotel v. Parrish* decision, which upheld a Washington State minimum wage law and overturned Adkins. In that decision, Chief Justice Charles Evans Hughes dismissed the primacy of freedom of contract and instead argued that due process was of paramount importance to the interests of the community.

With the repudiation of the Adkins decision and abandonment of a laissez-faire approach to social and economic problems, the roles of federal, state, and local governments clearly changed. The relative impact of the legislation that followed in the wake of the Court's later ruling remains a matter of considerable debate in the early twenty-first century.

Timothy E. Sullivan

Further Reading

Brandeis, Louis D., and Josephine Goldmark. *Women in Industry.* Reprint. New York: Arno Press, 1969. A summary of the Supreme Court's decision upholding the constitutionality of the ten-hour workday. Helps to place labor issues and the debate on gender and the workplace in the context of the early twentieth century.

Hall, Kermit L., ed. *The Oxford Companion to the Supreme Court of the United*

States. New York: Oxford University Press, 1992. A useful guide to the history of the Court, its major decisions, every justice who has served on the Court, and doctrines that have guided and influenced the Court since its founding in 1789. Concise yet detailed entries help to make landmark cases and legal terms accessible to a variety of users.

Levin-Waldman, Oren M. *The Case of the Minimum Wage: Competing Policy Models.* Albany: State University of New York Press, 2001. Discusses the evolution of minimum wage policy and law in the United States, focusing on how the nature of arguments concerning a minimum wage has changed over time as the strength of organized labor has declined. Includes tables and figures, bibliography, and index.

Nichols, Egbert Ray, and Joseph H. Baccus, eds. *Selected Articles on Minimum Wages and Maximum Hours.* New York: H. W. Wilson, 1936. Outlines and defines the debate on whether Congress has the power to fix minimum wages and maximum hours for workers. Reprints of editorials and other commentary offer a variety of legal, political, and economic interpretations.

Nordlund, Willis J. *The Quest for a Living Wage: The History of the Federal Minimum Wage Program.* Westport, Conn.: Greenwood Press, 1997. Traces the process through which the U.S. government has attempted to develop a fair method of ensuring that workers receive a living wage. Discusses the theories behind minimum wage programs and gives an overview of the first fifty years of the operation of the Fair Labor Standards Act. Includes tables and figures, bibliography, and index.

Stigler, George J. "The Economics of Minimum Wage Legislation." *American Economic Review* 36 (June, 1946): 358-365. Concise and nontechnical discussion of the relative efficiencies of minimum wage legislation. Provides and uses evidence on employment and wages in Minnesota in the late 1930's.

Welch, Finis. *Minimum Wages: Issues and Evidence.* Washington, D.C.: American Enterprise Institute for Public Policy Research, 1978. A reexamination of the issues forty years after the enactment of the federal minimum wage law.

See also *Bunting v. Oregon; Metro Broadcasting v. Federal Communications Commission; Morehead v. New York ex rel. Tipaldo; United States v. Darby Lumber Co.*

AFROYIM V. RUSK

Court: U.S. Supreme Court
Citation: 387 U.S. 253
Date: May 29, 1967
Issues: Citizenship; Immigration

- The Afroyim decision established that U.S. citizenship may not be revoked involuntarily for actions such as voting in a foreign country.

Beys Afroyim, a naturalized American citizen from Poland, moved to Israel and voted in an Israeli election in 1951. When he attempted to renew his U.S. passport in 1960, the U.S. State Department refused his request, based on the Nationality Act of 1940, which stipulated that voting in a foreign election would result in a loss of citizenship. In an earlier decision, *Perez v. Brownell* (1958), the U.S. Supreme Court had upheld the law by a 5-4 vote. In a civil action against the secretary of state, nevertheless, Afroyim argued that the revocation of his citizenship was unconstitutional.

By a 5-4 margin, The Supreme Court agreed with Afroyim's contention. Writing for the majority, Justice Hugo L. Black emphasized that the first clause of the Fourteenth Amendment was written in order to ensure that U.S. citizenship would be "permanent and secure." The decision had the result of encouraging the right of U.S. citizens to hold dual citizenship. In *Vance v. Terrazas* (1980), the Court held that the intent to give up one's citizenship must be proved by clear and convincing evidence, not simply inferred from acts such as voting in a foreign country. According to the State Department, citizenship may be revoked for treason. In a few other cases, particularly *Fedorenko v. United States* (1981), the Court would uphold the government's power to revoke citizenship if deception had been used in the naturalization process.

Thomas Tandy Lewis

See also *Fedorenko v. United States; Ozawa v. United States; Trop v. Dulles.*

Agostini v. Felton

Court: U.S. Supreme Court
Citation: 521 U.S. 203
Date: June 23, 1997
Issues: Establishment of religion

- The U.S. Supreme Court held that the establishment clause did not prevent the use of public funds for sending public schoolteachers into parochial schools to provide remedial services.

In *Aguilar v. Felton* (1985), the Supreme Court voted five to four to strike down a program in which public school teachers went to private schools to provide a variety of secular services for disadvantaged students. Emphasizing the separationist viewpoint, the majority explained that the program might convey a message of governmental endorsement of religion. After *Aguilar,* New York continued the program by providing remedial services in parked vans near the private schools. In 1995 the parents of affected students went to federal court asking for the reversal of *Aguilar,* which appeared inconsistent with several recent decisions.

In *Agostini v. Felton,* a 5-4 majority of the justices agreed with the petitioners and overturned *Aguilar.* Using an interpretation of the *Lemon* test (developed in *Lemon v. Kurtzman,* 1971) that favored accommodationists, Justice Sandra Day O'Connor argued that the placing of public employees in parochial schools did not result in any state-sponsored indoctrination nor did it constitute any symbolic union between government and religion. In dissent, Justice Ruth Bader Ginsburg argued that it was impossible to draw a clear line between religious and secular instruction in religious schools.

Thomas Tandy Lewis

See also *Abington School District v. Schempp; Everson v. Board of Education of Ewing Township; Lemon v. Kurtzman; Pierce v. Society of Sisters.*

AKRON V. AKRON CENTER FOR REPRODUCTIVE HEALTH

Court: U.S. Supreme Court
Citation: 462 U.S. 416
Date: June 15, 1983
Issues: Parental rights; Reproductive rights; Right to privacy;
Women's issues

• In the face of challenges to the *Roe v. Wade* trimester framework, the Court struck down a range of abortion regulations and reaffirmed *Roe*'s principle that the right of privacy encompasses a qualified right to obtain an abortion.

An Akron, Ohio, city ordinance required that (1) all abortions after the first trimester of pregnancy would be performed in hospitals; (2) parents of unmarried minors would be notified, and their consent would be obtained before such minors could have abortions; (3) physicians would advise their patients that "the unborn child is a human life from the moment of conception"; (4) except in an emergency, there would be a twenty-four-hour waiting period between the signing of a consent form and the abortion; and (5) fetal remains would be disposed of in a humane and sanitary fashion. The United States District Court for the Northern District of Ohio invalidated some of the provisions and upheld others. The U.S. Court of Appeals for the Sixth Circuit affirmed in part and reversed in part. On appeal, the U.S. Supreme Court found these provisions unconstitutional.

Justice Lewis Powell, joined by Chief Justice Warren Burger and Justices William Brennan, Thurgood Marshall, Harry Blackmun, and John Paul Stevens, wrote the majority opinion. Recalling *Roe v. Wade* (1973), Powell noted that the right of privacy encompasses the right to an abortion but that this right must be considered against important state interests. A state can regulate to further its "legitimate interest in protecting the potentiality of human life." This interest, however, becomes compelling only at the point of fetal viability. Further, a state has an important interest in safeguarding the health of women who undergo abortions, but this health interest does not become compelling until "approximately the end of the first trimester" of pregnancy. The majority was unconvinced that the challenged regulations furthered legitimate state interests and, citing the importance of the doctrine of *stare decisis*, reaffirmed *Roe*.

In a dissent joined by Justices Byron R. White and William Rehnquist, Justice Sandra Day O'Connor stopped short of advocating that *Roe* be overruled, but she did argue that "the trimester approach is a completely unworkable method." Improvements in medical technology will make later abortions safer, thus postponing the point at which the state's maternal health interests become compelling.

Conversely, technological developments will enable fetuses to reach viability earlier, thus advancing the point at which this state interest becomes compelling. Therefore, O'Connor wrote, "The *Roe* framework is clearly on a collision course with itself." Instead, O'Connor would hold that an abortion regulation "is not unconstitutional unless it unduly burdens the right to seek an abortion." The minority concluded that the Akron regulations were not unduly burdensome. This case is important because, although the *Roe v. Wade* decision survived, its analytical framework was severely challenged.

Joseph A. Melusky

See also *Doe v. Bolton; Planned Parenthood of Central Missouri v. Danforth; Planned Parenthood of Southeastern Pennsylvania v. Casey; Roe v. Wade; Thornburgh v. American College of Obstetricians and Gynecologists; Webster v. Reproductive Health Services.*

ALBEMARLE PAPER CO. V. MOODY

Court: U.S. Supreme Court
Citation: 422 U.S. 405
Date: June 25, 1975
Issues: Affirmative action; Civil rights and liberties; Employment discrimination; Labor law

- Based on Title VII of the Civil Rights Act of 1964, the U.S. Supreme Court found that an employer's screening tests were discriminatory and that the employer must provide back pay for employees who suffered monetary loss due to racial discrimination.

African American employees in a North Carolina paper mill, the Albemarle Paper Company, charged that the company's preemployment tests and seniority system perpetuated the discrimination that had existed before the passage of Title VII, and they sought back pay relief. By a 7-1 vote, the Supreme Court ruled in favor of the employees. Because the tests were judged to be not sufficiently job related to be valid, they had to be discontinued. The awarding of back pay, moreover, provided an appropriate incentive for compliance with the law. The *Albemarle Paper Co.* decision provided a useful framework for resolving numerous claims under Title VII.

Thomas Tandy Lewis

See also *Craig v. Boren; Fullilove v. Klutznick; Griggs v. Duke Power Co.; Local 28 of Sheet Metal Workers International Association v. Equal Employment Opportunity Commission; Metro Broadcasting v. Federal Communications Commission; United Steelworkers of America v. Weber.*

ALBERTSON V. SUBVERSIVE ACTIVITIES CONTROL BOARD

Court: U.S. Supreme Court
Citation: 382 U.S. 70
Date: November 15, 1965
Issues: Antigovernment subversion; Freedom of assembly and association; Immunity from prosecution; Self-incrimination

- In this case, one of a series of decisions undermining 1950's anti-communist legislation, the U.S. Supreme Court struck down registration provisions of the 1950 McCarran Act.

The Supreme Court unanimously ruled that the Subversive Activities Control Board could not prosecute Communist Party members for failing to register with the board as mandated by the McCarran Act of 1950. The Court held that forced registration meant self-incrimination in other prosecutions. Even provisions granting registrants immunity from prosecution were inadequate to protect Communist Party members from violations of their Fifth Amendment right against self-incrimination.

In an earlier decision, *Communist Party v. Subversive Activities Control Board* (1961), the Court had upheld the registration provisions of the act but declined to reach a conclusion on whether anyone could be prosecuted for refusing to register. Many legal authorities correctly surmised that the Court might not actually allow prosecutions. When enforcement of the act was attempted, the Court blocked it. Recognizing that the act was unenforceable, President Richard M. Nixon and Congress allowed the board to expire in the early 1970's.

Richard L. Wilson

See also *Aptheker v. Secretary of State*; *Communist Party v. Subversive Activities Control Board*; *Dennis v. United States*; *Scales v. United States*; *Yates v. United States*.

ALCOA V. FEDERAL TRADE COMMISSION

Court: U.S. Court of Appeals for the Third Circuit
Citation: 299 Fed. 361
Date: 1924
Issues: Antitrust law; Regulation of commerce

• A circuit court dismissed charges against Aluminum Company of America for acquisition of the Cleveland Products Company's stock, showing that not all monopolies would be prosecuted.

Founded in 1902, Aluminum Company of America (commonly known as Alcoa) immediately attained monopoly power in the aluminum industry. After signing a consent decree with the government in 1912, the company was charged by the Federal Trade Commission in 1918, under section 7 of the Clayton Antitrust Act of 1914, for acquiring stocks of the Cleveland Products Company. *Alcoa v. Federal Trade Commission* was dismissed in 1924, leaving Alcoa with monopoly status until it was prosecuted again in 1945.

The formation of Alcoa was a result of a patent for processing aluminum alloys by electrolysis, a process discovered by Charles Martin Hall in 1886. Despite the abundance of bauxite ore, until the discovery of the Hall process, aluminum had been difficult to extract and was used only in expensive costume jewelry. In 1888, a group of Pittsburgh investors including Alfred Hunt, Arthur Vining Davis, and Andrew and Richard B. Mellon formed the Pittsburgh Reduction Company and acquired the right to the Hall patent.

Meanwhile, Alfred and Eugene Cowles of Cowles Electric Smelting Company of Lockport also began using the Hall process to make aluminum alloys. After winning a patent infringement suit against the Cowles brothers in 1893, Pittsburgh Reduction became the sole producer of virgin aluminum by the Hall process until 1906. The Cowles brothers acquired rights to a process similar to Hall's that was patented in 1892 by Charles Schenck Bradley.

Growth of Pittsburgh Reduction

By 1891, Pittsburgh Reduction had been recapitalized as a million-dollar company. In 1907, after Hall's patent expired, the company changed its name to Aluminum Company of America to reflect the nature and national scope of its business. Between 1907 and 1910, Alcoa became the sole aluminum producer by purchasing the exclusive right to the Bradley patent from the Cowles brothers.

The Hall and Bradley processes dramatically reduced the cost of aluminum production. A few years after its formation, Pittsburgh Reduction was able to undercut most other smelting companies in aluminum price. By the beginning of the twentieth century, aluminum's price had fallen enough to make commercial aluminum production and use practical for the first time.

Immediately after its formation, Pittsburgh Reduction began the process of vertical integration to ensure the company's position against potential competition once Hall's patent expired. First, it integrated backward by acquiring bauxite mines to secure its own ore supply, aluminum refineries in Illinois, fabricating facilities in New Kensington, and a number of waterpower electricity-generating sites in New York State and Canada. By the late 1890's, Pittsburgh Reduction had purchased about 90 percent of bauxite reserves in the United States. Even after Hunt died during the Spanish-American War, the integration process continued under Richard B. Mellon and later under Arthur Davis, who became the presidents of Alcoa in 1899 and 1910, respectively.

With the increased production of and the creation of a potential market for aluminum, the Pittsburgh company began to make efforts to expand its demand. First, it began to integrate forward, acquiring consumers of its product. In 1901, it formed its own cookware subsidiary, Aluminum Cooking Utensil Company, to promote the use of aluminum cooking utensils. Through its efforts, aluminum came to be used in many household products ranging from cooking utensils and heat conductors to electric wire and cables, gradually replacing other metals, particularly steel.

In the 1910's, mass production of automobiles by the Ford Motor Company, the beginning of the aircraft industry, and the outbreak of World War I increased the demand for aluminum. By 1915, more than half of all aluminum production was devoted to automobile parts. Three years later, Alcoa's annual production reached 150 million pounds, much of the increase a result of military applications of aluminum during World War I.

As a result of increased demand for aluminum and economies of scale achieved through increased production, Alcoa expanded its production at an annual rate of 10 percent throughout the first two decades after its formation. Declining aluminum prices accompanied expanded production. During the 1910's, Alcoa had operations across most of the United States east of the Mississippi, including mining, reduction, fabricating, and electric power sites. It produced about 90 percent of primary aluminum alloy and mill-fabricated products used in the United States, with the other 10 percent accounted for by imports, mostly from Switzerland, France, and Great Britain.

Through its Canadian subsidiary, the Northern Aluminum Company, Alcoa joined European cartels between 1901 and 1912 in order to control its domestic markets. The United States contains only a small amount of the world's bauxite reserves. By the end of the 1920's, through the purchase of bauxite reserves in South America, waterpower plants on waterfalls in eastern Canada, and various aluminum smelting and fabricating companies, Alcoa controlled thirty-two operations in eleven countries.

Even after Hall's patent expired, Alcoa proved successful in maintaining its monopoly position in the aluminum industry. Attempts to enter the industry of primary aluminum failed to challenge Alcoa's dominant position. In 1912, for example, a group of French financiers representing the central sales agency of the French aluminum industry, L'Aluminum Français, organized the Southern Aluminum Company and began constructing aluminum reduction facilities in North Carolina. The company planned to use French imported bauxite ore, which was cheaper than the American counterpart. The outbreak of World War I in August, 1914, however, terminated the French financing and ended construction of the plant. A year later, Alcoa bought the Southern Aluminum Company. The Uihlein family, known for its Schlitz breweries, acquired some bauxite ore in Guyana but soon decided to quit aluminum production. The Guyana ore eventually was sold to Alcoa.

Antitrust Law

Passage of the Sherman Antitrust Act in 1890 had begun intense public scrutiny of "trusts," or holding companies, and monopolies in the U.S. market. Even though the prosperity of Alcoa was the result of a patent, the legality of the company's monopoly status was no longer warranted after 1907, when

Hall's patent expired. Throughout the 1910's and 1920's, Alcoa was able to continue expanding its operation by acquiring aluminum reduction plants, mines, and power-generating facilities not only in the United States but also in Canada, Western Europe, and Scandinavia.

Meanwhile, major victories over big trusts in the early 1910's encouraged the U.S. Department of Justice to prosecute other big corporations for violation of antitrust law. Alcoa was an obvious candidate for such action. In May, 1912, the Justice Department charged Alcoa with violating section 2 of the Sherman Act by monopolizing and restraining trade in the aluminum industry. The next month, the District Court of Western Pennsylvania ruled Alcoa guilty and ordered a consent decree in which Alcoa agreed to drop its participation in the international cartels through its Canadian subsidiary and to end its policy of restricting bauxite companies from supplying competing aluminum manufacturers. Alcoa denied the charges that it had controlled the price of aluminum and discriminated in price or service of primary aluminum against competing fabricators and in favor of its own subsidiary.

Largely because of abolition of the international agreement, aluminum imports to the United States increased sharply following the decree in 1912. Even though the decree signified a victory for the government and temporarily reduced public hostility against monopoly, it had little effect on Alcoa's industry position. Alcoa remained the dominant firm in the aluminum industry.

In 1914, new major antitrust legislation was passed in the form of the Clayton Antitrust Act and the Federal Trade Commission Act. The new laws resulted in a new government agency, the Federal Trade Commission, which was responsible for enforcing the modified antitrust law. Because the 1912 consent decree had not resulted in dissolution of Alcoa, the government continued to press charges. Between 1912 and 1940, Alcoa was subject to five major antitrust charges and three Federal Trade Commission complaints.

In 1915, the Cleveland Products Company's aluminum rolling mill in Ohio went bankrupt, largely because of the federal government's price control over aluminum sheet during World War I. Alcoa agreed to invest in the plant in return for a controlling stock interest. In 1922, the Federal Trade Commission challenged this transaction for violating section 7 of the Clayton Act, which prohibits both acquisitions of competing firms and interlocking directorates that may potentially lessen competition.

In February, 1923, in the Third Circuit Court of Appeals, the prosecution was sustained by a vote of two to one. Alcoa sold Cleveland Products stock interest to avoid further charges. Later, Cleveland Products found itself in debt again. Alcoa purchased the company's ingot supply in a government auction, and the Federal Trade Commission filed against the transaction. In 1924, the same judges in the Third Circuit Court, headed by Pierce Butler, unanimously ruled in favor of Alcoa. The court decision demonstrated the judiciary's tendency to be tolerant of monopolies if they were "well behaved." The government temporarily halted its actions against Alcoa.

Significance

Alcoa's history provides many interesting legal as well as economic lessons. The decision in the 1924 case, together with that in the U.S. Steel case in 1920, reflected the government's attitude toward existing monopolies. It reaffirmed the courts' principle of "rule of reason," established in the Standard Oil antitrust suit in 1911. It also reflected pressure from the administration favoring Alcoa, in which Secretary of the Treasury Andrew Mellon was a major stockholder. The court's interpretation that not all monopolies are offenses against the antitrust laws extended the era of the rule of reason as the basis of enforcing the antitrust laws. The rule of reason stated that large firms were legal as long as their size was not accompanied by "unreasonable" conduct.

After its victory over the government, Alcoa continued to expand. From 1925 to 1928, it acquired waterpower sites and expanded its reduction capacity in Canada. Alcoa's victory also initiated a new merger movement in many American industries over the next two decades. The president of Alcoa, Arthur Davis, began to refocus the company's attention on domestic operations. In 1928, he divested Alcoa of all overseas operations except for bauxite mines in South America. The assets were sold to Davis's brother, Edward, who operated Aluminum Limited in Montreal, Canada. The Canadian company, which was renamed Alcan Aluminum Limited in 1966, grew to become the dominant aluminum company in Canada.

After its early defeat, the Department of Justice did not give up on Alcoa. Before the second major antitrust suit, which began in 1937, the government made nearly 140 individual charges against Alcoa, including conspiracy with foreign aluminum manufacturers and monopolization of bauxite reserves, waterpower sites, alumina and ingot aluminum, and aluminum castings. In addition, the Federal Trade Commission continued to file charges against Alcoa for violating the 1912 consent decree by delaying shipment of ore supply to competitors and by discriminating in prices. In 1930, all these complaints were dismissed. Alcoa also successfully defended itself against charges by the Baush Company in 1935 and the Sheet Aluminum Corporation in 1934 that it had monopolized the industry through price discrimination.

The second major antitrust suit against Alcoa lasted for eight years, ending with a U.S. Supreme Court decision in 1945 that held Alcoa had monopolized virgin ingot aluminum. That court decision reversed the interpretation in the

1924 case and stressed that the sheer existence of a monopoly can be an offense against antitrust law.

Alcoa provides a classic example of monopoly in the United States. The company was able to maintain its monopoly power in the aluminum industry beyond that warranted by the government patent through the skilled management of full (forward and backward) integration in the aluminum business as well as by maintaining continued expansion of the demand for aluminum. Amid the government hostility against monopoly in the early twentieth century, the court ruling in favor of Alcoa reversed more than two decades of rulings against big corporations, notably Standard Oil and American Tobacco. The new judicial attitude toward big corporations led to the rise of many large companies and to mergers in the next few decades. As for the aluminum industry, Alcoa maintained its monopoly status until the second major antitrust suit ended in 1945. The period following that defeat saw the rise of two competitors, Reynolds Metals and Kaiser Aluminum & Chemical Corporation.

Jim Lee

Further Reading

Areeda, Phillip, Louis Kaplow, and Aaron Edlin. *Antitrust Analysis: Problems, Text, Cases.* 6th ed. New York: Aspen, 2004. Textbook containing case studies of the major antitrust cases in American history. Bibliographic references and index.

Armentano, Dominick T. *Antitrust and Monopoly: Anatomy of a Policy Failure.* 2d ed. Oakland, Calif.: Independent Institute, 1990. Covers major antitrust lawsuits since the Sherman Act. Discusses their relationship to economic theory and the development of antitrust legislation. Chapter 4 addresses the Alcoa case. Includes an appendix of relevant sections of antitrust laws. Written for an undergraduate audience.

Carr, Charles C. *Alcoa: An American Enterprise.* New York: Rinehart, 1952. Covers the birth of the modern aluminum industry and the history of Alcoa until the end of World War II. Also discusses Alcoa's labor relations and antitrust cases.

Hovenkamp, Herbert. *Federal Antitrust Policy: The Law of Competition and Its Practice.* 2d ed. Eagan, Minn.: West, 1999. Covers nearly all aspects of U.S. antitrust policy in a manner understandable to people with no background in economics. Chapter 2 discusses "history and ideology in antitrust policy."

Hylton, Keith N. *Antitrust Law: Economic Theory and Common Law Evolution.* New York: Cambridge University Press, 2003. Comprehensive text on economic principles behind antitrust and the development of American antitrust law over more than one hundred years of litigation. Includes a chapter on the Alcoa case. Bibliographic references and index.

Parry, Charles W. *Alcoa: A Retrospection.* New York: Newcomen Society of the United States, 1985. A pamphlet containing Parry's speech on the history of Alcoa, beginning with the life of Charles Martin Hall.

Peck, Merton J. *Competition in the Aluminum Industry, 1945-1958.* Cambridge, Mass.: Harvard University Press, 1961. An industry study of supply and demand conditions and of pricing behavior in the industry. Includes a chapter on economic theory and public policy.

Peritz, Rudolph J. R. *Competition Policy in America: History, Rhetoric, Law.* Rev. ed. New York: Oxford University Press, 2001. Explores the influences on U.S. public policy of the concept of free competition. Discusses congressional debates, court opinions, and the work of economic, legal, and political scholars in this area.

Smith, George David. *From Monopoly to Competition: The Transformation of Alcoa, 1888-1986.* Cambridge, England: Cambridge University Press, 1988. Provides interesting discussion of the changing dynamic structure of the aluminum industry over the course of the twentieth century.

Wallace, Donald H. *Market Control in the Aluminum Industry.* Cambridge, Mass.: Harvard University Press, 1937. A thorough study of the early development of the aluminum industry in the United States as well as in Europe before World War II. Includes an appendix that presents a record of the 1924 legal case.

Weiss, Leonard. *Economics and American Industry.* New York: John Wiley & Sons, 1961. Chapter 5 provides good coverage of the evolution of the structure of the aluminum industry. Offers a useful illustration of the industry's pricing behavior with economic models. Valuable for undergraduate economics students.

Whitney, Simon N. *Antitrust Policies: American Experience in Twenty Industries.* 2 vols. New York: Twentieth Century Fund, 1958. Chapter 2 of volume 2 contains succinct discussions of the antitrust cases in the aluminum industry in the first half of the twentieth century and a good end-of-chapter survey of events. Other chapters provide case studies of other major industries. Appendix contains critiques of the studies by economists and government officials.

See also *Gibbons v. Ogden; Muller v. Oregon; Northern Securities Co. v. United States; Standard Oil v. United States; United States v. American Tobacco Co.; United States v. United States Steel Corp.; West Coast Hotel Co. v. Parrish.*

Alexander v. Holmes County Board of Education

Court: U.S. Supreme Court
Citation: 396 U.S. 1218
Date: October 29, 1969
Issues: Desegregation; Education

• In this case, the U.S. Supreme Court ruled that southern school boards must desegregate their schools immediately and refused to grant several school districts a one-semester delay in proceeding with school desegregation.

In the late 1960's, many southern school districts still operated segregated schools, notwithstanding pressure from both the U.S. Office of Education and the federal courts to integrate. In the late 1960's, African American parents throughout Mississippi, with the assistance of the National Association for the Advancement of Colored People (NAACP) Legal Defense and Educational Fund, filed lawsuits challenging segregation in thirty Mississippi school districts.

In 1969, the U.S. Court of Appeals for the Fifth Circuit ordered the districts to file desegregation plans by August 11, 1969, to take effect by the beginning of the 1969-1970 school year. With the support of President Richard M. Nixon's Department of Justice, however, the school districts requested the court to allow them to postpone the submission of school desegregation plans until December 1, 1969. The proceedings, which marked the first time that the Department of Justice had asked for a delay in a school desegregation case, reflected the Nixon administration's lukewarm support for school desegregation. The Fifth Circuit granted the request, and the parents who had filed the original suits appealed to the U.S. Supreme Court.

The Supreme Court considered the case in an expedited fashion. On October 29, 1969—only twenty days after deciding to hear the case, and only six days after oral argument—the Court held that the court of appeals had erred in permitting the delay; the Court's decision stated that "the obligation of every school district is to terminate dual school systems at once." The Court ordered every affected school district to "begin immediately to operate as unitary school systems."

The *Alexander* decision signaled an unprecedented sense of urgency in school desegregation cases. After allowing local school boards to desegregate at a slow pace for much of the prior fifteen years, the Court had now indicated that further delays would not be tolerated—even delays until the end of a school semester or school year. In a sense, the *Alexander* decision constituted the Court's atonement for the "all deliberate speed" language of its 1954 decision in *Brown v. Board of Education*.

Although the *Brown* decision had been a landmark in the battle against segregation, the muted language of the Court's opinion had allowed another generation of African American children to remain in segregated schools. Beginning with its *Green v. County School Board of New Kent County* decision (1968), the Court had finally begun to insist upon meaningful desegregation. Faced for the first time with Justice Department recalcitrance in a desegregation case and a presidential administration with a questionable commitment to school integration, the Court acted in dramatic fashion to signal that the time for delay and "deliberate speed" had come to an end.

In the wake of the *Alexander* decision, courts throughout the South began to insist on immediate desegregation, in some instances in the middle of the school year. The *Alexander* decision dramatically altered the time frame within which school boards were required to meet their desegregation obligations.

Davison M. Douglas

See also *Brown v. Board of Education*; *Green v. County School Board of New Kent County*; *Griffin v. County School Board of Prince Edward County*; *Keyes v. Denver School District No. 1*; *Milliken v. Bradley*; *Swann v. Charlotte-Mecklenburg Board of Education*.

ALLEGHENY COUNTY V. AMERICAN CIVIL LIBERTIES UNION GREATER PITTSBURGH CHAPTER

Court: U.S. Supreme Court
Citation: 492 U.S. 573
Date: July 3, 1989
Issues: Establishment of religion

• The U.S. Supreme Court held that a Christmas display focusing predominantly on religious symbols violated the establishment clause of the First Amendment.

In *Lynch v. Donnelly* (1984), the Supreme Court voted five to four to approve a government-sponsored nativity scene that also included a reindeer, a clown, and a Santa Claus house. The majority found that the display was in conformity with the demands of the three-part *Lemon* test established in *Lemon v. Kurtzman* (1971). Justice Sandra Day O'Connor joined the majority because she concluded that the effect of the display was not to convey a message of either endorsing or disapproving a religion.

The *Allegheny County* case involved two holiday displays located on public property in Pittsburgh. The first was a pious nativity scene without any secular symbols. The judges voted five to four that this display was unconstitutional. Justice Harry A. Blackmun's opinion, which O'Connor joined, was based on the "no endorsement of religion" standard. The same 5-4 majority approved of the second display, a menorah placed next to a Christmas tree. Blackmun asserted that the second display did not promote any religious message. The requirement for including some secular symbols in a seasonal display is sometimes called the "Christmas tree rule." Justice Anthony M. Kennedy, a dissenter, wanted to rule on the basis of whether there was any "coercion." The case illustrated the deep divisions of the justices when interpreting the establishment clause.

Thomas Tandy Lewis

See also *Agostini v. Felton; Everson v. Board of Education of Ewing Township; Lemon v. Kurtzman; Lynch v. Donnelly; Mueller v. Allen.*

Allgeyer v. Louisiana

Court: U.S. Supreme Court
Citation: 165 U.S. 578
Date: March 1, 1897
Issues: Freedom of contract

• The U.S. Supreme Court first used the freedom of contract doctrine to overturn a state law as unconstitutional.

In order to regulate insurance businesses, Louisiana prohibited its residents from entering into most types of insurance contracts with companies located outside the state. Allgeyer and Company was fined one thousand dollars for making such a contract with a New York firm. By a 9-0 vote, the Supreme Court ruled that the law unconstitutionally violated the liberty of citizens to enter into business contracts without unwarranted interference by the state. Writing for the Court, Justice Rufus W. Peckham explained that his opinion

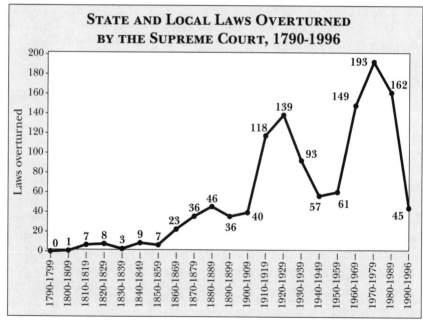

STATE AND LOCAL LAWS OVERTURNED BY THE SUPREME COURT, 1790-1996

Source: Lawrence Baum, *The Supreme Court* (6th ed. Washington, D.C.: Congressional Quarterly, 1998), p. 203.

was based on the concept that substantive economic liberties were protected by the due process clause of the Fourteenth Amendment. Further, having earlier ruled that insurance was not a form of commerce, the Court could not base the decision on the issue of state jurisdiction.

Although *Allgeyer* recognized the authority of states to regulate private companies, it insisted that states must justify the reasonableness of all such regulations. Freedom of contract was to be the rule, with exceptions allowed only when clearly necessary to protect the safety, health, or welfare of the public. Through the next four decades, the *Allgeyer* precedent provided a theoretical basis for overturning numerous laws that regulated terms of employment—such as laws requiring maximum working hours or minimum wages. The Court finally stopped giving special protection for the freedom of contract doctrine in *West Coast Hotel Co. v. Parrish* (1937).

Thomas Tandy Lewis

See also *Holden v. Hardy; Lochner v. New York; Mugler v. Kansas; Munn v. Illinois; West Coast Hotel Co. v. Parrish.*

ALSAGER V. DISTRICT COURT

Court: U.S. District Court of Polk County, Iowa
Citation: 545 F.2d 1137
Date: December 8, 1976
Issues: Children's rights; Parental rights

- This decision of a U.S. district court, upheld in a court of appeals, recognizes that parental rights cannot be terminated except for extremely good reasons.

Social workers in Polk County, Iowa, decided that Charles and Darlene Alsager were not taking good care of their six children. Circumstances included untidy living conditions, a lack of warm clothing in winter, and poor school attendance. After the case was referred to the county district court, the local judge, following the state's relevant statute, decided to terminate the Alsagers' parental rights over five of their children, after which the children were placed in foster homes. The parents challenged the action in the federal courts, where they prevailed.

The U.S. Court of Appeals made two major rulings. First, from the perspective of substantive due process the state had not shown any "high and substantial degree of harm to the children," and thus the state had not established an adequate basis for termination of parental rights. Second, from the perspective of procedural due process, the notice for the hearing had not included factual information necessary for the parents to prepare a defense. Thus, Iowa's parental termination statute was declared unconstitutional, and the case was sent back to the county court for resolution. This federal precedent requires courts to use the "compelling state interest test" to justify any termination of parental rights.

Thomas Tandy Lewis

See also *Meyer v. Nebraska; Zablocki v. Redhail.*

ALVAREZ-MACHAIN, UNITED STATES V. *See* UNITED STATES V. ALVAREZ-MACHAIN

AMERICAN BOOKSELLERS ASSOCIATION, INC. V. HUDNUT

Court: U.S. Supreme Court
Citation: 475 U.S. 1001
Date: February 24, 1986
Issues: Censorship; Pornography and obscenity

• In this case the U.S. Supreme Court summarily affirmed an appellate court's holding that an Indiana antipornography ordinance violated the First Amendment.

The *Hudnut* decision involved an Indianapolis-Marion County ordinance that defined pornography not a causal factor that harmed women but as an injury per se. The ordinance defined pornography as "graphic sexually explicit subordination of women through pictures and/or words" that dehumanized women as sexual objects, presented them in sexually degrading situations, showed them being sexually penetrated by objects or animals, or depicted them in other physically degrading situations in contexts that make the conditions sexual. After heated debate over the problems of pornography and sex discrimination in American society, the Indianapolis City-County Council enacted an ordinance that restricted the availability of materials depicting the sexual subordination of women.

A district court held that the state's interest in eradicating sex discrimination was insufficiently compelling to outweigh the public interest in free speech. The court paid particular attention to obscenity as the category of speech most closely resembling pornography. Defenders of the ordinance contended that because pornography was a broader category than obscenity the court should recognize it as a new category of unprotected speech. They also argued that the ordinance regulated conduct and not speech, since—by their own definition—pornography was more than a mere expression of ideas. They saw it as unconstitutional sex-based discrimination.

Opponents of the ordinance contended that it failed to provide fair notice to residents of Indianapolis and those doing business there as to what it covered or exempted, and that it thereby violated the Fifth and Fourteenth amendments of the U.S. Constitution. They also claimed that the ordinance had a "chilling effect" on the exercise of free speech rights and that its provision for cease and desist orders constituted an illegal prior restraint by allowing the government to act as a censor.

The district court ruled that it could not permit every group claiming to have been victimized by unfair expression special legislative exceptions to the First Amendment. Finally, the court suggested that while sociological patterns might need alteration, defendants should remember that free speech, "rather than being the enemy, is a long-tested and worthy ally," that could be used to protect against tyranny.

Barbara G. Kramer

See also *Ashcroft v. Free Speech Coalition; Hamling v. United States; Miller v. California; New York v. Ferber; Osborne v. Ohio; Roth v. United States; Times Film Corp. v. City of Chicago.*

AMERICAN COMMUNICATIONS ASSOCIATION V. DOUDS

Court: U.S. Supreme Court
Citation: 339 U.S. 382
Date: May 8, 1950
Issues: Freedom of assembly and association; Freedom of speech;
Interstate commerce

- At the height of the Cold War, the U.S. Supreme Court upheld the portions of the Taft-Hartley Act (1947) that required labor union leaders to sign an affidavit affirming that they were not presently members of the Communist Party.

The Communications union, which had a record of some Communist Party infiltration, charged that the registration provisions of the Taft-Hartley Act of 1947 violated the freedoms provided by the First Amendment. Speaking for a 5-1 majority, Chief Justice Fred M. Vinson interpreted the law as an attempt to prevent disruptive strikes in interstate commerce, a legitimate interest of Congress. Using an ad hoc balancing approach, Vinson made a distinction between freedom of speech, protected by the First Amendment, and political association, a form of action that deserved less protection than the communication of ideas. *Douds* may be contrasted with *United States v. Brown* (1965), in which the Supreme Court struck down a more restrictive law that prohibited people from serving as labor leaders if they had been affiliated with the Communist Party during the previous five years.

Thomas Tandy Lewis

See also *Albertson v. Subversive Activities Control Board; Aptheker v. Secretary of State; Communist Party v. Subversive Activities Control Board; DeJonge v. Oregon; Dennis v. United States; Kent v. Dulles; United States v. Robel.*

AMERICAN TOBACCO CO., UNITED STATES V. *See* UNITED STATES V. AMERICAN TOBACCO CO.

ANTELOPE, THE

Court: U.S. Supreme Court
Citation: 10 Wheat. (23 U.S.) 66
Date: March 16, 1825
Issues: International law

- While acknowledging that the slave trade was contrary to principles of natural justice, the U.S. Supreme Court nevertheless recognized the authority of sovereign nations to enact laws allowing the practice.

Pirates seized a Spanish vessel, *The Antelope*, carrying a large cargo of African slaves. A U.S. naval ship subsequently captured the ship with its cargo and took it to Savannah, Georgia. Spanish and Portuguese slave traders sued to have their property restored. Because Congress had outlawed U.S. participa-

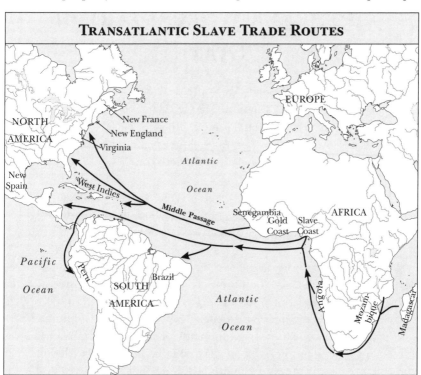

TRANSATLANTIC SLAVE TRADE ROUTES

tion in the slave trade in 1808, many jurists argued that the captured slaves should be repatriated to Africa.

Chief Justice John Marshall's opinion for the Supreme Court had three parts. First, the "abhorrent" trade in slaves was indeed "contrary to the law of nature"; however, the trade, long accepted throughout the world, was not condemned by the positive law of nations. Second, the United States had no power to impose its laws on other countries; therefore, a ship captured in a time of peace must be restored with its cargo. Third, based on the evidence for the claims of ownership, some of the slaves were returned to the Spanish claimants, and the remainder were repatriated to the American Colonization Society's colony in Liberia.

Thomas Tandy Lewis

See also *Cooley v. Board of Wardens of the Port of Philadelphia; Gibbons v. Ogden; Groves v. Slaughter; Johnson and Graham's Lessee v. McIntosh.*

APTHEKER V. SECRETARY OF STATE

Court: U.S. Supreme Court
Citation: 378 U.S. 500
Date: June 22, 1964
Issues: Antigovernment subversion; Freedom of assembly and association; Right to travel

- In this case, one of a series that undermined 1950's anticommunist legislation, the U.S. Supreme Court overturned the communist registration provision in the 1950 McCarran Act.

A six-vote liberal majority on the Supreme Court voided the part of the 1950 McCarran Act requiring Communist Party members to register with the Subversive Activities Control Board. This registration provision was upheld in *Communist Party v. Subversive Activities Control Board* (1961), but the Court said it would rule on the constitutionality of the registrations only if enforcement were attempted. The government had previously tried to block the issuance of passports to communists and other subversives under the

1926 Passport Act, but this was stricken as unconstitutional in *Kent v. Dulles* (1958).

Writing for the Court, Justice Arthur J. Goldberg called the statute overly broad, pointing out that the right to travel outside the United States, while not absolute, was valuable and that this act banned travel for subversive organization members without regard to the purpose of their travel and whether they were active or knowing members of the organization.

Richard L. Wilson

See also *Albertson v. Subversive Activities Control Board; Communist Party v. Subversive Activities Control Board; Dennis v. United States; Kent v. Dulles; Scales v. United States; Yates v. United States.*

ARGERSINGER V. HAMLIN

Court: U.S. Supreme Court
Citation: 407 U.S. 25
Date: June 12, 1972
Issues: Right to counsel

- The U.S. Supreme Court ruled that the Sixth and Fourteenth Amendments mandate that states must provide a poor defendant with a lawyer at the time of trial if the defendant could be imprisoned for any period of time.

In *Gideon v. Wainwright* (1963), the Supreme Court held that states must provide counsel for indigent defendants in felony cases. However, it was not clear whether this expanded right to an attorney applied to misdemeanor cases. Then the Court decided in 1968 that defendants had a right to a jury trial when they faced incarceration for six months or more. In this context, Argersinger was not provided counsel when he was convicted and sentenced to three months in jail for the misdemeanor of carrying a concealed weapon.

By a 9-0 vote, the Court reversed Argersinger's conviction. Writing for the majority, Justice William O. Douglas developed the one-day rule, which triggers the right to counsel whenever a person is deprived of liberty for even one day. The *Argersinger* decision was ambiguous about whether the right to counsel applied whenever a defendant was charged with a crime that could result in a jail term. The Court clarified the issue in *Scott v. Illinois* (1979), holding that counsel must be provided only if conviction would actually result in imprisonment.

Thomas Tandy Lewis

See also *Edwards v. California; Gideon v. Wainwright; Johnson v. Zerbst; Miranda v. Arizona; Powell v. Alabama.*

ARIZONA V. FULMINANTE

Court: U.S. Supreme Court
Citation: 499 U.S. 279
Date: March 26, 1991
Issues: Confessions; Evidence; Miranda rights

• The U.S. Supreme Court ruled that a coerced confession wrongly admitted as evidence could be subjected to "harmless error" analysis and might not be grounds for automatic invalidation of a criminal conviction.

In 1983, Oreste C. Fulminante, incarcerated in a federal prison for an unrelated crime, confessed to another inmate, a paid informant for the Federal Bureau of Investigation, that he had raped and murdered his eleven-year-old stepdaughter. He also confessed to a woman who later married the informant. The next year, when tried for first-degree murder in the Superior Court, Maricopa County, Arizona, Fulminante sought to have his confessions suppressed on grounds that they violated his due process rights guaranteed by the Fifth and Fourteenth Amendments.

The motion was denied, and Fulminante was convicted of first-degree murder and sentenced to death. On appeal, Fulminante's conviction was first upheld by the Arizona Supreme Court; later, however, under reconsideration, that same court ordered a retrial on the grounds that the "harmless error" basis of admitting Fulminante's confession was inapplicable because the first confession was coerced.

On *certiorari*, the U.S. Supreme Court upheld the ruling of the Arizona Supreme Court. It confirmed that Fulminante's first confession had been coerced and that admission of his confession was not harmless under the specific circumstances. However, part of the majority opinion, argued by Chief Justice William H. Rehnquist, advanced the 5-4 majority's conclusion that in a state criminal trial an involuntary confession admitted in violation of the Fourteenth Amendment's due process clause is, in fact, subject to harmless-error analysis.

This opinion was rooted in a distinction made between due process violations and "trial error," holding that the admission of an involuntary confession does not transcend the criminal trial process and that it is similar in kind and degree to other evidence admitted in court. It noted, too, that confessions secured in violation of *Massiah v. United States* (1964) and *Miranda v. Arizona* (1966) had already been subject to harmless-error analysis.

Justice Byron R. White, vigorously dissenting, argued that the admission of a coerced confession in a criminal trial violated the defendant's constitutional rights and should not be subject to harmless-error analysis, and, further, that no sufficient reason had been presented for departing from the Supreme Court's time-honored "rule of automatic reversal" in coerced-confession cases. According to that rule, if a coerced, involuntary confession was erroneously admitted in criminal proceedings, any conviction had to be overturned regardless of how much other evidence of guilt supported it.

In effect, the Supreme Court's *Fulminante* decision overturned earlier decisions such as that rendered in *Chapman v. California* (1967), one of the last cases prior to *Fulminante* upholding the rule of automatic reversal. This departure from that rule raised questions whether admission of a coerced confession as evidence must always be interpreted as a violation of a defendant's constitutional rights or of those protected by the rulings in the *Massiah* and *Miranda* decisions. The finding has been criticized for eroding those rights.

John W. Fiero

See also *Brecht v. Abrahamson; Brown v. Mississippi; Chambers v. Florida; Escobedo v. Illinois; Faretta v. California; Harris v. New York; Massiah v. United States; Miranda v. Arizona; United States v. Wade.*

ARLINGTON HEIGHTS V. METROPOLITAN HOUSING DEVELOPMENT CORP.

Court: U.S. Supreme Court
Citation: 429 U.S. 252
Date: January 11, 1977
Issues: Housing discrimination; Racial discrimination

- The U.S. Supreme Court reaffirmed the principle that a governmental policy will not be judged unconstitutional solely because it has a disproportionate impact on a particular race.

A nonprofit developer wanted to construct low- and moderate-income housing units in a largely white suburb of Chicago. A major goal of the project was to promote racial integration in the community. The suburb's board of trustees refused to rezone the region for multiple-family dwellings, thus killing the project. The federal court of appeals ruled that the denial of rezoning violated the Fourteenth Amendment because its "ultimate effect" was discrimination against racial minorities. By a 7-1 vote, the Supreme Court reversed the lower court's ruling. Based on the recent precedent, *Washington v. Davis* (1976), Justice Lewis F. Powell, Jr., explained that proof of a "racially discriminatory intent" was necessary in order to establish a constitutional violation. From the official minutes and other evidence of the case, Powell concluded that the challengers had "simply failed to carry their burden of showing that discriminatory purpose was a motivating factor in the Village's decision."

Thomas Tandy Lewis

See also *Buchanan v. Warley; Corrigan v. Buckley; Evans v. Abney; Reitman v. Mulkey; San Antonio Independent School District v. Rodriguez; Shelley v. Kraemer; Spallone v. United States; Washington v. Davis.*

ASHCROFT V. FREE SPEECH COALITION

Court: U.S. Supreme Court
Citation: 535 U.S. 234
Date: April 16, 2002
Issues: Freedom of expression; Pornography and obscenity

• The U.S. Supreme Court held that Congress has no constitutional authority to outlaw computer-generated depiction of children that is sexually oriented but not legally obscene.

The Child Pornography Prevention Act of 1996 (CPPA) criminalized all forms of child pornography, including computer-generated images that portray minors engaged in sexually explicit conduct. The act did not make any distinction between indecency and obscenity. The Free Speech Coalition, an adult entertainment commercial group, alleged in court that the statute was overly broad and vague, thereby restraining works protected by the First Amendment. The Court of Appeals agreed and held that the CPPA was unconstitutional because it banned material that was neither obscene according to the test under *Miller v. California* (1971), nor produced with the exploitation of children as in *New York v. Ferber* (1982).

The Supreme Court upheld the lower court's ruling. Writing for a 6-3 majority, Justice Anthony M. Kennedy found that the CPPA did not meet *Miller's* definition of obscenity because of its lack of reference to community standards. The CPPA lacked the support of *Ferber*, moreover, because it punished expression even though its production was not based on crime or the victimization of anyone. The *Ashcroft* opinion reaffirmed that when sexually oriented expression is neither obscene nor the product of sexual abuse, it falls under the protection of the First Amendment. Finally, Kennedy wrote that the potential misuse of material by pedophiles did not justify the statute, since almost all forms of expression are subject to abuse by some individuals.

Thomas Tandy Lewis

See also *Miller v. California; New York v. Ferber; Osborne v. Ohio; Stanley v. Georgia.*

Ashwander v. Tennessee Valley Authority

Court: U.S. Supreme Court
Citation: 297 U.S. 288
Date: February 17, 1936
Issues: Judicial powers

- The U.S. Supreme Court upheld the constitutionality of the Tennessee Valley Authority, including its right to sell electricity. In a concurring opinion, Justice Louis D. Brandeis formulated influential guidelines concerning when the Court will decide constitutional questions.

When the Tennessee Valley Authority (TVA) sold "surplus power" to a private utility company, minority shareholders went to court to annul the agreement. Speaking for an 8-1 majority, Chief Justice Charles Evans Hughes argued that the TVA had been built for national defense and for the improvement of navigation, which were legitimate interests of the national govern-

Justice James C. McReynolds on his seventy-eighth birthday in 1940. (Harris & Ewing Collection/ Library of Congress)

ment. He added that Article IV, section 3, of the U.S. Constitution authorized Congress to dispose of property legally acquired. Dissenting, Justice James C. McReynolds accused the majority of using a fictitious rationale, since the main purpose of the TVA was to produce and sell electricity.

Although concurring with the decision, Justice Brandeis argued that the Supreme Court should not have even addressed the constitutional question because the case involved only an internal dispute among shareholders. He codified rules for the Court to follow. First, the Court will not determine constitutional questions in a friendly, nonadversarial proceeding; second, the Court will not anticipate an issue of constitutional law; third, the Court will not decide a constitutional question unless necessary to resolving the case at hand; fourth, the Court will not formulate a principle of constitutional law broader than necessary for resolving the case; fifth, the Court will not decide on the validity of a statute unless a plaintiff has been injured by its operation; and sixth, before deciding that a statute is unconstitutional, the Court will first ascertain whether a reasonable interpretation of the statute permits avoidance of the constitutional issue.

Although not always followed, justices commonly refer to the *Ashwander* rules, or Brandeis rules, as established standards. At times the rules have encouraged the justices to exercise a degree of self-restraint, and sometimes they have served as an excuse to avoid awkward or difficult questions.

Thomas Tandy Lewis

See also *Chicago, Milwaukee, and St. Paul Railway Co. v. Minnesota; Coleman v. Miller; Kansas v. Hendricks; Smyth v. Ames; Tennessee Valley Authority v. Hill; Wolff Packing Co. v. Court of Industrial Relations.*

ATKINS V. VIRGINIA

Court: U.S. Supreme Court
Citation: 536 U.S. 304
Date: June 20, 2002
Issues: Capital punishment; Cruel and unusual punishment;
Medical ethics

• Directly overturning a decision of 1989, the U.S. Supreme Court disallowed the execution of offenders with mental disabilities, based on the Eighth Amendment's prohibition of cruel and unusual punishments.

After ruling in *Gregg v. Georgia* (1976) that the Eighth Amendment did not prohibit capital punishment in all instances, the Supreme Court was frequently called upon to decide when the penalty is unconstitutional because it offends society's "evolving sense of decency," a subjective standard enunciated in *Trop v. Dulles* (1958). Applying this standard in *Ford v. Wainwright* (1986), the justices voted five to four to disallow the execution of insane persons. However, in another 5-4 ruling, *Penry v. Lynaugh* (1989), the Court held that the Eighth Amendment did not automatically proscribe the execution of moderately retarded persons. The majority opinion, however, required juries to consider the issue of retardation when deciding on a penalty. Critics of the death penalty claimed that at least thirty-five mentally retarded persons were executed between 1976 and 2002.

In 1998, Daryl R. Atkins was prosecuted in York County, Virginia, on charges of abduction and first-degree murder. The jury heard uncontested evidence that he and a codefendant, William Jones, had randomly abducted U.S. airman Eric Nesbitt and then forced him to withdraw two hundred dollars from an automated teller machine before killing him. Atkins and Jones each claimed that the other was directly responsible for the murder. Jones pleaded guilty of participation in the crime in exchange for a reduced penalty. In view of Atkins's criminal record, the prosecution was determined that he should receive the maximum penalty. The jury concluded that Atkins was guilty as charged.

At the separate hearing to determine the punishment, two forensic psychologists presented contradictory conclusions about Atkins's mental capacity. Evan Nelson, the expert for the defense, reported that Atkins was "mildly" mentally retarded with an intelligence quotient (IQ) of 59—a figure well below the benchmark level of 70. Nelson also observed that the defendant had not succeeded in school and had never lived on his own or held a job. Testifying for the prosecution, Stanton Samenow, strongly disagreed and described the defendant as a man of normal intelligence who was able to "adapt and to take care of basic needs." Despite their different evaluations, both psychologists agreed that Atkins was competent to understand that the act of murder was wrong. They also agreed that his behavior corresponded to the standard criteria for an "antisocial personality disorder." Not surprisingly, Atkins was sentenced to death. When the Virginia Supreme Court upheld the sentence in a 5-2 decision, its opinion for the majority asserted that the relevance of Atkins's mental disability was a matter to be decided by the jury.

However, when the case reached the U.S. Supreme Court, its justices voted six to three to disallow Atkins's death sentence and to overturn the *Penry* precedent. Writing for the majority, Justice John Paul Stevens argued that offenders with "subaverage intellectual" ability are less likely to foresee the consequences of their actions, a consideration that "diminishes their personal culpability." Stevens observed that since 1989, sixteen state legislatures had enacted legislation disallowing executions of mentally disabled offenders and that only five states had executed such persons during the 1990's. These statistics demonstrated that executing such offenders had "become truly unusual" and that "a national consensus has developed against it." In addition to violating an evolving standard of decency, Stevens declared that the execution of the mentally retarded is excessive because it does not advance either the retributive or deterrent purposes of capital punishment.

Both Chief Justice William H. Rehnquist and Justice Antonin Scalia wrote dissenting opinions. Rehnquist insisted that legislatures, juries, and trial judges should be allowed to decide the proper punishments for particular offenders. Denying that there was a "national consensus" on the issue, he observed that twenty states continued to have laws permitting the execution of a retarded murderer, and he also criticized the majority for taking into account the views of judiciaries and legislatures of foreign countries. Writing in a more aggressive tone, Scalia denounced the "empty talk of a national consensus," and he castigated the "arrogance" of the presumption "that really good lawyers have moral sentiments superior to those of the common herd." Society's "moral outrage," he wrote, "sometimes demands execution of retarded offenders." Justice Clarence Thomas indicated his agreement with both opinions. Despite the protests of the three dissenters, the ruling in *Atkins* appeared to indicate that a firm majority of the justices disliked executions so strongly that they would only allow them in extremely limited conditions.

Thomas Tandy Lewis

Further Reading

Atwell, Mary Welek. *Evolving Standards of Decency: Popular Culture and Capital Punishment.* New York: Peter Lang, 2004. Referring to Chief Justice Warren's criterion of society's evolving standards of decency; Atwell explores views on the acceptability of capital punishment in the nation's popular culture.

Foley, Michael. *Arbitrary and Capricious: The Supreme Court, the Constitution, and the Death Penalty.* Westport, Conn.: Praeger, 2003. A professor of philosophy, Foley argues that the Supreme Court's jurisprudence in the area of capital punishment has been inconsistent and often based on questionable constitutional interpretations.

Latzer, Barry. *Death Penalty Cases: Leading U.S. Supreme Court Cases on Capital*

Punishment. 2d ed. Boston: Butterworth-Heinemann, 2002. Collection of twenty-five Supreme Court cases with introductory materials and relevant statistical data.

Parrish, Michael. *The Supreme Court and Capital Punishment.* Washington, D.C.: CQ Press, 2009. Includes a valuable historical account of the topic and analyses important issues such as the influence of race, public opinion, and financial resources available to defendants.

Walker, Thomas G. *Eligible for Execution: The Story of the Daryl Atkins Case.* Washington, D.C.: CQ Press, 2008. Fascinating and detailed examination of the Atkins case, based on interviews with major participants, personal observations of the hearings, and close examination of legal documents.

See also *Ford v. Wainwright; Gregg v. Georgia; Harmelin v. Michigan; Hutto v. Davis; McCleskey v. Kemp; Rhodes v. Chapman; Rummel v. Estelle; Stanford v. Kentucky; Weems v. United States.*

ATWATER V. CITY OF LAGO VISTA

Court: U.S. Supreme Court
Citation: 532 U.S. 318
Date: April 24, 2001
Issues: Police powers; Search and seizure

• A U.S. Supreme Court decision on warrantless arrests for minor criminal offenses, this case ratified routine arrests for minor crimes punishable only by a fine.

In 1997, Gail Atwater was driving her three-year-old son and five-year-old daughter home from soccer practice. Officer Barton Turek of Texas's City of Lago Vista police stopped Atwater because neither she nor the children were wearing seat belts, a violation of Texas law with a maximum fine of fifty dollars. Turek approached the car and began yelling at Atwater that she was going to jail.

Instead of following the common practice of issuing a citation, Turek arrested Atwater, handcuffed her, and transported her to the police station. There the booking officers took a "mug shot" and had her empty her pockets and remove her shoes, jewelry, and eyeglasses. She was placed alone in a jail cell for approximately an hour before appearing in front of a magistrate and posting a $310 bond. Eventually, she pleaded no contest to the seatbelt violations and paid the fines. She then filed a lawsuit against the city and Turek under the federal Civil Rights Act, claiming that her right to be free from unreasonable seizure had been violated.

In a 5-4 decision, the U.S. Supreme Court deemed the custodial arrest constitutional even though the justices thought the officer at best "exercis[ed] extremely poor judgment." The Court rejected Atwater's contention that the common law, at the time of the adoption of the Fourth Amendment, generally prohibited warrantless arrests for minor crimes unless special circumstances such as violence or a demonstrable threat existed. The Court also declined to establish a rule prohibiting routine warrantless arrests for fine-only offenses on the grounds that officers might not have the time or knowledge to make the distinction among the fine-only crimes and others. Instead, the Court focused on Turek's probable cause that Atwater committed a crime in his presence and that Texas law permitted such arrests.

Justice Sandra Day O'Connor, writing for the dissent, recognized that "significant qualitative differences" exist between a traffic stop and a full custodial arrest, a much greater infringement on a person's liberty and privacy interests. In weighing the competing interests of the state in enforcing traffic laws against the invasion of the individual's rights, she found arrests for fine-only offenses should be unreasonable unless special circumstances exist.

Atwater v. City of Lago Vista (2001) was immediately criticized by commentators from across the political spectrum. Even those who usually advocate stronger police powers were dismayed by this expansion of police discretion to permit someone to be jailed for a fine-only offense.

Susan Coleman

Further Reading

Katz, Jason. "*Atwater v. City of Lago Vista:* Buckle Up or Get Locked Up." *Akron Law Review* 491 (2003).

Milloy, Ross E. "Public Lives: For Seat-Belt Violator, a Jam, a Jail, and Unmoved Justices." *The New York Times*, April 28, 2001.

Osborne, Jonathan, and Bob Dart. "Lago Vista Mom Loses in High Court." *Austin American-Statesman*, April 25, 2001.

See also *Chimel v. California; Marshall v. Barlow's; Maryland v. Buie; Miranda v. Arizona; Tennessee v. Garner; United States v. Ross.*

AUTOMOBILE WORKERS V. JOHNSON CONTROLS

Court: U.S. Supreme Court
Citation: 499 U.S. 187
Date: March 20, 1991
Issues: Employment discrimination; Reproductive rights; Women's issues

- Based on an interpretation of the Pregnancy Discrimination Act of 1983, the U.S. Supreme Court struck down a private company's fetal-protection policy that barred all women with childbearing capacity from jobs involving significant lead exposure.

The Pregnancy Discrimination Act of 1983, an amendment to Title VII of the Civil Rights Act of 1964, required that pregnant employees must be "treated

Justice Harry A. Blackmun.
(Library of Congress)

the same" as other employees unless there was a bona fide occupational qualification for different treatment. By a 6-3 vote, the Supreme Court held that there was no bona fide occupational qualification justification for Johnson Controls' policy of exclusion. Justice Harry A. Blackmun's majority opinion emphasized that the policy did not seek to protect the future children of all employees equally because it did not apply to male employees despite evidence of the debilitating effect of lead exposure on the male reproductive system. In addition, he wrote that the 1983 act permitted a safety exception only in instances in which the employee's sex or pregnancy actually interfered with the worker's ability to perform the job and that decisions about the welfare of future children must be left to parents rather than the employer. Rejecting the argument about the need of the company to protect itself from tort liability, Blackmun noted that the Occupational Safety and Health Administration required safety standards designed to minimize the risk to an unborn child and that it would be difficult for a court to find liability without negligence.

Thomas Tandy Lewis

See also *Geduldig v. Aiello; General Electric v. Gilbert; Monell v. Department of Social Services.*

BABY M, IN RE. *See* IN RE BABY M

BAILEY V. DREXEL FURNITURE CO.

Court: U.S. Supreme Court
Citation: 259 U.S. 20
Date: May 15, 1922
Issues: Federal supremacy; Regulation of commerce; Taxation

• The U.S. Supreme Court ruled that Congress could not use its taxing power to impose regulations on production, which were powers reserved to the states by the Tenth Amendment.

In *Hammer v. Dagenhart* (1918), the Supreme Court struck down the first federal child labor statute as an unconstitutional use of the commerce power. In response, Congress enacted the Child Labor Act of 1916, which imposed a 10 percent tax on the net profits of companies employing children under the age of fourteen. Supporters of the law noted that the Court had approved of a prohibitive excise tax on oleomargarine in *McCray v. United States* (1904).

In *Bailey*, the justices voted eight to one to strike down the law. Chief Justice William H. Taft's opinion for the majority declared that the "so-called" tax was really a disguised regulation designed to stop child labor. To allow taxes to be used for such purposes, he declared, would give Congress almost unlimited powers and "completely wipe out the sovereignty of the states." In *McCray*, the Court had approved of a tax that provided only "incidental restraint and regulation," but the child labor tax, in contrast, had a "prohibitory and regulatory effect." Modern commentators usually find that Taft's distinction lacks merit. Although the *Bailey* decision remained good law for two decades, the Court rejected its theoretical foundations in *Mulford v. Smith* (1939).

Thomas Tandy Lewis

See also *Hammer v. Dagenhart*; *McCray v. United States*; *Mulford v. Smith*; *United States v. Butler.*

BAKER V. CARR

Court: U.S. Supreme Court
Citation: 369 U.S. 186
Date: March 26, 1962
Issues: Reapportionment and redistricting; Voting rights

- In a series of cases over a two-year period, the U.S. Supreme Court issued decisions requiring election districts to be determined by population. The decisions affirmed the principle that each voter in the United States should have comparable power by ensuring that each voter represented roughly the same percentage of a congressional representative's constituency.

Among the many profound changes ushered in by the twentieth century, none has had a more far-reaching effect on U.S. society than urbanization. The United States has not always adjusted well to the changes wrought by urbanization. This has been especially true in the area of democratic political representation in the various states. By 1960, there were flagrant examples of malapportionment in the majority of states, both in state legislatures and in delegations to the U.S. House of Representatives. Incumbent state legislatures, dominated by rural elements, had refused to reapportion representation to reflect population shifts accurately; to do so would have strengthened urban areas at the expense of the rural groups in control. Delaware, for example, had not reapportioned its legislature since 1897; Tennessee and Alabama had not done so since 1901. These were only the worst cases. In all but six states, less than 40 percent of the population could elect a majority of the legislature.

State legislatures frequently ignored provisions in their state constitutions that required periodic reapportionment on the basis of the decennial census. Such a situation imperiled the very basis of democracy. However, before 1962, the Supreme Court had refused to intervene on the grounds that apportionment was a political question and thus outside the jurisdiction of the Court. This dictum had been handed down in the case *Colegrove v. Green* (1946). The resulting malapportionment has been likened to the eighteenth century English "rotten boroughs."

In 1962, the Court finally abandoned its unwillingness to act on the matter of apportionment and took a strong stand in favor of democratic representation in *Baker v. Carr,* a case challenging the apportionment of the Tennessee state legislature. The Tennessee state constitution called for reapportionment every ten years, although none had taken place since 1901. As a result, urban areas were greatly underrepresented in the legislature, while rural areas were overrepresented. Moore County, with a population of 3,454, elected one legislator, while Shelby County (which includes Memphis), with a population of 627,019, elected only three. The inequities were starkly evident.

The Supreme Court Ruling

The federal district court in Tennessee, in which the suit had been filed originally, refused to take action on the basis of the precedent established in *Colegrove v. Green*. When the case was appealed to the Supreme Court, however, that body ruled by a 6-2 margin that the Tennessee case was justiciable and returned it to the lower court for a decision. With this decision, issued on March 26, 1962, political reformers finally had realized their aim: The Court, under Chief Justice Earl Warren, had agreed to deal with the problem of equitable apportionment of representation, although it had made no actual decision on the subject. Justices Felix Frankfurter and John M. Harlan II dissented in *Baker v. Carr,* again arguing that apportionment was a political question and therefore not within the Court's jurisdiction.

As a result of *Baker v. Carr*, a spate of litigation and legislation regarding apportionment followed. By the end of 1963, federal suits had been filed in thirty-one states and state suits in nineteen others. During that same period, twenty-six states adopted new legislative apportionment plans. Nevertheless, these plans did not always satisfy political reformers. The plans varied greatly in intent and effect, because the Court had not actually ruled on apportionment and therefore had not established guidelines for the states to follow.

This confusion over the Court's views was partially remedied in March of 1963, when *Gray v. Sanders* struck down Georgia's so-called county unit rule. That rule assigned a certain number of units, or votes, to each county in elections for statewide offices and operated in a manner similar to the federal electoral college. The result of the county unit rule was severe discrimination against voters in the more populous areas. The Court ruled eight to one, Justice Harlan dissenting, that the Georgia system violated the equal protection clause of the Constitution, and Justice William O. Douglas, in writing the majority opinion, used the momentous phrase "one man, one vote." Again, the Court had not ruled directly on the question of apportionment, but it had given a broad hint as to what it expected.

Gray v. Sanders foreshadowed *Wesberry v. Sanders*, a landmark case decided on February 17, 1964, in which the Court used the "one man, one vote" principle to void a 1931 Georgia congressional apportionment law. Justice Harlan again dissented, contending that the Court was intruding upon the proper province of Congress. The Court, however, was now clearly committed to guaranteeing equitable apportionment and democratic representation in the United States House of Representatives as well as in state legislatures. Later in 1964, the Court further delineated its standards in six cases involving Alabama, New York, Maryland, Virginia, Delaware, and Colorado.

The cases in Alabama and New York were particularly important, because, in addition to rural-urban issues, they also presented strong race issues. As cities such as Birmingham and New York grew after World War I, their most densely populated sections became predominantly African American. Not only was the "one man, one vote" ideal not being met, but racial minorities were also grossly underrepresented. In Alabama, *Reynolds v. Sims* (1964) challenged apportionment policies set up in 1901, when the state constitution was designed to preserve rule by white, conservative Democrats. The New York case of *WMCA v. Lomenzo* received national attention when New York City radio station WMCA decided early in 1961 to begin challenging state apportionment policies outlined in the state constitution of 1894. The Supreme Court ruled in favor of reapportionment in the WMCA case on June 1, 1965; Justice Harlan again dissented.

Significance

One effect of these decisions was to create a movement for a remedial constitutional amendment in Congress—a movement that failed, as did a vigorous effort to call a federal constitutional convention to consider apportionment. The Court had served notice that malapportionment would not be tolerated, and in 1967 it reaffirmed its endorsement of the "one man, one vote" principle in *Swann v. Adams.* From that point onward, it became an established constitutional precedent that each congressional district must contain roughly the same number of potential voters such that each member of the House of Representatives is answerable to roughly the same number of constituents.

Fredrick J. Dobney and Geralyn Strecker

Further Reading

Ball, Howard. *The Warren Court's Conceptions of Democracy: An Evaluation of the Supreme Court's Apportionment Opinions.* Rutherford, N.J.: Fairleigh Dickinson University Press, 1971. Explores the political dynamics within the Supreme Court and the effects they had on the outcomes of apportionment cases. Particularly interesting are Ball's discussions of Justice Harlan's dissenting opinions.

Buchman, Jeremy. *Drawing Lines in Quicksand: Courts, Legislatures, and Redistricting.* New York: Peter Lang, 2003. A study of the Supreme Court reapportionment decisions, responses by legislatures and commissions, and the state of political redistricting in the early twenty-first century. Bibliographic references and index.

Cortner, Richard C. *The Apportionment Cases.* Knoxville: University of Tennessee Press, 1970. Explores the genesis and impact of the apportionment cases, paying particular attention to *Baker v. Carr* and *Reynolds v. Sims.*

Graham, Gene. *One Man, One Vote: Baker v. Carr and the American Levellers.* Boston: Little, Brown, 1972. Follows the *Baker* case from its beginnings, through its effects on other apportionment cases, to its residual impact a decade after the decision.

Lee, Calvin B. T. *One Man, One Vote: WMCA and the Struggle for Equal Representation.* New York: Scribner, 1967. This study follows the *WMCA v. Lomenzo* case from the radio station's first decision to fight apportionment in 1961 to the Supreme Court decision in 1965. Much discussion of the dissenting arguments.

Maveety, Nancy. *Representation and the Burger Years.* Ann Arbor: University of Michigan Press, 1991. Examines the impact of reapportionment after twenty-five years. Particularly examines the post-1965 debate over group rights versus individual rights in regard to representation.

O'Rourke, Timothy G. *The Impact of Reapportionment.* New Brunswick, N.J.: Transaction Books, 1980. Charts the effects of reapportionment on elections in legislative districts in Delaware, Kansas, New Jersey, Oregon, South Dakota, and Tennessee.

Zelden, Charles L. *The Supreme Court and Elections: Into the Political Thicket.* Washington, D.C.: CQ Press, 2010. Collection of historical essays and documents tracing the U.S. Supreme Court's rulings on voting rights issues throughout U.S. history.

See also *Colegrove v. Green; Gomillion v. Lightfoot; Gray v. Sanders; Reapportionment Cases; Reynolds v. Sims; Wesberry v. Sanders.*

BAKER V. VERMONT

Court: Vermont Supreme Court
Citation: 744 A.2d 864
Date: December 20, 1999
Issues: Gay and lesbian rights; Marriage

- The Vermont U.S. Supreme Court's unanimous ruling extended to same-sex couples the right to treatment equivalent to that of traditionally married couples.

Three same-sex couples applied for and were denied marriage licenses in Vermont under the rationale that the dictionary definition of "marriage" as well as the legislative intent indicated a union between a man and a woman. The couples submitted that the denial of marriage licenses abridged one of their basic constitutional rights. Each sued their respective towns, and the state of Vermont moved to dismiss the lawsuits on the grounds that no relief could be granted for the plaintiffs' grievances. The trial court granted the defendants' motion, ruling that the marriage statutes could not be interpreted as allowing same-sex marriages and that the statutes were constitutional because they furthered the public interest by promoting a link between procreation and child rearing. After an initial dismissal by the Vermont Superior Court in 1997, plaintiffs appealed and presented their arguments before the Vermont Supreme Court. That court held unanimously that the state could not deprive same-sex couples of the statutory benefits and protections conferred on persons of the opposite sex who choose to marry.

Having determined that Vermont marriage statutes excluded same-sex couples from marrying, the court rejected the state's argument that same-sex marriages would harm citizens by weakening the link between marriage and child rearing. Responding to an argument that potential lack of interstate conformity might result from a legal recognition of same-sex marriages in Vermont, the court pointed out that Vermont allowed for certain marriage contracts not recognized by other states, such as first-cousin marriages, and noted that such concerns had not prevented the passage of similarly unique laws allowing same-sex couples to adopt. Further, the court held that the state is required to extend to same-sex couples the benefits and protections that flow from marriage, whether the goal is procreation or some equivalent domestic partnership. Dismissing other arguments, such as those concerning the "stability" of same-sex couples, the court held that that reasoning was too nebulous or speculative to be considered. That contention would not justify the inequalities placed on those couples in permanent relationships. The same situation could exist as well in male-female partnerships.

The *Baker* decision led to Vermont's and the nation's first civil union law, intended to provide committed same-sex Vermont couples with the benefits and obligations parallel to those afforded to married heterosexual couples. In the years following this decision, most states in the United States have confronted the issue of same-sex marriage with varying results.

Marcia J. Weiss

Further Reading

Eskridge, William N. *Equality Practice: Civil Unions and the Future of Gay Rights.* New York: Routledge, 2002.

Mello, Michael. *Legalizing Gay Marriage.* Philadelphia: Temple University Press, 2004.

Wolfson, Evan. *Why Marriage Matters: America, Equality, and Gay People's Right to Marry.* New York: Simon & Schuster, 2004.

See also *Bowers v. Hardwick; Goodridge v. Department of Public Health; Romer v. Evans.*

BALLARD V. UNITED STATES

Court: U.S. Supreme Court
Citation: 329 U.S. 187
Date: December 9, 1946
Issues: Sex discrimination

- The U.S. Supreme Court held that women may not be excluded from jury service in federal trials taking place in states where women were eligible for service under state law.

After Edna Ballard, a leader of the "I Am" movement, was convicted for fraudulent use of the mails, she appealed her conviction on the grounds that the federal courts in California systematically excluded women from juries. At the time federal law required federal courts to maintain the same jury requirements as those of state courts. Although California made women eligible for juries, the state courts did not summon women to serve, and the federal courts in California followed the same practice.

By a 5-4 vote, the Supreme Court reversed Ballard's conviction. Speaking for the majority, Justice William O. Douglas reasoned that the various federal statutes on the topic demonstrated that Congress desired juries to represent a cross section of the community. Because women were eligible for jury service under California law, they must be included in the federal trial juries. Although the Ballard decision was an interpretation of congressional statutes, its reasoning was used to arrive at basically the same requirement under the Sixth Amendment in *Taylor v. Louisiana* (1975).

Thomas Tandy Lewis

See also *County of Washington v. Gunther; Frontiero v. Richardson; Geduldig v. Aiello; Grove City College v. Bell; Hoyt v. Florida; Meritor Savings Bank v. Vinson; Phillips v. Martin Marietta Corp.; Rosenfeld v. Southern Pacific; Taylor v. Louisiana.*

Ballew v. Georgia

Court: U.S. Supreme Court
Citation: 435 U.S. 223
Date: March 21, 1978
Issues: Juries

• The U.S. Supreme Court held that juries must be composed of a minimum of six persons.

Historically, the Anglo-American trial jury has been composed of twelve members. In *Williams v. Florida* (1970), nevertheless, the Supreme Court approved of the use of six-person juries in all noncapital cases. The state of Georgia, attempting to save time and money, instituted a five-person jury for misdemeanor cases. By a 9-0 vote, the Court ruled that five-person juries were inconsistent with the demands of due process. Justice Harry A. Blackmun's opinion for the majority cited studies showing that the purpose and functioning of the jury "is seriously impaired" if the size is reduced to less than six members. Blackmun concluded that at least six jurors was necessary to promote group deliberation and to "to provide a representative cross section of the community."

Thomas Tandy Lewis

See also *Duncan v. Louisiana; Johnson v. Louisiana; Williams v. Florida.*

Bank of Augusta v. Earle

Court: U.S. Supreme Court
Citation: 38 U.S. 519
Date: March 9, 1839
Issues: Interstate commerce; Regulation of commerce

• The U.S. Supreme Court recognized that the comity clause gave corporations a conditional right to do business in other states, but it also allowed states to regulate or even prohibit such business by explicit legislation.

An Alabama citizen refused to pay the bills of exchange of an out-of-state bank on the grounds that a foreign corporation had no legal right to make and enforce contracts in Alabama. The bank responded that a corporation, like a citizen, was guaranteed basic privileges and immunities in all the states, including the right to conduct business.

Writing for an 8-1 majority, Chief Justice Roger Brooke Taney ruled in favor of the bank. The comity principle was operative in the absence of clear laws to the contrary, which was the situation in Alabama. Taney refused to recognize corporations as possessing all the rights of natural persons. Based on the *Bank of Augusta* principle, state legislatures enacted a great deal of legislation restricting business practices of out-of-state corporations. Although it never overturned the decision, the Supreme Court has subsequently held that regulations must not impose an undue burden on interstate commerce.

Thomas Tandy Lewis

See also *Citizens United v. Federal Election Commission; Cooley v. Board of Wardens of the Port of Philadelphia; Garcia v. San Antonio Metropolitan Transit Authority; Louisville, Cincinnati, and Charleston Railroad Co. v. Letson; Northern Securities Co. v. United States; Paul v. Virginia; Santa Clara County v. Southern Pacific Railroad Co.; Younger v. Harris.*

BANK OF THE UNITED STATES V. DEVEAUX

Court: U.S. Supreme Court
Citation: 5 Cranch (9 U.S.) 61
Date: March 15, 1809
Issues: Citizenship; Diversity jurisdiction; Regulation of commerce

- The U.S. Supreme Court held that although a corporation was a citizen for the purpose of diversity jurisdiction, the location of its citizenship was determined by the citizenship of its shareholders.

The Bank of the United States attempted to sue a Georgia tax collector for recovery of property. The issue was whether the bank (as a corporation) could sue in federal court under diversity of citizenship jurisdiction. The Supreme Court's unanimous ruling made the suit impossible, because some of the bank's shareholders lived in Georgia. The *Deveaux* restriction on diversity jurisdiction was overruled in *Louisville, Cincinnati, and Charleston Railroad Co. v. Letson* (1844), which recognized corporate citizenship in the state granting the charter.

Thomas Tandy Lewis

See also *Louisville, Cincinnati, and Charleston Railroad Co. v. Letson; Paul v. Virginia.*

Barenblatt v. United States

Court: U.S. Supreme Court
Citation: 360 U.S. 109
Date: June 8, 1959
Issues: Antigovernment subversion; Self-incrimination

• Previously, the Court had recognized the Fifth Amendment's privilege against compulsory self-incrimination as a legal limit upon the authority of congressional investigating committees; here the Court held that the First Amendment provides less protection against congressional interrogations.

Congress has long conducted legislative investigations and provided criminal penalties for uncooperative witnesses. In *Kilbourn v. Thompson* (1881), the Court ruled that Congress can investigate only where it has the power and intent to legislate. During the Cold War era, congressional committees had roving commissions to investigate subversive activities. Some congressmen noted that public exposure of persons of questionable loyalty—rather than crafting new legislation—was a primary function of such investigations. In *Watkins v. United States* (1957), the Court ruled, on Fifth Amendment due process grounds, that congressional investigations must clearly relate to legislating.

Lloyd Barenblatt, a former psychology instructor at Vassar College, was called to testify before a subcommittee of the House Committee on Un-American Activities (HUAC) investigating communist infiltration into the field of education. He invoked the First Amendment rather than the Fifth Amendment in refusing to answer questions about his affiliation with the Communist Party and was convicted for contempt of Congress in the United States District Court for the District of Columbia. The Court of Appeals for the District of Columbia Circuit affirmed—and subsequently reaffirmed—his conviction. In light of *Watkins'* ban on exposure "for the sake of exposure," some observers expected the U.S. Supreme Court to shut down HUAC. Instead, on *certiorari*, the U.S. Supreme Court upheld Barenblatt's conviction.

Justice John M. Harlan wrote the majority opinion in this 5-4 decision. Harlan found that the subcommittee was authorized to conduct this investigation and that Barenblatt could ascertain the pertinency of the subcommittee's questions to the subject of the inquiry. First Amendment protections against government interrogations involve "a balancing by the courts of . . . competing private and public interests." Harlan balanced the public's interest in preventing government overthrow against an individual's right to refrain from revealing Communist Party affiliations, and he found the former to be weightier.

Justice Hugo L. Black, joined by Chief Justice Earl Warren and Justice William O. Douglas, dissented on grounds that the committee's mandate to investigate "un-American" activities was vague and that First Amendment freedoms should not be evaluated through a balancing test. Further, Black argued that the majority overstated the government's self-preservation interests and understated the interest of the people as a whole to be able to join organizations, advocate causes, and make political mistakes without being penalized. Black found these societal interests to be weightier. In a separate dissent, Justice William Brennan agreed with Black that the only purpose for the investigation was "exposure purely for the sake of exposure."

This case is important because the Court refused to provide legislative witnesses with a "right to silence" based on the First Amendment. In the 1960's, however, the Court did recognize the related claim of "associational privacy."

Joseph A. Melusky

See also *Albertson v. Subversive Activities Control Board; Boyd v. United States; Counselman v. Hitchcock; Griffin v. California; Kastigar v. United States; Kilbourn v. Thompson; Malloy v. Hogan; Minnick v. Mississippi; Murphy v. Waterfront Commission of New York.*

Barker v. Wingo

Court: U.S. Supreme Court
Citation: 407 U.S. 514
Date: June 22, 1972
Issues: Trial by jury

- The U.S. Supreme Court, for the first time, gave substantive content to the Constitution's guarantee of a speedy trial.

In 1958 Silas Manning and Willie Barker were arrested for the murder of an elderly Kentucky couple. Kentucky had a stronger case against Manning, and the state decided to try him first. If Manning were convicted, then he could be required to testify against Barker. Kentucky sought and obtained the first of what would be sixteen continuances of Barker's trial. Meanwhile, the prosecution had great difficulty in getting a conviction against Manning. The first trial ended in a hung jury, and a second trial, at which Manning was convicted, was annulled because of the admission of illegally seized evidence.

Barker finally objected to additional delay when the state requested a twelfth continuance. Even after Manning's conviction—after a third trial—became final, the Kentucky court granted a further continuance because of the illness of the former sheriff who had been the investigating officer in the case. Barker finally came to trial in 1963, more than five years after his arrest. During ten months of that period he had been held in jail. He moved to dismiss the charge on the ground that his right to a speedy trial had been violated. After several unsuccessful appeals, Barker asked the U.S. Supreme Court to review his claim.

In an opinion for a unanimous Supreme Court, Justice Lewis F. Powell, Jr., held that Barker's right to a speedy trial had indeed been violated. Justice Powell pointed out that the notion of a "speedy" trial is slippery because there is no clearly definable standard. The circumstances of each case are likely to determine whether any postponements are reasonable. Powell saw two possible alternatives. The first would be to set a rigid time period and to apply it to every case. This the Court rejected because it would amount to lawmaking, a function reserved to the legislature. The second alternative would be to restrict the speedy trial right to defendants who demand it. Justice Powell rejected that solution because it would amount to waiving constitutional rights except for those who ask for them. That would be inconsistent with the Court's general approach to constitutional liberties.

The Court adopted a "balancing test" in which the conduct of both the prosecution and the defendant is considered. This approach requires courts to approach speedy trial issues on an ad hoc basis, but once the defendant has asserted the right to a speedy trial, the state must move forward expeditiously. Among the factors which courts must consider are the reasons for any delays, the strength and frequency of the defendant's objections, if any, and the length of any pretrial incarceration defendants have suffered.

The *Barker v. Wingo* balancing test did not prove satisfactory in practice, and the federal government and many states passed statutes to establish rigid time limits for trial. Typically, if no continuances are at the defendant's request, trial must proceed within ninety to one hundred days or the charges against the defendant must be dismissed with prejudice.

Robert Jacobs

See also *Brown v. Mississippi; Duncan v. Louisiana; Klopfer v. North Carolina; Sheppard v. Maxwell.*

Barnes v. Glen Theatre, Inc.

Court: U.S. Supreme Court
Citation: 501 U.S. 560
Date: June 21, 1991
Issues: Censorship; Freedom of speech; Symbolic speech

- In this case the U.S. Supreme Court recognized that nude dancing was a form of expression but held that a public indecency statute which prohibited nude dancing did not violate the First Amendment's free speech clause.

An Indiana statute prohibited individuals from appearing in a public place nude. Dancers in adult establishments were effectively required by the statute to wear "pasties" and "G-strings." Two establishments and the dancers employed by them wished to offer totally nude dancing for their customers and brought suit seeking to enjoin enforcement of the statute. They claimed that it violated the First Amendment's freedom of speech guarantee since the dancing they wished to provide was a form of communication.

In a narrowly divided decision, five members of the Court concluded that the Indiana public indecency statute was constitutional, although the justices disagreed on the reasons for this holding. Chief Justice William Rehnquist, joined by Justices Sandra Day O'Connor and Anthony Kennedy, argued that the statute was constitutional because it only incidentally limited expressive activity and was not expressly intended to suppress speech, because it furthered the state's substantial interests in protecting morals and public order, and because its requirement that dancers wear "pasties" and "G-strings" was narrowly tailored to achieve these interests.

Justice David Souter also believed that the statute was constitutional, but he differed from the chief justice in concluding that the interest served by the statute was not in protecting morals but in preventing certain secondary effects of nude dancing, such as prostitution. Justice Antonin Scalia found the statute constitutional as well but believed that it did not even raise a First Amendment issue since the state of Indiana had not specifically targeted expressive conduct for restraint.

Four dissenters who joined in an opinion by Justice Byron White argued that the very purpose of the statute as applied to dancing was to prevent the communication of the message conveyed by nude dancing: thoughts of eroticism and sensuality. This kind of censorship was, the dissenters contended, the very kind prohibited by the First Amendment.

Barnes v. Glen Theatre, Inc. revisited a constitutional issue most famously addressed in the 1960's when opponents of the Vietnam War burned their draft cards in symbolic protest of the war. Congress responded to these protests by making it a criminal offense to burn a draft card. In *United States v. O'Brien* (1968), the Supreme Court held that protesters of the Vietnam War could be punished for destroying their draft cards, even though the destruction was a kind of speech. Ever since, speakers who wished to express their ideas through nonverbal conduct have not fared well against general laws prohibiting the conduct they wished to use expressively. *Barnes* is one example. So long as government does not appear to target only the individuals who wish to convey a message through particular conduct, its ability to proscribe such conduct is broad.

Timothy L. Hall

See also *Erznoznik v. Jacksonville; Miller et al. v. Civil City of South Bend; Osborne v. Ohio; Safford Unified School District v. Redding; United States v. O'Brien.*

Barron v. Baltimore

Court: U.S. Supreme Court
Citation: 32 U.S. 243
Date: February 16, 1833
Issues: Incorporation doctrine; Property rights

• The U.S. Supreme Court held that the Bill of Rights did not protect citizens from actions by their state governments, a ruling that stood largely unaltered until the 1920's.

The First Amendment begins with the word "Congress," apparently making the federal government its only target, but none of the other amendments in the Bill of Rights include this language. John Barron, a Baltimore businessperson, sought to test the possibility that the Fifth Amendment in the Bill of Rights might protect him from actions of the Maryland state government.

The city of Baltimore repaired the streets and dumped the leftover construction materials into the water near the wharf Barron owned, raising the bottom of the bay so much that ships could no longer dock there, depriving Barron of his property interest and his livelihood without due process or just compensation. Barron sued Baltimore to recover damages, but Baltimore was a subunit of Maryland, whose constitution, unlike the U.S. Constitution, did not provide a guarantee against eminent domain.

Because Barron could not succeed in Maryland courts, he turned to the federal courts. However, the Supreme Court ruled that the Fifth Amendment applied only to the federal government and not to the states and that therefore Barron was not entitled to protection against state action under this amendment. After *Barron*, the courts applied this ruling consistently. Although the passage of the Fourteenth Amendment would seem to have reversed this decision, the Court did not initially agree, essentially continuing *Barron* in force until justices holding different views began to serve on the Court in the 1920's. Gradually, the incorporation doctrine effectively overturned the principles set out in *Barron*.

Richard L. Wilson

See also *Chicago, Burlington, and Quincy Railroad Co. v. Chicago; Gideon v. Wainwright; Hurtado v. California; Maxwell v. Dow; Pointer v. Texas; Presser v. Illinois; Rochin v. California.*

BATES V. STATE BAR OF ARIZONA

Court: U.S. Supreme Court
Citation: 433 U.S. 350
Date: June 27, 1977
Issues: Freedom of speech

- The U.S. Supreme Court held that states could not prohibit lawyers from advertising the prices of routine legal services.

In 1974 lawyers John Bates and Van O'Steen placed an advertisement in a newspaper that announced "legal services at very reasonable fees" and listed several examples. Because the Arizona bar association's ethics code prohibited such advertisements, the two lawyers were censored and suspended from legal practice for one week. They appealed on First Amendment grounds. Meanwhile, the Supreme Court, in *Virginia Pharmacy Board v. Virginia Citizens Consumer Council* (1976), struck down a state law that made it illegal for pharmacists to advertise the prices of prescription medications. For the Court, Justice Harry A. Blackmun explained that the First Amendment protected the right of pharmacists to communicate truthful information about lawful products and services.

In *Bates*, the justices voted five to four to extend the *Virginia Pharmacy Board* principles to commercial advertising by lawyers. Justice Blackmun's majority opinion held that the protection of commercial speech under the First Amendment outweighed any possible "adverse effect on professionalism." He noted that the decision did not endorse in-person solicitation of clients or advertisements about the quality of legal services. Also, he recognized the need to restrain false, deceptive, or misleading advertising as well as the legitimacy of reasonable time, place, and manner regulations.

After *Bates*, the Court endorsed several restrictions on the commercial speech of lawyers. In *Florida Bar v. Went for It* (1995), for example, the Court upheld the Florida bar's prohibition of written solicitations to personal injury victims for thirty days following an accident or natural disaster.

Thomas Tandy Lewis

See also *Bigelow v. Virginia; Edmonson v. Leesville Concrete Co.; Goldfarb v. Virginia State Bar; Williams v. Mississippi.*

BATSON V. KENTUCKY

Court: U.S. Supreme Court
Citation: 476 U.S. 79
Date: April 30, 1986
Issues: Equal protection of the law; Juries

- The U.S. Supreme Court ruled that the equal protection clause of the Fourteenth Amendment forbids a prosecutor from using peremptory challenges to remove potential jurors because of their race.

James Batson, an African American, was indicted for second-degree burglary. When the judge conducted a *voir dire* examination (preliminary check of suitability and qualifications) of the potential jurors, the prosecutor used his peremptory challenges to remove all four African Americans from the panel, resulting in an all-white jury. The Supreme Court had refused to disturb the same development in *Swain v. Alabama* (1965). After Batson's conviction, nevertheless, his lawyers asserted that the process of jury selection violated his rights to equal protection and to a jury drawn from a cross section of the community.

By a 7-2 majority, the Court accepted Batson's claim. Speaking for the majority, Justice Lewis F. Powell, Jr., remanded the case and instructed the trial court to require the prosecutor to justify the exclusion of members of the defendant's race from the jury. If the prosecutor were unable to give a racially neutral explanation, Batson's conviction would have to be reversed. Powell's opinion formulated a framework for future *voir dire* proceedings. The basic idea is that a pattern of exclusion based on race creates an inference of discrimination. Once such an inference is established, the prosecutor has the burden of showing that the peremptories are not discriminatory. Emphasizing that the Constitution does not guarantee a right to peremptory challenges, Powell wrote that potential jurors may not be eliminated simply because of the assumption that people of a particular race might be more sympathetic to a particular defendant. Thus, Powell's opinion requires color-conscious rather than color-blind procedures in jury selection, and it tends to encourage the use of racial quotas.

The *Batson* principles have been significantly expanded. In *Powers v. Ohio* (1991), the Court held that criminal defendants may object to race-based peremptory challenges even if the defendant and the excluded jurors do not belong to the same race. Later that year, in *Edmondson v. Leesville Concrete Co.*, the Court applied the *Batson* framework to the selection of juries in civil trials. In *Georgia v. McCollum* (1992), the Court decided that the *Batson* ruling applies to defense attorneys. In *J. E. B. v. Alabama* (1994), moreover, the Court held that the equal protection clause prohibits discrimination in jury selection on the basis of gender.

Thomas Tandy Lewis

See also *Civil Rights Cases; Edmonson v. Leesville Concrete Co.; Hernández v. Texas; Norris v. Alabama; Powers v. Ohio; Strauder v. West Virginia.*

BELLE TERRE V. BORAAS

Court: U.S. Supreme Court
Citation: 616 U.S. 1
Date: April 1, 1974
Issues: Due process of law; Right to privacy

• The U.S. Supreme Court upheld the constitutionality of a local zoning ordinance that prohibited most unrelated groups from living together in a single-unit dwelling.

The owner of a house in the small village of Belle Terre, New York, leased it to six unrelated college students. When cited for violating a zoning ordinance, the owners and tenants went to court, claiming that the ordinance violated their constitutional right of privacy. Speaking for a 7-2 majority, Justice William O. Douglas used the rational basis test of economic and social legislation, and found the ordinance to be a valid exercise of the community's police power. The ordinance bore a rational relationship with a permissible governmental objective of maintaining a quiet place to raise a family. In dissent, Justice Thurgood Marshall argued that the ordinance infringed on fundamental rights of privacy and association and that the village had the burden of showing a "compelling and substantial" justification for the infringement.

Although upholding the ordinance, the *Belle Terre* decision demonstrated the Supreme Court's developing commitment to the doctrine of substantive due process, requiring that any restraints on liberty must be justified by an adequate state interest. The decision should be compared with *Moore v. City of East Cleveland* (1977), in which the Court struck down an ordinance that had the effect of prohibiting an extended family from living together.

Thomas Tandy Lewis

See also *Euclid v. Ambler Realty Co.*; *First English Evangelical Lutheran Church of Glendale v. County of Los Angeles*; *Griswold v. Connecticut*; *Moore v. City of East Cleveland*; *Young v. American Mini Theatres.*

BENTON V. MARYLAND

Court: U.S. Supreme Court
Citation: 395 U.S. 784
Date: June 23, 1969
Issues: Double jeopardy; Incorporation doctrine

- The U.S. Supreme Court ruled that the protection against double jeopardy, guaranteed at the federal level, also applied at the state level. The decision was one of a series that extended most of the provisions contained in the Bill of Rights to apply to the states.

Protection against double jeopardy is widely regarded in Western culture as one of the most basic of an individual's legal rights, equal in importance to the right to a trial by jury. The term refers to the principle that no person should be at risk twice—that is, be put in "double jeopardy"—for one alleged criminal act. So basic is this concept that its roots can be traced back to Greek, Roman, and canon law. In the United States, this principle is incorporated in the Fifth Amendment to the Constitution, stating that no one is to "be subject for the same offence to be twice put in jeopardy of life and limb."

Theoretically, this protective principle is a humane acknowledgment of the discrepancy in power between an ordinary citizen and the government. Private individuals, with limited resources, are protected from harassment by the ubiquitous and mightier powers of the government, which, with its greater resources, could continue to investigate and charge any person for any crime any number of times over an indefinite period were it not for this protection against double jeopardy. This protection also allows an accused person to be given a final judgment, eliminating the anxiety and uncertainty that could be caused if an accusation of criminal wrongdoing could be levied repeatedly. Finally, it acknowledges that the verdict delivered after the due process of the law must be allowed to stand, even if the evidence would seem to indicate a different result.

In practice, such a balance between the individual's rights and the government's need to maintain law and order is difficult either to identify clearly or to administer consistently. It is an area of the law so fraught with practical problems that several aspects of the definition of double jeopardy have had to be tested and judged repeatedly. So many issues have had to be determined on a case-by-case basis in court that the set of standards has been left unclear.

Understanding the significance of any one specific case, therefore, requires keeping in mind that the practice of double jeopardy has evolved over many years. In the United States, history illustrates the power of the Supreme Court in directing the course of human rights. From the beginning, for example, there arises the question of when an accused person might be placed in double jeopardy. Logically, it would seem clear that a person who has been tried initially and found not guilty could claim "double jeopardy" if he or she were to be tried again. It took the Supreme Court's *Crist v. Bretz* decision in 1978 to determine that the initial jeopardy attaches when a jury is sworn in, not necessarily upon completion of a trial. On the other hand, what happens in the case of a mistrial? In a landmark case (*United States v. Perez*) in 1824, the Court ruled that a person cannot claim double jeopardy on the second trial if the judge in the first trial correctly declared a mistrial.

Other seemingly basic definitions have been subject to court rulings. Legal and scholarly debate has tried, for example, to determine what constitutes the "same offense," because one criminal act could be construed to break several laws. The Court has ruled that the same criminal action could involve several different offenses, so that a person could be charged several times and not be in double jeopardy.

The Court's Ruling

One of the major decisions in the history of double jeopardy protection and the United States Supreme Court came in 1969, in the case of *Benton v. Maryland*. Appreciation of the significance of this one specific decision requires understanding of an old conceptual problem, that of dual sovereignty. In the United States, the Constitution and the first ten amendments to it—the Bill of Rights—were framed with the federal government in mind. While an individual is protected against the danger of being tried twice for the same offense by a federal prosecutor, if the same criminal offense also breaks a state law, a person may be tried by the state. Many but not all states had evolved their own codes protecting an individual from double jeopardy, but the standards tended to differ from state to state and were not always consistent with federal standards. In an important case in 1937, *Palko v. Connecticut*, the Supreme Court had declared that the Fourteenth Amendment's due process clause did not guarantee double jeopardy protection in state actions.

In August, 1965, John Dalmer Benton was tried in the state of Maryland on charges of larceny and burglary. He was convicted of burglary, but the jury found him not guilty of the larceny charges. Benton was given a ten-year sentence. He filed an appeal in the Maryland Court of Appeals. Meanwhile, in another case, the same court had ruled that the section of the state constitution requiring jurors to swear their belief in the existence of God was invalid. Because the jurors in Benton's trial had been asked to so swear, he was given the option of asking for a reindictment and retrial, which he did. Benton appealed the charge of larceny, however, claiming that he had been found not guilty of that charge in the first trial and to be tried again would put him in double jeopardy. This appeal was denied, and Benton was tried again on both burglary and larceny charges.

Ironically, this time the jury found him guilty of both offenses, and he was given fifteen years for burglary and five years for larceny. Benton's case was appealed to the Maryland Court of Special Appeals on the double jeopardy claim, but it was rejected. When the case reached the Supreme Court in 1968, the Court decided to hear the case to the extent of asking two questions. First, is the double jeopardy clause of the Fifth Amendment applicable to the states through the Fourteenth Amendment? Second, if double jeopardy applies to states as well as to federal prosecutions, was Benton put in double jeopardy?

On the merits of the case, the Supreme Court ruled, on June 23, 1969, that the double jeopardy clause of the Fifth Amendment is applicable to the states through the Fourteenth Amendment. Benton's conviction for larceny was reversed. Writing the majority opinion for the Court, Justice Thurgood Marshall rejected the opinion of the *Palko* case that basic constitutional rights could be denied by the states as long as the totality of the circumstances does not result in a denial of "fundamental fairness." Instead, once it is decided that a particular Bill of Rights guarantee is fundamental to the American scheme of justice, the same constitutional standards apply against both the state and federal governments. Justices John M. Harlan II and Potter Stewart dissented from the majority opinion, objecting to the continuing incorporation of the Bill of Rights into the due process clause.

Significance

The exact origin of the concept of an individual's protection against double jeopardy remains unclear. Even a brief sampling of the historical development of the practice of this ideal suggests how much the political and social

*Thanks to the protection against double jeopardy, the moment defendants are ac-
quitted, they are cast free of the criminal justice system and cannot be tried again
on the same criminal charges.* (Brand-X Pictures)

environments influence the nature of human rights, such as protection
against double jeopardy, in any one country in any one time period. In the
1969 case of *Benton v. Maryland*, the Supreme Court clarified at least one very
important aspect in the United States system of government, that double
jeopardy protection, previously limited to federal prosecution, also extends to
state prosecution.

In the broader historical context, the impact of this decision can be seen as
analogous to the situation in England in the twelfth century. Considerable
tension resulted from the skirmishes between the head of the state, Henry II,
and the representative of the church in England, the Archbishop of Canter-
bury, Thomas Becket. To protect clerks from being tried and punished by
both the ecclesiastical and the king's courts, the protection against double
jeopardy was sometimes cited. The Framers of the U.S. Constitution included
this protection in the Bill of Rights in 1789. Although the relationship between the states and the federal government is nowhere near as adversarial as
the reference to twelfth century English politics might suggest, the two were
conceived and remain as separate sovereignties. Thus the Fourteenth Amendment declares, ". . . nor shall any State deprive any person of life, liberty, or

property, without due process of law." The Fifth Amendment, referring only to the federal government, explicitly protects against double jeopardy.

That the Court ruling linking these two amendments came in the 1960's may also provoke some reflections on the fragility of any human right. During the 1960's, the nation as a whole put great faith in the power of the federal government to undertake the responsibility of finding solutions to national social problems and protecting the rights of individuals. Such an attitude was a considerable change from the historical view of the federal government.

It is dangerous to overstate the importance of the *Benton* case. Dual sovereignty still exists—the states and the federal government are separate entities, with their own rights to prosecution. In practice, both are leery of wasting effort on prosecuting twice and tend not to do so. What was clarified in 1969 was the basic human right to be judged by some uniform standard by both sovereignties.

The practice of the ideal of double jeopardy protection remains riddled with confusion, inconsistencies, and questions. Progress toward smooth implementation of this ideal has been, and will no doubt continue to be, rocky. The *Benton* case, no matter how technical the victory may seem, was a symbolic step toward protecting an individual from getting lost in the battle between two much more powerful entities.

Shakuntala Jayaswal

Further Reading

Garcia, Alfredo. *The Fifth Amendment: A Comprehensive Approach.* Westport, Conn.: Greenwood Press, 2002. Explains holistically and in detail each element of the Fifth Amendment to the Constitution, including the double jeopardy prohibition. Bibliographic references and index.

Kirchheimer, Otto. "The Act, the Offense, and Double Jeopardy." *Yale Law Review* 58 (March, 1949): 513-544. A scholarly analysis of one specific aspect of double jeopardy, the difference between a single criminal act and the many categories of law one such act may violate. Discusses the potential dangers of this dichotomy and the differences between legal substance and legal procedures. Notes.

Parker, Frank J. "Some Aspects of Double Jeopardy." *St. John's Law Review* 25 (May, 1951): 188-202. A discussion by a state's attorney of some of the issues in double jeopardy cases. Uses specific cases to illustrate the problems of dual sovereignty when a state as well as a federal law has been violated; the issue of closely related offenses which may be tried separately; and the problem of retrials when the first is terminated. Notes.

Rudstein, David S. *Double Jeopardy: A Reference Guide to the United States Constitution.* Westport, Conn.: Praeger, 2004. Comprehensive review of the consti-

tutional protection against double jeopardy, its philosophical underpin-
nings, and the history of its application. Bibliographic references and
index.

Schulhofer, Stephen J. "Jeopardy and Mistrials." *University of Pennsylvania Law
Review* 125 (January, 1977): 452-539. Detailed discussion of the issues involved when mistrials occur. A brief summary of the double jeopardy concept is followed by an analysis of a landmark decision, the *Perez* case in
1824, as well as other specific cases of mistrials. Classification of the kinds
of mistrials that may occur. Notes.

Sigler, Jay A. *Double Jeopardy: The Development of a Legal and Social Policy.* Ithaca,
N.Y.: Cornell University Press, 1969. Traces the history and development of
double jeopardy as a legal and social policy, both federal and state, in the
United States. Includes comparisons of the policy with practice in other
nations and a discussion of the possibilities for doctrinal reform. An often-
cited study, particularly useful for its extensive bibliography of both primary and secondary sources. Index.

Slovenko, Ralph. "The Law on Double Jeopardy." *Tulane Law Review* 30 (April,
1956): 407-430. A discussion of the law on double jeopardy with specific
reference to one state. Although it refers to aspects of the criminal code of
Louisiana, it provides a brief overview of basic concepts, such as the tests
for determining double jeopardy, and is useful as a supplementary reference for the general reader.

Westen, Peter, and Richard Drubel. "Toward a General Theory of Double
Jeopardy." *Supreme Court Review,* 1978, 81-169. Often-cited article in the discussion of double jeopardy. Argues that the shifts and inconsistencies in
double jeopardy applications are a result of flaws in the fundamental theory. Addresses three distinct issues: finality, double punishment, and ac-
quittal against evidence. Specific court cases are analyzed as illustrations.

See also *Kansas v. Hendricks; Palko v. Connecticut; United States v. Lanza; United
States v. Ursery.*

Berman v. Parker

Court: U.S. Supreme Court
Citation: 348 U.S. 26
Date: November 22, 1954
Issues: Land law

- The U.S. Supreme Court interpreted the term "public use" to refer to any policy that reasonably promotes the public interest, providing legislatures with great discretion in deciding how to use the eminent domain power.

The District of Columbia Redevelopment Act of 1945 used the eminent domain power to condemn land for slum eradication and for beautification projects. Some of the land was sold to private developers, who developed it according to the urban renewal plan. A landowner challenged the constitutionality of the statute. He argued that the property was not taken for public use because it was sold to private interests and for the purpose of beautification.

By a 9-0 vote, the Supreme Court upheld the statute. Speaking for the Court, Justice William O. Douglas suggested that eminent domain might be used to advance any of the legitimate purposes of government. The term "public use" did not imply that the property must be publicly owned or used directly by the general public. Reaffirming several Court precedents, Douglas wrote that the role of the judiciary in the matter is "extremely narrow." The Court would not substitute its judgment for a legislature's judgment about what constitutes a public use, but it would insist only that the use must not be "palpably without reasonable foundation."

Subsequent decisions have endorsed Douglas's broad understanding of the public use doctrine, the most notable case being *Hawaii Housing Authority v. Midkiff* (1984).

Thomas Tandy Lewis

See also *Barron v. Baltimore; Hawaii Housing Authority v. Midkiff; Kelo v. City of New London; Nollan v. California Coastal Commission; West River Bridge Co. v. Dix.*

BETTS V. BRADY

Court: U.S. Supreme Court
Citation: 316 U.S. 455
Date: June 1, 1942
Issues: Right to counsel

• Until the *Betts* ruling was reversed in 1963, indigent criminal defendants in state trials did not have the constitutional right to a lawyer's assistance.

Betts, a poor defendant prosecuted for robbery in Maryland, asked his trial court to appoint a lawyer for his defense. The local policy, however, was to appoint counsel only in cases of murder or rape. After his conviction, Betts filed habeas corpus petitions, alleging that his rights under the Sixth Amendment had been violated. The lower courts rejected his petitions, based on the principle that the first eight amendments generally applied only to the federal government. The U.S. Supreme Court then granted *certiorari*.

The issue before the Court was whether the right to counsel should be incorporated into the due process clause of the Fourteenth Amendment. The justices voted six to three to uphold the lower courts. Speaking for the majority, Owen J. Roberts noted that most states did not require appointment of counsel in all criminal trials, and he argued that counsel was not necessary for a fair trial in Betts's circumstances. Counsel was required only in special situations such as *Powell v. Alabama* (1932), when illiterate defendants had been charged with a capital offense.

Three dissenters—Hugo L. Black, William O. Douglas, and Frank Murphy—argued that the constitutional right to counsel should be recognized in all criminal trials. In *Gideon v. Wainwright* (1963), the Court finally accepted the position of the dissenters.

Thomas Tandy Lewis

See also *Argersinger v. Hamlin; Escobedo v. Illinois; Faretta v. California; Hague v. Congress of Industrial Organizations; Johnson v. Zerbst; Massiah v. United States; Minnick v. Mississippi; Miranda v. Arizona.*

BIGELOW V. VIRGINIA

Court: U.S. Supreme Court
Citation: 421 U.S. 809
Date: June 16, 1975
Issues: Freedom of speech

- The U.S. Supreme Court declared that the First Amendment protects commercial advertising to "some degree" and overturned a state statute prohibiting advertisements of abortion services.

In 1971 the *Virginia Weekly* of Charlottesville published an advertisement for an organization that helped women obtain legal abortions in the state of New York. The newspaper's editor, Jeffrey Bigelow, was convicted for violating a state statute that made it a misdemeanor to encourage or help a woman to have an abortion. Bigelow argued that the statute infringed on his free press rights under the First Amendment. In response, the state referred to *Valentine v. Chrestensen* (1942), in which the Supreme Court ruled that the First Amendment placed no restrictions on governmental regulations of "purely commercial advertising."

By a 7-2 vote, the Court overturned the statute and greatly limited the *Valentine* ruling. Justice Harry A. Blackmun's opinion for the Court emphasized that the spirit of the First Amendment favors the widespread dissemination of information and opinions. Blackmun noted that the advertisement contained truthful information about a legal service. The Court refused to decide the extent to which states might regulate commercial advertisements, especially those dealing with harmful activities. It was clear, nevertheless, that commercial speech merited a lesser degree of constitutional protection than political and religious speech.

Subsequent to *Bigelow*, the Court issued a series of decisions, such as *Bates v. State Bar of Arizona* (1977), that continued to expand First Amendment protection for commercial advertising. In *44 Liquormart v. Rhode Island* (1996), the Court struck down a state ban on the advertising of alcoholic beverage prices, even though the Twenty-first Amendment gives states broad authority to regulate the sale of the product.

Thomas Tandy Lewis

See also *Akron v. Akron Center for Reproductive Health*; *Bates v. State Bar of Arizona*; *Doe v. Bolton*; *44 Liquormart, Inc. v. Rhode Island*; *Harris v. McRae*; *Maher v. Roe*; *Roe v. Wade*; *Thornburgh v. American College of Obstetricians and Gynecologists*; *Webster v. Reproductive Health Services*.

BIVENS V. SIX UNKNOWN NAMED AGENTS

Court: U.S. Supreme Court
Citation: 403 U.S. 388
Date: June 21, 1971
Issues: Immunity from prosecution; Right to privacy; Search and seizure

- This case established that, under certain conditions, plaintiffs have the right to claim civil damages when federal officials violate the Fourth Amendment guarantee against unreasonable search and seizure.

The plaintiff in this case filed a civil action against federal employees of the Federal Bureau of Narcotics who had entered his house, searched it, and arrested him for possession of narcotics. He alleged that the entry and search had been without probable cause and was therefore in violation of the Fourth Amendment of the U.S. Constitution. He sought $15,000 in damages from each federal official.

The lower courts denied him relief on the ground that in the absence of a federal statute giving him the right to sue federal officials for violation of his constitutional rights, he could not sue the federal officials in a federal court for monetary relief. The U.S. Supreme Court disagreed. In his opinion for the Court, Justice William J. Brennan held that federal law permitted the plaintiff to bring the action. He reserved the question of whether the action might nevertheless be defeated by a claim of immunity by the officials.

Justice Brennan reasoned that the Fourth Amendment "guarantees to citizens of the United States the absolute right to be free from unreasonable searches and seizures carried out by virtue of federal authority" and that, "where federally protected rights have been invaded, it has been the rule from the beginning that courts will be alert to adjust their remedies so as to grant the necessary relief." He saw no reason to depart from this rule simply because there was no specific congressional authorization of the suit or because the plaintiff might have been able to bring an action under state law for the invasion of his privacy.

Dissenting opinions argued against the decision on the grounds that it invaded Congress's prerogative to define the rights of persons to sue in federal courts, that it would result in an avalanche of unmeritorious claims against federal officials, and that, like the exclusionary rule in criminal prosecutions, it would hamper the capacity of law-enforcement officers to carry out their duties because they would be fearful of direct personal liability for violation of the Fourth Amendment.

Bivens established that federal courts may, at least in some circumstances, hear and adjudicate civil actions for monetary damages against federal officials predicated on violation of constitutional rights even though Congress has not explicitly created the right to sue. It therefore raises questions regarding the distribution of lawmaking (or "right-creating") power between the judicial and the legislative branches of the federal government. The issue, generally referred to as the "implication of a private right of action," continues to be a difficult and challenging one for the courts: When should the courts find that the existence of a federal law (a statute, a constitutional provision, a treaty, or even a prior decision) gives a plaintiff a right to seek damages for violation of the law? Despite *Bivens* and numerous other cases since, the Supreme Court has failed to give a clear and concise answer to the question and has proceeded on a case-by-case basis.

Maxwell O. Chibundu

See also *Carroll v. United States; Chimel v. California; Knowles v. Iowa; Terry v. Ohio.*

BMW OF NORTH AMERICA V. GORE

Court: U.S. Supreme Court
Citation: 517 U.S. 559
Date: May 20, 1996
Issues: Due process of law

• The U.S. Supreme Court held that a punitive damage award of five hundred times the amount of actual damages was "grossly excessive" and therefore contrary to the due process clause of the Fourteenth Amendment.

After Ira Gore purchased a new BMW, he found that it had been repainted by the manufacturer. Alleging fraud according to Alabama law, Gore brought suit against BMW for failure to disclose a defect. He was awarded four thousand dollars in compensatory damages and $2 million in punitive damages. By a 5-4 margin, the Supreme Court found that BMW's conduct was not egregious enough to justify such an extreme sanction. Writing for the Court, Justice John Paul Stevens emphasized that there must be a "reasonable relationship" between a punitive damages award and any conceivable harm that the plaintiff might suffer. In dissent, Justice Antonin Scalia criticized the expansion of the substantive due process doctrine to include jury decisions in civil suits.

Thomas Tandy Lewis

See also *Gertz v. Robert Welch; New York Times Co. v. Sullivan; Pacific Mutual Life Insurance Co. v. Haslip.*

BOARD OF EDUCATION OF OKLAHOMA CITY V. DOWELL

Court: U.S. Supreme Court
Citation: 498 U.S. 237
Date: January 15, 1991
Issues: Desegregation; Education

• The U.S. Supreme Court held that federal district courts may end court-supervised busing plans when the "effects of past intentional discrimination" have been removed "as far as practicable" and a local school board has complied with a desegregation order for a "reasonable period of time."

In 1985 the Oklahoma City school district requested dissolution of a desegregation decree that had been in effect for nineteen years. Approving the request, the district judge observed that the school board had done nothing to promote residential segregation for twenty-five years and that it had bused students in good faith for more than a decade. The court of appeals reversed the judgment because the majority of children in the district continued to attend one-race schools, reflecting demographic residential patterns mostly developed after the decree had gone into effect. By a 5-3 vote, the Court ruled in favor of the district judge's decision. Chief Justice William H. Rehnquist argued that desegregation decrees had never been intended to "operate in perpetuity" and that the tradition of local control over public schools justified the dissolution of court-supervised desegregation plans as long as present residential segregation was a result of private decisions and economic factors rather than official policies.

The Court amplified the *Dowell* decision in *Freeman v. Pitts* (1992), holding that district judges have discretion to withdraw supervision of school districts once officials have shown good faith compliance with a court-ordered desegregation plan, even if some vestiges of de jure segregation continued.

Thomas Tandy Lewis

See also *Brown v. Board of Education; Columbus Board of Education v. Penick; Keyes v. Denver School District No. 1; Lemon v. Kurtzman; Milliken v. Bradley; Missouri v. Jenkins; Parents Involved in Community Schools v. Seattle School District No. 1; Swann v. Charlotte-Mecklenburg Board of Education.*

Boerne v. Flores

Court: U.S. Supreme Court
Citation: 521 U.S. 507
Date: June 25, 1997
Issues: Freedom of religion; Separation of powers

• In striking down the Religious Freedom Restoration Act of 1993, the U.S. Supreme Court declared that congressional enforcement powers in the Fourteenth Amendment may not be used to override the Court's interpretations of the Constitution.

In *Sherbert v. Verner* (1963), the Supreme Court required a compelling state interest as justification for any indirect restraint on religion. In *Employment Divi-*

sion, Department of Human Resources of Oregon v. Smith the Court allowed the states more discretion when balancing claims of religious freedom against the states' interests in enacting and enforcing reasonable laws of general application. Congress responded to the controversial *Smith* decision with the Religious Freedom Restoration Act of 1993, which required states to apply the more demanding *Sherbert* standards. A Roman Catholic Church in Boerne, Texas, desired to replace its old and small church building, but the city had classified the structure as an historic landmark that must be preserved. The bishop sued in federal court, asserting that the 1993 act prevented the city from interfering with the church's decision to construct a new building.

By a 6-3 vote, the Court ruled that the 1993 act was unconstitutional. Justice Anthony M. Kennedy's opinion argued that section 5 of the Fourteenth Amendment gave Congress the power only to enforce the rights protected by the amendment, not to decree the substantive meaning of the amendment. The clear intent of the 1993 act was to veto a constitutional interpretation made by the Court. Kennedy insisted that such a challenge to the Court's proper authority is contrary to the U.S. tradition of separation of powers. Three justices dissented from the majority's continued support for the *Smith* decision.

Thomas Tandy Lewis

See also *Employment Division, Department of Human Resources of Oregon v. Smith; Lemon v. Kurtzman; Sherbert v. Verner.*

BOLLING V. SHARPE

Court: U.S. Supreme Court
Citation: 347 U.S. 497
Date: May 17, 1954
Issues: Desegregation; Due process of law; Education

• In ruling that racially segregated schools in the District of Columbia were a violation of the Fifth Amendment, the U.S. Supreme Court interpreted the due process clause to prohibit invidious racial discrimination.

In this companion case to *Brown v. Board of Education*, the issue of segregated public schools in the nation's capital, a matter of congressional jurisdiction, was treated in an opinion separate from *Brown* because the Fourteenth Amendment did not apply to the federal government and because the applicable Fifth Amendment did not include an equal protection clause. From the perspective of practical politics, it would have been highly embarrassing for the Court to allow segregated schools in Washington, D.C., while ruling them unconstitutional in the rest of the country.

Speaking for a unanimous Supreme Court, Chief Justice Earl Warren first noted that the petitioners were African American minors who had been refused admission to a public school "solely because of their race." He then declared that the Court had long recognized that certain forms of governmental discrimination violated the constitutional mandate for due process of law. For precedents, he looked to an 1896 dictum by Joseph M. Harlan and to *Buchanan v. Warley*, a 1917 decision that had defended the equal right of citizens to own property based on a substantive due process reading of the Fourteenth Amendment. Also, Warren referred to *obiter dicta* in the Japanese American cases which acknowledged that racial classifications were inherently suspect, requiring that they be "scrutinized with particular care."

Warren gave an expansive interpretation of the "liberty" protected by the Fifth Amendment, explaining that it extended to the "full range of conduct which the individual is free to pursue." The government could restrict liberty only when justified by a "proper governmental objective," and racial segregation in education was not related to such an objective. Thus, the Washington schools were imposing an "arbitrary deprivation" on the liberty of black children. In addition, Warren noted that it was "unthinkable" that the federal government might practice the kind of discrimination prohibited in the states.

Bolling v. Sharpe had major theoretical implications, for the case indicated that the Supreme Court continued to interpret the due process clauses as protecting substantive rights as well as procedures, although the substantive focus had shifted from property interests to liberty interests. Also, the decision affirmed that the ideas of liberty and equality are often overlapping and that constitutional due process of law prohibits government from practicing invidious discrimination.

Thomas Tandy Lewis

See also *Adarand Constructors v. Peña; Board of Education of Oklahoma City v. Dowell; Brown v. Board of Education; Buchanan v. Warley; Keyes v. Denver School District No. 1; Lemon v. Kurtzman; Milliken v. Bradley; Parents Involved in Community Schools v. Seattle School District No. 1; Swann v. Charlotte-Mecklenburg Board of Education.*

BOOTH V. MARYLAND

Court: U.S. Supreme Court
Citation: 482 U.S. 496
Date: June 15, 1987
Issues: Capital punishment; Evidence

• In this case, a sharply divided U.S. Supreme Court ruled that victim impact evidence was not admissible in capital sentencing proceedings.

John Booth and an accomplice robbed and murdered an elderly couple in West Baltimore, Maryland, to obtain money to buy heroin. A jury sentenced Booth to die after considering information contained in a victim impact statement (VIS). The VIS emphasized the victims' outstanding personal characteristics and stressed how deeply the murdered couple would be missed. The VIS also reported the emotional and personal problems suffered by family members as a result of the murders. Finally, the VIS set forth the family members' opinions and characterizations of the crime and of Booth.

In death penalty cases, the Supreme Court requires the jury to make an individualized determination about whether the defendant should be executed, based on the character of the defendant and the circumstances of the crime. Booth argued that the victim impact evidence presented in his case was irrelevant to the question of his character and/or the circumstances of his crime. Worse, because of its inflammatory nature, the VIS had unduly influenced the jury to return a death sentence.

By a 5-4 vote, the Supreme Court agreed. Writing for the majority, Justice Lewis F. Powell, Jr., said that permitting the jury to consider the VIS in Booth's case had violated the Eighth Amendment by increasing the risk that Booth's death sentence was arbitrary and capricious. Justice Powell said that victim impact evidence diverts the jury's attention from the defendant's background and record and focuses it on the victim and surviving family members. Consequently, whether a defendant is sentenced to death might turn on such irrelevant factors as the degree to which surviving family members are willing and able to articulate their grief, or the relative worth of the victim's character. Thus, defendants whose victims were assets to the community would be punished more harshly than those whose victims were considered less worthy. This in turn would run contrary to the promise, engraved on the Supreme Court building itself, of "Equal Justice Under Law."

Four justices dissented. Justice Byron White argued that because victim impact evidence was admissible in noncapital cases it should also be permitted in death penalty cases. In Justice Antonin Scalia's view, a criminal's personal responsibility is very much a function of how much harm he or she causes. Victim impact evidence provides a more complete picture of the defendant's personal responsibility. Justice Scalia also wrote that admitting victim impact evidence in death penalty cases would accomplish an additional benefit: It would help offset the evidence the defendant offered to mitigate his moral guilt.

In 1989, only two years after *Booth*, the Court reaffirmed its principles in *South Carolina v. Gathers*, again by a 5-4 margin. In *Gathers*, a bare majority extended the rule in *Booth* to prohibit prosecutors from commenting on the personal characteristics of the victim during closing arguments to the jury. Nevertheless, the *Booth* decision proved to be impermanent. After two members of the *Booth* majority retired and were replaced by more conservative justices, the Court decided to revisit the victim impact evidence issue. In a dramatic reversal in 1991, only four years after *Booth* and two years after *Gathers*, the Court overruled both decisions in *Payne v. Tennessee*.

Randall Coyne

See also *Furman v. Georgia; Maher v. Roe; Payne v. Tennessee.*

BOUMEDIENE V. BUSH

Court: U.S. Supreme Court
Citation: 553 U.S. 723
Date: June 12, 2008
Issues: Due process of law; Habeas corpus; Military law;
Warfare and terrorism

- In this decision, the U.S. Supreme Court ruled that noncitizens who were suspected of terrorism and detained at the Guantánamo Bay detention center had the constitutional right to challenge their detention by petitioning U.S. federal courts for writs of habeas corpus, requiring the government to provide justification for continuing to hold them at the center.

Following the terrorist attacks of September 11, 2001, the policies of President George W. Bush raised a number of controversial issues about civil rights and due process. U.S. courts have always acknowledged that enemy combatants captured and detained in foreign countries do not have any access to U.S. courts. After the Bush administration began to imprison several hundred terrorist suspects on the U.S. Naval Base at Guantánamo in Cuba, lawyers for some of the prisoners claimed the right to petition federal courts for writs of habeas corpus that would disallow the government from keeping them imprisoned indefinitely without good evidence of wrongdoing.

The lawyers referred to the U.S. Constitution's suspension clause, which stipulates that writs of habeas corpus could be suspended only in cases of "rebellion or invasion." The Bush administration argued that the US. naval base at Guantánamo was actually part of Cuba, a foreign country, whereas the prisoners' lawyers answered that because the United States exercised exclusive control and jurisdiction over the base, persons detained there could claim the protections of the U.S. Constitution.

The Boumediene Case

The case of Lakhdar Boumediene began in October, 2001, when American intelligence analysts obtained information that the Middle East terrorist organization known as al-Qaeda was planning to attack the American embassy in Bosnia. At the request of the analysts, the Bosnian government arrested the principal suspect, an Algerian named Bensayah Balkacem, as well as five other Algerians, including Boumediene. In January, 2002, the Bosnian supreme court found that there was no evidence to hold the six men and ordered their release. As soon as they were released, however, American officials in Bosnia had them arrested and transported to Guantánamo Bay, where they were classified as "enemy combatants." Boumediene denied that he had ever been associated with any terrorist organizations such as al-Qaeda or the Taliban. However, the Combatant Status Review Tribunal, which was created to determine which of the detainees were dangerous, concluded in three annual reviews that because Boumediene had associated with known terrorists he should not be released.

Boumediene joined with other detainees to petition the federal courts for habeas corpus review. Their lawyers alleged that their imprisonment violated principles of due process under the U.S. Constitution, the common law, federal statutes, and the Geneva Conventions. Both the district court and court of appeals for the D.C. Circuit denied the motion on the grounds that U.S. courts had no jurisdiction over aliens kept in captivity by the military overseas. Meanwhile, the Supreme Court issued the landmark decision, *Rasul v. Bush* (2004), which established that the U.S. courts had the authority to consider whether foreign nationals at Guantánamo were wrongfully imprisoned. In a related case, *Hamdan v. Rumsfeld* (2006), the high Court held that the president did not have the authority to establish military commissions without congressional authorization. Congress and the Bush administration reacted to the two decisions by enacting the Military Commissions Act (MCA) of 2006, which authorized trials by military commissions and also disallowed suspected enemy combatants detained abroad from gaining access to U.S. courts.

When the Boumediene group's petition reached the D.C. Circuit for the second time, its lawyers argued that the MCA's suspension of the privilege of habeas corpus was unconstitutional. The district court rejected the argument, holding that habeas corpus, as understood when the Constitution was written in 1787, could not have applied to any military bases located in a foreign country. The petitioners then appealed their case to the Supreme Court, which granted *certiorari* and heard oral arguments in December, 2007. The case before the Court included four complex questions:

- Should the MCA be interpreted as eliminating the federal courts' jurisdiction over writs of habeas corpus by foreign citizens at Guantánamo?
- If so, was the MCA inconsistent with the Constitution's suspension clause?
- Did the United States government exercise enough control over the Guantánamo base to guarantee its prisoners the protections of due process under the Fifth Amendment?
- Could the detainees challenge the procedures of the MCA before their cases had been reviewed under that law?

The Court's Ruling

In *Boumediene v. Bush*, a 5-4 majority of the Supreme Court reversed the ruling of the lower appeals court and answered with a resounding yes to each of the four questions. Justice Anthony Kennedy's seventy-page opinion for the Court emphasized the central importance of habeas corpus protection in the American legal tradition and affirmed that all alien prisoners at Guantánamo were entitled to the equivalence of this protection. Based on this premise, Kennedy struck down the portion of the MCA that denied access to habeas corpus as an unconstitutional violation of the suspension clause. He acknowledged that the Court had upheld the constitutionality of a 1996 statute, the Antiterrorism and Effective Death Penalty Act (AEDPA), which put restrictions on the filing of habeas corpus petitions, but he wrote that unlike the MCA, the AEDPA had not completely suspended the right to such petitions. In regard to the legal status of the Guantánamo naval base, Kennedy wrote that even if the United States did not have complete de jure (legal) sovereignty over the base, it did exercise enough de facto (functional) sovereignty to extend the protections of the U.S. Constitution to the prisoners.

Justice David Souter's concurring opinion, joined by Justices Ruth Bader Ginsburg and Stephen Breyer, agreed with the opinion of the Court in recognizing the right of petitioners to habeas corpus relief. However, Souter wrote that the right was based entirely on the Constitution rather than on acts of Congress. He also criticized the four dissenting justices for insufficiently appreciating that many prisoners at Guantánamo had been detained for more than six years without any impartial review to determine their guilt or innocence. In view of their long imprisonment, he wrote that the Court's dissenters had no basis for suggesting that the military and the D.C. Circuit were able to resolve the case within a "reasonable period of time."

Dissenting Opinions

Justice Antonin Scalia, joined by three other conservative justices, wrote a forceful dissent, arguing that the Military Commission Act did not violate either the suspension clause or any other provision in the Constitution. Reminding his audience that the country "is at war with radical Islamists," he emphasized two major points: U.S. courts had never made the privilege of habeas corpus available to aliens abroad; the Guantánamo base was part of Cuba and therefore outside the sovereign territory of the United States.

The suspension clause, therefore, did not apply in the case. As a result of

Suspected terrorist at the U.S. detention center at Cuba's Guantánamo Bay being escorted to an interrogation in early 2002. (AP/Wide World Photos)

the majority's opinion, the fate of "enemy prisoners in this war will ultimately lie with the [judicial] branch," which is the branch that is the least prepared to deal with "national security concerns." Scalia added that the Constitution allows suspension of the writ of habeas corpus in cases of rebellion or invasion, and observing that the members of the majority expanded the scope of the writ on "functional" considerations, he asked why the majority narrowly limited its suspension almost entirely to domestic crises.

Chief Justice John Roberts wrote a more moderate dissent, arguing that the procedures in the Detainee Treatment Act of 2005 were an adequate substitute for the habeas corpus privilege in the Constitution.

Not long after the Court's decision was announced, a U.S. district judge in Washington found that there was insufficient evidence to continue detaining Boumediene and four of the other Algerians, and he ordered their release. In 2009, at the request of President Barack Obama's administration, the French government agreed to allow Boumediene to settle in France. In an interview, Boumediene said that he was going file suit against the U.S. government for his imprisonment, which he described as cruel and inhumane. It appeared unlikely, however, that he would be able to prevail in such a suit, especially after April, 2009, when the D.C. Court of Appeals dismissed a civil suit of four former Guantánamo detainees who claimed to have suffered torture and other indignities. The court found that the military officials responsible for the alleged abuses had immunity because they could not have known that the treatment of the prisoners was illegal at the time it occurred. On December 14, 2009, the Supreme Court declined to review the appeals court's decision.

Thomas Tandy Lewis

Further Reading

Berkowitz, Peter, ed. *Terrorism, The Laws of War, and the Constitution.* Stanford, Calif.: Hoover Institution Press, 2005. Collection of scholarly essays from different perspectives, addressing primarily the cases of Padilla, Hamdi, and Rasul.

Cole, David, and James Dempsey. *Terrorism and the Constitution: Sacrificing Civil Liberties in the Name of National Security.* New York: New Press, 2006. Two constitutional scholars argue that many of the antiterrorism measures have needlessly sacrificed civil liberties without promoting national security.

Evangelista, Matthew. *Law, Ethics, and the War on Terror.* New York: John Wiley & Sons, 2008. Explores the key legal and ethical controversies related to the struggle against radical Jihadists since the attacks on September 11, 2001.

Federman, Cary. *The Body and the State: Habeas Corpus and American Jurisprudence.* Albany: University of New York Press, 2007. Historical account of the application of the writ since 1789.

Hafetz, Jonathan, and Mark Denbeaux. *The Guantánamo Lawyers: Inside a Prison Outside the Law.* New York: New York University Press, 2009. Stories of the lawyers who represented the 750 men held at the naval base at Guantánamo Bay.

McDonald, Nicole. *Prisoner of War or Illegal Enemy Combatant?* Saarbrücken, Germany: VDM Verlag, 2008. Examination of the legal status and rights of detainees in the war on terrorism, with an emphasis on the policies of the Bush administration.

Pohlman, H. L. *Terrorism and the Constitution: The Post-9/11 Cases.* Lanham, Md.: Rowman & Littlefield, 2008. Dispassionate examination of the difficulties inherent in attempting to balance individual rights and national security.

See also *Frank v. Mangum; Hamdan v. Rumsfeld; McCleskey v. Zant; Stone v. Powell.*

BOWE V. COLGATE-PALMOLIVE

Court: U.S. Court of Appeals for the Sixth Circuit
Citation: 416 F.2d 711
Date: September 26, 1969
Issues: Employment discrimination; Labor law; Sex discrimination; Women's issues

- This case determined that excluding women from positions that required lifting more than thirty-five pounds was discriminatory.

Thelma Bowe filed a lawsuit against Colgate-Palmolive that questioned gender as a bona fide occupational qualification under Title VII of the Civil Rights Act of 1964. The circuit court stated that the company's weight- lifting requirement could be retained "as a general guideline for *all* of its employees, male or female." All employees had to be allowed to bid on all jobs requiring heavy lifting.

In this court decision, the seniority system of Colgate-Palmolive, which used separate lists for men and women, was also judged to be discriminatory. Men were eligible for any job in the plant, while women were eligible for only those jobs without the heavy-lifting requirement. Female plaintiffs were laid off, while male employees with less seniority kept their jobs. The company's seniority system based on departments was ruled discriminatory as well. Women who transferred to higher jobs in another department lost their seniority and were subject to layoffs. The court observed that when a plaintiff has suffered discrimination because of a class characteristic, the trial court may identify facts broader than those related to the plaintiff and allow the action to become a class action. Each person seeking relief need not have filed a charge with the Equal Employment Opportunity Commission (EEOC) previously in order to join in the lawsuit. Because the court's action was based on a class characteristic, "similarly situated" female employees could apply for back pay.

Glenn Ellen Starr

See also *Bradwell v. Illinois; County of Washington v. Gunther; Frontiero v. Richardson; Geduldig v. Aiello; Grove City College v. Bell; Phillips v. Martin Marietta Corp.; Rosenfeld v. Southern Pacific.*

BOWERS V. HARDWICK

Court: U.S. Supreme Court
Citation: 478 U.S. 186
Date: June 30, 1986
Issues: Gay and lesbian rights; Right to privacy

- In this case the U.S. Supreme Court held that the fundamental right to privacy protected by the due process clause of the Fourteenth Amendment did not extend to create a right for homosexuals to engage in consensual acts of sodomy.

Bowers v. Hardwick involved a Georgia statute making it a criminal offense to commit sodomy. Hardwick was charged with violating the statute by committing sodomy with another male in Hardwick's bedroom, but the district attorney in charge of the prosecution ultimately decided not to pursue a conviction. Hardwick then brought suit, seeking a declaration that the Georgia statute was unconstitutional. In a 5-4 decision, the Supreme Court held that the statute did not violate the due process clause of the Fourteenth Amendment.

Prior to the decision in *Bowers*, the Supreme Court had held that the Constitution protected a right to privacy in matters such as abortion and the use of contraceptives. In *Bowers*, Hardwick argued that consensual sexual acts, including sodomy, should also fall within this right to privacy and should therefore be free from government regulation. In an opinion by Justice Byron R. White, a narrowly divided Court emphasized that previous privacy cases had involved family, marriage, and procreation. White insisted that homosexual conduct fell into a different category. Normally, he wrote, the Court determined whether a particular interest was a fundamental right by considering whether the interest was "implicit in the concept of ordered liberty" such that "neither liberty nor justice would exist if [it] were sacrificed," or whether the interest was "deeply rooted in this Nation's history and tradition."

Sodomy, Justice White suggested, clearly failed to satisfy either of these definitions of a fundamental right. Nor was it fatal to the statute that it used the criminal sanction to enforce morality. The law, Justice White declared, "is constantly based on notions of morality, and if all laws representing essentially moral choices are to be invalidated under the due process clause, the courts will be very busy indeed."

Justice Harry Blackmun, joined by Justices William Brennan, Thurgood Marshall, and John Paul Stevens, vigorously dissented from the majority's holding, arguing that the right to engage in intimate sexual relationships should be considered a fundamental right. For the dissenters, at issue in *Bowers* was the right that Justice Louis Brandeis had once described as "the most comprehensive of rights and the right most valued by civilized men": "the right to be let alone."

Bowers is significant because it signified a reluctance by the Court to recognize fundamental rights not explicitly guaranteed by the Constitution. Prior to the decision in *Bowers* it had seemed that the Court might soon recognize a fundamental right to sexual privacy between consenting adults protected by the due process clauses of the Fifth and Fourteenth Amendments. *Bowers* disappointed these expectations. It also suggested that the era in which the Court had looked to the doctrine of "substantive due process" to declare certain rights "fundamental" might be nearing a close.

Timothy L. Hall

See also *Lawrence v. Texas; Pierce v. Society of Sisters; Romer v. Evans; Stanley v. Georgia.*

BOWSHER V. SYNAR

Court: U.S. Supreme Court
Citation: 478 U.S. 714
Date: July 7, 1986
Issues: Separation of powers

- The U.S. Supreme Court ruled that it was unconstitutional for Congress to invest one of its own legislative officers with powers belonging to the executive branch.

Faced with continuing budget deficits, Congress set annual ceilings for deficits in the Balanced Budget and Emergency Deficit Control Act of 1985. If Congress failed to make the necessary budget cuts, the statute authorized the comptroller general to instruct the president concerning where to make the reductions. Representative Mike Synar and eleven other members of Congress challenged the constitutionality of the statute in the Supreme Court.

Speaking for a 7-2 majority, Chief Justice Warren E. Burger wrote that Congress could not delegate the comptroller general with powers to make decisions properly belonging to the president. Because the comptroller general was an agent of Congress and independent of the executive departments, the statute encroached on the president's duty to execute the laws. Thus, Burger's opinion relied on the relatively narrow principle of separation of powers and avoided the much broader nondelegation doctrine, which would have had great implications for the modern administrative state. Burger approved of the fallback provision of the 1985 statute, which allowed Congress to make the final budget decision by joint resolution, subject to presidential veto.

Thomas Tandy Lewis

See also *Immigration and Naturalization Service v. Chadha; Morrison v. Olson; Panama Refining Co. v. Ryan.*

BOY SCOUTS OF AMERICA V. DALE

Court: U.S. Supreme Court
Citation: 530 U.S. 640
Date: June 28, 2000
Issues: Gay and lesbian rights; Right to privacy

- In *Boy Scouts of America v. Dale*, the U.S. Supreme Court upheld the right of the Boy Scouts to exclude gay leaders, dealing a blow to the efforts of gay rights advocates.

In the United States, the issue of gay rights has been the subject of debate since the 1960's, when gay men and lesbians began to assert their rights to certain civil liberties, in part as a response to the gains of the Civil Rights movement. The U.S. Supreme Court has rarely ruled directly on gay and lesbian issues, and the Court made no such rulings until the late twentieth century.

One question related to the rights of gays and lesbians in American society is how much organizations are allowed to discriminate based on sexual orientation in such areas as hiring and membership; another is how sexual orientation is weighed against a person's or a group's rights. A related, implied question, rarely stated, involves whether sexual orientation is a choice or predetermined. Advocates for the rights of gay men and lesbians generally believe that it should not matter whether sexual orientation is a choice or a genetic predetermination. Others, however, believe that if sexual orientation is a choice, then homosexuals do not deserve legal protection, but if sexual orientation is genetically predetermined, then homosexuals deserve legal protection as minorities.

The state of New Jersey passed a law that prohibited discrimination on the basis of sexual orientation by any groups that use public places for their meetings. The Boy Scouts of America prohibited openly homosexual men from becoming Boy Scout leaders, and James Dale, an openly gay Eagle Scout, sued the Scouts, claiming that the organization violated New Jersey's law when it refused to allow him to continue in the position of assistant scoutmaster. The question in the case, however, ultimately came down not to questions of gay and lesbian rights but to the question of whether New Jersey's law violated the right of the Boy Scouts to control its own association through the right to freedom of association contained in the First Amendment to the U.S. Constitution.

The Court's Ruling

The U.S. Supreme Court ruled for the Boy Scouts in the case of *Boy Scouts of America v. Dale*, holding that New Jersey's law violated the organization's right to "expressive association." This right, located in the First Amendment's freedom of association, has been construed to hold that groups engaged in public discussion of ideas have a right to pick their own members. The reason for this right is that if the government can force groups to admit people, then the government is interfering with the groups' right to advocate positions. This right has not been held to be absolute, as a government can limit it, but only if there is a "compelling state interest."

The Court's decision was written by Chief Justice William H. Rehnquist, who first noted that the Boy Scouts of America, as an organization, was engaged in the expression of ideas—a requirement for groups that want to claim they are engaged in expressive association. He then looked at the policies of the Boy Scouts and held that the organization had a clear policy against homosexual leaders, which was a criterion for the Court to support the Scouts in this case. If no such policy had existed, then the organization's desire to exclude all homosexual leaders would not have been clearly sincere, and its application in Dale's case might also have been arbitrary.

The question then became whether New Jersey's claimed interest in the public accommodations statute outweighed the right of the Boy Scouts to control its own membership and whether forcing the Boy Scouts to admit Dale would limit the organization's right to expressive association. In the past, U.S. courts had ordered private groups to admit women, but in those cases the courts had held that admitting women to groups such as the Jaycees did not harm the groups' right to expressive association. In this case, Rehnquist held that admitting Dale would harm the right of the Boy Scouts of America to advocate its values, which the organization believed to be at variance with homosexuality.

The Court also held that the positions of the state and federal governments regarding the view of the Boy Scouts organization that homosexuality is immoral were irrelevant to the group's right to expressive association. Rehnquist used this argument as part of his response to the dissent's argument that homosexuality was becoming more accepted and so New Jersey should be allowed to force the Boy Scouts to admit gay leaders.

The dissent, written by Justice John Paul Stevens, disagreed with the majority in a number of areas, but not in the conclusion. Stevens first looked at the teachings of the Boy Scouts, and, although he agreed that the organization was expressing values, he held that it did not, in fact, publicly state clearly that homosexuality was wrong or have a clear policy forbidding homosexual leaders. Instead, Stevens asserted, the group avoided the issue of homosexuality. If this was the case, then admitting Dale as a leader could not possibly contradict the group's values. Stevens also argued that the Boy Scouts had no clear public policy of rejecting homosexual leaders, merely a quiet, unwritten policy. Finally, he argued that homosexuality was becoming more accepted in American society. Stevens stated that the Boy Scouts could have taken less drastic steps to protect the organization's right to advocate certain views while still admitting Dale as a leader. He suggested that forbidding Dale to discuss the issue of homosexuality would have been one possible solution and that this policy would have allowed the Boy Scouts its right to association while not violating New Jersey's public accommodations law.

Significance

The Supreme Court decision in the *Dale* case, which legitimated the right of certain kinds of groups to exclude homosexuals, was a blow to the efforts of gay rights activists. The decision also represented another check by the Rehnquist Court against government efforts in some states to encourage equality by protecting the rights of homosexuals.

In 2003, the Supreme Court, in *Lawrence and Garner v. Texas*, struck down a law forbidding homosexual sodomy. In that case, the Court held that the right to privacy, another traditional right like the freedom of association, extends to gays and lesbians and prevents the government from criminalizing sodomy. The difference between the *Dale* ruling and the one in *Lawrence and Garner v. Texas* was that in *Dale*, the group aiming to restrict homosexuals was advancing the traditional right, whereas in *Lawrence and Garner v. Texas*, the homosexual couple was advancing the traditional right. In the latter case, the Court overturned its 1986 ruling that had upheld such laws.

Scott Allen Merriman

Further Reading

Koppelman, Andrew. *The Gay Rights Question in Contemporary American Law.* Chicago: University of Chicago Press, 2003. Critiques arguments on both sides of the gay rights issue, discussing whether discrimination against gays is legally or morally defensible. Also provides some history regarding court decisions concerning gay rights.

Mechling, Jay. *On My Honor: Boy Scouts and the Making of American Youth.* Chicago: University of Chicago Press, 2001. Examines masculinity in the Scouts through extensive study of a summer camp. Argues that the Boy Scouts aim to produce "normal" boys—meaning heterosexual ones.

Pinello, Daniel R. *Gay Rights and American Law.* New York: Cambridge University Press, 2003. Examines the development of gay rights throughout the American legal system, including both the Supreme Court and appellate courts. Covers nearly four hundred court decisions between 1980 and 2000.

Rosenthal, Michael. *The Character Factory: Baden-Powell and the Origins of the Boy Scout Movement.* New York: Pantheon Books, 1986. Looks at the original goals of Robert Stephenson Smyth Baden-Powell in the creation of the Boy Scouts, among which were the development of honor and character.

Warren, Mark E. *Democracy and Association.* Princeton, N.J.: Princeton University Press, 2001. Discusses the fundamental freedom defended in the *Dale* case, freedom of association. Focuses extensively on the benefits of associations and those who participate in them.

See also *Hurley v. Irish-American Gay, Lesbian, and Bisexual Group of Boston; Lawrence v. Texas; Rotary International v. Duarte.*

BOYD V. UNITED STATES

Court: U.S. Supreme Court
Citation: 116 U.S. 616
Date: February 1, 1886
Issues: Common law; Right to privacy; Search and seizure; Self-incrimination

• The U.S. Supreme Court made expansive interpretations of the constitutional guarantees against compulsory self-incrimination and unreasonable searches and seizures.

The federal government charged New York merchants George Boyd and Edward Boyd with a civil offense for importing plate glass without paying the required duty. Using a federal statute, officials obtained a court order instructing the Boyds to produce the invoices for the goods. When the invoices were used as evidence, the Boyds claimed that the government had violated their rights under the Fourth and Fifth Amendments. The government argued that there had been no physical invasion of property and that the amendments applied only to criminal trials.

A unanimous Supreme Court ruled in favor of the Boyds and found part of the customs statute unconstitutional. Justice Joseph P. Bradley reasoned that the Fourth and Fifth Amendments combined with the common law to

Justice Joseph P. Bradley.
(Library of Congress)

protect "the sanctity of a man's house and the privacies of life." The Fourth Amendment protected individuals from any procedures that had the same effect as a physical search. It applied to all proceedings with government penalties and permitted searches only for contraband articles, not for mere evidence of an illegal action. A warrantless seizure, moreover, violated the Fifth Amendment prohibition against compulsory self-incrimination. Bradley declared that the courts should guard against any "stealthy encroachments" of constitutional rights.

The *Boyd* decision was a watershed in providing a liberal interpretation of privacy rights by joining the Fourth and Fifth Amendments to common law principles. Also, the decision initiated the development of the exclusionary rule. *Boyd*'s mere evidence rule, however, was eventually abandoned in *Warden v. Hayden* (1967).

Thomas Tandy Lewis

See also *Albertson v. Subversive Activities Control Board; Griffin v. California; Kastigar v. United States; Kilbourn v. Thompson; Minnick v. Mississippi; Murphy v. Waterfront Commission of New York; Slochower v. Board of Education of New York City; Weeks v. United States.*

Bradwell v. Illinois

Court: U.S. Supreme Court
Citation: 83 U.S. 130
Date: April 15, 1873
Issues: Employment discrimination; Labor law; Sex discrimination;
Women's issues

- The U.S. Supreme Court upheld a state's denial of the right of women to enter a profession traditionally reserved for men.

Myra Bradwell studied law with her attorney husband, and she edited and published the *Chicago Legal News*, a leading publication of the Midwest. Although she had passed the bar exam, her application for a state license to practice law was rejected solely because of her sex. She argued that her rights under the privileges or immunities clause of the Fourteenth Amendment were violated. By an 8-1 vote, the Supreme Court rejected her claim. Speaking for the Court, Justice Samuel F. Miller applied the restrictive interpretation of the Fourteenth Amendment that he had announced the previous day in the *Slaughterhouse Cases*. The granting of licenses to practice law was entirely in the hands of the states and therefore not related to any question of national citizenship. In a concurring opinion, Joseph P. Bradley noted: "The natural and proper timidity and delicacy which belongs to the female sex evidently unfits it for many of the occupations of civil life."

Although the Illinois Supreme Court allowed Bradwell to practice law in 1890, it was not until *Reed v. Reed* (1971) that the Court applied the Fourteenth Amendment to overturn discriminatory laws based on sex.

Thomas Tandy Lewis

See also *County of Washington v. Gunther; Frontiero v. Richardson; Grove City College v. Bell; Hoyt v. Florida; Meritor Savings Bank v. Vinson; Reed v. Reed; Rosenfeld v. Southern Pacific; Slaughterhouse Cases; Stanton v. Stanton.*

BRADY V. UNITED STATES

Court: U.S. Supreme Court
Citation: 397 U.S. 742
Date: May 4, 1970
Issues: Self-incrimination

- In this decision the U.S. Supreme Court first acknowledged the validity of plea bargaining, asserting that it offered a "mutuality of advantage" for both the defendant and the state.

In 1959, Robert M. Brady, in a kidnapping case that involved the death of the victim, changed a plea of innocent to guilty when a codefendant in the case pled guilty and became available as a witness against him. Before admitting the new plea, the judge twice asked Brady if his plea was voluntary. Brady was convicted, but in 1967 he sought a reversal of his conviction in the U.S. District Court for the District of New Mexico, arguing that his guilty plea had not been voluntary. The petitioner argued that the death-penalty provisions of the Federal Kidnapping Act had coerced his plea. The district court denied Brady relief, upholding the constitutionality of the federal statute and arguing that Brady changed his plea because of his codefendant's confession. The Court of Appeals for the Tenth Circuit affirmed the lower court's finding.

On *certiorari*, the U.S. Supreme Court concurred. In the various opinions issued by the Court, it was argued that an earlier case, *United States v. Jackson* (1968), which struck down the section of the Federal Kidnapping Act under which Brady had originally been tried, did not mandate that every guilty plea previously entered under the statute be deemed invalid, even when the threat of death was a consideration. It was further argued that a guilty plea was not a violation of the Fifth Amendment protection against self-incrimination when it was entered to ensure a lesser penalty than the maximum provided for by a criminal statute.

It was also noted that the Fifth Amendment did not bar prosecutors or judges from accepting pleas of guilty to lesser, reduced, or selected charges in order to secure milder penalties. Brady's guilty plea was held to have been made voluntarily, despite the fact that it was influenced by the death-penalty provision of the statute that *United States v. Jackson* later declared unconstitutional.

The formal recognition of plea bargaining as a valid procedure for obtaining criminal convictions was very important because plea bargaining has been widely used in the United States, despite the fact that there is no statutory or constitutional basis for it. In fact, almost four-fifths of all convictions in serious state and federal criminal cases are obtained through guilty pleas made to secure either reduced charges or milder punishments. Although the procedure has its critics, it is a practical way of speeding up justice and clearing court dockets. It also mitigates against long pretrial imprisonment and anxiety and protects the public from the criminal activities of habitual offenders who would be free on bail for indefinite periods.

John W. Fiero

See also *Albertson v. Subversive Activities Control Board; Boyd v. United States; Griffin v. California; Kastigar v. United States; Kilbourn v. Thompson; Malloy v. Hogan; Murphy v. Waterfront Commission of New York; Santobello v. New York; Twining v. New Jersey.*

BRANDENBURG V. OHIO

Court: U.S. Supreme Court
Citation: 395 U.S. 444
Date: June 9, 1969
Issues: Freedom of speech

• Climaxing a long line of cases about the limits of free expression, the Court ruled that government may not punish the advocacy of illegal actions except when the advocacy is aimed at imminent action and is likely to have such a result.

Charles Brandenburg, a Ku Klux Klan leader, had addressed a rally of twelve hooded men on a farm near Cincinnati and declared that if the government continued "to suppress the white, Caucasian race, it's possible that there might have to be revengeance taken." Based on films of the rally, Brandenburg was convicted under the Ohio Criminal Syndicalism statute of 1919 for advocating unlawful or violent means in pursuit of political reform, and he was fined one thousand dollars and sentenced to imprisonment from one to ten years. Although the Court had protected the advocacy of abstract beliefs in *Yates v. United States* (1957), the precedent of *Whitney v. California* (1927) still allowed government to prosecute the advocacy of illegal acts when such advocacy tended to cause such acts.

At conference, the judges voted unanimously to reverse *Whitney*, to overturn Brandenburg's conviction, and to rule the Ohio law a violation of the First and Fourteenth Amendments. Chief Justice Earl Warren assigned Justice Abe Fortas to write the opinion for the Court, but after Fortas resigned from the Court in May, the Court issued its ruling as an unsigned, *per curiam* opinion. The Court declared that the constitutional guarantees of free speech and free press meant that government might not "forbid or proscribe advocacy of the use of force or of law violation except where such advocacy is directed to inciting or producing imminent lawless action and is likely to incite or produce such action."

Brandenburg v. Ohio did not make use of the exact words of the controversial "clear and present danger" test, but in referring to imminence and likelihood, the opinion seemed to accept Judge Learned Hand's modification of the basic idea. Justices Hugo Black and William Douglas wrote concurring opinions to explain that while they agreed with the outcome of the case, they took an absolutist view on freedom of expression and believed that the clear and present danger test had no place in the interpretation of the First Amendment.

Since 1969, the Court has pointed to *Brandenburg* as controlling precedent in regard to First Amendment protection for advocating those very evils against which the state may act. While it is impossible to know how the courts might interpret the *Brandenburg* standard in an emergency or wartime situation, the standard presents the state with a hurdle that makes it very difficult to prosecute most forms of advocating illegal actions.

Thomas Tandy Lewis

See also *Feiner v. New York*; *Whitney v. California*; *Yates v. United States*; *Younger v. Harris*.

BRANZBURG V. HAYES

Court: U.S. Supreme Court
Citation: 408 U.S. 665
Date: June 29, 1972
Issues: Freedom of speech; Freedom of the press

• The Supreme Court ruled that the First Amendment did not provide journalists with a special testimonial privilege not enjoyed by other citizens.

Paul Branzburg, a reporter of a Louisville newspaper, wrote a series of articles about traffic in illegal drugs, using information from drug users who insisted on their anonymity. Subpoenaed by a grand jury, he refused to answer questions about his confidential sources. The Supreme Court consolidated the case with those of two other journalists who had refused to provide information to grand juries. By a 5-4 vote, the Court found that requiring their testimony was not an unconstitutional infringement on the freedom of the press. Justice Byron R. White's plurality opinion concluded that the public interest in law enforcement outweighed any incidental burden that journalists might have in obtaining confidential information. Throughout U.S. history, White wrote, the press had "operated without protection for press informants." In response to the media's vehement opposition to the *Branzburg* decision, thirty-six states and the District of Columbia had enacted shield laws by 2009. These laws allow reporters to refuse to divulge their sources in limited circumstances.

Thomas Tandy Lewis

See also *Cohen v. Cowles Media Co.*; *Grosjean v. American Press Co.*; *Miami Herald Publishing Co. v. Tornillo*; *Richmond Newspapers v. Virginia.*

Brecht v. Abrahamson

Court: U.S. Supreme Court
Citation: 507 U.S. 619
Date: April 21, 1993
Issues: Habeas corpus; Miranda rights

- When federal courts review challenges to trial errors involving Miranda violations, the U.S. Supreme Court held that the courts may overturn convictions only when the errors result in "a substantial and injurious effect or influence" on the outcome of the trial.

In a trial that resulted in Todd Brecht's conviction on charges of first-degree murder, the prosecutor made statements that were contrary to the Supreme Court's binding interpretations of *Miranda v. Arizona* (1966). The Court had previously held that the state had the burden of proving beyond a reasonable doubt that any constitutional error was harmless. In *Brecht*, a 5-4 majority of the Court voted to expand the "harmless error" standard in cases involving Miranda rights. Chief Justice William H. Rehnquist's opinion for the majority had the result of shifting the burden of proof from the state to the defendant filing a petition for a habeas corpus hearing in federal court.

Thomas Tandy Lewis

See also *Arizona v. Fulminante; Brown v. Mississippi; Chambers v. Florida; Escobedo v. Illinois; Faretta v. California; Gideon v. Wainwright; Harris v. New York; Mallory v. United States.*

Breedlove v. Suttles

Court: U.S. Supreme Court
Citation: 302 U.S. 277
Date: December 6, 1937
Issues: Voting rights

• The U.S. Supreme Court upheld the constitutionality of a state's poll tax that did not treat all people equally.

A Georgia law levied a poll tax of one dollar per year on all people between the ages of twenty-one and sixty, except for the blind and women who had not registered to vote. Payment of the tax was a prerequisite for voter registration. A white male citizen asserted that the law was an invidious discrimination, contrary to the principles of the Fourteenth and Nineteenth Amendments. The Supreme Court unanimously rejected the claim. In the opinion for the Court, Justice Pierce Butler declared that the exclusions from tax liability were reasonable in view of the special circumstances of the exempted groups. Butler also noted that the use of poll taxes as a condition for voting had long been accepted in U.S. traditions. The *Breedlove* decision was overturned in *Harper v. Virginia State Board of Elections* (1966).

Thomas Tandy Lewis

See also *Dunn v. Blumstein; Guinn v. United States; Harper v. Virginia State Board of Elections; South Carolina v. Katzenbach.*

BRISCOE V. BANK OF THE COMMONWEALTH OF KENTUCKY

Court: U.S. Supreme Court
Citation: 11 Pet (36 U.S.) 257
Date: February 11, 1837
Issues: Fiscal and monetary powers

• Reflecting Chief Justice Roger Brooke Taney's bias toward states' rights, the U.S. Supreme Court allowed a state-owned bank to issue notes for public circulation as legal tender.

The U.S. Constitution prohibited states from issuing bills of credit, but the exact meaning of the term was unclear. In *Craig v. Missouri* (1830), the Supreme Court ruled that interest-bearing certificates issued by a state were unconstitutional bills of credit. In *Briscoe v. Bank of the Commonwealth of Kentucky,* however, the justices voted six to one to allow a state-owned bank to issue circulating notes. Justice John McLean wrote for the Court that the notes at issue were not unconstitutional because they were not issued directly by the state or backed by the faith and credit of the state. The justices at the time were very sensitive to the rights of the states and recognized the need for a circulating medium following the demise of the Bank of the United States. The decision allowed for greater state controls over banking and currency in the years before the Civil War.

Thomas Tandy Lewis

See also *Craig v. Missouri; Legal Tender Cases; Ware v. Hylton.*

BRONSON V. KINZIE

Court: U.S. Supreme Court
Citation: 42 U.S. 311
Date: February 23, 1843
Issues: Bankruptcy law; Freedom of contract; Property rights

• Based on the contracts clause, the U.S. Supreme Court overturned debtor-relief laws restricting the rights of creditors to foreclose on mortgages.

Although the Supreme Court under Chief Justice Roger Brooke Taney sometimes limited the scope of the contract clause, *Bronson v. Kinzie* demonstrated its continuing commitment to enforce property rights under the clause. With the Panic of 1837, several states passed laws providing relief for debtors unable to make mortgage payments. Illinois passed two such laws.

By a 6-1 vote, the Court ruled that the contract clause prohibited state legislatures from modifying the terms of an existing mortgage. The purpose of the clause, wrote the chief justice, "was to maintain the integrity of contracts, and to secure their faithful execution throughout this Union." Although the *Bronson* precedent was upheld for many years, it was almost entirely abandoned in *Home Building and Loan Association v. Blaisdell* (1934).

Thomas Tandy Lewis

See also *Charles River Bridge v. Warren Bridge; Home Building and Loan Association v. Blaisdell; Powell v. Alabama; Sturges v. Crowninshield.*

Brown v. Board of Education

Court: U.S. Supreme Court
Citation: 347 U.S. 483
Date: May 17, 1954
Issues: Civil rights and liberties; Desegregation; Education;
Racial discrimination

- For almost sixty years, racial segregation had been established by law in the United States. The U.S. Supreme Court decision in *Brown v. Board of Education* changed race relations, mandating an end to segregation in public education.

Segregation of blacks and whites in the United States is the most obvious of the racial problems that have faced the nation, because black people form one of its largest racial minorities and have been the object of laws, as well as customs, which have kept them from full participation in social and economic life. Many of the laws imposing racial segregation dealt with public schools' segregation of children based on their race.

Legal segregation began in the United States in the years following the Civil War. Since black people were declared equal citizens to whites by the Fourteenth and Fifteenth Amendments to the Constitution, a new basis for race relations needed to be worked out to replace the prewar master-slave status. Because most black people lived in the states which had formed the Confederacy, the problem of race relations was more intense in the South.

In 1896, the Supreme Court of the United States was asked to settle the question of whether forcing black people to use separate facilities was a violation of the constitutional guarantees of equality. The case in question, *Plessy v. Ferguson*, involved streetcars in New Orleans, Louisiana. In that case, the Supreme Court ruled that "equal but separate" facilities did not violate the demands of the Constitution. (The more commonly quoted phrase "separate but equal" is taken from the dissenting opinion in that case, as well as from the decision in *Brown v. Board of Education*.) Based on this decision, a number of states passed laws that demanded racial segregation in almost every aspect of life, from restaurants to public schools to the ballot box, with most black people losing the right to vote.

Many African American leaders, such as Booker T. Washington, accepted the reality of segregation and did not openly challenge the system. White political leaders, in southern and border states, found they could whip up enthusiasm for their candidacies and could win votes by making strong and emotional supports of segregation. This separation of the races was reinforced by the economic conditions of the period from 1920 to 1940, when agricultural and blue-collar industrial workers were competing for jobs. In this economic competition, race was an easily identified and easily exploited factor. Black workers were accused of accepting lower wages and of being strikebreakers.

"Separate but Equal" Principle

If the "separate" aspect of the *Plessy v. Ferguson* decision was honored, the "equal" was quickly forgotten. In the twenty-one states which either required or permitted segregation, salaries for African American teachers were about one-half those for white teachers, and the amount of money spent for each black pupil was about one-fourth that spent on each white pupil. In the states of the old Confederacy and in the border states, separate schools with enrollment based on race were a universal practice. Such segregation was not uncommon in the rest of the nation. In some cases separate schools were maintained contrary to state law. Hispanics, Asians, and Native Americans were often the subjects of segregation in western states.

Although segregation was widespread, the practice was under attack by 1950. President Harry S. Truman had ordered the desegregation of facilities belonging to the federal government, and the armed forces were beginning to integrate their units. Also, five suits challenging the validity of public school segregation had been introduced before the federal courts of various districts. These cases involved the public schools of Clarendon County, South Carolina; Prince Edward County, Virginia; Topeka, Kansas; Wilmington, Delaware; and Washington, D.C. These were all "class action" suits, meaning that any decision reached in them would apply not just to the people who had brought suit but also to any others in the same district who suffered the same discrimination.

All five of these cases were heard by the Supreme Court of the United States under Chief Justice Earl Warren. In order to make sure that all aspects of this sensitive and important issue were covered, the Supreme Court ordered certain aspects of the cases reargued in 1953. At this point, all five cases were consolidated and listed alphabetically. This listing meant that the first case on the docket would be *Brown, et al. v. the Board of Education of Topeka, Kansas*, or as it would be better known, simply *Brown v. Board of Education*.

The Legal Teams

The nation's oldest civil rights organization is the National Association for the Advancement of Colored People (NAACP). This group traditionally has challenged discriminatory practices through lawsuits. The chief counsel for this group, who would argue the case before the Supreme Court, was Thurgood Marshall. Marshall was a veteran of many court battles over racial discrimination and was eager to demonstrate not only that segregation was unfair under the Constitution but also that the practice was psychologically damaging to African Americans, especially black children. To assist him in making this point, Marshall invited several prominent social scientists to study the situation in Topeka, Kansas, and to comment on the psychological impact of segregation. It was the opinion of this group that assigning a particular group to separate facilities identified this group as having a lower status than other people. This evaluation of having a lower status became damaging to the segregated group by lowering its members' self-esteem.

The defendants in the case assembled a team of lawyers led by John W. Davis, a corporate lawyer from New York City. Davis was a former Democratic presidential nominee and solicitor general of the United States. In his government capacity, he had successfully prosecuted the Ku Klux Klan and had won cases which restored the right to vote to black citizens in some states. He took the line of defense taken by Davis was not based on racial prejudice but on the matter of states' rights, a troublesome issue that, along with slavery, had led to the Civil War almost a century before. Davis argued that the federal govern-

Thurgood Marshall, who joined the Supreme Court in 1967, was the chief counsel for the group who argued the Brown case before the Supreme Court. (Joseph Lavenburg, National Geographic, courtesy the Supreme Court of the United States)

ment generally and the Supreme Court specifically were not qualified to take over and conduct the business of state operations such as schools.

Chief Justice Earl Warren had only recently been appointed to his post by newly elected President Dwight D. Eisenhower. Warren was thought to be of a conservative point of view, and many people favorable to civil rights were unsure how he would vote, especially since his record when he was governor of California gave few hints as to what his judicial opinions might be.

Both sides presented their arguments in December, 1953. On May 17, 1954, the Supreme Court ruled that "separate but equal" had ceased to be the law of the land. State-enforced racial segregation in the public schools would no longer be permitted. This ruling meant that while the school districts covered in the five combined cases should be desegregated quickly, the way was also open for all other court districts to hear suits on the same basis. The unanimous opinion of the Supreme Court, written by Chief Justice Warren, left no doubt as to the outcome of future suits. The chief justice wrote, "We conclude that in the field of public education the doctrine of 'separate but equal' has no place. Separate educational facilities are inherently unequal." This decision in *Brown v. Board of Education* may well be the most momentous and far-reaching court order in the area of civil rights in the twentieth century.

Significance

It would be no exaggeration to say the decision in *Brown v. Board of Education* completely changed the face of the United States. Although some states tried to resist the process of integration of public schools for a time, their resistance was doomed to fail. When President Eisenhower sent U.S. Army troops to Little Rock, Arkansas, in 1957 to enforce school desegregation, it became clear that the impact of *Brown v. Board of Education* would be universal. No state would be able to impose its will on the national Supreme Court.

Within ten years, many public schools had been integrated by race. After fifteen years, virtually all public schools had ended segregation. One reaction to desegregation was the creation of numerous private schools, often connected with churches, in which the student body was all white. Students in the integrated public schools found common ground, and joint achievement in extracurricular activities such as music and sports soon drew favorable public attention. For example, in 1964 three civil rights workers were murdered near Philadelphia, Mississippi. In 1980, the same town held a parade honoring Marcus Dupree, a black football player at the local high school. With the breakdown of segregation in public schools, the task of attacking race separation in other aspects of life also became easier.

The integration of public schools did not produce national heroes such as Martin Luther King, Jr. Instead, there were many heroic individuals such as the black children who walked through crowds of yelling protesters to enter the schools, the white students who violated the customs of their communities to welcome their black classmates, and community leaders such as the *Nashville Tennessean* newspaper editor who advocated peaceful acceptance of integration as the proper action.

It should not be assumed that integration of public schools solved the matter of race relations in the schools or in society at large. Issues such as busing students to other schools to achieve racial balance, employment opportunities for black teachers and administrators, "white flight" to private or suburban schools, inclusion of black history in the curriculum, and the events and ideas to be emphasized in teaching the history of the Civil War would all cause problems and debate following 1954. Indeed, some black leaders would come to call for all-black schools and colleges as a means of preserving a black culture and heritage.

Leslie W. Dunbar, a white Southern teacher, consultant, and community organizer, sums up the impact of the Supreme Court decision very well:

> I think *Brown v. Board of Education* has a very special historical claim. I guess you could say the same thing, in a way, about 1865, with the Thirteenth Amendment [which abolished slavery and involuntary servitude]. But that got ignored. Up until *Brown v. Board of Education*, in 1954, segregation had been legal. Up to *Brown v. Board of Education*, the Constitutional rights of black people not to be discriminated against were, to say the least, unclear. After that, they were not. From 1954 on, it was as though the Constitution had been clarified.

Michael R. Bradley

Further Reading

Branch, Taylor. *Parting the Waters: America in the King Years, 1954-1963*. New York: Simon & Schuster, 1988. This book won the 1989 Pulitzer Prize for its historical and personal portrayal of all the major, and many minor, characters involved in what the author calls "The King Years." The first volume of a three-volume series.

Cottrol, Robert J., Raymond T. Diamond, and Leland B. Ware. *Brown v. Board of Education: Caste, Culture, and the Constitution*. Lawrence: University Press of Kansas, 2003. Places the decision in its broad historical context, while also discussing the specific institutions and individuals at the heart of the case.

Fireside, Harvey, and Sarah Betsy Fuller. *Brown v. Board of Education: Equal Schooling for All*. Berkeley Heights, N.J.: Enslow, 1994. Designed for young-adult readers, this volume examines the issues leading up to *Brown v. Board of Education*, people involved in the case, the legal development of the case, and the historical impact of the ruling. Includes chapter notes, further reading list, and index.

Franklin, John Hope, and Isidore Starr. *The Negro in the Twentieth Century.* New York: Vintage Books, 1967. Franklin is the "dean" of African American history. This book gives a survey of blacks in America. Book 3 contains a section dealing especially with *Brown v. Board of Education.*

Friedman, Leon. *The Civil Rights Reader: Basic Documents of the Civil Rights Movement.* New York: Walker, 1968. The value of this book is found in its reprinting of original interviews and documents from the civil rights years.

Lewis, Anthony. *Portrait of a Decade: The Second American Revolution.* New York: Random House, 1964. Lewis was a reporter who covered in person the events he describes. His firsthand involvement is backed with accurate historical research.

Patterson, James T. *Brown v. Board of Education: A Civil Rights Milestone and Its Troubled Legacy.* New York: Oxford University Press, 2001. This historical and legal analysis of Brown also delves into the issue of the limits of the courts' abilities to bring about social change.

Powledge, Fred. *Free at Last? The Civil Rights Movement and the People Who Made It.* Boston: Little, Brown, 1991. The author is a journalist, born in North Carolina, who covered the Civil Rights movement for the *Atlanta Journal* and *The New York Times.* Valuable because the author has interviewed participants in the movement and has allowed them to tell their own stories of these events.

Rasmussen, R. Kent. *Farewell to Jim Crow: The Rise and Fall of Segregation in America.* New York: Facts On File, 1997. Brief but comprehensive survey of the history of segregation with special attention to the struggle to desegregate schools.

Tushnet, Mark, ed. *I Dissent: Great Opposing Opinions in Landmark Supreme Court Cases.* Boston: Beacon Press, 2008. Collection of dissenting opinions in thirteen major Supreme Court cases, including *Marbury v. Madison, Brown v. Board of Education, Griswold v. Connecticut,* and *Lawrence v. Texas.* Tushnet places each case in its historical perspective, with an overview of the principal issues at stake.

Woodward, C. Vann. *The Strange Career of Jim Crow.* New York: Oxford University Press, 1974. "Jim Crow" was the nickname for discriminatory laws and practices. This book is the standard history of racial segregation. Frequent revisions have kept it up to date with legal, social, and historical trends.

See also *Bolling v. Sharpe; Green v. County School Board of New Kent County; Lau v. Nichols; Lemon v. Kurtzman; Muller v. Oregon; Plessy v. Ferguson; Swann v. Charlotte-Mecklenburg Board of Education.*

BROWN V. MARYLAND

Court: U.S. Supreme Court
Citation: 12 Wheat. (25 U.S.) 419
Date: March 12, 1827
Issues: Taxation

- The U.S. Supreme Court held that a state tax on imported goods that were still in the original packaging and not mixed with other goods violated both the imports-exports and the commerce clause.

A Maryland statute required importers of foreign goods to purchase a license. The state claimed that a license tax on the importer was different from a tax on the import itself. By a 6-1 vote, the Supreme Court struck down the law. Chief Justice John Marshall enunciated the original packaging rule, which said that as long as imported goods were in the original packaging, a state tax was an unconstitutional violation of both the imports-exports and the commerce clause. Once imported goods became mixed up with other property, the state could tax them. This ruling enhanced federal powers without permanently insulating imported goods from state taxation.

In 1869 the Court decided that the original packaging rule did not apply to goods moving in interstate commerce. In *Michelin Tire Corp. v. Wages* (1976), the Court almost entirely abandoned the rule when it allowed states to assess nondiscriminatory property taxes on foreign imports in storage.

Thomas Tandy Lewis

See also *Dobbins v. Erie County; Graves v. New York ex rel. O'Keefe; Weston v. Charleston; Woodruff v. Parham.*

BROWN V. MISSISSIPPI

Court: U.S. Supreme Court
Citation: 297 U.S. 278
Date: February 17, 1936
Issues: Confessions; Due process of law

• This was one of the first cases in which the U.S. Supreme Court held that a state's criminal process had deprived the defendant of due process of law under the Fourteenth Amendment; it paved the way for later cases requiring states to exclude coerced confessions and to provide humane and fair procedures for defendants.

Brown and his two codefendants were tried and convicted of murder in Mississippi in 1934. Confessions had been obtained from them by deputy sheriffs and jailers by means of torture. They were repeatedly hanged until nearly dead and then flogged unmercifully with a leather strap with buckles on it. After initially denying their guilt they confessed, adjusting or changing their statements until these had been provided in the exact form demanded by the deputies. After being allowed to recuperate for a day, they were put through the farce of repeating these confessions to witnesses. On the basis of the confessions alone, the defendants were convicted of murder and condemned to death. Although the deputies and others who had participated in the whippings freely admitted to the fact on the witness stand, the trial judge and later the Mississippi Supreme Court refused to reverse the convictions. The defendants appealed to the U.S. Supreme Court.

Under the Fourteenth Amendment, states are forbidden to "deprive any person of life, liberty, or property without due process of law." At that time this clause had been interpreted to mean that states had to provide a fundamentally fair procedure in criminal cases. Although they could establish their own court policies, the policies could not "offend some principle of liberty and justice so rooted in the traditions of conscience of our people as to be ranked as fundamental."

Under this rule the Supreme Court reversed Brown's conviction. Chief Justice Charles Evans Hughes, writing for a unanimous Court, held that Mississippi could not substitute the rack and torture chamber for the witness stand. The defendants had been deprived of a fundamental aspect of due process of law. Hughes gave short shrift to Mississippi's argument that

Brown's counsel had made a technical procedural error in not asking more clearly to have the confessions suppressed: "The duty of maintaining constitutional rights of a person on trial for his life rises above mere rules of procedure."

Brown v. Mississippi was the first case in which the Supreme Court held that a coerced confession was inadmissible in a state criminal trial. It mirrored *Weeks v. United States* (1914), in which the same rule had been applied to federal trials. In the three decades that followed *Brown*, the rule was broadened to include more and more forms of coercion. This line of cases culminated in 1966 when, in *Miranda v. Arizona*, the Court decided that no confession obtained once a defendant is in custody is admissible unless the defendant has been fully informed of his constitutional rights.

Robert Jacobs

See also *Chambers v. Florida; Miranda v. Arizona; Weeks v. United States.*

BRYANT V. YELLEN

Court: U.S. Supreme Court
Citation: 447 U.S. 352
Date: June 16, 1980
Issues: Environmental issues and animal rights;
Regulation of commerce

- The *Bryant v. Yellen* decision overturned rulings that would have restricted delivery of irrigation water to large landholders in California's Imperial Valley. The decision confirmed the status quo, but it did not address the issue of aridity in California's valleys.

In 1991, California experienced its fifth consecutive dry year in a cycle of drought. Californians were then consuming thirty-five million acre-feet of water annually, and there was a deficiency of nine million acre-feet to be made up from reservoirs and other sources. (An acre-foot of water covers one acre to a depth of one foot.) Emergency restrictions were imposed on the state's cities. Southern California's Metropolitan Water District, which includes Los Angeles, cut its flow to consumers by more than 30 percent. Severe restrictions also affected the heartland of the state's huge agribusinesses, the Central and Imperial valleys. The state's water project stopped delivering water to farmers, and the Central Valley project reduced its deliveries, mostly to farmers, by nearly two-thirds. Californians reported in some polls that the wastage of water ranked second, after crime, as their major concern. Clearly, water could no longer be treated as if it were free.

Much of California, like most of the western United States, is naturally arid. Authors of nineteenth century textbooks guessed correctly when they described much of the vast trans-Mississippi region (even before it was explored in detail) as the "Great American Desert." Eastern and inherited European farming techniques and crops could not be transplanted there successfully.

As a result, from the 1870's to the early twentieth century, congressional, California, and territorial legislation grappled experimentally with the unfolding difficulties posed by the aridity of the West. Irrigation seemed an immediate answer, with the achievements of Utah's Mormon community setting the example. Aridity and irrigation both raised issues that John Wesley Powell, an explorer of the West and later director of the U.S. Geological Survey, sought to unravel in studies of the West and to explain in his prophecies about the limitations of irrigation. Powell's cautionary studies elicited positive responses in California from William Hammond Hall, a California engineer and an advocate of state water control, and from Elwood Mead, who pursued land and water reform during the early twentieth century.

Powell's studies on the nature of the West largely were ignored by California's miners, by its land speculators, by its railroad barons, and by those who dreamed of making the state a commonwealth of small landholders, all of whom were eager to exploit whatever scarce water was available. In Washington, the outcome of trying to satisfy such interests was reflected by the federal government's sale of 610 million acres of public land through the Desert Land Act of 1875, the Timber and Stone Act of 1878, the Carey Act of 1894, and the Newlands Act of 1902. In California, litigation sometimes resulted from water disputes. The most famous case involved Charles Lux and James Ben Ali Haggin and lasted years. Legislation that emerged from further clashes of the state's diverse peoples involved the complex blending and compromise of riparian rights and appropriator rights known as the California Doctrine.

These elements mingled in the legal origins of *Bryant v. Yellen*, decided by the U.S. Supreme Court on June 16, 1980. Retired dentist Ben Yellen and his allies hoped to displace the subsidized agribusinesses that controlled the land and produced the commodities in California's Imperial Valley, and that also consumed the water brought there. Yellen hoped to replace industrial farms with smaller individual farms.

The Issue

The issue before the Court involved application of a general rule of federal reclamation laws that limited delivery of irrigation waters from federal reclamation projects to single-ownership farms smaller than 160 acres. If the rule applied in the Imperial Valley, owners of more than 160 acres would be forced to sell their surplus lands at prices affordable to small farmers, and California's richest agricultural region might be transformed into a bastion of family farms. The Imperial Valley otherwise would remain the preserve of large landholders and agribusinesses.

Until 1929, the privately owned Imperial Irrigation District supplied irrigation water to the valley through its own distribution system. That year, however, the federal Boulder Canyon Project Act (BCPA), which was signed into law in 1928, became effective. Under the BCPA and contracts subsequent to it, the federal government agreed to construct and pay for a new irrigation system drawing water from the Colorado River. In contracting with the Imperial Valley Irrigation District, the government agreed that the provisions of the Colorado River Compact, involving seven western states, left Imperial Valley landowners with their "present perfected rights," unaffected by the 160-acre limitation. Officials of the Department of the Interior sustained that position until 1964, when it was abruptly repudiated. Repudiation at once brought Imperial Valley landowners under provisions of the 1926 Omnibus Adjustment Act, which prohibited delivery of reclamation project waters to one-owner private lands in excess of 160 acres. The repudiation prompted legal battles.

In the Supreme Court's ruling in *Bryant v. Yellen,* Justice Byron White, at times a liberal but more often a strict constructionist legal scholar, rejected the contentions of lower court rulings that would have restricted water rights of large farms. A critical section of the BCPA, White noted, stipulated that project waters were to be applied to irrigation, domestic uses, "and satisfaction of present perfected rights." Before 1929, under California law, the Imperial Valley District had supplied irrigation waters to individual farmers regardless of the size of their landholdings. Moreover, from 1929 until 1964, the Interior Department had made no effort to invoke the 160-acre limitation. Thus, in White's view, the interior secretary's reversal of long-accepted practice ignored "unavoidable limitations" imposed on his authority. Neither state nor federal laws, White concluded, sanctioned the 160-acre limitation on the perfected rights of Imperial Valley landholders.

Significance

The *Bryant v. Yellen* decision legally confirmed the status quo in the Imperial Valley, a garden spot that before irrigation appeared on many maps as the Colorado Desert. The agribusiness saved by the Court was an outgrowth of the BCPA, which after 1932 brought enough Colorado River water to the valley to irrigate 440,000 acres. The prosperity that ensued raised land prices. Most small farmers sold out to wealthy purchasers, creating two classes. One has been described as an elite of large, often absentee, landholders irrigating an average of five hundred acres each, in several cases nearly ten thousand acres. This group has been successfully represented through its numerous associations and its lobbyists in Sacramento and in Washington. The other class, by 1970 one of the nation's most impoverished, was composed chiefly of Chicano or Mexican laborers who maintained irrigation canals and harvested the owners' crops. The status quo thus did nothing to nurture small landholdings or to foster social reform.

What the Supreme Court decreed and agribusiness applauded, nature treated with indifference. The West, California included, remained as arid as ever in affirmation of geographic, geological, and meteorological realities. Irrespective of spectacular public and private efforts, westerners by 1990 were able to irrigate only 69,000 square miles out of millions of dry acres. Even in Utah, where Mormons had pioneered irrigation and paved the way for federal reclamation laws, the limits of assaults on nature were manifest. After heroic labors, only 3 percent of the land had been irrigated. California, despite the construction of twelve hundred dams, the creation of two of the world's largest irrigation projects, and expenditures that spiraled into the billions of dollars, had irrigated about 9,200 of its 156,537 square miles of land area. Some desert had been made to bloom, but not enough even to blemish the complexion of a vast arid region.

A California drought lasting from 1987 to 1992 drew public attention to the issues raised in *Bryant v. Yellen* and to the effects of the status quo in the Imperial Valley and elsewhere. Into the 1980's, the state had continued evasive actions to preclude application of the 160-acre limitation embodied in federal reclamation laws. During the early 1990's, Californians examined their prodigal uses of the West's most essential commodity.

State officials and the public acknowledged that water could no longer be treated as if it were virtually free. Even so, indications were that it cost less for some than for others. About 85 percent of California's water, for example, went to its farmers, mostly agribusinesses, whose products earned revenues of $18 billion a year but constituted only about 3 percent of the state's economy. These farmers, in turn, paid only 10 percent of the cost of their water, about $10 per acre-foot. California's cities paid up to two hundred dollars per acre-foot. Part of the bill fell on taxpayers. Agribusinesses using the Central Valley's federal irrigation system were allowed to pay the Boulder Canyon Project's cost, interest free, over a fifty-year period. With water furnished so cheaply to them, Imperial Valley farmers lacked incentives to conserve. They had pros-

214 • BRYANT V. YELLEN

pered from growing notoriously thirsty crops such as alfalfa, cotton, and rice, each federally subsidized ($400 million annually for rice alone) and each a surplus crop. Few farmers drilled wells, and few tried the economical drip irrigation common in Israel and other dry parts of the world. Few bothered to prevent leakage on their lines and aqueducts.

Some experts argued that California possessed adequate water and that the problem was maldistribution. Most Californians live in the southern portions of the state and most water is in the north. Southern Californians demanded more dams, aqueducts, and canals, although in the 1990's environmental groups posed opposition. Some pointed to the availability of the huge aquifer that underlies the state, estimated in 1991 to contain 850 million acre-feet of water, for which farmers could pay as little as twenty dollars per acre-foot.

Tapping the aquifer at 1990 levels of usage reportedly would exhaust it within decades. Many believed in addition that continuing the subsidization of agribusinesses' surplus crops and cattle, and thereby wasting water, was a recipe for economic and political disaster. Environmentalists refused to support expenditures for new irrigation projects. They regarded water as a finite resource that was being applied to inefficient agriculture to produce nonessential commodities. They opposed further damage to California's landscape and wildlife that would be caused by dam building and by the neutering of the soil resulting from saline deposits from irrigation reservoirs and canals.

Nothing is likely to cure California's or the West's aridity or, in the short term, drastically alter lifestyles. The coincidence in 1991 of prolonged drought and the expiration of many old water contracts favored plans to conserve and to price water realistically. Schemes were proposed to reclaim waste waters and to desalinate seawater. Southern California's Metropolitan Water District allocated $30 million to purchase water from farmers, while Sacramento rice growers were offered $250 an acre to save water by not growing rice. In addition, early in the 1990's the trading of water rights within irrigation projects and between cities and farmers was being explored. In 1991, Los Angeles entered into the Inyo-Los Angeles Long Term Water Agreement to address both water needs and the effects of underground pumping on affected environments. This was followed in 1997 by a Memorandum of Understanding among Los Angeles, Inyo County, the Owens Valley Committee, and the Sierra Club to restore the integrity of the lower Owens River, which had been damaged by overpumping.

Clifton K. Yearley

Further Reading

Beck, Warren A., and David A. Williams. *California: A History of the Golden State.* Garden City, N.Y.: Doubleday, 1972. Standard introduction to the general context of events. Easy to read. Many illustrations and maps. Water problems are dealt with throughout.

Carle, David. *Introduction to Water in California.* Berkeley: University of California Press, 2004. An engaging history of water in California. Maps and many photographs.

Fellmeth, Robert C. *Politics of Land.* New York: Grossman, 1973. An informative, challenging, critical study of the power of California's large landowners and agribusinesses. Detailed tables and abundant appendixes.

Hundley, Norris, Jr. *The Great Thirst: Californians and Water, a History.* Rev. ed. Berkeley: University of California Press, 2001. Fine, informative, well-written scholarship. Essential for a full grasp of the subject. Suggests that changes in Californians' attitudes can help reverse water wastage; others argue nothing can be done to overcome natural aridity. Many photos and maps; valuable index.

Pisani, Donald J. *From the Family Farm to Agribusiness.* Berkeley: University of California Press, 1984. A balanced historical view to 1931 of California water policies, of those who made them, and of failed dreams of a small farmers' commonwealth. Excellent research and writing, enlivened by depiction of many fascinating individuals. Many maps and photos; superb bibliography and index.

Reisner, Marc. *Cadillac Desert: The American West and Its Disappearing Water.* Rev. ed. New York: Penguin Books, 1993. An excellent source for understanding the politics involved in water use in the western states.

See also *Katzenbach v. McClung; Mulford v. Smith; Pennsylvania Coal Co. v. Mahon.*

BUCHANAN V. WARLEY

Court: U.S. Supreme Court
Citation: 245 U.S. 60
Date: November 5, 1917
Issues: Housing discrimination; Private discrimination

• Emphasizing property rights, the U.S. Supreme Court struck down state laws that mandated racial segregation in housing.

Early in the twentieth century, many southern cities enacted ordinances that mandated residential segregation. Louisville, Kentucky, prohibited both African Americans and European Americans from living on blocks where the majority of residents were persons of the other race. The National Association for the Advancement of Colored People arranged a sale of property to test the law. Although the Supreme Court had consistently sanctioned segregation, it ruled unanimously that the Louisville ordinance was unconstitutional. In his opinion for the Court, Justice William R. Day stated that the ordinance was an unreasonable restriction on the liberty of all people to buy and sell property, as protected by the due process clause of the Fourteenth Amendment. The decision showed that the protection of property rights and economic liberty could sometimes have the effect of promoting civil equality.

The *Buchanan v. Warley* decision, however, was of limited impact for two reasons. First, it did not question the constitutionality of de jure racial segregation in areas such as education and transportation. Second, many private citizens began to enter into racially restrictive contracts, which were not rendered unenforceable until *Shelley v. Kraemer* (1948).

Thomas Tandy Lewis

See also *Bolling v. Sharpe; Corrigan v. Buckley; Shelley v. Kraemer.*

BUCK V. BELL

Court: U.S. Supreme Court
Citation: 274 U.S. 200
Date: May 2, 1927
Issues: Medical ethics; Reproductive rights

- This case upheld the authority of states to require sterilization of any person deemed to be mentally defective.

In 1924 the Virginia legislature passed a statute that required the sexual sterilization of many "feebleminded" persons in state mental institutions. The law provided for procedural rights, including a hearing, appointment of a guardian, approval of an institution's board, and appeals to the courts. The superintendent of the Virginia State Colony for Epileptics and Feebleminded recommended sterilization for Carrie Buck, who was classified as feebleminded and a "moral delinquent." Because Buck's mother and daughter were also alleged to be mentally deficient, she was considered an ideal test case for the law. After state courts decided in favor of the state's position, the U.S. Supreme Court upheld the lower court decisions by an 8-1 vote.

Justice Oliver Wendell Holmes, writing the opinion for the majority, found that the law did not violate any principles of equal protection and that its procedural guarantees were more than adequate. Accepting the eugenics notions of the day, Holmes argued that if society could call on its "best citizens" to sacrifice their lives in war, it could "call upon those who already sap the strength of the State for these lesser sacrifices." In this context, he made the notorious statement that "three generations of imbeciles are enough." Holmes had no way of knowing that Carrie Buck's child was the result of a rape and that she had actually done acceptable work in school until withdrawn by her guardians to do housework.

Subsequent to *Buck v. Bell*, many states passed similar sterilization laws, and more than fifty thousand persons were sterilized nationwide. The practice of sterilization, however, was generally discontinued by the 1970's. Although *Buck* was never directly overturned, it was based on eugenics theories later considered invalid and appears inconsistent with several of the Court's decisions upholding reproductive freedom.

Thomas Tandy Lewis

See also *Plyler v. Doe; Skinner v. Oklahoma.*

BUCKLEY V. VALEO

Court: U.S. Supreme Court
Citation: 424 U.S. 1
Date: January 30, 1976
Issues: Political campaigning

• This decision upheld the constitutionality of publicly financed presidential election campaigns while striking down limitations on the amount of money that candidates may spend in their own behalf.

Growing concern over the political influence wielded by large contributors and the potential for corruption that such activities represented led Congress to pass the Federal Election Campaign Act (FECA) in 1971 and to strengthen its provisions substantially in the wake of the Watergate scandal in 1974. The major provisions of the act as amended included the establishment of the Federal Elections Commission (FEC), whose members would be appointed by Congress; restrictions on the amount that individuals or political action committees might contribute to campaigns; restrictions on the amount that candidates or their organizations might spend on campaigns; and provision of public financing of presidential campaigns.

FECA sought to bring about significant changes in the ways political campaigns were financed, and many opposed the act. A challenge to the act was mounted by New York's Republican senator James Buckley. The U.S. Supreme Court took the case as an opportunity to review FECA's constitutionality.

The Court's decision in the case was given in a long and complicated *per curiam* opinion (one not signed by individual justices). Different majorities of justices decided different points of controversy that the law had raised. Ultimately, the decision upheld some parts of the act while invalidating others. The decision had four major points. First, the appointment of the members of the FEC by Congress was held to be an unconstitutional violation of the appointments clause. (This part of the act was subsequently rewritten to provide for appointment by the president.) Second, restrictions on campaign contributions were upheld as a valid exercise of Congress's responsibility to provide for the general welfare. Third, restrictions on expenditures by candidates themselves were struck down as violating their right of free expression. In addition, it was noted that candidates spending their own money were less susceptible to corruption than those dependent on contributions from others. Finally, the decision upheld the provision of public financing of presidential campaigns.

The decision in the *Buckley* case left standing some of the most significant campaign-reform legislation in American history. Nevertheless, the scope of FECA was restricted in important ways. The invalidating of limits on campaign expenditures allowed an advantage to wealthy candidates. The court also found that indirect expenditures in behalf of candidates were not limited by the act. This left an important loophole through which increasing numbers of political action committees could operate.

William C. Lowe

See also *First National Bank of Boston v. Bellotti; McConnell v. Federal Election Commission; Pacific States Telephone and Telegraph Co. v. Oregon.*

BUDD V. NEW YORK

Court: U.S. Supreme Court
Citation: 143 U.S. 517
Date: February 29, 1892
Issues: Judicial review; Regulation of business

- The U.S. Supreme Court reaffirmed that state legislatures had great discretion in regulating businesses "affected with a public interest."

In 1888 the New York legislature passed a statute establishing maximum rates that grain elevators might charge. The Supreme Court had approved similar regulations of large and strategic businesses in *Munn v. Illinois* (1877), but it had ruled that rates of regulatory commissions were subject to judicial review in *Chicago, Milwaukee, and St. Paul Railway Co. v. Minnesota* (1890).

In *Budd*, the justices voted six to three to approve the New York law. State legislatures, in contrast to regulatory commissions, had the authority to decide on the fairness of rates without judicial review. The dissenters argued that the law violated the rights to property and liberty protected by the due process clause of the Fourteenth Amendment. The Court read *Munn* and *Budd* narrowly early in the twentieth century, but legislative discretion was restored during the New Deal period.

Thomas Tandy Lewis

See also *Chicago, Milwaukee, and St. Paul Railway Co. v. Minnesota*; *Legal Tender Cases*; *Munn v. Illinois*; *Nebbia v. New York*; *Wolff Packing Co. v. Court of Industrial Relations*.

BUNTING V. OREGON

Court: U.S. Supreme Court
Citation: 243 U.S. 426
Date: April 9, 1917
Issues: Labor law

- In upholding a state's maximum-hour law, the U.S. Supreme Court weakened but did not overturn the freedom of contract doctrine.

An Oregon law of 1913 established a maximum ten-hour working day for all men and women who worked in factories, mills, and other manufacturing plants. The law required time-and-a-half pay for any additional hours. Bunting, foreman of a mill, was convicted of violating the law. After Louis D. Brandeis was named to the Supreme Court, the National Consumers' League obtained the services of Felix Frankfurter to defend the constitutionality of the law. In *Muller v. Oregon* (1908), the Court had upheld a maximum-hour law for women, but it had stated that such a policy could not be justified if applied to men. By a 5-3 vote, nevertheless, the Court upheld the 1913 law as a reasonable way to preserve the health of workers. Although the majority of the justices were strongly opposed to minimum-wage laws, they approved of the time-and-a-half provision as a penalty designed to discourage overtime work, not as a regulation of wages. Justice Joseph McKenna's opinion for the majority was wholly inconsistent with the reasoning and conclusion of *Lochner v. New York* (1905), but the opinion omitted any reference to *Lochner.* Despite *Bunting,* the Court reaffirmed its commitment to the freedom of contract doctrine in *Adkins v. Children's Hospital* (1923).

Thomas Tandy Lewis

See also *Adkins v. Children's Hospital; Allgeyer v. Louisiana; Lochner v. New York; Muller v. Oregon.*

Burstyn v. Wilson

Court: U.S. Supreme Court
Citation: 343 U.S. 495
Date: May 26, 1952
Issues: Censorship; Freedom of speech

- The U.S. Supreme Court held, for the first time, that films were a medium for expressing ideas and therefore deserved a degree of protection under the First and Fourteenth Amendments.

The film in question, *The Miracle*, was an Italian import that told the story of a peasant girl who, after being seduced by a stranger, gave birth to a son she believed to be Jesus Christ. The New York censors ruled that the film was "sacrilegious," and it was banned from the state. The practice of film censorship had been approved by the Supreme Court in its first ruling on films, *Mutual Film Corp. v. Industrial Commission of Ohio* (1915), which held that films were not covered by any constitutional guarantee of free expression because they were "business pure and simple."

The Court unanimously reversed the 1915 ruling and ruled that the vague concept "sacrilegious" was unacceptable as a standard for prior restraint. Justice Tom C. Clark's opinion for the majority argued that pre-exhibition censorship was justified only in exceptional cases, and that standards must not permit unfettered discretion by censors. Clark acknowledged that films, because of their special potential for harm, might enjoy less First Amendment protection than printed materials, but he refused to discuss whether states had a legitimate interest in censoring pornographic films.

The prerogative of states to engage in film censorship was further restricted in *Roth v. United States* (1957), when the Court narrowly defined obscenity and ruled that any nonobscene expression of ideas was protected by the First and Fourteenth Amendments. In *Freedman v. Maryland* (1965), the Court continued to allow censorship of films but only under stringent procedures that include prompt judicial review.

Thomas Tandy Lewis

See also *Freedman v. Maryland; Mutual Film Corp. v. Industrial Commission of Ohio; Roth v. United States.*

BURTON V. WILMINGTON PARKING AUTHORITY

Court: U.S. Supreme Court
Citation: 365 U.S. 715
Date: April 17, 1961
Issues: Civil rights and liberties; Equal protection of the law

- The U.S. Supreme Court held that a state agency may not lease public property to a private restaurant on terms inconsistent with the equal protection clause of the Fourteenth Amendment.

In *Burton*, the Supreme Court was asked to decide on the constitutionality of a segregated private restaurant located within a parking garage owned and operated by the city. William Burton, an African American, sued the city agency after he was denied service in the restaurant. By a 6-3 vote, the Court found that the city's association with the restaurant was sufficient to make it a party to the discrimination in violation of the Fourteenth Amendment. *Burton* illustrates the willingness of the Court under Chief Justice Earl Warren to expand the definition of state action in support of the Civil Rights movement. The public/private distinction became much less important after the Civil Rights Law of 1964 prohibited racial discrimination in private businesses open to the public. The doctrine of state action, nevertheless, continues to have significance in cases involving private clubs, as in *Moose Lodge v. Irvis* (1972).

Thomas Tandy Lewis

See also *Katzenbach v. McClung; Klopfer v. North Carolina; Moose Lodge v. Irvis; Shelley v. Kraemer.*

Bush v. Gore

Court: U.S. Supreme Court
Citation: 531 U.S. 98
Date: December 12, 2000
Issues: Equal protection of the law; Federalism; Political campaigning;
Voting rights

- By ordering the end to all recounts of Florida's presidential ballots
in the 2000 election, the U.S. Supreme Court in effect decided that
George W. Bush, not Albert Gore, would be the next president.

After votes were counted on the evening of the presidential election of November, 2000, the outcome depended on whether George W. Bush or Albert
Gore would be able to claim the electoral votes of Florida. Although it initially appeared that Bush had probably won the state's popular vote by a few
hundred votes, the Gore campaign demanded manual recounts of ambiguous punch-out ballots in four heavily Democratic counties. They argued that
perhaps fifty thousand of the ballots had not been counted because the
punch-out holes, or chads, were not entirely removed, and that it would nevertheless be possible to discern the voters' intents in many instances. Bush's
legal team, happy with the initial count, naturally tried to prevent all hand
recounts.

The controversy produced a complex series of legal maneuverings. On
November 21, the Florida Supreme Court ordered Florida's Secretary of State
Katherine Harris to include the results of manual recounts as part of the final
tally. After reviewing the order, the U.S. Supreme Court issued *Bush v. Palm
Beach County*, asking unanimously for the Florida court to clarify whether its
order was based on state or federal law. Informed observers understood that
the Court's conservative wing was attempting to establish that the Florida
court had based the order on federal law in violation of Article I, section 2 of
the Constitution, which left the manner of selecting electors to the state legislatures.

On December 8, before responding to the inquiry, the Florida Supreme
Court pleased the Gore camp when it ordered hand recounts to begin in
counties having significant numbers of "undercounted" ballots. In response,
Bush's lawyers petitioned the U.S. Supreme Court for an emergency review.
The next day, the Court issued a 5-4 emergency injunction which stopped the

recount, Justice Antonin Scalia explaining that the recount threatened "irreparable harm" to the country and to Bush's reputation as the legitimately elected president. On December 11, the Court heard oral arguments, and the following day, it announced *Bush v. Gore*, which was a *per curiam* opinion containing two rulings.

The first ruling, based on a 7-2 vote, announced that Florida's recount order was inconsistent with the equal protection principle because it used different standards of counting in different areas without any clear directions on how the chads were to be assessed. The second ruling, based on a 5-4 vote, which reflected the conservative-liberal split on the Court, declared that there was insufficient time to carry out a recount, referring to Florida's legislature's presumed desire to take advantage of the federal "safe harbor" deadline, the date that would ensure that Florida's electoral vote would not be contested. The two justices agreeing with the first ruling but not with the second ruling argued that the case should be remanded to the state court to resolve the equal protection problem. Concurring with both majority rulings, Chief Justice William H. Rehnquist denounced the Florida Supreme Court for substituting its judgment for that of the state legislature.

Dissenting Opinions

Each of the four dissenters of the second ruling wrote separate opinions, arguing that the dispute should have been left up to Florida's court and legislature. Finding that no federal questions were involved, the four liberals suggested that the five-justice majority, who usually defended states' rights, had been motivated by an ideological bias. They noted, moreover, that the Constitution authorized Congress rather than the Court to resolve disputed presidential elections and other political controversies. Judge John Paul Stevens wrote that the legacy of the decision would be a decline in "the Nation's confidence in the judge as an impartial guardian of the rule of law." Many people in the country, especially those sympathetic to the Democratic Party, agreed with this statement.

Bush v. Gore is one of the most controversial rulings in Supreme Court history. Critics have noted that the majority's application of the equal protection clause to demand the same standard for deciding voters' intent was contrary to tradition. A particular weakness was the acknowledgment in the *per curiam* opinion that the requirement for a uniform standard would apply only to the "present circumstances," and that in future elections different standards might be decided in different parts of a state. Despite the Court's disclaimer, it is nevertheless possible that the application of the equal protection principle might again be applied to the way that votes are counted.

Thomas Tandy Lewis

Further Reading

Dershowitz, Alan. *Supreme Injustice: How the High Court Hijacked Election 2000.* New York: Oxford University Press, 2002.

Dworkin, Ronald, ed. *A Badly Flawed Election: Debating Bush v. Gore, the Supreme Court, and American Democracy.* New York: W. W. Norton, 2002.

Gilman, Howard. *The Votes That Counted: How the Courts Decided the 2000 Presidential Election.* Chicago: University of Chicago Press, 2001.

Hasen, Richard L. *The Supreme Court and Election Law: Judging Equality from Baker v. Carr to Bush v. Gore.* New York: New York University Press, 2003.

Ryden, David K. *The U.S. Supreme Court and the Electoral Process.* 2d ed. Washington, D.C.: Georgetown University Press, 2002.

Whitman, Mark, ed. *Florida 2000: A Sourcebook on the Contested Presidential Election.* Boulder, Colo.: Lynn Rienner, 2004.

See also *Buckley v. Valeo; McConnell v. Federal Election Commission.*

BUTLER, UNITED STATES V. *See* UNITED STATES V. BUTLER

BUTZ V. ECONOMOU

Court: U.S. Supreme Court
Citation: 438 U.S. 478
Date: June 29, 1978
Issues: Immunity from prosecution

• The U.S. Supreme Court held that high officials of the executive branch, with rare exceptions, do not have absolute immunity from civil suits.

Economou, a commodities dealer, filed a civil suit for $32 million, claiming that Secretary of Agriculture Earl Butz had entered a false claim against him because of his criticisms of the department's policies. Citing Supreme Court precedents, Butz responded that he had absolute immunity from such a suit.

Speaking for a 5-4 majority, however, Justice Byron R. White declared that executive officials are entitled only to qualified good-faith immunity. Thus, officials are liable for damages if their illegal actions actually deprived a person of clearly established rights or if they acted with malicious intention in an attempt to cause harm or to deprive a person of constitutional rights. The Court allowed for exceptions for prosecutors and judicial officials within administrative agencies.

In *Harlow v. Fitzgerald* (1982), the Court modified the *Economou* ruling by eliminating the malicious intention test as a basis for bringing suits against officials. In *Harlow*'s companion case, *Nixon v. Fitzgerald* (1982), the Court found that the president did have absolute immunity for any actions stemming from his official duties.

Thomas Tandy Lewis

See also *Clinton v. Jones; United States v. Nixon.*

CALDER V. BULL

Court: U.S. Supreme Court
Citation: 3 U.S. 386
Date: August 8, 1798
Issues: Judicial review

- While ruling that the ex post facto limitation did not apply to civil laws, the U.S. Supreme Court's justices debated the concepts of judicial review and natural law.

The Connecticut legislature passed a resolution that granted a new hearing in a probate trial. The disappointed litigants, Calder and his wife, contended that the resolution was an ex post facto law, which was prohibited to the states by the U.S. Constitution. By a 4-0 vote, the Supreme Court concluded that the term "ex post facto" applied only to retroactive criminal laws and not to laws dealing with civil matters. After much controversy, the Court reaffirmed this definition in *Collins v. Youngblood* (1990).

In *Calder*, the justices wrote seriatim opinions, discussing possible ways to decide the case. Justice Samuel Chase denied the "omnipotence" of the legislatures and asserted that "the very nature of our free Republican govern-

Justice James Iredell.
(Albert Rosenthal/
Collection of the
Supreme Court of the
United States)

ments" will override and invalidate laws contrary to fundamental principles of "reason and justice." Justice James Iredell answered that judges did not have any right to invalidate a statute simply because they might consider it "contrary to the principles of natural justice," but he explicitly recognized the duty of the Court to strike down legislative acts that violate the Constitution. Beginning in the 1820's, the Court has assumed the validity of Iredell's theoretical perspective, but the natural law approach has sometimes reappeared, most often in the form of substantive due process.

Thomas Tandy Lewis

See also *Cummings v. Missouri; Fletcher v. Peck; Kansas v. Hendricks.*

CALIFORNIA, UNITED STATES V. *See* UNITED STATES V. CALIFORNIA

CALIFORNIA V. ACEVEDO

Court: U.S. Supreme Court
Citation: 500 U.S. 565
Date: May 30, 1991
Issues: Right to privacy; Search and seizure

- The U.S. Supreme Court held that the police may search either an automobile or a closed container in an automobile without a search warrant provided that the search is supported by probable cause.

The *Acevedo* decision established "one clear-cut rule" for searches of both automobiles and containers within automobiles. After 1925, the Supreme Court had allowed the police to stop and search moving vehicles on probable cause without a search warrant. In *United States v. Chadwick* (1977), however, the Court held that the police needed a warrant to search a sealed container, even when the container was located in an automobile. Then in *United States v. Ross* (1982), the Court allowed the police to search any containers that happened to be located in an automobile that was being searched on the basis of probable cause. The combination of *Chadwick* and *Ross* often confused judges and the police.

When the police observed Charles Acevedo put a brown bag into the trunk of his car, they had probable cause to think that the bag contained marijuana. Although the police had no other justification to search the car, they nevertheless took the bag from the trunk and opened the bag without getting a warrant. California courts, in conformity with *Chadwick*, ruled that the marijuana in the bag could not be used as evidence in a criminal trial. By a 6-3 vote, however, the Supreme Court reversed the *Chadwick* ruling. Justice Harry A. Blackmun's majority opinion argued that the Fourth Amendment's protection of privacy should not depend on "coincidences" such as whether the probable cause referred to the automobile or to the container.

Thomas Tandy Lewis

See also *Carroll v. United States; Harris v. United States; Illinois v. Caballes; Illinois v. Krull; Knowles v. Iowa; United States v. Ross.*

CALIFORNIA V. CABAZON BAND OF MISSION INDIANS

Court: U.S. Supreme Court
Citation: 480 U.S. 202
Date: February 25, 1987
Issues: Native American sovereignty; Treaties

- Based on a combination of federal law and the doctrine of Native American sovereignty, the U.S. Supreme Court held that if a particular kind of gambling is legal within a state, tribes occupying reservations in that state have the right to engage in all legal forms of gambling, and the state has no authority to regulate such activities without a tribe's consent. Based on federal legislation, however, the Court also acknowledged that a tribe does not have the right to engage in any form of gambling that is prohibited by criminal law of the state in which it is based.

The nature of Native American sovereignty is quite complex. Since the 1830's, the Supreme Court has consistently held that the tribes are not independent foreign nations, but rather they are "domestic, dependent nations" that retain "attributes of sovereignty." However, in cases such as *Lone Wolf v. Hitchcock* (1903), the Court has also acknowledged that the U.S. Congress has unlimited power to rescind treaties and place restrictions on tribal sovereignty. Based on the U.S. Constitution's supremacy and commerce clauses, however, state governments do not possess any power to regulate tribal affairs except when explicitly authorized in federal law. In effect, the tribes possess almost complete sovereignty in their relationships with the state governments, but the national government possesses plenary powers to place limitations on that sovereignty.

Public Law 280

In 1953, the U.S. Congress enacted Public Law 280, which authorized the states to take jurisdiction over all criminal offenses committed on Indian reservations. The statute, however, did not give states the right to enforce their civil regulatory laws on Indian lands. In *Bryan v. Itasca County* (1976), the U.S. Supreme Court broadly interpreted the statute and established a test to distinguish between criminal laws and civil regulatory laws. Only activities prohibited by state law belonged in the latter category and were thus enforceable under P.L. 280. As increasing numbers of tribes turned to gaming activities, distinctions between criminal proscription and civil regulatory authority became crucially important.

The small Cabazon and Morongo bands of Mission Indians controlled reservations in Riverside County, California. During the 1980's, both bands were conducting high-stakes bingo games on their reservations. The Cabazon Band also operated a card club for the playing of poker and other card games. These gaming activities were open to the general public, and the majority of the clients were non-Indians. California's laws specifically allowed smaller bingo games when conducted by charitable organizations, and the state did not explicitly criminalize the kinds of games played in the Cabazon Card Club. The activities were generating large sums of money. By 1986, the Cabazon tribe, which had only twenty-five members, grossed $5 million from its bingo hall. State officials took note of the bingo hall's success and began the process of extending its gambling regulations to the reservations. As a justification, the state officials noted that oversight was necessary because games such as high-states bingo risked infiltration by organized crime. The Cabazon Band argued in federal district court that the potential threat of criminal infiltration was not an adequate justification for civil regulations. After both the district court and the court of appeals ruled in favor of the tribes, the state of California appealed the case to the U.S. Supreme Court, which granted *certiorari*.

The Court's Ruling

In its *California v. Cabazon Band of Mission Indians* decision, the Supreme Court justices voted by a 6-3 margin to uphold the lower courts' rulings. In the official opinion for the majority, Justice Byron White concluded that "California regulates rather than prohibits gambling in general and bingo in particular," and he argued that neither Public Law 280 nor the Organized Crime Control Act of 1970 authorized the state to regulate noncriminal activities on federally recognized Indian land. The state's interest in preventing crime, moreover, did not justify state regulations that would "impermissibly infringe on tribal government." White explained that the majority decision was made in the light of traditional notions of Indian sovereignty and the congressional goal of Indian self-government, including the "overriding goal of encouraging tribal self-sufficiency and economic development."

In a strong dissent, Justice John Paul Stevens took issue with much of White's analysis. In particular, he noted that California law permitted only bingo games to be operated by nonprofit charitable organizations, and that none of these organizations were allowed to conduct high-stakes bingo games.

He found it disingenuous for White to argue "that the operation of high-stakes bingo games does not run afoul of California's public policy because the State permits some forms of gambling and, specifically, some forms of bingo." Likewise, he pointed out that the state did not authorize any other groups to maintain card clubs like the Cabazon enterprise.

The *Cabazon* decision created significant concerns in states that contained recognized Indian territory, except for the states of Utah and Hawaii, which were unaffected because they criminalized all forms of gambling. In 1988, Congress responded with the Indian Gaming Regulatory Act, which modified *Cabazon* by distinguishing among three categories of gambling and establishing the National Indian Gaming Commission to regulate all forms of gambling except for traditional Indian games. The statute supported tribal interests by requiring states that allowed legal casino-type gambling to negotiate compacts in good faith for the creation of Indian casinos. As a result of *Cabazon* and the Indian Gaming Regulatory Act, gambling casinos soon developed into economic windfalls for many tribes, particularly those with small memberships that were located near large cities, such as the Shakopee Mdewakanton Sioux tribe, which is located near Minneapolis. In 2004, 228 tribes in thirty states were operating 367 casinos and bingo halls that earned an estimated $19.6 billion. However, these casinos provided little help to large and impoverished tribes located in more isolated regions.

Thomas Tandy Lewis

Further Reading

Duthu, N. Bruce. *American Indians and the Law.* New York: Penguin Books, 2008. Concise and accessible summary of Native American law, including a useful summary of the court decisions relevant to modern casinos.

Eadington, William, ed. *Indian Gaming and the Law.* Reno, Nev.: Institute for the Study of Gambling and Commercial Gaming, 1998. Helpful collection of essays and documents, with readable introductions.

Fromson, Brett. *Hitting the Jackpot: The Inside Story of the Richest Indian Tribe in History.* New York: Atlantic Monthly Press, 2003. The fascinating story of how the tiny Mashantucket Pequot tribe of Connecticut gained legal recognition and used a gigantic casino to become the most prosperous tribe in U.S. history.

Kallen, Stuart, ed. *Indian Gaming.* Farmington, Conn.: Greenhaven Press, 2005. Small volume that includes a selection from primary and secondary sources expressing a variety of perspectives.

Light, Steven Andrew, and Kathryn R. L. Rand. *Indian Gaming and Tribal Sovereignty: The Casino Compromise.* Lawrence: University Press of Kansas, 2005. Concise description of the contemporary gaming industry, with recommendations for tribal and governmental policymakers that can help promote shared goals while recognizing tribal sovereignty.

Rand, Kathryn R. L., and Steven Andrew Light. *Indian Gaming Law: Cases and Materials*. Durham, N.C.: Carolina Academic Press, 2008. Comprehensive casebook that includes the laws and court cases that resulted in a very prosperous industry.

See also *Cherokee Cases; Ex parte Crow Dog; Johnson and Graham's Lessee v. McIntosh; Lone Wolf v. Hitchcock; Santa Clara Pueblo v. Martinez; United States v. Kagama; Worcester v. Georgia.*

CALIFORNIA V. GREENWOOD

Court: U.S. Supreme Court
Citation: 486 U.S. 35
Date: May 16, 1988
Issues: Illegal drugs; Police powers; Right to privacy; Search and seizure

- This case expanded the ability of all levels of law-enforcement bodies to conduct searches, without judicial warrants, for things in which persons are considered to have no reasonable expectation of privacy—such as garbage left out for collection.

In 1984, police in Laguna Beach, California, received information that a man named Billy Greenwood was selling drugs out of his home. However, there was not sufficient evidence for the police to obtain a warrant to search Greenwood's home. Consequently, the police asked the local trash collection company to turn over to them garbage they collected from Greenwood's house.

Greenwood was in the habit of leaving his garbage in opaque plastic bags at the curbside in front of his house. When officers searched the bags that had been collected at this house, they found evidence of illegal drug use. Citing that evidence, they obtained a warrant to search Greenwood's house, in which they found hard evidence of drug trafficking and then arrested Greenwood. While Greenwood was out on bail, officers searched his garbage again, found more incriminating evidence, obtained a second search warrant, and eventually arrested Greenwood on additional charges.

During Greenwood's ensuing criminal trial, the court found that the searches of his trash bags without a warrant were illegal. Without the evidence obtained from the trash, there would have been no probable cause to obtain the search warrants. Therefore, under what is known as the "fruit of the poisonous tree" doctrine, the warrants were invalid, and the charges against Greenwood were dropped. The state of California then appealed the decision to a higher court but lost. The state's own supreme court did not agree to hear the case, but the U.S. Supreme Court did because the case touched on an issue of broad national importance.

In previous cases, the Supreme Court had held that the Fourth Amendment to the U.S. Constitution requires police to obtain search warrants when subjects of their investigations have a "reasonable expectation of privacy" in the places or items to be searched. In *Katz v. United States* (1967), for example, the Court had held that a person had a reasonable expectation of privacy in the content of a phone conversation he had conducted in a public phone booth.

In the *Greenwood* case, the defendant argued that he had a reasonable expectation of privacy in the contents of his trash bags. Although the opaque bags were placed on a public street, Greenwood argued that he did not suppose that anyone was likely to inspect the contents of those bags. He assumed that, as always, his trash would be picked up by the trash company and mingled with that of his neighbors. However, a majority of justices on the Supreme Court ruled that while Greenwood might have expected that his garbage was private, that was not a *reasonable* expectation, as anyone—"animals, children, scavengers, [or] snoops"—could have gone through the contents of his trash bags after he placed them on the curb. The Court's ruling in his case, therefore, narrowed the range of searches for which law-enforcement officers had to obtain search warrants, thereby making it easier to collect evidence.

Phyllis B. Gerstenfeld

Further Reading

Kennedy, Caroline, and Ellen Alderman. *The Right to Privacy*. New York: Vintage, 1997.

Sykes, Charles. *The End of Privacy: The Attack on Personal Rights at Home, at Work, On-Line, and in Court*. New York: St. Martin's Griffin, 2000.

See also *Bivens v. Six Unknown Named Agents; Boyd v. United States; California v. Acevedo; Carroll v. United States; Katz v. United States; Knowles v. Iowa*.

CANTWELL V. CONNECTICUT

Court: U.S. Supreme Court
Citation: 310 U.S. 296
Date: May 30, 1940
Issues: Freedom of religion

- The U.S. Supreme Court broadly interpreted the religious exercise clause of the First Amendment and held that the clause was applicable to the states through the Fourteenth Amendment.

Newton Cantwell, an active member of the Jehovah's Witnesses, went door to door trying to make converts. A few people complained about his diatribes against the Roman Catholic Church. Cantwell was arrested and convicted for violating a state law that required a license for soliciting funds.

By a 9-0 vote, the Supreme Court reversed the conviction and invalidated the law. Justice Owen J. Roberts's opinion for the Court emphasized that the Constitution protected religious conduct such as proselytizing. He wrote that a state may reasonably regulate the time, place, and manner of activities to prevent fraud or disorder, but it cannot entirely forbid unpopular conduct. The Connecticut law constituted a form of religious censorship because it gave public officials excessive discretion for approving or rejecting applications for licenses.

Thomas Tandy Lewis

See also *Brown v. Mississippi; Cox v. New Hampshire; Lovell v. City of Griffin; Murdock v. Pennsylvania; Reynolds v. United States; West Virginia State Board of Education v. Barnette.*

CAROLENE PRODUCTS CO., UNITED STATES V. *See* UNITED STATES V. CAROLENE PRODUCTS CO.

CARROLL V. UNITED STATES

Court: U.S. Supreme Court
Citation: 267 U.S. 132
Date: March 2, 1925
Issues: Search and seizure

- The U.S. Supreme Court held that the Fourth Amendment permits the police to stop and search a vehicle without a warrant when there is probable cause that it contains illegal contraband.

Based on a combination of circumstances, federal agents had reason to think that George Carroll was illegally transporting liquor in his automobile. Following a chase, the agents searched his automobile without a warrant and found bottles of liquor concealed in the back seat. After Carroll's conviction, his lawyers argued that the evidence should have been excluded from his trial because it violated the requirements of the Fourth Amendment.

By a 6-2 margin, the Supreme Court rejected the claim. Speaking for the majority, Chief Justice William H. Taft wrote that the U.S. legal tradition had long accepted a distinction between stationary buildings and means of transportation such as boats or automobiles, in which mobility often made it impractical for the police to secure a warrant. At the same time, Taft insisted that the Fourth Amendment prohibited all "unreasonable searches and seizures." Trying to reconcile these two considerations, he wrote that the police must not stop and search highway travelers unless there is probable cause that the vehicles are carrying contraband.

Carrol's so-called "automobile exception" is well established. Since the 1970's, however, the Court had to decide many difficult questions about the implications and limits of the decision. In *California v. Carney* (1985), for example, the Court held that a motor home, unless situated in a residential location, falls under the *Carroll* ruling.

Thomas Tandy Lewis

See also *California v. Acevedo; Harris v. United States; Illinois v. Caballes; Illinois v. Krull; Knowles v. Iowa; New York v. Belton; United States v. Ross; Whren v. United States.*

CARTER V. CARTER COAL CO.

Court: U.S. Supreme Court
Citation: 298 U.S. 238
Date: May 18, 1936
Issues: Regulation of business

• The decision declared unconstitutional the chief provisions of the Bituminous Coal Conservation Act of 1935 and helped provoke the "Court-packing" controversy.

When the National Industrial Recovery Act of 1933, a New Deal program, was held unconstitutional in 1935, Congress attempted to reenact parts of the program for individual industries to relieve the impact of the economic depression. The [Guffey] Bituminous Coal Act of August, 1935, created the Bituminous Coal Commission to help formulate and administer a Bituminous Coal Code. The country was divided into twenty-three districts, each with a board, including representatives of management and labor. These organizations were empowered to fix minimum prices for coal and to negotiate

Editorial cartoon from the March 24, 1937, San Francisco Chronicle ridiculing President Franklin D. Roosevelt's effort to put into effect his New Deal programs. (FDR Library)

labor provisions limiting hours of work and setting minimum wages. Coal producers were subjected to a 15 percent sales tax, 90 percent of which would be refunded to producers who accepted the code. The goal was to raise the market price of coal and thereby to enable coal producers to pay higher wages.

A number of lawsuits were initiated to block payment of the tax and adherence to the codes. These were consolidated on *certiorari* from federal district and appellate courts. The U.S. Supreme Court decision thus involved several cases, though it is best known for the first, namely *Carter.*

The Court's decision closely resembled that in *Schechter Poultry Corp. v. United States* (1935). Delegation of code-drafting authority to representatives of industry and labor was held to be improper. Neither the production and sale of coal nor the employment of labor in the mines constituted interstate commerce: "Production is a purely local activity." Granting the hardships faced by coal miners, "the evils are all local evils over which the federal government has no legislative control."

The *Carter* case, with the better-known *Schechter* case and *United States v. Butler* (1936), placed the Supreme Court squarely in opposition to measures which President Franklin D. Roosevelt considered central to his program for economic recovery. The Court came under heavy criticism. After President Roosevelt's landslide reelection in 1936, he proposed a number of "reforms" which would have enabled him to appoint new Supreme Court justices. The proposal aroused a storm of protests and was withdrawn, but the Court gave way to the political pressures of the times. The decision in *National Labor Relations Board v. Jones & Laughlin Steel Corp.* (1937) essentially reversed the *Carter* position regarding labor relations. The restrictive view of the commerce clause with regard to commodities was removed in *United States v. Darby Lumber Co.* (1941) and *Wickard v. Filburn* (1942).

Congress passed a second Bituminous Coal Act in 1937 with provisions very similar to those of 1935. The detailed labor provisions of the 1935 law were omitted, and the authority of the commission was clarified. It remained in effect until August, 1943.

Paul B. Trescott

See also *Panama Refining Co. v. Ryan; Schechter Poultry Corp. v. United States; United States v. Butler; United States v. Darby Lumber Co.; United States v. Lopez; Wickard v. Filburn.*

CHAMBERS V. FLORIDA

Court: U.S. Supreme Court
Citation: 309 U.S. 227
Date: February 12, 1940
Issues: Confessions

- This case established that confessions elicited by compulsion short of actual physical duress cannot be used in state criminal proceedings.

In May, 1933, an elderly white man was murdered in Pompano, Florida. Within the next twenty-four hours, twenty-five to forty black men were arrested. Isaiah Chambers and three others were questioned by relays of law-enforcement officers and deputies continuously for the next five days. There were two all-night sessions. During this period they were not permitted to consult counsel or to see family or friends. On the fifth day they confessed. Although Florida admitted that they had been held incommunicado, there was considerable dispute whether physical force had been used against the four defendants. The Florida state courts found that all allegations of physical coercion were false and that the confessions were therefore admissible. On the basis of the confessions, Chambers and his codefendants were convicted and sentenced to death.

The U.S. Supreme Court unanimously reversed the convictions. At that time the only relevant precedent was *Brown v. Mississippi* (1936). In that case the Court reversed a conviction based on a confession which had been obtained by torture. Forced by jurisdictional rules to accept the Florida state court findings that Chambers and the others had not been tortured, the Court nevertheless held the convictions invalid. Justice Hugo L. Black wrote the Court's opinion. He stated that the circumstances by which the confessions had been obtained rendered them involuntary even though physical coercion may not have been applied.

Justice Black focused on incommunicado interrogation. The defendants had been questioned for five days; they were held at the will of their jailers without formal charges having been brought against them. They were terrified: "[T]he haunting fear of mob violence was around them in an atmosphere charged with excitement and public indignation." They had no opportunity to consult friends or family. Once they did confess, the interrogators insisted that they redo the confessions so as to conform their words to the physical facts of the crime. Black insisted that the confessions were compelled, not voluntary, and consequently they were inadmissible.

In the immediate sense, *Chambers v. Florida* establishes that compulsion that stops short of physical coercion can still render a confession invalid. It prevents incommunicado and protracted interrogation of criminal suspects. In the broader development of American criminal procedure, this case is an important precursor of *Miranda v. Arizona* (1966), which requires law-enforcement officers to obtain a knowing waiver of a potential defendant's right to remain silent in situations of custodial interrogation.

Robert Jacobs

See also *Arizona v. Fulminante; Brown v. Mississippi; Escobedo v. Illinois; Harris v. New York; Massiah v. United States; Minnick v. Mississippi; Miranda v. Arizona.*

CHAMPION V. AMES

Court: U.S. Supreme Court
Citation: 188 U.S. 321
Date: February 23, 1903
Issues: Admiralty law; Regulation of commerce

- The U.S. Supreme Court, through its broad interpretation of the commerce clause in the case of *Champion v. Ames*, sustained federal powers to prohibit and regulate commerce.

In 1903, the U.S. Supreme Court upheld the federal government's potential to prohibit or restrict commerce. The case of *Champion v. Ames*, also known as the *Lottery Case*, altered the delineation between interstate and intrastate commerce under Article I, section 8, clause 3, of the U.S. Constitution, the so-called commerce clause.

The circumstances brought before the Court originated in 1895 with an act of Congress. This act made it illegal to transport or conspire to transport lottery tickets from state to state. On February 1, 1899, C. F. Champion sent two Pan-American Lottery Company lottery tickets from Dallas, Texas, to Fresno, California. The tickets were transported by a vehicle owned by the Wells-Fargo Express Company. Champion was arrested in Chicago under a warrant based on his alleged violation of the act and was subsequently convicted.

The case was appealed to the U.S. Supreme Court for final review, and on February 23, 1903, the Court upheld the conviction in a 5-4 decision. Justice John Marshall Harlan delivered the majority opinion of the Court, and Chief Justice Melville W. Fuller wrote the dissenting opinion.

When the *Lottery Case* appeared before the Court, the power to regulate interstate commerce was a concurrent power shared by the states and the federal government. Prior to the *Lottery Case*, several Court decisions had begun the process of liberalizing the connotation of "interstate," favoring federal control. One such case was *Gibbons v. Ogden* (1824). This decision played a major role in the Court's final disposition of the *Lottery Case* by initiating a method for analyzing commerce issues. A review of the facts in Gibbons shows that the state of New York granted a monopoly to Robert Livingston and Robert Fulton in the operation of steamboats in the waterways of New York. Under the monopoly, Aaron Ogden managed two licensed steamboats that ferried between New York and New Jersey. Thomas Gibbons obtained a coasting license under a 1793 act of Congress and began competing with Ogden.

The Court's Ruling

Gibbons's steamboat was not licensed to operate under the New York monopoly. The pressure of additional competition encouraged Ogden to bring action in a New York court to prohibit Gibbons from operating. Writing for the majority in Gibbons, Chief Justice John Marshall delivered the opinion of the Supreme Court, which held the New York monopoly law to be unconstitutional. In *Gibbons*, the Court aspired to denote interstate commerce. Gibbons's attorneys argued that interstate commerce is traffic to buy and sell, or the interchange of commodities. The Court agreed that interstate commerce includes traffic but added the notion of intercourse.

Generally, the term "intercourse" connotes exchange between persons or groups. With this notion, the Court reasoned that interstate commerce does not end at external boundary lines between states but may be introduced into the interior. The justices determined that commerce may pass the jurisdictional line of New York and act upon the waters to which the monopoly law applied, thus concluding that the transportation of passengers between New York and New Jersey constituted interstate commerce.

In the *Champion v. Ames* decision, the Court went on to reference other decisions that sanction federal authority. These cases continued to expand the essence of interstate commerce. Consequently, the Court resolved that commerce embraces navigation, intercourse, communication, traffic, the transit of persons, and the transmission of messages by telegraph.

In the *Lottery Case*, the use of a vehicle from Wells-Fargo Express traveling from state to state was relevant. The Court held that this travel provided sufficient intercourse with interstate commerce to allow federal domination. Further, the Court viewed the congressional justification for the creation of the act as being rational. It determined that the federal government is the proper means for protecting U.S. citizens from the widespread pestilence of lotteries. The Court deemed that such an evil act of appalling character, carried through interstate commerce, deserves federal intervention.

In his dissenting opinion, Chief Justice Fuller asserted that the Court had imposed a burden on the state's powers to regulate for the public health, good order, and prosperity of its citizens. To hold that Congress has general police power would be to defeat the operation of the Tenth Amendment. This argument would constitute the foundation of many later dissenting opinions. This particular conviction never became the majority view.

At the time of the *Lottery Case*, an escalating struggle was taking place between a desire for a strong federal government, called federalism or nationalism, and the states' right to regulate themselves. This conflict goes as far back in U.S. history as the Constitution itself. After the Revolutionary War, the states regarded themselves as independent sovereigns. The Articles of Confederation allowed only minimal intrusion into states' internal affairs by the Continental Congress.

Faced with the inability of the confederation to function properly, provincial patriotism had to concede. The delegates at the Constitutional Convention, in an effort to fabricate a more concentrated federal government, made many compromises. They maintained within the Constitution, however, certain seemingly insurmountable limits on the federal government. As a consequence, the judiciary generally discerns the Constitution as being a limitation on federal power. Without an expressed or implied grant of authority from within the Constitution, the federal government cannot regulate.

This policy is not easily implemented in cases concerning commerce. Under the commerce clause, Congress has the authority to regulate commerce with foreign nations and among the several states and with Native Americans. The commerce clause seems to conflict with the Tenth Amendment, which assigns all rights to the states unless such control is prohibited or delegated to the U.S. government by the Constitution. The Tenth Amendment is said to contain the states' police powers. Further, the Constitution does not expressly exclude states from regulating interstate commerce. It simply limits the federal government's jurisdiction over interstate trade and precludes interference with purely local activities.

To add another complication, consider the Constitution's supremacy clause, Article VI, paragraph 2. This states that if legitimate state and federal powers are in conflict, then the national interest will prevail. This power is enhanced by the Court's broad interpretation of the "necessary and proper clause" (Article I, section 8) in *McCulloch v. Maryland* (1819). This ruling gave Congress a discretionary choice of means for implementing implied powers.

From a political perspective, it is notable that both the McCulloch and Gibbons cases came before the Court while John Marshall was chief justice. Marshall served under President John Adams as the secretary of state and was a devout federalist. During Marshall's tenure as chief justice, the Court vested within its jurisdiction an unusual allotment of power. It assigned to itself final interpretation rights over the constitutionality of all federal and state laws brought before the Court.

Significance

The ruling in the *Lottery Case* had an immediate influence on U.S. society. Social reformers quickly seized on the rationale provided by the Court and began prompting Congress to regulate. In 1906, Senator Albert J. Beveridge of Indiana successfully proposed a meat inspection amendment to an appropriations bill. The amendment, which prohibited the interstate shipment of meats that had not been federally inspected, received an influential recommendation from President Theodore Roosevelt. Additionally, Upton Sinclair's novel *The Jungle* (1906) greatly intensified popular support for Beveridge's cause. In this novel, Sinclair, an active socialist, characterized the life of a worker in the Chicago stockyards in such a compelling manner that President Roosevelt was induced to investigate the meatpacking industry. During the same term, Congress also approved the Pure Food and Drug Act.

Later, Beveridge proposed another bill based on the commerce clause. This legislation attempted to exclude from commerce goods produced by child labor. Beveridge was certain that the *Lottery Case* settled the constitutionality of his proposal, but convincing his colleagues of this proved to be arduous and unsuccessful. Congress finally passed the Child Labor Act in 1916, but the Court declared it unconstitutional in *Hammer v. Dagenhart* (1918). It would be another decade before such a law would be held valid under constitutional scrutiny by the Court.

Despite this setback, the precedent established in the *Lottery Case* was adequate to sustain a wide variety of laws intended to limit the movement of harmful goods. During the early twentieth century, the Court upheld the exclusion from interstate commerce of impure foods, white slavery (involuntary prostitution), obscene literature, and articles designed for indecent and immoral use.

With only some antithesis, the Court continued to reform the meaning of interstate commerce to enhance federal control. A greatly extended application of the clause can be found in *Heart of Atlanta Motel v. United States* (1964). This case implicated the constitutionality of Title II of the Civil Rights Act of 1964. The act strives to eliminate racial discrimination in hotels, motels, restaurants, and similar places. The owners of the Heart of Atlanta Motel disputed the constitutionality of the act. It was the motel's policy to refuse lodging to people of color. It advertised in several surrounding states, and approximately 75 percent of its guests were from other states.

The Court upheld the constitutionality of the act. The tests employed by the Court were whether the activity is commerce that concerns more than one state and whether the act showed a substantial relation to a national interest. The Court postulated that the operation of a motel might appear local in nature, but it does affect interstate commerce. The Court resolved that a motel accommodating interstate travelers is engaged in commerce that concerns more than one state.

Again, as in the *Lottery Case*, the Court determined that the evil averted by the act was a legitimate national concern. The rationale offered by the Court in *Heart of Atlanta Motel* exhibits the accumulation of many years of precedents. The Court asserted that the same interest that led Congress to deal with segregation prompted it to control gambling, criminal enterprises, deceptive practices in the sale of products, fraudulent security transactions, improper branding of drugs, wages and hours, members of labor unions, crop control, discrimination against shippers, the protection of small business from injurious price cutting, and resale price maintenance at terminal restaurants. The Court affirmed that Congress, in many of these examples, was regulating against moral wrongs. It concluded that segregation is a valid moral issue that would support the enactment of the Civil Rights Act.

The Court has applied various constitutional tests to interstate commerce throughout its history. Initially, the Court viewed interstate commerce as physical movement between states. Soon it began examining federal jurisdiction based on the direct versus indirect influences of the law in questions on interstate commerce. By the middle of the twentieth century, the Court began examining whether the purely local activity had an appreciable effect on interstate commerce.

Another offspring of the commerce clause is the Interstate Commerce Commission (ICC). The ICC consists of experts who aspire to protect and represent the public in matters of transportation in interstate commerce. This agency has immense powers and is not without its opponents.

The need to unite the country necessitated a strong centralized government, but debates persist over the effects ensuing from the expanding role of the federal bureaucracy. Some critics perceive the federal government as an inadequate regulator of business, particularly in the area of environmental protection. Other commentators reason that businesses have become dependent on the government as a form of protection from competition. Still others assert that business enterprises cannot mature and flourish because of excessive government control.

The judiciary appears to recognize one conspicuous restriction on the federal government's authority. Regardless of how significant the legal arguments are, most courts hesitate to make decrees that will prohibit major industries from operating. In addition, certain potentially negative economic effects, such as the loss of many jobs, particularly in the automotive, steel, and oil industries, act as subtle legal shields from overly zealous government intrusion.

Brian J. Carroll

Further Reading

Amar, Akhil Reed. *America's Constitution: A Biography.* New York: Random House, 2005. Examines in turn each article of the Constitution and explains how the Framers drew on English models, existing state constitutions, and other sources in structuring the three branches of the federal government and in defining the relationship of that government to the states.

Breyer, Stephen. *Active Liberty: Interpreting Our Democratic Constitution.* New York: Alfred A. Knopf, 2005. In this book, which is based on the Tanner Lectures on Human Values that he delivered at Harvard University in November, 2004, Stephen Breyer, associate justice of the United States, defines the term "active liberty" as a sharing of the nation's sovereign authority with its citizens. He argues that the Constitution is a guide for the application of basic principles to a changing society rather than a rigid legal means for restricting that society. Presents examples in the areas of free speech, federalism, privacy, affirmative action, statutory interpretation, and administrative law.

Cox, Archibald. *The Court and the Constitution.* Boston: Houghton Mifflin, 1987. A well-organized approach to major Court decisions. The author was a former solicitor general and the first Watergate special prosecutor. He details how the Court has kept the Constitution an important instrument.

Fellmeth, Robert C. *The Interstate Commerce Omission.* New York: Grossman, 1970. Presents an encompassing view of the problems haunting the Interstate Commerce Commission. The Center for Study of Responsive Law produced the report, and Ralph Nader wrote the introduction.

Gunther, Gerald. *Cases and Materials on Constitutional Law.* 10th ed. Mineola, N.Y.: Foundation Press, 1980. A well-written textbook that discusses the immense area of constitutional law. The text has remarkable depth but has a tendency to ask more questions than it answers. Provides a superior foundation in beginning constitutional research.

Hilsman, Roger. *To Govern America.* New York: HarperCollins, 1979. An admirable compilation of data describing all features of government, including many peripheral aspects, such as philosophy and the future of American democracy.

Mason, Alpheus T., and Donald Grier Stephenson, Jr. *American Constitutional Law: Introductory Essays and Selected Cases.* 12th ed. Englewood Cliffs, N.J.: Prentice Hall, 1998. A commendable review and analysis of constitutional law. The authors present this complex subject in a clear manner.

Tindall, George B. *America: A Narrative History.* 5th ed. New York: W. W. Norton, 1999. A constricted narrative that shapes U.S. history into an eventful story. Presents history organized in themes such as "judicial nationalism."

See also *Gibbons v. Ogden; Hammer v. Dagenhart; Heart of Atlanta Motel v. United States; McCulloch v. Maryland.*

CHAPLINSKY V. NEW HAMPSHIRE

Court: U.S. Supreme Court
Citation: 315 U.S. 568
Date: March 9, 1942
Issues: Freedom of speech

• The U.S. Supreme Court upheld a man's conviction for derisive speech of name-calling in public, reasoning that "fighting words" were not subject to First Amendment protection.

Writing for a unanimous Supreme Court, Justice Frank Murphy upheld a state statute under which the defendant was convicted for calling a city marshal a "racketeer" and "fascist" and referring to other officials as "agents of fascists." The relevant state law prohibited derisive speech or name calling in public. Murphy created a two-tier theory of free speech protection in which certain "well-defined and narrowly limited" types of speech do not have First Amendment protection. "Fighting words" as well as lewd, profane, obscene, and libelous words fell outside the boundaries of constitutional protection because they did not represent a free speech value such as the search for truth.

Justice Frank Murphy in 1940, shortly after joining the Supreme Court. (Harris & Ewing Collection/Library of Congress)

Although *Chaplinsky* was never overturned and the two-tier theory remains valid regarding business advertising, public swearing, and pornography, the thrust of this decision has been considerably narrowed. Libelous publications are judged by the standards set in *New York Times Co. v. Sullivan* (1964), and verbal challenges to police officers enjoy constitutional protection, so *Chaplinsky* is only a shell of its former self.

Richard L. Wilson

See also *Cohen v. California; New York Times Co. v. Sullivan; Terminiello v. Chicago; Tinker v. Des Moines Independent Community School District; United States v. O'Brien; Whitney v. California.*

CHARLES RIVER BRIDGE V. WARREN BRIDGE

Court: U.S. Supreme Court
Citation: 11 Pet. (36 U.S.) 420
Date: February 12, 1837
Issues: Freedom of contract; Property rights

- In holding that only clear and explicit terms of contracts were legally binding, the U.S. Supreme Court increased the power of state legislatures to regulate private corporations.

Under Chief Justice John Marshall's leadership, the Supreme Court had used a broad construction of the contract clause to protect vested rights in private property. *Charles River Bridge v. Warren Bridge* demonstrated that Chief Justice Roger Brooke Taney and his colleagues wanted to give state legislatures greater latitude in formulating economic policy.

In 1785 the Massachusetts legislature had granted the Charles River Bridge Company a charter to build and operate a toll bridge between Boston and Cambridge. In 1828 the legislature authorized the Warren River Bridge Company to erect a second bridge that would eventually become toll-free. The Charles River Bridge Company sought an injunction against construction of the new bridge on the grounds that the older charter implied the company's exclusive right to operate a bridge at that location during the life of the charter. The issue was whether the Court would make a broad or a narrow interpretation of the charter under the contract clause.

By a 4-3 margin, the Court rejected the company's claim. Writing for the Court, Taney held that legislative charters must be interpreted literally and that charters did not convey any implied corporate privileges. Unless restrained by explicit language in a charter, state legislatures were free to make reasonable regulations and to authorize new projects for the public good. With his distrust of monopolistic power, Taney did not want vested property rights to get in the way of innovation and progress. However, he did not reject the idea that the contract clause required legislatures to honor the explicit terms of their charters. In a strongly worded dissent, Justice Joseph Story accused the majority of diminishing protection for property rights and contended that lawmakers should be required to respect implied promises in charters.

The *Charles River Bridge* decision reflected and encouraged a new emphasis on competition within the capitalistic system. Under Taney, however, the Court did not at all abandon the contract clause. In *Bronson v. Kinzie* (1843), for example, the Court overturned debtor-relief legislation as an unconstitutional abrogation of contracts.

Thomas Tandy Lewis

See also *Bronson v. Kinzie; Fletcher v. Peck; Home Building and Loan Association v. Blaisdell; Powell v. Alabama; Providence Bank v. Billings.*

CHEROKEE CASES

CHEROKEE NATION V. GEORGIA

Court: U.S. Supreme Court
Citation: 5 Pet. (30 U.S.) 1
Date: March 18, 1831

WORCESTER V. GEORGIA

Court: U.S. Supreme Court
Citation: 31 U.S. 515
Date: March 3, 1832
Issues: Land law; Native American sovereignty; Treaties

• Although these two U.S. Supreme Court rulings on cases involving the Cherokees and the state of Georgia had little practical impact on those cases, they would serve to limit the sovereignty of all Native American tribes by placing them under federal protection.

In 1823, the U.S. Supreme Court made its first notable ruling that helped to define the relationship between the federal government and Native Americans. *Johnson v. McIntosh,* the case then under review, concerned disputed land titles. The Court ruled that the federal government was, in effect, the ultimate landlord over Native Americans, who were thus the government's tenants. Chief Justice John Marshall and the Court majority thus ruled that the

Artist Robert Lindneux's 1942 somewhat fanciful painting Trail of Tears depicts the arduous removal of Cherokee and other Native American societies during the 1830's. (Woolaroc Museum, Bartlesville, Oklahoma)

federal government was responsible for Native American affairs, including the protection of Native American peoples against state actions, which often materially affected Native American lives and property.

The Supreme Court considered the *Johnson* case at a time when the federal government and the states were locked in disputes about where the U.S. Constitution intended ultimate sovereignty to reside. Federal authority seemed unsure, and Georgia contemplated removing its Cherokee and Creek peoples from the northern and western portions of the state. To legitimate its plans, Georgia charged that when it had agreed, in 1802, to cede its western land claims to the federal government, the latter had agreed to invalidate Native American titles to those lands and then return the lands to the state. However, the federal government never followed through, and Georgia had had to deal with the presence of a sovereign Native American state within its borders.

Land-hungry as a result of expansive pressures from the cotton culture, Georgians themselves initiated steps to remove Native Americans, primarily Cherokees. They denied the relevance of federal treaties with the Cherokees and threatened to use force against federal troops if they were dispatched to protect the tribe. Andrew Jackson's election as president in 1828 accelerated Georgia's actions to begin removing the Cherokees, because Jackson, a veteran Indian fighter who deemed Native Americans "savages," was a strong proponent of removal.

In December, 1828, the Georgia legislature added Cherokee lands to a number of Georgia counties. Far from being "savages," the Cherokees who protested this action had become a successful farming people. Thanks to a syllabary produced by their own Sequoyah, they were literate and produced their own newspaper, the *Cherokee Phoenix*. In response to the Georgia action, they instantly assembled a distinguished delegation to appeal to Congress for assistance. Their course was applauded by a host of congressmen and public officials—including Daniel Webster and William Wirt—who proclaimed Georgia's legislation unjust, on moral as well as legal grounds.

In December, 1829, Georgia's legislature went even further by enacting a comprehensive law that essentially nullified all Cherokee laws. Further aggravating the Cherokees' plight was the discovery of gold on Cherokee land in western Georgia during the following year. A gold rush flooded Cherokee land with white gold seekers, whose presence violated Cherokee treaties. Under great pressure, Georgia governor George Gilmer claimed the gold as state property and threatened to oust the Cherokees forcibly. Having failed in Georgia's courts, the Cherokees, as a last peaceful resort and encouraged by missionaries such as Jeremiah Evarts and public officials such as Webster and Wirt, appealed to the U.S. Supreme Court under Article III, section 2 of the Constitution, which gave the Court original jurisdiction in cases brought under treaties or by foreign nations.

The Court's Rulings

In *Cherokee Nation v. Georgia*, Chief Justice Marshall, who had been sympathetic to Cherokee claims but also was aware of Jackson's hostility toward both Native Americans and the Supreme Court, dismissed the case on March 18, 1831. Marshall asserted that the Court lacked the jurisdiction to halt Georgia's sequestration, or legal seizure, of Cherokee lands. In making that ruling, Marshall defined the relationship of the Cherokees—and, by inference, all other Native American tribes—to the federal government as that of a "domestic, dependent nation," rather than a sovereign one.

On March 3, 1832, however, Marshall modified his earlier ruling while deciding *Worcester v. Georgia*. The *Worcester* case arose from a Georgia law enacted in 1831 that forbade whites from residing on Cherokee lands without a state license. The law was aimed primarily at white missionaries who were encouraging Cherokee resistance to removal. Under its new law, Georgia arrested, convicted, and sentenced two unlicensed missionaries, Samuel Worcester and Elizur Butler, whom the American Board of Commissioners for Foreign Missions promptly defended by engaging William Wirt as their counsel. Wirt then was running as a vice presidential candidate for the National Republican Party and as a presidential candidate for the Anti-Masonic Party. Therefore, he hoped for a decision that would embarrass Jackson.

Because the plaintiff in *Worcester* was a white missionary and the defendant the state of Georgia, the Supreme Court had clear jurisdiction in this case. Without overruling his *Cherokee Nation* decision, Marshall ruled that the Georgia law was unconstitutional and therefore void, because it violated treaties, as well as the commerce and contract clauses of the U.S. Constitution. Furthermore, Marshall declared, Georgia's laws violated the sovereignty of the Cherokee nation, and, in this case, the Court was constrained to define relationships between Native Americans and a state. The ruling overturned Worcester's and Butler's convictions but did nothing to save the Cherokees from eventual removal from their homeland.

Significance

As historians and legal scholars later observed, the Cherokee cases advanced two contradictory descriptions of Native American sovereignty. In *Cherokee Nation v. Georgia*, Marshall delineated the dependent relationship of Native American tribes to the federal government. In *Worcester*, sympathetically stressing historic aspects of Native American independence, nationhood, and foreignness rather than their domestic dependency, he defined the relationship of Native American tribes to the states. Together, these decisions suggested that although Native American tribes lacked sufficient sovereignty to claim political independence and were therefore wards of the federal government, they nevertheless possessed sufficient sovereignty to guard themselves against intrusions by the states, and that it was a federal responsibility to preserve that sovereignty. In subsequent years, these conflicting interpretations were exploited by both the federal government and Native Americans to serve their own purposes.

Marshall's pronouncements were one thing; making them effective was yet another thing. President Jackson who, as chief executive, was the only party capable of enforcing the Court's decision, chose to ignore it. Instead, Jackson threw federal troops into the removal of Cherokees and others of the so-called Five Civilized Tribes to the newly created Indian Territory beyond the Mississippi River. The resulting tragedy became known as the Trail of Tears.

Mary E. Virginia

Further Reading

Deloria, Vine, Jr., and Clifford M. Lytle. *The Nations Within.* New York: Pantheon Books, 1984. Traces the past and weighs the future of Native American sovereignty, from the Doctrine of Discovery through the shift from tribal and federal notions of self-government to self-determination.
Duthu, N. Bruce. *American Indians and the Law.* New York: Penguin Books,

2008. Concise and accessible summary of Native American law, including a useful summary of the court decisions relevant to modern casinos.

Gold, Susan Dudley. *Worcester v. Georgia: American Indian Rights.* Tarrytown, N.Y.: Marshall Cavendish Benchmark, 2009. Part of its publisher's Supreme Court Milestones series designed for young-adult readers, this volume offers an accessible history and analysis of the *Worcester v. Georgia* case that examines opposing sides in the case, the people involved, and the case's lasting impact. Includes bibliography and index.

Guttmann, Allen. *States' Rights and Indian Removal: The Cherokee Nation v. the State of Georgia.* Boston: D. C. Heath, 1965. Brief documentary history of the Cherokees' legal struggle to keep their land.

McLoughlin, William G. *Cherokees and Missionaries, 1789-1839.* New Haven, Conn.: Yale University Press, 1984. Study of the missionaries, who played such an important role in supporting the Cherokees.

Prucha, Francis Paul. *American Indian Treaties.* Berkeley: University of California Press, 1994. Unravels the political anomaly of the treaty system, a system devised according to white perspectives that made the relationships between Native Americans and the federal government unlike the legal and political relationships of any other two peoples.

_____. *The Great Father.* Vol. 1. Lincoln: University of Nebraska Press, 1984. A masterful, detailed analysis of historical relationships—political, economic, and social—between the federal government and Native Americans through cultural changes affecting both groups, from the Revolutionary War to 1980. Chapter 2 discusses the Cherokee cases and American Indian removal.

Remini, Robert V. *Andrew Jackson.* 3 vols. Baltimore: Johns Hopkins University Press, 1998. Nearly definitive biography of the most fervid and effective advocate of Indian removal.

_____. *The Legacy of Andrew Jackson: Essays on Democracy, Indian Removal, and Slavery.* Baton Rouge: Louisiana State University Press, 1988. The leading biographer of Andrew Jackson discusses Jackson's role in Indian removal and other social and political issues of his time.

Satz, Ronald N. *American Indian Policy in the Jacksonian Era.* Lincoln: University of Nebraska Press, 1974. Excellent coverage of the Cherokee cases; also clarifies the complex political climate in which the cases developed around conflicts between the Jackson administration, Georgia, and the Cherokees.

Vinzant, John Harlan. *The Supreme Court's Role in American Indian Policy.* El Paso, Tex.: LFB Scholarly Publications, 2009. Study of the U.S. Supreme Court's role in reducing the sovereignty of Native American tribes.

Wallace, Anthony F. C. *The Long, Bitter Trail: Andrew Jackson and the Indians.*

New York: Hill & Wang, 1993. Brief overview of the removal policies, the Trail of Tears, and the implications of both for U.S. history.

Wilkins, David E., and K. Tsianina Lomawaima. *Uneven Ground: American Indian Sovereignty and Federal Law.* Norman: University of Oklahoma Press, 2002. Reviews the often inconsistent federal legal precedents related to issues concerning Native Americans.

Williams, Robert A. *The American Indian in Western Legal Thought.* New York: Oxford University Press, 1990. Starting with the thirteenth century notion that the West had a mandate to conquer the earth, this intriguing study explores the laws that evolved to legitimate this mandate, specifically as the mandate was interpreted by Spanish, English, and U.S. laws regarding relations with Native Americans.

See also *California v. Cabazon Band of Mission Indians; Employment Division, Department of Human Resources of Oregon v. Smith; Ex parte Crow Dog; Lone Wolf v. Hitchcock; Santa Clara Pueblo v. Martinez; Talton v. Mayes; United States v. Kagama; Worcester v. Georgia.*

CHICAGO V. MORALES

Court: U.S. Supreme Court
Citation: 527 U.S. 41
Date: June 10, 1999
Issues: Due process of law

• The U.S. Supreme Court held that an antiloitering ordinance was unconstitutionally vague, failing to give ordinary citizens fair notice about the kinds of conduct that are prohibited and allowing the police too much unguided discretion.

In 1992, the Chicago City Council enacted a law making it a misdemeanor to remain in one place with "no apparent purpose" while in the presence of a suspected gang member and when ordered to move by a police officer. During its three years of application, forty-two thousand people were arrested under the law. Many cities looked to the law as a model for reclaiming streets from gangs that used loitering as a strategy to control territory. A 6-3 majority of the justices found that the law violated due process standards because of the vagueness issue. Three members of the majority wanted to rule that the freedom to loiter for innocent purposes was part of the "liberty" protected by the Fourteenth Amendment. In a strong dissent, Justice Clarence Thomas accused the majority of sentencing "law-abiding citizens to lives of terror and misery." The justices appeared to agree that a law narrowly worded to prohibit intimidating conduct on the streets would be constitutional.

Because the Supreme Court recognized the problems associated with city gangs, the tone of the *Chicago* decision was quite different from *Papachristou v. City of Jacksonville* (1972), in which the Court, in an opinion written by Justice William O. Douglas, struck down a vagrancy law by referring to the values of nonconformity and the open road as extolled by poets Walt Whitman and Vachel Lindsay.

Thomas Tandy Lewis

See also *Hurtado v. California*; *Jackson v. Metropolitan Edison Co.*

Chicago, Burlington, and Quincy Railroad Co. v. Chicago

Court: U.S. Supreme Court
Citation: 166 U.S. 226
Date: March 1, 1897
Issues: Due process of law; Incorporation doctrine

- The U.S. Supreme Court held that the due process clause of the Fourteenth Amendment applied to the states and that, therefore, the state needed to compensate a railroad adequately when it converted private property to a public purpose.

Justice John Marshall Harlan wrote the 7-1 majority opinion with Justice David J. Brewer dissenting in part and Chief Justice Melville W. Fuller not participating. The Supreme Court unanimously held that the Fourteenth Amendment's due process clause required the states to grant just compensation

DUE PROCESS AND THE FOURTEENTH AMENDMENT

Ratified in 1868, the 433-word Fourteenth Amendment is the lengthiest amendment in the U.S. Constitution. It addressed a variety of important constitutional issues, but its central relevance to criminal justice is contained in this single sentence that concludes the amendment's first section:

> No State shall make or enforce any law which shall abridge the privileges or immunities of citizens of the United States; nor shall any State deprive any person of life, liberty, or property, without due process of law; nor deny to any person within its jurisdiction the equal protection of the laws.

when it took private property for a public purpose. The ruling was unanimous because Justice Brewer concurred on this point even though he dissented on other issues.

The Illinois Supreme Court had upheld a jury verdict of one dollar awarded to the Chicago, Burlington, and Quincy Railroad for loss of its money-making ability when the city of Chicago created a street across its railroad track. *Chicago, Burlington, and Quincy Railroad Co.* was one of the earliest attempts to use the right of substantive due process to control a state's attempt to regulate economic behavior. Although this latter purpose has been set aside by other decisions, this case remains valid law for the proposition that the Fourteenth Amendment's due process clause incorporates specific guarantees for the Bill of Rights. In this case, the Fifth Amendment's guarantee of just compensation when private property is taken for public purpose was incorporated and applied to the states.

Richard L. Wilson

See also *Chicago, Milwaukee, and St. Paul Railway Co. v. Minnesota; Munn v. Illinois; Shreveport Rate Cases; Wabash, St. Louis, and Pacific Railway Co. v. Illinois.*

Chicago, Milwaukee, and St. Paul Railway Co. v. Minnesota

Court: U.S. Supreme Court
Citation: 134 U.S. 418
Date: March 24, 1890
Issues: Due process of law; Judicial review; Takings clause

- The U.S. Supreme Court, in holding that the courts had the power to review utility rates, incorporated part of the due process clause of the Fourteenth Amendment and applied it to the states.

Justice Samuel Blatchford wrote the 6-3 majority opinion in this case, which struck down a statute forbidding judicial review of railroad shipping rates set by a state commission. The case laid the foundation for the modern regulatory state by departing from the Supreme Court's ruling in *Munn v. Illinois* (1877). Although the decision was vague, the general direction was to break away from the Court's past constitutional standard in which the Court was able to judge only whether a particular branch could act in an area, not whether it acted reasonably in doing so. One basic modern administrative law principle is that due process requires judicial review of bureaucratic decisions to determine compatibility with constitutional standards. The Court stated that courts had the authority to judge the reasonableness of utility rates set by other branches of government. After this decision, the Court began to review not only whether one of the three branches had the authority to act but also whether the government procedures arrived at reasonable decisions.

Richard L. Wilson

See also *Budd v. New York; Calder v. Bull; Chicago, Burlington, and Quincy Railroad Co. v. Chicago; Fletcher v. Peck; Hayburn's Case; Hylton v. United States; Marbury v. Madison; Stuart v. Laird; Yakus v. United States.*

CHIMEL V. CALIFORNIA

Court: U.S. Supreme Court
Citation: 395 U.S. 752
Date: June 23, 1969
Issues: Search and seizure

- *Chimel v. California* was the U.S. Supreme Court's most significant pronouncement concerning the permissible extent of a warrantless search of a criminal suspect conducted pursuant to making a lawful arrest.

Chimel, who was suspected of having committed a burglary at a coin shop a month earlier, was arrested at his home, where the police—who had a warrant for his arrest but not one authorizing a search—at the same time conducted a search. Over Chimel's objections, police searched his entire three-bedroom house, seizing some coins found there that were later entered into evidence at Chimel's trial. Chimel was convicted, and his conviction was twice upheld by California state courts before he petitioned the Supreme Court for review, claiming that the warrantless search of his house had been unreasonable and violated the Fourth Amendment.

In overturning Chimel's conviction, the Supreme Court held that police may search only the person of the arrested criminal suspect and the area "within his immediate control" in order to uncover a concealed weapon and prevent the destruction of evidence. In so deciding, the Court overruled two earlier precedents, *Harris v. United States* (1947) and *United States v. Rabinowitz* (1950), in which a warrantless search was limited only by the nature of what was sought.

As Justice John M. Harlan had stated in *Katz v. United States*, which the Court decided the year before *Chimel* was handed down, "searches conducted outside the judicial process [that is, without a warrant] are per se unreasonable under the Fourth Amendment—subject only to a few specifically established and well-delineated exceptions." One long-standing exception is that of permitting a warrantless search that is made incident to a lawful arrest.

The justification for this exception is often that the police have not had time to obtain a search warrant, but the open-ended interpretation given the exception by the Harris-Rabinowitz rule gave police tremendous latitude for abuse. In *Chimel,* the offense precipitating the search and the arrest was committed a month before police arrested Chimel, and in the interim Chimel clearly had neither fled nor destroyed all the evidence against him. After obtaining the arrest warrant, police delayed several days before serving it, and they provided no explanation of why there was no time to obtain a search warrant from the court.

In *Weeks v. United States* (1914), the Court made the exclusionary rule, banning introduction at trial of evidence obtained in any unconstitutional fashion, binding on federal courts. Because most crimes are tried at the state level, however, reaction against the exclusionary rule became pronounced only when the Court, led by Chief Justice Earl Warren, extended it to state court proceedings in *Mapp v. Ohio* (1961). The Warren Court was accused of coddling criminals, and when Earl Warren retired in 1969, President Richard Nixon, who had made the Warren Court a campaign issue in 1968, replaced him with an outspoken critic of the exclusionary rule, Warren Burger.

Lisa Paddock

See also *Harris v. United States; Katz v. United States; Mapp v. Ohio; New York v. Belton; Weeks v. United States.*

CHINESE EXCLUSION CASES

CHEW HEONG V. UNITED STATES; UNITED STATES V. JUNG AH LUNG; CHAE CHAN PING V. UNITED STATES; FONG YUE TING V. UNITED STATES; WONG QUAN V. UNITED STATES; AND LEE JOE V. UNITED STATES

Court: U.S. Supreme Court
Citations: 112 U.S. 536; 124 U.S. 621; 130 U.S. 581; 149 U.S. 698
Dates: December 8, 1884; February 13, 1888; May 13, 1889; May 15, 1893
Issues: Immigration; Right to travel

• Using the Fourteenth Amendment, the U.S. Supreme Court first ruled in favor of challenges to laws excluding the Chinese from immigrating and becoming U.S. citizens, then succumbed to popular sentiment and upheld exclusionary statutes.

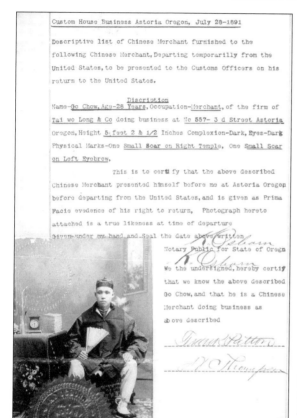

Custom House Business Astoria Oregon, July 28-1891

Descriptive list of Chinese Merchant furnished to the following Chinese Merchant, Departing temporarily from the United States, to be presented to the Customs Officers on his return to the United States.

Discription

Name-Go Chow, Age-28 Years, Occupation-Merchant, of the firm of Tai wo Long & Co doing business at No 557- 3 d Street Astoria Oregon, Height 5 feet 2 & 1/2 Inches Complexion-Dark, Eyes-Dark Physical Marks-One Small Scar on Right Temple, One Small Scar on Left Eyebrow,

This is to certify that the above described Chinese Merchant presented himself before me at Astoria Oregon before departing from the United States, and is given as Prima Facie evedence of his right to return, Photograph hereto attached is a true likeness at time of departure given under my hand and Seal the date above written

Notary Public for State of Oregn

We the undersigned, hereby certify that we know the above described Go Chow, and that he is a Chinese Merchant doing business as above described

Reentry documents carried by a Chinese immigrant in 1891. (NARA)

In 1882 Congress enacted the first Chinese Exclusion Act, prohibiting Chinese laborers and miners from entering the United States. An 1884 amendment required resident Chinese laborers to have reentry certificates if they traveled outside the United States and planned to return. The 1888 Scott Act prohibited Chinese laborers temporarily abroad from returning, thereby stranding thousands of Chinese. Merchants and teachers were exempted from the Scott Act if they had "proper papers," thereby beginning the practice of using "paper names" to create new identities so that Chinese could return. The 1892 Geary Act banned all future Chinese laborers from entry and denied bail to Chinese in judicial proceedings. All Chinese faced deportation if they did not carry identification papers. The 1893 McCreary Act further extended the definition of laborers to include fishermen, miners, laundry owners, and merchants. The 1902 Chinese Exclusion Act permanently banned all Chinese immigration.

The Supreme Court initially attempted to defend Chinese rights under the Fourteenth Amendment; however, as anti-Chinese sentiment grew more pronounced, it withdrew even its limited protections from Chinese immigrants. The Court defended the right of Chinese to reenter the United States in *Chew Heong* and *Jung Ah Lung*. In *Chae Chan Ping*, it found the Scott Act unconstitutional. However, in the three 1893 cases, it upheld a law retroactively requiring that Chinese laborers have certificates of residence or be deported.

Richard L. Wilson

See also *Lau v. Nichols; Ozawa v. United States; United States v. Wong Kim Ark; Yick Wo v. Hopkins.*

CHISHOLM V. GEORGIA

Court: U.S. Supreme Court
Citation: 2 Dall. (2 U.S.) 419
Date: February 18, 1793
Issues: State sovereignty

• In its first major decision, the U.S. Supreme Court held that the U.S. Constitution allowed a citizen of one state to sue another state in federal court.

Article III of the U.S. Constitution granted federal jurisdiction over "controversies between a state and citizens of another state." During ratification of the Constitution, Federalists asserted that this provision would not override the doctrine of sovereign immunity, which meant that the government may be sued only with its consent. Two South Carolina citizens, executors of an estate of a British decedent, attempted to recover property that Georgia had confiscated during the American Revolution. Georgia refused to appear, claiming immunity as a sovereign state.

By a 4-1 vote, the Supreme Court ruled against the state and endorsed the authority of the federal judiciary over the states. In seriatim opinions, Justices John Jay and James Wilson emphasized strong nationalistic views. They declared that the people of the United States had acted "as sovereigns" in establishing the Constitution and that the states, by virtue of membership in a "national compact," could be sued by citizens throughout the nation. In dissent, Justice James Iredell, a southerner who had participated in a ratifying convention, argued that the English common law doctrine of sovereign immunity had not been superseded by constitutional provision or by statute.

The *Chisholm* decision was bitterly denounced by partisans of states' rights. The controversy resulted in the drafting and ratification of the Eleventh Amendment, the first of four amendments to directly overrule a decision of the Court.

Thomas Tandy Lewis

See also *Cohens v. Virginia; Edelman v. Jordan; Ex parte Young; Strawbridge v. Curtiss.*

CHURCH OF LUKUMI BABALU AYE V. HIALEAH

Court: U.S. Supreme Court
Citation: 508 U.S. 520
Date: June 11, 1993
Issues: Environmental issues and animal rights; Freedom of religion

• Striking down a ban on animal sacrifices, the Court ruled that a law targeting religious conduct for special treatment must be justified by compelling state interests and must be narrowly tailored to advance those interests.

Santeria, a religion combining East African traditions with elements of Roman Catholicism, teaches that rituals of animal sacrifice influence benevolent spirits, and believers perform sacrifices for the cure of the sick and at ceremonies such as marriages and funerals. After most sacrifices, the resulting meat is cooked and eaten by church members. In 1987 a Santeria church was announced for Hialeah, Florida, and the Hialeah City Council responded to a public outcry by passing a series of ordinances which had the effect of outlawing the killing of animals in religious rituals while allowing such killing when exclusively done for food or other secular reasons.

Church attorneys attacked the ordinances as a violation of freedom of religion under the First and Fourteenth Amendments. After federal district and appellate courts upheld the ordinances, the church then appealed the case to the U.S. Supreme Court, where the justices voted unanimously that the ordinances were unconstitutional.

Justice Anthony Kennedy's opinion for the Court explained that when a law, as in the Hialeah ordinances, is plainly directed at restricting a religious practice, the law must satisfy two tests: justification by a compelling state interest and use of the least restrictive means to promote that interest. Kennedy, however, displeased libertarians in reaffirming *Employment Division, Department of Human Resources of Oregon v. Smith* (1990), a rule that a neutral law of general applicability would not be required to pass the two tests when the law burdens religion incidentally. General and neutral laws might proscribe cruelty to animals or require the safe disposal of animal wastes; however, Hialeah could not place a direct burden on unpopular religious rituals without a secular justification.

Justices David Souter, Harry Blackmun, and Sandra Day O'Connor issued concurring opinions expressing agreement with the ruling while disagreeing with the *Smith* precedent. These three justices wished to return to *Sherbert v. Verner* (1963) and require a compelling state interest and narrowly tailored laws for both direct and indirect burdens on religious practice.

While *Lukumi Babalu* gave First Amendment protection against direct assaults on unpopular religions, many agreed with the concurring justices' opposition to the *Smith* rule. Congress in 1993 responded with the Religious Freedom Restoration Act, which mandated the compelling state interest test when a federal or state restriction imposed a "cruel choice" by penalizing any significant practice based on sincere religious convictions.

Thomas Tandy Lewis

See also *Employment Division, Department of Human Resources of Oregon v. Smith; 44 Liquormart, Inc. v. Rhode Island; Sherbert v. Verner.*

CITIZENS UNITED V. FEDERAL ELECTION COMMISSION

Court: U.S. Supreme Court
Citation: 558 U.S. ____
Date: January 21, 2010
Issues: Freedom of expression; Political campaigning;
Regulation of commerce

- In this landmark decision that overturned two precedents, the U.S. Supreme Court held that corporations and labor unions have a First Amendment right to spend unlimited amounts of money to distribute independent broadcasts that support or oppose political candidates at any time, even during elections.

Before the presidential primaries of 2008, a conservative nonprofit corporation called Citizens United produced a ninety-minute documentary film, *Hillary: The Movie*, which was highly critical of then-Senator Hillary Clinton, who was the leading Democratic candidate. The corporation wanted to distribute the film over television and as a video-on-demand during the primary season. There was, however, a serious obstacle to this distribution: a provision in the Bipartisan Campaign Reform Act (BCRA) of 2002, commonly known as the McCain-Feingold Law, banned corporations and unions from broadcasting "electioneering communications" that expressly endorsed or opposed a particular candidate three months before a primary election or six months before a general election. The purpose of the law was to prevent "big money" from unfairly influencing federal elections. Although some jurists questioned the constitutionality of the BCRA, the Supreme Court had upheld the right of Congress to place limits on political speech by corporations in *Austin v. Michigan Chamber of Commerce* (1990). In *McConnell v. Federal Election Commission* (2003), the Court had voted five to four to uphold major restrictions on campaign expenditures in the BCRA.

Citizens United petitioned the U.S. District Court for the District of Columbia for a preliminary injunction forbidding the Federal Election Commission from restricting the dissemination of *Hillary: The Movie*. The group's major argument was that the film was a nonpartisan, fact-based documentary—not a political advertisement. On January 15, 2008, however, the district court concluded that the primary purpose of the film was to discredit candidate *Clinton*, and it therefore rejected the motion for an injunction. The U.S. Supreme Court agreed to review the dismissal and heard oral arguments in March, 2009. A few months later, however, the Court took the unusual step of announcing that it would rehear the case, and it directed the lawyers on both sides to prepare new briefs concerning two issues not considered in the earlier hearing:

- whether Congress had the authority to ban or restrict books containing advocacy for or against candidates in elections
- whether the Court should overrule its precedents on campaign finance regulations

The Court's Ruling

After the second hearing, a bitterly divided Supreme Court decided by a 5-4 majority that the First Amendment protects the right of any association of individuals to make unrestricted expenditures for the purpose of communicating political messages, including advocacy for or against particular candidates running in public elections. By equating money with speech in the political context, the ruling struck down an important portion of the BCRA as unconstitutional, and it entirely overruled *Austin v. Michigan Chamber of Commerce* and partially overturned *McConnell v. Federal Election Commission*. It is important to note, however, that the ruling also upheld important provisions of the BCRA, including the requirements for disclosures by sponsors of advertisements and the many restrictions on direct contributions to candidates from corporations, unions, and other organizations.

Writing in behalf of the Court's majority, Justice Anthony Kennedy declared: "If the First Amendment has any force, it prohibits Congress from fining or jailing citizens for simply engaging in political speech." Any laws, moreover, that stifle or place a burden on political speech are subject to "strict scrutiny," which requires the government to prove that the limitation "furthers a compelling interest and is narrowly tailored to achieve that interest." Because it is impossible to distinguish media corporations from other corporations, allowing restrictions on corporations would provide Congress with the power to restrict political speech in books, newspapers, television, and even Internet blogs. Kennedy further asserted that when government uses its great power to command where people may get their information or what distrusted sources they may not hear, it uses censorship to control thought unlawfully. "The First Amendment," he stated, "confirms the freedom to think for ourselves."

Chief Justice John Roberts wrote a concurring opinion that addressed the issue of when it was appropriate for the Court to overturn its precedents. Observing that to follow precedents (or *stare decisis*) was secondary to making a correct decision, he referred to numerous historical instances in which the Court decided that a prior decision had not given adequate protection to constitutional rights. Justice Antonin Scalia also wrote a concurrence, explaining why he believed that the decision was supported by the original understanding of the First Amendment. Even if modern corporations did not exist when the amendment was written, he could not find any reason to conclude that the Framers had intended that the freedom of speech guaranteed to individuals should not also apply to "the freedom to speak in association with other individuals, including association in corporate form." Rejecting the dissenters' distinction between individuals and corporations, he argued that because the text of the First Amendment mentions protection for "speech, not speakers," it therefore "offers no foothold for excluding any category of speaker."

Dissenting Opinion

In a ninety-page dissent, Justice John Paul Stevens rebutted the arguments of the majority and warned that their decision "threatens to undermine the integrity of elected institutions across the Nation." Observing that restrictions on corporate financing of campaigns had been in effect since the Tillman Act of 1907, he accused the majority of making a dramatic break from the past and of rejecting the "common sense of the American people," who have struggled "against the distinctive corrupting potential of corporate electioneering since the days of Theodore Roosevelt." He emphasized that U.S. laws had always recognized a distinction between corporations and human beings; for example, only the latter can vote or hold office. The Court had long recognized, moreover, that corporations might be subject to special regulations in the public interest. By refusing to acknowledge a distinction between a person and a corporation, the majority had failed to consider the government's legitimate interest in limiting the influences that wealthy corporations might have on the outcome of elections. "While American democracy is imperfect," Stevens concluded, "few outside the majority of this Court would have thought its flaws included a dearth of corporate money in politics."

Soon after the Court announced *Citizens United*, retired justice Sandra Day O'Connor delivered a speech in which she publicly indicated her disagreement with the majority opinion. Expressing particular concern that unlimited corporate spending in elections for state judgeships could threaten the independence of the judiciaries, she declared, "No state can possibly benefit from having that much money injected into a political campaign." It is interesting to note that O'Connor had voted with the majority in the 2003 *McConnell* ruling. Had she not been replaced by Justice Samuel Alito in 2006, the Court almost certainly would not have ruled the way it did in *Citizens United*.

Public Reactions

Because of its potential impact, *Citizens United v. FEC* brought forth a wide range of strong reactions from journalists, politicians, legal scholars, and advocacy groups. Many conservatives and libertarians praised the ruling as a victory for free speech, whereas the vast majority of liberals agreed with Justice Stevens's dissent. Professor Bradley A. Smith, a a former chairman of the FEC and a longstanding opponent of campaign finance limits, wrote that the decision would "empower small and midsize corporations—and every incorporated mom-and-pop falafel joint, local firefighters' union, and environmental group—to make its voice heard in campaigns." President Barack Obama, in contrast, declared in his 2010 state of the union address that "the Supreme Court reversed a century of law to open the floodgates for special interests— including foreign corporations—to spend without limit in our elections." Some Democratic members of Congress advocated new legislation to limit the impact of the ruling, but most of their suggestions appeared impractical. Senator John Kerry, among others, advocated a constitutional amendment that would make a distinction between persons and corporations, but not many observers thought his proposal would attract the support necessary for success. Some Democratic members of Congress advocated new legislation to limit the impact of the ruling, but most of their suggestions appeared impractical. Senator John Kerry, among others, advocated a constitutional amendment making a distinction between persons and corporations, but not many

President Barack Obama delivering his state of the union address to a joint session of Congress on January 27, 2010. Vice President Joe Biden and House Speaker Nancy Pelosi are seated behind him.
(AP/Wide World Photos)

observers thought that the proposal would attract the support necessary for success.

Although most journalists and legal scholars focused on *Citizens United*'s impact on the McCain-Feingold Law, the ruling also invalidated twenty-four state laws prohibiting independent campaign expenditures by corporations and unions. Experts on campaign finance nevertheless disagreed about the possible unintended consequences of the ruling. Numerous commentators suggested that it would probably result in a significant increase in the number of campaign advertisements financed by large corporations, but others answered that unions and liberal advocacy groups would also increase their advertisements, thereby providing balance in campaigns. A number of moderate observers predicted that corporations would be hesitant to spend large sums of money on political elections because of concerns that too much overt partisanship might anger customers and thus harm business.

Thomas Tandy Lewis

Further Reading

Corrado, Anthony, et al. *The New Campaign Finance Sourcebook*. Washington, D.C.: Brookings Institution Press, 2005. Convenient sourcebook that includes the history of campaign finance regulations and an overview of legislation and case law prior to the *Citizens United* decision.

La Raina, Raymond J. *Small Change, Political Parties, and Campaign Finance Reform*. Ann Arbor: University of Michigan Press, 2008. History of the campaign finance system from the late nineteenth century through the BCRA of 2002, concluding that legislatures have intentionally designed regulations to gain partisan advantage.

Samples, John. *The Fallacy of Campaign Finance Reform*. Chicago: University of Chicago Press, 2006. Finds no evidence that campaign contributions do not influence members of Congress and argues that because restrictions on campaign finance protect incumbents, they are not good for democracy.

Slabach, Frederick F., ed. *The Constitution and Campaign Finance Reform: An Anthology*. Durham, N.C.: Carolina Academic Press, 2006. Collection of prominent legal scholars' writings on the First Amendment and restrictions on the financing of campaigns.

Smith, Rodney A. *Money, Power, and Elections: How Campaign Finance Reform Subverts American Democracy*. Baton Rouge: Louisiana State University Press, 2006. A prominent Republican, Smith argues that campaign finance laws have had unintended consequences, giving advantages to incumbents and wealthy candidates, while harming the chances of outsiders.

Urofsky, Melvin. *Money and Free Speech: Campaign Finance Reform and the Courts*.

Lawrence: University Press of Kansas, 2005. An outstanding legal historian, Urofsky provides a balanced and thoughtful review of court decisions from the Progressive era through *McConnell v. Federal Election Commission* (2003).

See also *Bank of Augusta v. Earle; Louisville, Cincinnati, and Charleston Railroad Co. v. Letson; McConnell v. Federal Election Commission; Northern Securities Co. v. United States; Paul v. Virginia; Santa Clara County v. Southern Pacific Railroad Co.*

City of Renton v. Playtime Theaters

Court: U.S. Supreme Court
Citation: 475 U.S. 41
Date: February 25, 1986
Issues: Censorship; Local government; Zoning

• In rejecting a First Amendment challenge to a dispersal zoning ordinance specifically directed at motion picture theaters that show sexually explicit films, the U.S. Supreme Court substantially expanded the authority available to local governments seeking to limit the sites at which adult film theaters might be located in a community.

The city of Renton, Washington, adopted an ordinance prohibiting any adult film theater from locating within one thousand feet of any residential area, school, church, or park. The new owners of two theaters who intended to show sexually explicit films to the public at their theaters brought suit in federal court to enjoin (negate) the ordinance on the grounds that it unconstitutionally regulated their expressive activities. The federal court of appeals held that the ordinance violated the First Amendment. The U.S. Supreme Court reversed the decision and ruled that the ordinance was constitutional.

Laws that regulate expressive activity based on the content of speech are presumed to violate the First Amendment. Such content-discriminatory laws receive strict scrutiny and are struck down in all but the most compelling of circumstances. Since the ordinance in question in *Renton* restricted the location of theaters showing sexually explicit films but did not regulate the location of other movie theaters, the ordinance appeared to be directed at the content of speech in violation of this basic rule of First Amendment jurisprudence.

By a 7-2 vote, however, the Supreme Court held that a different free speech principle applied to the Renton zoning law. While "the ordinance treats theaters that specialize in adult films differently from other kinds of theaters," Justice William Rehnquist, writing for the majority, explained, "the Renton ordinance is aimed not at the *content* of the films shown at 'adult motion picture theaters,' but rather at the *secondary effects* of such theaters on the surrounding community." The city's goal in adopting the ordinance was not to suppress the presentation of adult films, but rather to prevent the crime and neighborhood blight that adult movie theaters may cause. Since these objectives are unrelated to an attempt to silence the message being communicated by adult films, the Renton ordinance was more properly characterized as a content-neutral regulation. Accordingly, the ordinance could be upheld under a relatively lenient standard of review.

The importance of the *Renton* decision extends beyond its particular facts. The secondary-effects analysis utilized by the Court in *Renton* not only makes it easier for cities to regulate the location of adult theaters and bookstores but also arguably creates a new basis for justifying restrictions on other kinds of speech. In *Boos v. Barry* (1988), for example, the District of Columbia unsuccessfully attempted to justify a content-discriminatory ordinance prohibiting protests outside foreign embassies on the grounds that the challenged law was aimed at the secondary effects of speech. Although the Court did not accept the District's argument in *Boos*, the applicability of the secondary effects doctrine to speech that lies at the core of the First Amendment, such as political speech, remains unresolved.

Alan E. Brownstein

See also *Belle Terre v. Boraas; Euclid v. Ambler Realty Co.; First English Evangelical Lutheran Church of Glendale v. County of Los Angeles; Moore v. City of East Cleveland; Young v. American Mini Theatres.*

CIVIL RIGHTS CASES

UNITED STATES V. STANLEY; UNITED STATES V. RYAN; UNITED STATES V. NICHOLS; UNITED STATES V. SINGLETON; ROBINSON AND WIFE V. MEMPHIS & CHARLESTON RAILROAD COMPANY

Court: U.S. Supreme Court
Citation: 109 U.S. 3
Date: October 15, 1883
Issues: Civil rights and liberties; Equal protection of the law; Private discrimination; Racial discrimination

• In a set of five cases consolidated in a single decision, the U.S. Supreme Court found the Civil Rights Act of 1875 unconstitutional. The decision affirmed the premise that the Fourteenth Amendment gave Congress the power to prohibit discrimination only by state governments and not by private individuals or businesses.

The Civil Rights Act of 1875 proved to be the last piece of Reconstruction law passed by Congress to ensure that former slaves and their descendants would not be denied their rights as citizens. Partly as a tribute to Senator Charles Sumner, who had fought tirelessly for civil rights during his lifetime and who had died the previous year, his fellow senators approved the legislation. Sumner had held that the Thirteenth Amendment, in addition to abolishing the institution of slavery, also raised former slaves to a status of legal equality. On that basis, Congress had the power to pass laws that would guarantee African Americans freedom from discriminatory treatment, whether by public authorities or by private individuals. As Congress debated the Civil Rights Bill during the early 1870's, the most visible signs of African Americans' legal inferiority were restrictions and segregation in public facilities. Hotels, inns, theaters, trains, and ships routinely denied accommodations to black patrons.

Anticipating questions about the constitutionality of his proposals, Sumner tied his advocacy of free access to public facilities directly to the abolition of slavery, arguing that because one of the disabilities of slavery was the prohibi-

Harper's Weekly *illustration depicting the response of people gathered outside the galleries of the House of Representatives after the passage of the Civil Rights Act of 1866.* (Library of Congress)

tion against entering public places, the end of slavery should mean freedom to enter the establishments of one's choosing. Restrictions on that freedom based on race constituted a "badge of slavery."

Supporters of the public accommodations law also argued that it could be sustained on Fourteenth Amendment grounds. Representative Robert Brown Elliott insisted that the amendment's equal protection clause required that states secure equality before the law for all citizens as part of their responsibility to advance the common good. He cited the Supreme Court's position in the 1872 Slaughterhouse cases that the purpose of the Thirteenth and Fourteenth Amendments was to protect African Americans from those who had formerly enslaved them.

The Republicans lost their majority in Congress in the 1874 elections. They passed the Civil Rights Act in a lame duck session in early 1875, as a last effort to secure the rights of African Americans before Congress became dominated by Democrats and pro-white southerners. The original version of the bill was drafted by African American civil rights activist John Mercer Langston, who gave it to Sumner. As passed, the Civil Rights Act of 1875 included five sections. Section 1 provided for equal access for all Americans to public accommodations and places of amusement. Section 2 defined violations and penalties for violating the equal access provisions. Section 3 gave federal courts, rather than state, jurisdiction in civil rights cases and required that law-enforcement agencies cooperate to enforce the law. This section was an attempt to ensure that the act would be enforced and violations prosecuted even in states where local authorities were reluctant to do so. Section 4 forbade racial discrimination in federal or state juries, and section 5 provided for Supreme Court review of cases arising under the act. An additional provision extending the equal access guarantees to public education was dropped from the bill.

In the year after the passage of the Civil Rights Act, neither Republican presidential candidate Rutherford B. Hayes nor Democratic candidate Samuel Tilden received a majority of the electoral votes. As the outcome of the presidential election remained in doubt, a special commission was appointed to resolve the constitutional crisis. A settlement was reached that allowed Hayes to assume the presidency. This settlement included an agreement that the federal government would stop trying to enforce civil rights legislation, including the new law passed in 1875. Even so, the law remained on the books until a group of cases, known collectively as the Civil Rights Cases, came before the Supreme Court in 1883.

The Cases

The challenges to the law arose from four criminal prosecutions of persons who had excluded African Americans from their hotels or theaters and a fifth case brought by a black woman who had been excluded from a white railroad car reserved for women. All five cases fell under sections 1 and 2 of the 1875 law, and the Supreme Court was asked to decide whether these provisions were constitutional under the Thirteenth and Fourteenth Amendments. Could private discrimination be prohibited as one of the "badges of slavery"? Could Congress prevent discrimination by individuals on the grounds that the state was involved when it tolerated or ignored such actions by its citizens?

On October 15, 1883, Justice Joseph P. Bradley delivered the opinion of the Court. Seven justices joined his opinion; only Justice John Marshall Harlan dissented. Bradley's ruling effectively established a narrow scope for the Fourteenth Amendment, which was determined to apply only to the official actions of state governments. Congress, he maintained, did not have the power to prohibit discrimination by private individuals. Bradley asserted that such legislation was a "municipal law for the protection of private rights," far beyond the scope of congressional authority. He considered that under the Fourteenth Amendment, Congress's power to ensure that no state deprived a citizen of equal protection of the law meant that Congress could provide relief only after a state agency had acted to deny equal protection.

Bradley's interpretation of the Fourteenth Amendment left African Americans largely at the mercy of state governments, since they could appeal to

Congress for relief only after a state had acted to deprive them of their civil rights. As for the acts of individuals that interfered with other persons' enjoyment of their rights of other persons, the Court's opinion termed such situations "simply a private wrong." The remedy for such discrimination was to bring action in a state court. According to this ruling, private interference, even with the right to hold property, to vote, or to serve as a witness or a juror, could not be prohibited by federal law.

Bradley reasoned that federal laws could only prohibit or prevent the "denial" of rights—that is, the elimination of those rights in principle. Because a private individual did not have the power to deny rights but only to "interfere with the enjoyment of the right in a particular case," such an individual's actions fell outside the scope of federal power to enforce the Fourteenth Amendment. It remained up to each state to enforce its laws against instances of "force or fraud" that interfered with the enjoyment of civil rights, just as it was up to the state to enforce laws against any other instance of "force or fraud."

Bradley further denied that the Thirteenth Amendment had any relevance to the case. In the opinion of the Court, "mere discrimination on account of race or color" could not be considered among the badges of slavery. In abolishing slavery, the amendment was not intended to adjust the "social rights" in the community. According to Bradley's opinion, it was time for African Americans to stop being "the special favorite of the laws" and to assume "the rank of a mere citizen." In ruling the Civil Rights Act of 1875 unconstitutional, the Supreme Court advised African Americans that their rights would be protected in the same way as other citizens' rights, by the state governments.

Justice John Marshall Harlan, a former slave owner, wrote the only dissent in the Civil Rights Cases. As he would do later in *Plessy v. Ferguson*, Harlan criticized his colleagues for distorting the intent of the Fourteenth Amendment by their narrow definition of state action. He asserted that public establishments were agents of the state, as they operated under state licenses and regulations. Harlan also argued that, because race had served as a justification for slavery, racial discrimination qualified as a badge of slavery. Emancipation raised the former slaves to the status of freedom and entitled them to the same civil rights as their fellow citizens. The Thirteenth Amendment, in its enforcement clause, gave Congress the power to ensure the enjoyment of those rights, including equal access. Harlan concluded that the constitutional amendments passed after the Civil War had prohibited any race or class of people from deciding which rights and privileges their fellow citizens could enjoy.

Significance

Through its narrow definition of state action and of the Fourteenth Amendment's equal protection clause, the Supreme Court effectively limited the federal government's power to outlaw racial discrimination. Rather than affirming that the federal government had the constitutional authority to ensure equal citizenship for African Americans, the justices supported the principle of states' rights, opting for a limited definition of congressional authority and deferring to the states to safeguard the welfare of their citizens.

Among those who protested the Court's decision in the Civil Rights Cases was a group of black lawyers called the Brotherhood of Liberty. They argued that leaving the enforcement of civil rights to the states would be a disaster for African Americans. They criticized Republican federal judges as well as Republican legislators for betraying the purposes of the Reconstruction amendments out of political self-interest. Some black journalists compared the Civil Rights Cases to the Court's decision in *Scott v. Sandford* (1857), which had denied that any African American could ever be a U.S. citizen.

Mary Welek Atwell

Further Reading

Hyman, Harold M., and William M. Wiecek. *Equal Justice Under Law: Constitutional Development, 1835-1875*. New York: Harper & Row, 1982. Emphasizes issues concerning the Thirteenth Amendment as a source of federal power to enforce civil rights.

Lewis, Thomas T., and Richard L. Wilson, eds. *Encyclopedia of the U.S. Supreme Court*. 3 vols. Pasadena, Calif.: Salem Press, 2001. Comprehensive reference work on the Supreme Court that contains substantial discussions of the Civil Rights Cases and of all of the Court's other major civil rights decisions.

Litwack, Leon, and August Meier, eds. *Black Leaders of the Nineteenth Century*. Urbana: University of Illinois Press, 1988. Profiles of prominent African American activists.

Lively, Donald E. *The Constitution and Race*. New York: Praeger, 1992. A careful analysis of constitutional interpretation based on primary sources.

Nelson, William E. *The Fourteenth Amendment: From Political Principle to Judicial Doctrine*. Cambridge, Mass.: Harvard University Press, 1988. A valuable study of the changing application and meaning of the amendment.

Perry, Michael J. *We the People: The Fourteenth Amendment and the Supreme Court*. New ed. New York: Oxford University Press, 2002. Examines the controversies historically surrounding interpretation of the Fourteenth Amendment by the Supreme Court.

See also *Jones v. Alfred H. Mayer Co.*; *Plessy v. Ferguson*; *Scott v. Sandford*.

CLARK DISTILLING CO. V. WESTERN MARYLAND RAILWAY CO.

Court: U.S. Supreme Court
Citation: 242 U.S. 311
Date: January 8, 1917
Issues: Regulation of commerce

• The U.S. Supreme Court upheld the constitutionality of the Webb-Kenyon Act of 1913, forbidding the shipment of alcoholic beverages into a state in violation of its laws.

The Webb-Kenyon Act, passed in 1913 over President William H. Taft's veto, assisted the Prohibition states in enforcing their laws against the sale or shipment of intoxicating liquors to customers within their borders. By a 7-2 vote, the Supreme Court upheld the law, recognizing that Congress had broad discretion in choosing how to regulate interstate commerce. Speaking for the Court, Chief Justice Edward D. White argued that the law applied uniformly throughout the nation and that it did not delegate the commerce power to the states.

Thomas Tandy Lewis

See also *44 Liquormart, Inc. v. Rhode Island; License Cases; Mugler v. Kansas.*

CLASSIC, UNITED STATES V. *See* UNITED STATES V. CLASSIC

Clinton v. City of New York

Court: U.S. Supreme Court
Citation: 524 U.S. 417
Date: June 25, 1998
Issues: Presidential powers

- By a vote of six to three, the U.S. Supreme Court ruled in the case of *Clinton v. City of New York* that the U.S. Constitution forbids passing a law to revise the process of how a bill may be vetoed. The law at issue would have allowed the president to reject only parts of a bill passed by Congress rather than the entire bill.

The line-item veto is a variant of regular veto power given to executives, whereby an executive may reject a part of a bill rather than the entire bill. The U.S. Constitution does not specify such authority for the American president in the enumeration of the veto power, but by the early years of the twenty-first century, forty-three U.S. state governors had line-item veto power.

In the nineteenth century, the president of the Confederate States of America possessed a line-item veto under that government's constitution. After the Civil War, President Ulysses S. Grant became the first chief executive of the United States to make a formal proposal concerning the additional authority of the line-item veto; he was followed in this by most of the remaining presidents in the nineteenth century. In the twentieth century, the idea was renewed in the 1980's, partly as a result of the growing complexities of the federal budget and regular annual deficits after 1969.

The Contract with America, a compendium of promises promoted by Republican congressional candidates during the 1994 midterm election campaign, contained a proposal for the line-item veto. When, as a result of that election, Republicans gained control of both chambers of Congress, Senate Majority Leader Bob Dole led the fight to pass the Line Item Veto Act. The bill was quickly passed and was signed into law by President Bill Clinton on April 9, 1996. The Clinton White House supported the legislation for several reasons. First, because it would delegate additional authority to the chief executive, the law was seen as strengthening the institution of the presidency. Second, the law was viewed as necessary to control wasteful spending and thus as beneficial to the effort to reduce budget deficits. Finally, Clinton's backing of the law enabled the administration to cite it as an example of bipartisan cooperation.

The Case

Claiming that the 1996 Line Item Veto Act violated the veto provisions in Article I, section 7, of the U.S. Constitution, Senator Robert Byrd, a Democrat from West Virginia, immediately challenged the act in the courts. In April, 1997, U.S. district court judge Thomas Penfield Jackson declared the law unconstitutional. On appeal, the U.S. Supreme Court vacated and remanded that decision due to a lack of standing by the plaintiffs. In February, 1998, U.S. district court judge Thomas Hogan ruled that the Line Item Veto Act violated the rights of two sets of litigants who had been affected by President Clinton's use of the line-item veto, including the City of New York and the Snake River Potato Growers. The decision was appealed directly to the U.S. Supreme Court.

On June 25, 1998, the U.S. Supreme Court struck down the 1996 Line Item Veto Act in a 6-3 decision, thereby affirming the second district court ruling on the law. Writing for the majority, Justice John Paul Stevens initially rejected the government's contention that the controversy was nonjusticiable. Second, he noted the adverse effects suffered by the appellees as a result of President Clinton's employment of the line-item veto. Third, he contrasted the presentment clause in the Constitution with the wording of the Line Item Veto Act, noting that the procedures provided in the latter were not found in the former. In doing so, he construed the silence of the presentment clause on the line-item veto tool as a clear prohibition of its use. Fourth, he asserted that Congress cannot alter the language and meaning of Article I, section 7, of the Constitution except by way of an amendment.

Justice Anthony Kennedy issued a concurrence. He stated that failure of political will did not justify resorting to an unconstitutional remedy. Kennedy found that the principle of separation of powers was violated in that the executive branch alone was making spending decisions as a result of the use of the line-item veto. He highlighted federalism and accountability of the political branches to the electorate as two mechanisms by which spending could be controlled.

Justice Antonin Scalia authored an opinion that concurred in part and dissented in part with the majority; his opinion was joined by Justice Sandra Day O'Connor and by Justice Stephen G. Breyer in part. Justice Scalia believed that one of the challenges to the Line Item Veto Act should be dismissed for lack of standing. Although he found the other challenge valid, he held that the Constitution had not been violated by the provisions of the act. His reasoning centered on the authority of Congress to delegate power to the president to decline to spend on any item of a bill.

Justice Breyer wrote a dissent that was joined by Justice O'Connor and by Justice Scalia in part. He first stated his view that the parties had standing in the case. He disagreed that the Line Item Veto Act violated the literal wording of the presentment clause in the Constitution, finding the law to be a means to an end rather than an end in itself. He extensively reviewed Supreme Court holdings that upheld congressional delegation of rule-making and adjudicatory power. Finally, he did not find any violation of the separation of powers principle or any violation of individual liberties.

Significance

Prior to suspending use of the line-item veto due to pending legal action, President Clinton employed the device eighty-three times on eleven different spending bills. As a result of the Supreme Court's decision in *Clinton v. City of New York*, those vetoes were rendered moot, as was an estimated $1.9 billion in savings attributed to the tool. It is evident from an examination of Clinton's second-term veto use, however, that the line-item veto replaced regular veto issuance during 1997. Clinton's aggressive use of the veto in all its forms had discernible impacts: The annual budget was balanced during the final two years of his tenure in the White House, marking the first time that had occurred in more than three decades.

From the Civil War until the 1980's, some 150 proposals to grant the president a line-item veto power were initiated in the U.S. Congress. The 1996 Line Item Veto Act was in many ways an extension of this movement, albeit one that finally achieved fruition. Surprisingly, the law's demise did not stop efforts to imbue the president with the tool without resorting to a constitutional amendment. For example, President George W. Bush proposed the Legislative Line Item Veto Act of 2006 in March of that year. Considered a weaker version of the 1996 Line Item Veto Act, the bill was passed by the full House of Representatives in June, 2006, by a 247-172 vote. It was not approved by the Senate and therefore would have to be reintroduced in a new Congress. Senator Robert Byrd again promised to oppose granting the chief executive the line-item veto by any means other than a constitutional amendment.

Samuel B. Hoff

Further Reading

Brownell, Roy E., II. "The Unnecessary Demise of the Line Item Veto Act: The Clinton Administration's Costly Failure to Seek Acknowledgment of 'National Security Rescission.'" *American University Law Review* 47 (1997/1998): 1273-1353. Posits that the Line Item Veto Act could have been saved with limited use of the tool in the national security area.

Calabresi, Stephen G. "Separation of Powers and the Rehnquist Court: The Centrality of *Clinton v. City of New York.*" *Northwestern University Law Review* 99 (2004/2005): 77-87. Places the case in the pantheon of Supreme Court decisions regarding the separation of powers during the Rehnquist era.

Kennedy, J. Stephen. "How a Bill Does Not Become Law: The Supreme Court Sounds the Death Knell of the Line Item Veto." *Mississippi College Law Review* 20 (1999/2000). Traces the legal controversy over the line-item veto that culminated in the Supreme Court's decision in *Clinton v. City of New York* in 1998.

Spitzer, Robert J. *The Presidential Veto: Touchstone of the American Presidency.* Albany: State University of New York Press, 1988. Includes a chapter on the development of proposals for a presidential line-item veto.

"Symposium on the Line-Item Veto." *Notre Dame Journal of Law, Ethics, and Public Policy* 1 (1985): 157-283. Offers a comprehensive overview of the arguments for and against the line-item veto.

See also *Dames and Moore v. Regan; Goldwater v. Carter; Humphrey's Executor v. United States; Immigration and Naturalization Service v. Chadha; McCulloch v. Maryland; Martin v. Mott; Mississippi v. Johnson; Myers v. United States.*

CLINTON V. JONES

Court: U.S. Supreme Court
Citation: 520 U.S. 681
Date: May 27, 1997
Issues: Immunity from prosecution

• The U.S. Supreme Court unanimously rejected President Bill Clinton's claim of immunity from a civil suit while in office.

In 1994 Paula Jones brought a sexual harassment suit against President Bill Clinton. She alleged that an incident had taken place in 1991, when he was governor of Arkansas and she a state employee. President Clinton asserted that the suit should be postponed until after his term of office expired. He argued that the separation of powers doctrine places limits on the authority of the judiciary over the executive branch, and he also referred to *Nixon v. Fitz-*

gerald (1982), which provided presidents with absolute immunity from suits arising from their official duties of office.

Writing for the Supreme Court, Justice John Paul Stevens reasoned that a president was not totally immune from the jurisdiction of the federal courts and that it was appropriate for the courts to determine the legality of a president's conduct, both official and unofficial. Stevens suggested that the suit should not be especially "onerous" in time and efforts. A delay in the trial, he argued, would be unfair to Jones because it would increase the danger of prejudice from lost evidence.

Thomas Tandy Lewis

See also *Davis v. Beason; Employment Division, Department of Human Resources of Oregon v. Smith; Reynolds v. United States; Wiener v. United States.*

COHEN V. CALIFORNIA

Court: U.S. Supreme Court
Citation: 403 U.S. 15
Date: June 7, 1971
Issues: Symbolic speech

• The U.S. Supreme Court overturned the conviction of a man for wearing a jacket emblazoned with a profanity in a courthouse, thereby establishing the concept of symbolic speech and limiting the concept of "fighting words."

By a 5-4 vote, the Court overturned the conviction of a defendant who wore a jacket with the words "Fuck the draft" emblazoned across its front into a Los Angeles courthouse, where profanity was prohibited. Justice John M. Harlan II, a generally conservative justice, wrote the opinion for the 5-4 majority, which held that symbolic speech, even if provocative in nature, was protected by the First Amendment.

Although the Court substantially broadened the range of provocative speech under First Amendment protection, it left limits. For example, when young men protested the Vietnam War by burning their draft cards, the Court upheld their conviction in *United States v. O'Brien* (1968). In that case, the protection extended to symbolic speech was judged not to extend to violations of otherwise valid laws. In *Tinker v. Des Moines Independent Community School District* (1969), the Court ruled that schools cannot stop students from protesting by wearing black arm bands. In *Texas v. Johnson* (1989), the Court voided a Texas law that banned the burning of the U.S. flag, finding the act to be protected symbolic speech because it was a form of political protest.

Richard L. Wilson

See also *Texas v. Johnson; Tinker v. Des Moines Independent Community School District; United States v. O'Brien; Village of Skokie v. National Socialist Party of America.*

COHEN V. COWLES MEDIA CO.

Court: U.S. Supreme Court
Citation: 501 U.S. 663
Date: June 24, 1991
Issues: Freedom of the press

- The U.S. Supreme Court held that the First Amendment does not protect newspapers from civil suits for breaking a promise of confidentiality.

Dan Cohen, a political consultant, was fired from his job after two newspapers identified him as the source of information about a political candidate. Having been promised confidentiality, he sued for breach of contract. Based on the state's contract law, the jury awarded him $200,000 in compensatory damages. The Minnesota Supreme Court, however, overturned the award, concluding that protection for the First Amendment's freedom of the press outweighed the state's interest in enforcing contractual obligations.

By a 5-4 margin, the Supreme Court directed Minnesota's high court to reconsider the judgment according to the relevant state laws. Speaking for the majority, Justice Byron R. White reasoned that the First Amendment did not give the publisher of a newspaper any special immunity from the enforcement of general laws and that the application of a general law against the press is not subject to any heightened scrutiny simply because its incidental effect is to make it more difficult for the press to gather and report the news. In contrast, the dissenters argued that an indirect restraint on the truthful reporting of political speech should be judged by the compelling state interest test.

Thomas Tandy Lewis

See also *Branzburg v. Hayes*; *Grosjean v. American Press Co.*; *Miami Herald Publishing Co. v. Tornillo*; *Richmond Newspapers v. Virginia.*

COHENS V. VIRGINIA

Court: U.S. Supreme Court
Citation: 6 Wheat. (19 U.S.) 264
Date: March 3, 1821
Issues: Federal supremacy; Judicial powers; State sovereignty

- Chief Justice John Marshall used a minor dispute over the sale of lottery tickets in Virginia to assert the U.S. Supreme Court's jurisdiction over state court decisions.

After Congress authorized a lottery sale for the District of Columbia, a Virginia court fined the Cohen brothers one hundred dollars for selling tickets in Virginia in violation of a state statute. The two brothers appealed their fine to the Supreme Court, asserting that the Virginia court had acted unconstitutionally. Virginia claimed immunity from review, based on the Eleventh Amendment and on principles of state sovereignty. Speaking for a unanimous Court, Chief Justice John Marshall made a narrow ruling in favor of Virginia, with the rationale that Congress had not intended lottery tickets to be sold in states where they were illegal.

Marshall's opinion in *Cohens v. Virginia* is memorable because of its vigorous defense of the Court's broad jurisdiction and the principle of national supremacy. In regard to states' rights, Marshall argued that the states had surrendered much of their sovereignty when they joined a national union. Taking a narrow reading of the Eleventh Amendment, Marshall wrote that the amendment did not apply when the sole purpose of a suit was to inquire about whether a state court had violated the U.S. Constitution or federal law. Marshall's lengthy opinion presented a sweeping interpretation of the Court's appellate jurisdiction over all state court decisions involving issues of national authority. Defenders of states' rights, including Thomas Jefferson, denounced *Cohens* as an extreme step toward the consolidation of federal power.

Thomas Tandy Lewis

See also *Craig v. Missouri; Gibbons v. Ogden; McCulloch v. Maryland; Martin v. Hunter's Lessee.*

COKER V. GEORGIA

Court: U.S. Supreme Court
Citation: 433 U.S. 584
Date: June 29, 1977
Issues: Capital punishment; Cruel and unusual punishment; Women's issues

- The Court ruled that capital punishment for the crime of rape is an excessive and disproportionate penalty that violates the Eighth Amendment.

While serving sentences for murder, rape, kidnapping, and other crimes, Erlich Anthony Coker escaped from a Georgia prison in 1974. That same evening he entered the private home of a couple, tied up the husband in the bathroom, raped the wife, and then forced her to leave with him in the car belonging to the couple. Apprehended by the police, Coker was tried and convicted on charges of rape, armed robbery, and kidnapping. Based on procedures that had been approved by the U.S. Supreme Court in *Gregg v. Georgia* (1976), the jury found Coker guilty of rape with aggravating circumstances and sentenced him to death. After the Georgia Supreme Court upheld the conviction and sentence, the U.S. Supreme Court accepted the case for review.

The Supreme Court limited its review to the single question whether capital punishment for rape is a cruel and unusual punishment that violates the Eighth and Fourteenth Amendments. Ruling seven to two in the affirmative, the Court reversed Coker's death sentence and remanded the case to the Georgia courts for a new sentencing.

Writing the majority opinion, Justice Byron R. White argued that the sentence of death for the crime of rape is unconstitutional because it is an excessive and disproportionate punishment. As evidence that the public judgment agreed with this conclusion, White pointed to the fact that Georgia was the only state to authorize the death penalty for the rape of an adult woman. Although the crime of rape deserved serious punishment, it was disproportionate to inflict the defendant with a more severe punishment than he inflicted on his victim. Although rape was not equivalent to the unjustifiable taking of a human life, the crime of deliberate murder in Georgia was not a basis for the death penalty except where there were aggravating circumstances. White wrote that it was disproportionate to punish a rapist more severely than a deliberate killer.

As in other cases dealing with capital punishment, the justices expressed a variety of views. Two concurring justices opposed all use of capital punishment, while two dissenters would have allowed it for rape. One justice, Lewis F. Powell, Jr., joined the majority because the rapist did not inflict great brutality or serious injury on the victim.

The *Coker* decision underscored the extent to which the Court had accepted the view that the Eighth Amendment prohibited excessive and disproportionate punishments. It appeared that the Court would not approve the use of the death penalty for any crime other than deliberate murder, but it was not certain how the Court would react to capital punishment for rape with excessive brutality or when the victim sustained serious injury. Some observers noted that *Coker* appeared to indicate that the Court was becoming more reliant upon the doctrine of substantive due process.

Thomas Tandy Lewis

See also *Furman v. Georgia; Gregg v. Georgia; Harmelin v. Michigan; Hutto v. Davis; Louisiana ex rel. Francis v. Resweber; McCleskey v. Kemp; Rhodes v. Chapman; Robinson v. California; Rummel v. Estelle.*

COLEGROVE V. GREEN

Court: U.S. Supreme Court
Citation: 328 U.S. 549
Date: June 10, 1946
Issues: Equal protection of the law; Reapportionment and redistricting; Voting rights

• In this case, which remained as a precedent until the 1960's, the U.S. Supreme Court decided that it could not decide whether congressional districts were properly drawn because this issue constituted a "political question" that had to be decided by elected officials.

Three voters who resided in Illinois districts with much larger populations than other congressional districts in the state filed an action to challenge the unequal sizes of Illinois legislative districts. In Illinois and other states, state legislatures had marked out legislative districts of unequal size or else had failed to draw new district boundaries when population patterns changed. One congressional district in Illinois, for example, contained 914,000 people while another district contained only 112,000.

The effect of such maldistribution was to dilute the voting strength of voters in larger districts and enhance the power of voters in smaller districts. In Congress, two representatives from districts containing fewer than 150,000 people could outvote a representative from a district containing more than 900,000. Thus government was more responsive to and controlled by people from smaller districts than representative of the wishes of the majority of voters, whose votes would be diluted in larger districts. Rural interests in many states controlled political power and the development of public policy, despite the fact that a majority of citizens lived in urban and suburban areas.

In an opinion by Justice Felix Frankfurter, the Supreme Court declined to decide whether unequal legislative districts violated the equal protection rights of voters in larger districts. On behalf of a five-member majority, Frankfurter declared that issues concerning legislative districting were "beyond [the] competence" of courts because such issues were "of a peculiarly political nature and therefore not meant for judicial determination." By labeling legislative districting a "political question" unsuited for judicial resolution, the majority of justices avoided any examination of questions about discrimination and voting rights that were raised by the existence of unequal districts.

Three dissenting justices, Hugo Black, William O. Douglas, and Frank Murphy, complained that the Court was improperly permitting state legislatures to violate the rights of voters in larger districts. One justice, Robert H. Jackson, did not take part in the case.

The Court's decision left districting temporarily in the hands of state legislatures. Justices Black and Douglas were still on the Court two decades later, however, when a new set of justices revisited the issue and decided that districts must be designed with comparable populations in order to avoid violating citizens' equal protection rights. In *Baker v. Carr* (1962), the Supreme Court decided that such legislative districting questions were not reserved for the legislative branch alone but could also be examined by the judiciary. In the subsequent cases of *Wesberry v. Sanders* (1964) and *Reynolds v. Sims* (1964), the *Colegrove* precedent was completely eliminated when the Court mandated that federal and state legislative districts be of equivalent sizes.

Christopher E. Smith

See also *Baker v. Carr; Gomillion v. Lightfoot; Reynolds v. Sims; Wesberry v. Sanders.*

COLEMAN V. MILLER

Court: U.S. Supreme Court
Citation: 307 U.S. 433
Date: June 5, 1939
Issues: Constitutionalism

• In deciding three issues regarding the ratification of a child labor constitutional amendment, the U.S. Supreme Court introduced the Fourteenth Amendment, adding considerable confusion to the process.

Chief Justice Charles Evans Hughes wrote the opinion for the 7-2 majority with Justices Pierce Butler and James C. McReynolds dissenting. The Court left standing a lower court's decision that the lieutenant-governor of Kansas could cast a tie-breaking vote in the constitutional amendment ratification process. It also found the state's ratification of an amendment it had previously rejected and the issue of whether time limits should exist for ratification of amendments to be political questions for Congress to resolve. Congress later began to add time limits to all proposed constitutional amendments. The vagueness of *Coleman* confused the ratification process for amendments to the U.S. Constitution by introducing Fourteenth Amendment considerations. Subsequently, *Coleman* was limited by *Idaho v. Freeman* (1981), in which the Court allowed a state to rescind its ratification of the Equal Rights Amendment after the original deadline was extended by Congress.

Richard L. Wilson

See also *Dillon v. Gloss; Edelman v. Jordan; Frontiero v. Richardson.*

COLLECTOR V. DAY

Court: U.S. Supreme Court
Citation: 78 U.S. 113
Date: April 3, 1871
Issues: Federalism

• In a series of decisions on tax immunities, the U.S. Supreme Court held that the federal government could not tax the income of a state judge, based on dual sovereignty of the state and the federal government.

Collector is of historical interest for its place in a line of opinions on tax immunities that began with Chief Justice John Marshall's opinion in *McCulloch v. Maryland* (1819). Marshall held that the state could not impose a tax on an institution created by the federal government. Following this line, the Court held in *Dobbins v. Erie County* (1842) that the state could not tax the income of a federal official.

In *Collector,* the opposite situation from *Dobbins,* the Court held that the federal government could not tax the income of a state judge. Justice Samuel Nelson wrote the 8-1 majority opinion; only Justice Joseph P. Bradley dissented. Nelson relied on the Tenth Amendment and on the theory of dual sovereignty to hold that both the state and federal governments were independent of each other and states retain all aspects of sovereignty not delegated to the national government. This was the strongest view of dual sovereignty presented by the Court, but it could not be sustained over time. *Collector* was substantially weakened by *Helvering v. Gerhardt* (1938) and directly overturned in *Graves v. New York ex rel. O'Keefe* (1939).

Richard L. Wilson

See also *Dobbins v. Erie County; Graves v. New York ex rel. O'Keefe; Helvering v. Davis; McCulloch v. Maryland.*

COLUMBUS BOARD OF EDUCATION V. PENICK

Court: U.S. Supreme Court
Citation: 443 U.S. 449
Date: July 2, 1979
Issues: Desegregation; Education

- The U.S. Supreme Court supported the use of a districtwide urban desegregation plan at a time when many observers thought the Court was unwilling to uphold the use of busing to correct de facto school segregation.

By 1979, as the result of *Milliken v. Bradley* (1974) and *Pasadena Board of Education v. Spangler* (1976), the Supreme Court appeared no longer willing to impose on urban districts large, complicated school desegregation plans involving busing. However, in a 7-2 vote, the Court supported such a system in Columbus, Ohio. It reaffirmed the basic principles it announced in *Swann v. Charlotte-Mecklenburg Board of Education* (1971). The Court insisted that purposeful segregation in a substantial portion of a metropolitan school district created a strong presumption that the board or system had practiced systemwide segregation or tolerated its existence, thereby mandating widespread extraordinary relief. It ruled that as long as a system seemed infected with segregative intent when *Brown v. Board of Education* (1954) was decided, that school board remained under an obligation to dismantle the segregated system if it had not already done so. This was true even if innocent behavior had produced segregated results. In dissent, Justice Lewis F. Powell, Jr., restated his belief that the de facto/de jure distinction made no sense, and Justice William H. Rehnquist objected to making an improper intrusion into local education decision making.

Richard L. Wilson

See also *Board of Education of Oklahoma City v. Dowell; Brown v. Board of Education; Keyes v. Denver School District No. 1; Lemon v. Kurtzman; Milliken v. Bradley; Parents Involved in Community Schools v. Seattle School District No. 1; Pasadena Board of Education v. Spangler; Swann v. Charlotte-Mecklenburg Board of Education.*

COMMONWEALTH V. HUNT

Court: Massachusetts Supreme Judicial Court
Citation: 45 Mass. 111, 4 Met.
Date: March, 1842
Issues: Common law; Labor law

• This Massachusetts court ruling articulated the first legal basis for American workers to organize and strike.

Although its impact was not felt for almost three-quarters of a century, the case of *Commonwealth v. Hunt*, which was decided by the Supreme Judicial Court of Massachusetts in March, 1842, was a major event in the evolution of the legal status of organized labor. The case dealt with one of the most difficult problems encountered in Anglo-American law: the definition and treatment of combinations of employers or employees (or both) engaged in the restraint of trade.

Analyses of nineteenth century American labor were complicated by the questions of whether a given trade union itself was unlawful as an organization or, instead, had become unlawful through the way it was utilized to achieve demands. Answers to those queries were required before any law applying to organized labor could be stated with any degree of certainty. They were provided, for the most part, by the decision of *Commonwealth v. Hunt*, which helped to fix principles by which the rights of labor might be definitely ascertained.

Beginning with the Philadelphia Shoemakers' case in 1806, courts in the United States had followed the lead of English courts and the common-law doctrine of criminal conspiracy by punishing persons seeking to form labor organizations. Precedence for that American decision had been provided by the 1721 English case of *Rex v. Journeyman Tailors of Cambridge*, in which a labor union seeking higher wages for its members was treated as a criminal conspiracy. In 1800, Parliament assigned criminal penalties for workers entering "any combination to obtain an advance of wages or to lessen or alter the hours of work." This British doctrine was in accord with the generally accepted opinion that the demands of labor organizations would upset the economic laws of supply and demand, artificially increase the prices of goods and services, and interfere with the freedom to contract. Ultimately, it was believed, the organization of labor would upset the natural relationship between population and food supply.

Commonwealth v. Hunt tested those concerns in the United States. The case stemmed from the activities and policies of the Boston Journeymen Bootmakers' Society. In 1841, this society sought to establish a "closed shop," a plan whereby employers would hire only workers who were approved by the society's union and who would agree to follow a strict set of labor rules. Society member Jeremiah Horne violated one of those rules when he agreed to do extra work without receiving extra pay. The union immediately organized a work stoppage, to continue until Horne either paid a stiff fine for violating union rules or was fired by his employer. Horne's employer, Isaac Wait, was reluctant to lose a good employee, so he offered to pay Horne's fine to help him comply. However, Horne refused to allow payment of his fine, and Wait was forced to fire him.

Horne later took up the matter with the state prosecutor, district attorney Samuel D. Parker, who presented the case to a grand jury. Parker secured an indictment against the shoemakers' union. The indictment charged that the union had criminally conspired to control Wait's employment practices and had made efforts to bring economic ruin upon Horne, Wait, and other union members. In short, Parker accused the union of attempting to create a closed shop.

The Court's Ruling

The trial was heard in Boston Municipal Court before Judge Peter O. Thatcher. Thatcher ran his courtroom under the assumption that the future welfare of the state and the nation depended upon the jury's assistance in preventing labor unions from gaining recognition in society. Defense counsel Robert Rantoul, Jr., argued that labor organizations were analogous to professional organizations and that the common-law doctrine of criminal conspiracy should be rejected as hostile to American freedom. Thatcher rejected these arguments and suggested to the jury that, as a matter of law, the Boston Journeymen Bootmakers' Society—and, by implication, other labor unions—constituted an unlawful conspiracy. The jury returned a guilty verdict.

When the case was appealed to the Judicial Court, Rantoul's main argument was that the common-law doctrine of criminal conspiracy was not a part of the law of Massachusetts. Once again, Rantoul's line of reasoning was not accepted. However, Chief Justice Lemuel Shaw did provide a legal reinterpretation of the law, creating a foundation on which to overturn the society's conviction. A conspiracy, said Shaw, must be a combination (of employers and/or employees) united for an unlawful purpose or a combination united to accomplish an innocent purpose by unlawful means. By that standard, Shaw went on to find that a combination united for the purpose of inducing fellow workers to join a given organization and to follow its rules was not unlawful. It was an unwarranted assumption, he reasoned, to conclude that the society would have abused its power. Had it done so, it would have been answerable to the criminal law, but it was not unlawful for workers to have organized, even for the purpose of forming a closed shop to demand higher wages.

In refusing to work so long as Horne was not discharged, the court ruled, the journeymen had merely been exercising their lawful right to work or not to work. Shaw decided that it was lawful, however, to demand that the individual worker in question be fired, since the union had not relied on force or fraud to expel him, nor had it insisted that his employer violate the provisions of a contract. Finally, Shaw rejected the prosecution's argument that the union was conspiring to impoverish Horne, Wait, or others. He justified his rejection by pointing out that the evenhanded, mechanical enforcement of the rule against combinations united to impoverish third parties by indirect means would result in an excessive stifling of open competition, the basic premise of a capitalist society.

Thus, the rule of *Commonwealth v. Hunt* may be stated as follows: While the common law of conspiracy is a part of the Massachusetts common law, the mere formation and operation of a labor organization in the interest of its members does not constitute a criminal conspiracy.

Significance

The impact of the decision in *Commonwealth v. Hunt* as legal precedent was sufficiently great, according to some labor historians, to deter the use of the doctrine of criminal conspiracy against unions for some forty years after its implementation. However, when the courts revived the doctrine during the 1880's, its effectiveness was soon eclipsed by the more versatile method of securing injunctions against labor organizing activity. The injunction clause, and not the criminal conspiracy doctrine, was used in connection with the Sherman Antitrust Act of 1890 to force the breakup of monopolistic combinations engaged in the restraint of free enterprise.

Commonwealth v. Hunt nevertheless remained a piece of prolabor legislation worthy of veneration by those disposed to the cause of workers. Justice Oliver Wendell Holmes, Jr., while serving on the Supreme Judicial Court of Massachusetts, spoke highly of Shaw's reasoning in the influential dissent in *Vegelahn v. Guntner* (1896). *Commonwealth v. Hunt* thus ultimately earned high recognition by becoming associated with Holmes and the cause of labor reform.

James J. Bolner,
updated by Thomas J. Edward Walker and Cynthia Gwynne Yaudes

Further Reading

Green, James, and Hugh Carter Donahue. *Boston's Workers: A Labor History.* Boston: Trustees of the Boston Public Library, 1979. Community history that analyzes the significant contributions of Boston's working classes, describing the independent initiatives of community labor organizers. Index, bibliography.

Gregory, Charles O. *Labor and the Law.* New York: W. W. Norton, 1949. Provides a concise summary of *Commonwealth v. Hunt* and its significance for the history of labor law. Index.

Juravich, Tom, William F. Hartford, and James R. Green. *Commonwealth of Toil: Chapters in the History of Massachusetts Workers and Their Unions.* Amherst: University of Massachusetts Press, 1996. Comprehensive history of labor unions in the Commonwealth of Massachusetts.

Levy, Leonard W. *The Law of the Commonwealth and Chief Justice Shaw: The Evolution of American Law, 1830 to 1860.* Cambridge, Mass.: Harvard University Press, 1957. A "judicial biography" that discusses Shaw's contributions to the law of criminal conspiracy; contains some thought-provoking chapters on Shaw's concept of objectivity. Index, bibliography.

Mason, Alpheus T. *Organized Labor and the Law.* Durham, N.C.: Duke University Press, 1925. Presents the fundamental legal doctrines that have guided the courts of the United States in defining and setting limits upon the rights of organized labor. Index, bibliographical essay.

Rayback, Joseph G. *A History of American Labor.* Rev. ed. New York: Free Press, 1966. Detailed survey of the history of workers and labor unions in the United States.

Tomlins, Christopher L. *The State and the Unions: Labor Relations, Law, and the Organized Labor Movement in America, 1880-1960.* New York: Cambridge University Press, 1985. An institutional history of both unions and the legal regulation of labor organization and activity. Discusses the impact of *Commonwealth v. Hunt* on "modern" labor legislation. Index, bibliography.

See also *Adair v. United States; Duplex Printing Co. v. Deering; In re Debs; Thornhill v. Alabama.*

COMMUNIST PARTY V. SUBVERSIVE ACTIVITIES CONTROL BOARD

Court: U.S. Supreme Court
Citation: 367 U.S. 1
Date: June 5, 1961
Issues: Antigovernment subversion; Freedom of assembly and association; Right to travel

• The U.S. Supreme Court upheld the registration provisions of the McCarran Act of 1950, although it declined to rule on the constitutionality of sanctions written into the act.

A five-member majority of the Supreme Court upheld the McCarran Act of 1950, which required members of the Communist Party to register and file financial statements with the Subversive Activities Control Board, making them subject to sanctions such as being banned from work in the defense industry. Justice Felix Frankfurter wrote the opinion for the Court and Chief Justice Earl Warren and Justices Hugo L. Black, William J. Brennan, Jr., and William O. Douglas dissented. Although the Court upheld the act's registration provisions, it declined to rule on enforcement until enforcement was attempted. This led some observers to believe that the Court might rule against the McCarran Act. In *Aptheker v. Secretary of State* (1964), the Court ruled the denial of passports to Communist Party members to be an unconstitutional violation of the right to travel. The next year, the Court struck down the registration provisions in *Albertson v. Subversive Activities Control Board* (1965), calling them a violation of Fifth Amendment rights as registration led to sanctions. These decisions destroyed the effectiveness of the Subversive Activities Control Board, and Congress allowed the board to expire in the early 1970's.

Richard L. Wilson

See also *Albertson v. Subversive Activities Control Board; Aptheker v. Secretary of State; Scales v. United States; Yates v. United States.*

Cooley v. Board of Wardens of the Port of Philadelphia

Court: U.S. Supreme Court
Citation: 12 How. (53 U.S.) 299
Date: March 2, 1852
Issues: Interstate commerce

• In upholding a state statute regulating navigation standards for ships, the U.S. Supreme Court formulated the doctrine of selective exclusiveness, allowing states to regulate aspects of interstate commerce in the absence of federal laws.

A Pennsylvania law required each ship entering or leaving Philadelphia to hire a local pilot for navigation purposes. When Aaron Cooley was fined for disobeying the law, he argued that it was an unconstitutional regulation of interstate commerce. By a 6-2 vote, the Supreme Court rejected his argument. Speaking for the majority, Justice Benjamin R. Curtis made a distinction between activities needing a single national rule and other activities, such as pilotage laws, that were essentially local in nature. In the latter category, states retained a concurrent authority until Congress exerted its paramount power. The *Cooley* rule was essentially a compromise that allowed states to exercise limited control over interstate commerce, and it operated as a practical formula for nearly a century.

Thomas Tandy Lewis

See also *License Cases; Passenger Cases; Pennsylvania v. Wheeling and Belmont Bridge Co.; Prudential Insurance Co. v. Benjamin.*

Cooper v. Aaron

Court: U.S. Supreme Court
Citation: 358 U.S. 1
Date: September 12, 1958
Issues: Desegregation; Education; Equal protection of the law;
Judicial powers

- The U.S. Supreme Court held that fear of violence did not provide justification for postponing school desegregation, and it also affirmed that its constitutional interpretations were legally binding on governors and state legislators.

In *Brown v. Board of Education* (1954), the Supreme Court ruled that racial segregation of the public schools violated the equal protection clause of the Fourteenth Amendment. The next year, in *Brown II*, the Court ordered desegregation to proceed "with all deliberate speed." The Little Rock crisis of 1957-1958 occurred after a federal district judge approved a desegregation plan that scheduled nine African American students to enter Little Rock's Central High School in September, 1957. When classes began, Arkansas Governor Orville Faubus and the state legislature acted on the premise that they had no legal obligation to enforce the *Brown* decision. Confronted with an open defiance to federal authority, President Dwight D. Eisenhower dispatched federal troops to restore order and to enforce the desegregation order.

With tensions in Little Rock continuing in 1958, the school board asked the district judge to withdraw the African American students from the school and to postpone desegregation until September, 1960. The judge accepted the proposal. In expedited proceedings, the Supreme Court reversed the judge's ruling. Justice William J. Brennan, Jr., prepared a draft of an opinion, which was then reworked and signed by all nine justices. The joint opinion held that postponement was unacceptable because it would violate the constitutional rights of the African American students. In addition, the Court declared that "the federal judiciary is supreme in the exposition of the law of the Constitution," meaning that state governments must recognize the *Brown* holding as "the supreme law of the land." Never before had the Court expressed the doctrine of judicial supremacy in such strong terms.

Although President Eisenhower personally disagreed with the *Brown* decision, he made it manifestly clear that he would use his executive powers to enforce the decrees and interpretations of the Court. Confident of presidential enforcement, the justices were encouraged to take a firm stand in the *Cooper* ruling. It was not until the Civil Rights Act of 1964 that Congress provided statutory support for the desegregation effort.

Thomas Tandy Lewis

See also *Alexander v. Holmes County Board of Education; Board of Education of Oklahoma City v. Dowell; Brown v. Board of Education; Columbus Board of Education v. Penick; Green v. County School Board of New Kent County; Keyes v. Denver School District No. 1; Milliken v. Bradley; Pasadena Board of Education v. Spangler; Swann v. Charlotte-Mecklenburg Board of Education.*

Corrigan v. Buckley

Court: U.S. Supreme Court
Citation: 271 U.S. 323
Date: May 24, 1926
Issues: Housing discrimination; Private discrimination

- The U.S. Supreme Court upheld a restrictive covenant in the District of Columbia, a ruling that would stand until 1948, more than twenty years later.

Restrictive covenants blocked the sale of properties owned by whites to members of minority groups and were designed to maintain segregation in an area. When a white owner of property controlled by a restrictive covenant subsequently contracted to sell it to an African American, other white owners asked the District of Columbia federal court to enforce the covenant and block the sale. The district court upheld the covenant. The Supreme Court unanimously affirmed the lower court's decision. Justice Edward T. Sanford, writing the opinion for the Court, disposed of various constitutional provisions. He noted that the Fifth Amendment was limited to the federal government (not individuals), that the Thirteenth Amendment protected African Americans only in their personal liberty (not contracts), and that the Fourteenth Amendment applied to states (not the District of Columbia).

The Court further held that the 1866 Civil Rights Act granted all people the legal authority to contract but did not prohibit or invalidate contracts between private individuals such as restrictive covenants. Sanford also said that judicial enforcement of covenants was not the same as state action denying people their Fourteenth Amendment rights. This decision closed the door to racially integrated housing that had been partially opened by *Buchanan v. Warley* (1917). It lasted more than two decades until *Shelley v. Kraemer* (1948) upheld such covenants but banned judicial enforcement as a form of state action prohibited by the Fourteenth Amendment.

Richard L. Wilson

See also *Buchanan v. Warley; Evans v. Abney; Reitman v. Mulkey; Shelley v. Kraemer; Spallone v. United States.*

COUNSELMAN V. HITCHCOCK

Court: U.S. Supreme Court
Citation: 142 U.S. 547
Date: January 11, 1892
Issues: Immunity from prosecution; Self-incrimination

• The U.S. Supreme Court upheld a person's refusal to testify before a grand jury, stating that the privilege against self-incrimination extends beyond criminal trials to investigations such as grand jury proceedings.

In *Counselman v. Hitchcock*, the Court considered a federal statute that granted witnesses immunity from criminal prosecution based on their testimony during judicial proceedings but not on their testimony before a federal grand jury. Charles Counselman asserted his Fifth Amendment privilege against self-incrimination in refusing to answer questions before a federal grand jury and asked for a writ of habeas corpus when he was confined for contempt of court for not answering.

The Court unanimously upheld his refusal to testify. In his opinion for the Court, Justice Samuel Blatchford stated that the privilege against self-incrimination could be used by an accused not only in a criminal trial but also in any investigation including grand jury proceedings. Federal immunity law could

Justice Samuel Blatchford. (Library of Congress)

not compel the appellant to testify because its protective scope was less than the Fifth Amendment guarantee. The statute prohibited the direct use of testimony in subsequent prosecution of the witness but not the testimony's use to search for other evidence. This broad privilege was narrowed substantially in *Kastigar v. United States* (1972) when the Court allowed evidence obtained independently to be used against a person who had testified under an immunity agreement.

Richard L. Wilson

See also *Adamson v. California; Boyd v. United States; Griffin v. California; Kastigar v. United States; Kilbourn v. Thompson; Malloy v. Hogan; Minnick v. Mississippi; Murphy v. Waterfront Commission of New York.*

COUNTY OF WASHINGTON V. GUNTHER

Court: U.S. Supreme Court
Citation: 452 U.S. 161
Date: June 8, 1981
Issues: Civil rights and liberties; Labor law; Sex discrimination;
Women's issues

- This case ruled that the parties alleging sex-based wage discrimination under Title VII of the Civil Rights Act of 1964 are required to show that a member of the opposite sex who holds the same position is receiving a higher rate of pay.

Female guards in an Oregon county jail were performing jobs similar to that of their male counterparts, but with more clerical work. The female guards were paid only 70 percent of the amount that the male guards were paid. These female guards filed suit under Title VII of the Civil Rights Act of 1964. The women contended that the difference in their wages was attributable solely to sex discrimination.

When hearing *County of Washington v. Gunther*, the U.S. Supreme Court dismissed any connection between its holding and the doctrine of comparable

---

SEEKING EQUAL PAY FOR EQUAL WORK

American women have struggled for equal pay for many years, and thousands of women have joined together to file class-action sex-discrimination suits against large corporations. The first major victory came in 1973 in a suit against American Telephone and Telegraph (AT&T); the giant communications company paid out $38 million to more than 13,000 women. In a class-action suit filed against Wal-Mart during the first years of the twenty-first century, hourly and salaried female employees of the world's largest retailer sought lost wages and punitive damages. Both sex discrimination cases were based on claims of unequal pay when compared with men in similar positions and failure of the companies to promote women to management positions.

worth. The theory of comparable worth holds that whole classes of jobs are traditionally underpaid because they are held by women. The Court's decision indicated that the Equal Pay Act of 1963 and the sex discrimination provisions of Title VII were directed toward the same goal of eliminating sex discrimination in employment. The Equal Pay Act affords a remedy only in limited situations involving wage-based discrimination claims. The Court's decision opened another avenue for female plaintiffs to seek legal remedies under Title VII. After this decision, women could pursue remedies under Title VII for sex-based wage discrimination even in situations in which their job descriptions were not substantially equal to those of their male counterparts.

Susan M. Taylor

See also *Bowe v. Colgate-Palmolive; Bradwell v. Illinois; Frontiero v. Richardson; Grove City College v. Bell; Hoyt v. Florida; Meritor Savings Bank v. Vinson; Rosenfeld v. Southern Pacific; Weeks v. Southern Bell.*

Cox v. Louisiana

Court: U.S. Supreme Court
Citation: 379 U.S. 536
Date: January 18, 1965
Issues: Civil rights and liberties; Freedom of assembly and association; Local government

- The U.S. Supreme Court overturned the conviction of a group of civil rights demonstrators, arguing that the group had a right to demonstrate peacefully even if local government officials disliked their political views.

By a 7-2 vote, the Supreme Court ruled that the conviction of civil rights demonstrators in Louisiana must be reversed because the state had allowed other approved groups to block traffic in similar ways to those convicted in this case. In *Cox*, it appeared that the state had improperly convicted these demonstrators because of the unpopularity of their views. In its decision, the Court was following the logic of time, place, and manner regulations that allow for safe, orderly streets but require like treatment of all demonstrators. Assembly is not as protected as speech is because the First Amendment qualifies assembly by the use of the word "peaceably." This case should be contrasted with *Adderley v. Florida* (1966), in which the Court upheld the conviction of people who had demonstrated on the grounds of a county jail.

Richard L. Wilson

See also *Adderley v. Florida; Cox v. New Hampshire; Whitney v. California.*

Cox v. New Hampshire

Court: U.S. Supreme Court
Citation: 312 U.S. 569
Date: March 31, 1941
Issues: First Amendment guarantees; Freedom of assembly and association; Local government

• The U.S. Supreme Court's decision protected the right of local government officials to place nondiscriminatory time, place, and manner restrictions on demonstrators.

Cox is part of a series of cases establishing the government's right to place reasonable time, place, and manner regulations on assemblies as long as these laws do not prevent people from speaking out or favor some speakers over others. It is also one of a number of cases in which the Jehovah's Witnesses challenged various laws as denials of their free exercise of religion. Although the Jehovah's Witnesses were often successful, they did not prevail in *Cox*.

A Manchester, New Hampshire, city ordinance required groups to have a parade license and pay a fee. Some Jehovah's Witnesses marched single file through city streets carrying placards to advertise a meeting but refused to get a license or pay the fee. Upon their arrest, their leader argued that they were not having a parade. Further, they also asserted that the Manchester ordinance was vague, unreasonable, and arbitrary and deprived them of their First Amendment rights as guaranteed by the Fourteenth Amendment. In its unanimous decision, the Court upheld the ordinance solely as a means of regulating traffic and reasonably providing for orderly, safe streets.

Richard L. Wilson

See also *Adderley v. Florida; Cox v. Louisiana; Whitney v. California.*

Coyle v. Smith

Court: U.S. Supreme Court
Citation: 221 U.S. 559
Date: May 29, 1911
Issues: States' rights

- The U.S. Supreme Court, citing the equality of states, ruled that Congress could not impose conditions on a territory that remained valid after it had become a state.

When Congress passed legislation admitting Oklahoma as a state, it stipulated that Guthrie was to be the capital until 1913. Oklahoma accepted this provision when it became a state in 1907, but after three years, it decided to move the capital to Oklahoma City. Some citizens asked the Supreme Court to decide if Congress could impose conditions that remained valid after ad-

Justice Horace H. Lurton. (Harris and Ewing/ Collection of the Supreme Court of the United States)

mission. After examining cases relating back to the Northwest Ordinance of 1787, the Court, by a vote of 7-2, found that congressional restrictions were an impermissible infringement that made Oklahoma unequal with other states. Justice Horace H. Lurton, writing for the majority, stated that although the Constitution did not explicitly deal with this issue, the Court viewed state equality as an unwritten tradition.

Richard L. Wilson

See also *Cohens v. Virginia; National League of Cities v. Usery; Texas v. White; United States v. Cruikshank.*

CRAIG V. BOREN

Court: U.S. Supreme Court
Citation: 429 U.S. 190
Date: December 20, 1976
Issues: Affirmative action; Judicial review; Sex discrimination

• The U.S. Supreme Court adopted a heightened level of judicial scrutiny when dealing with gender-based classifications alleged to be discriminatory.

Oklahoma law permitted eighteen-year-old women to purchase beer with 3.2 percent alcohol but required men to be twenty-one years old for the same privilege. Curtis Craig and a licensed vendor challenged the law. The state had statistical evidence demonstrating a reasonable basis for the law. The Supreme Court had recognized since 1971 that the equal protection clause of the Fourteenth Amendment applied to classifications based on sex. The issue in the *Craig* case was whether the law should be evaluated according to the rational basis test or the very demanding standard of strict scrutiny, as used in classifications based on race.

By a vote of seven to two, the Court found that the Oklahoma law was unconstitutional. Writing for the majority, Justice William J. Brennan, Jr., demanded that any statute classifying by gender "must serve important governmental objectives and must be substantially related to these objectives." Although the justices were badly divided, *Craig* established the intermediate level of scrutiny for determining whether particular gender distinctions are constitutional, and the compromise has continued ever since. Apparently, the decision did not apply to cases involving affirmative action programs.

Thomas Tandy Lewis

See also *County of Washington v. Gunther; Frontiero v. Richardson; Geduldig v. Aiello; Grove City College v. Bell; Hoyt v. Florida; Michael M. v. Superior Court of Sonoma County; Mississippi University for Women v. Hogan; Reed v. Reed; Rostker v. Goldberg.*

CRAIG V. MISSOURI

Court: U.S. Supreme Court
Citation: 29 U.S. 410
Date: March 12, 1830
Issues: Fiscal and monetary powers; State sovereignty; States' rights

• The U.S. Supreme Court's split decision in a case involving loan certificates issued by the state of Missouri showed the beginning of the Court's evolution away from the influence of Chief Justice John Marshall.

Article I, section 10, of the U.S. Constitution bans states from emitting "bills of credits." Nonetheless, Missouri had authorized circulating loan certificates, arguing that they were a legitimate exercise of state sovereignty. The state further challenged the constitutionality of section 25 of the 1789 Judiciary Act. In a 4-3 split decision—unusual for the Supreme Court at the time—the Court overturned the Missouri law authorizing the certificates. In his opinion for the Court, Chief Justice John Marshall used a historical analysis of paper money in America to explain why the Constitution's prohibition on state bills of credit voided the Missouri statute. In keeping with his *Cohens v. Virginia* (1821) opinion, Marshall also defended section 25 of the 1789 Judiciary Act, which granted nondiscretionary authority to the Court.

The three dissenters—Justices William Johnson, Smith Thompson, and John McLean—believed that there was enough variation in the statutory language to exempt the Missouri law from the constitutional provision. Seven years later, the new chief justice, Roger Brooke Taney, upheld a variant of the Missouri currency arrangement in *Briscoe v. Bank of the Commonwealth of Kentucky* (1837).

Richard L. Wilson

See also *Briscoe v. Bank of the Commonwealth of Kentucky; Cohens v. Virginia; Collector v. Day; National League of Cities v. Usery.*

CROW DOG, EX PARTE. *See* EX PARTE CROW DOG

CRUIKSHANK, UNITED STATES V. *See* UNITED STATES V. CRUIKSHANK

CRUZAN V. DIRECTOR, MISSOURI DEPARTMENT OF HEALTH

Court: U.S. Supreme Court
Citation: 497 U.S. 261
Date: June 25, 1990
Issues: Medical ethics; Parental rights

• A milestone U.S. Supreme Court decision in 1990 established the constitutional right of terminally ill patients to refuse or discontinue medical interventions necessary to sustain their lives under conditions that were specified by the court. This ruling intensified debate concerning the "right to die."

The topic of "passive euthanasia," allowing hopelessly afflicted patients to die by withdrawing life-support measures, was brought to the forefront of the public consciousness in 1976 when Karen Ann Quinlan's family successfully petitioned the New Jersey Supreme Court for permission to turn off her respirator. Quinlan had been rendered comatose in 1975, with a total loss of brain function. She could not breathe properly without a respirator and received food and water through a tube. When Quinlan remained alive without a respirator, state courts refused the family's requests to remove her feeding tube, and she lived for nine more years before dying in 1985.

The distinction made by the New Jersey courts between the termination of breathing assistance and the allowance of death by starvation and dehydration in the Quinlan case proved to be extremely relevant to the case of Nancy Beth Cruzan. Cruzan also lapsed into an irreversible coma, termed a "persistent vegetative state," in 1983, after she was thrown facedown, while unconscious, into a water-filled ditch during an automobile accident. She could breathe without assistance, and her family asked that she be fed through a tube to keep her alive. In 1987, doctors told Cruzan's parents that she could live in a permanent comatose condition for years, but there was no hope of recovery. The parents requested that the feeding tube be removed and that their daughter be allowed to die, but the hospital insisted on a court order authorizing the removal. Thus began a three-year legal odyssey that resulted in the U.S. Supreme Court's hearing its first "right to die" case.

A Missouri district court ruled in July, 1988, that Cruzan's parents could act on her behalf and order that the feeding tube be removed. However, William L. Webster, the Missouri state attorney general, and Robert G. Harmon, director of the Missouri Department of Health, appealed the decision to the Missouri Supreme Court. The higher court said that for life support to be discontinued, state law required "clear and convincing evidence" that a person, before becoming comatose, had expressed a desire to be allowed to die. The higher court ruled that testimony by a former housemate of Cruzan, in which the housemate claimed that Cruzon had said that she would not want to live as a "vegetable," did not constitute such definitive evidence and reversed the district court's decision. The only legal recourse left to the parents at this juncture was to appeal to the U.S. Supreme Court.

By 1990, when the U.S. Supreme Court agreed to hear *Cruzan v. Director*, there had already been widespread media coverage of both the first two trials and the contentious debates and confrontations between "pro-life" groups and those supporting the "right to die." The attorneys for Missouri included Webster and Kenneth Starr, U.S. solicitor general. They urged the Court to uphold the Missouri Supreme Court's decisions that all human life must be preserved regardless of its quality and that removing a comatose patient's feeding tube was murder.

The attorneys for Cruzan's parents, headed by William H. Colby, argued that the suffering of Cruzan and her family showed that family members and health care professionals should be able to make decisions about withdrawing life support. Cruzan's attorneys also argued that the Missouri Supreme Court's decision was primarily influenced by concerns that an affirmation of the district court's ruling would be used as precedent in cases involving suicide or abortion. This position was supported by the American Medical Association, the American Nurses Association, the Society for the Right to Die, and the American Academy of Neurology. Cruzan's parents, and those who strongly held either of the polarized positions in the debate on the "right to die," anxiously awaited the Court's decision.

The Court's Ruling

On June 25, 1990, in a 5-4 ruling, the U.S. Supreme Court upheld the Missouri Supreme Court's decision, saying that the testimony did not constitute the "clear and convincing evidence" that the state required because there was no specific mention of withdrawing life support and, therefore, that Cruzan's feeding tube could not be removed. This decision, delivered by Chief Justice William H. Rehnquist, established precedents that went far beyond Missouri's ruling in the Cruzan case. The Court stated that a person who had made it known through an advance directive, like a "living will" or "clear and convincing" statements, that he or she did not wish to be kept alive with artificial life-support measures, did have the constitutional right to have life support, including nutrition and hydration, halted. The decision also said that states were allowed, but not required, to demand "clear and convincing evidence" before ordering life support terminated. Furthermore, the ruling stated that the U.S. Constitution's guarantee of "liberty" was probably a more valid justification of a patient's right to refuse medical treatment than the "right to privacy" often cited in state court cases.

Armed with the U.S. Supreme Court ruling, Cruzan's parents filed suit in a probate court in Jasper County, Missouri. Three close friends of Cruzan testified that she had clearly stated to them that she would want life support, including the use of a feeding tube, halted rather than live in a permanently comatose condition. On December 14, 1990, the judge ruled that Cruzan's feeding tube could be removed, which was done immediately following the decision at the request of Cruzan's parents. After the feeding tube was removed, fifteen members of a pro-life group stormed the medical facility in an attempt to reinsert the tube, and all were arrested. Nancy Cruzan died on December 26, 1990.

Significance

About ten thousand people across the United States were living in a "persistent vegetative state" when the Cruzan case was heard by the Supreme

Court in 1990. There was no nationwide legal precedent to answer the questions of whether a person had the right to chose in advance when life-sustaining medical interventions should be abandoned if the patient were rendered irreversibly comatose, or if third parties or a state had such a right. The media attention leading up to and following this Supreme Court decision stirred public and political interest in the importance of honoring written and oral advance directives.

On November 5, 1990, Congress passed the Patient Self-Determination Act. This act required all health care facilities receiving Medicare or Medicaid funding (95 percent of all health care facilities in the nation) to advise patients of the facilities' policies regarding the administration of artificial life-support measures and of each patient's right to make an advance directive in the form of a living will or to appoint a proxy to state the patient's wishes regarding the use, or withholding, of such measures. By the early years of the twenty-first century, every U.S. state had laws in place providing for living wills or proxies.

The legal precedents established in *Cruzan v. Director*, also intensified the debate over "active euthanasia," or assisted suicide. Many advocates of the so-called right to die thought that it should be legal to end the suffering of terminally ill people, if requested by the individual, with lethal doses of drugs. This issue proved to be very controversial, with forty-four states declaring assisted suicide to be illegal. Oregon, on the other hand, passed a law in 1994 that made it legal for doctors to prescribe lethal drugs for terminally ill patients but forbade physicians to administer the drugs. Subsequent Supreme Court decisions have upheld the Oregon law but rejected the right to assisted suicide under the U.S. Constitution.

Jack Carter

Further Reading

Colby, William. *Long Goodbye: The Deaths of Nancy Cruzan.* Carlsbad, Calif.: Hay House, 2002. Written by the attorney who represented the Cruzan family, this book chronicles the legal battles that culminated in the landmark 1990 Supreme Court decision.

Filene, Peter G. *In the Arms of Others: A Cultural History of the Right-to-Die in America.* Chicago: Ivan R. Dee, 1998. Discusses how the Cruzan case and others like it became centers of contention and the focus of religious, political, and philosophical debates regarding America's changing attitudes toward dying.

Glick, Henry R. *The Right to Die: Innovation and Its Consequences.* New York: Columbia University Press, 1992. Focuses on policy changes that resulted in state laws that allowed the withholding or withdrawing of life support. Posits that the media attention on cases like Cruzan's helped to sway public and political opinion in favor of right-to-die legislation.

Larson, Edward J., and Darrell W. Amundsen. *A Differential Death: Euthanasia in the Christian Tradition.* Downers Grove, Ill.: InterVarsity Press, 1998. Addresses some differences of opinion regarding the history of the Christian perspective on euthanasia, but mainly presents nontheological objections to the right-to-die movement.

Pence, Gregory E. *Classical Cases in Medical Ethics.* New York: McGraw Hill, 2004. Includes a chapter on the Karen Quinlan and Nancy Cruzan cases, and another on Oregon's assisted suicide law. Examines the legal and ethical controversies surrounding the issue.

Poe, Lila. *Cruzan v. Missouri: The Right to Die.* Tarrytown, N.Y.: Marshall Cavendish Benchmark, 2008. Part of its publisher's Supreme Court Milestones series designed for young-adult readers, this volume offers an accessible history and analysis of the *Cruzan* case that examines opposing sides in the case, the people involved, and the case's lasting impact. Includes bibliography and index.

See also *Griswold v. Connecticut; Washington v. Glucksberg.*

CUMMING V. RICHMOND COUNTY BOARD OF EDUCATION

Court: U.S. Supreme Court
Citation: 175 U.S. 528
Date: December 18, 1899
Issues: Education; Racial discrimination

• The U.S. Supreme Court refused to enforce the equal stipulation in the separate but equal doctrine governing segregated schools that had been established in its landmark 1896 decision.

Just three years after announcing the separate but equal doctrine in *Plessy v. Ferguson* (1896), the Supreme Court unanimously refused to take action in a case in which school facilities for blacks and whites were definitely unequal. *Cumming*, which amounted to the Court's first approval of racially segregated public schools, was never overturned. John Marshall Harlan, who wrote the opinion for the Court, had dissented vigorously in *Plessy* but was unable to find a clear, unmistakable disregard of equality in *Cumming*.

In 1879 the Augusta, Georgia, school board had established the first African American public high school in the state. The board closed the school in 1897, claiming that the money was needed for black primary school education. Because a Georgia statute explicitly provided for separate but equal facilities, the local judge did not bother to consider the U.S. Constitution in overturning the board's judgment. Still, the Georgia supreme court, without offering any significant reasons, overturned the local judge's opinion.

African Americans argued that under the Fourteenth Amendment's equal protection clause, they were entitled to a high school if one was provided for white students, but Harlan asserted that the African American plaintiffs had to prove the board decision was motivated exclusively by hostility toward African Americans, which was impossible to prove. To reach his decision, Harlan ignored several lower court precedents that went in the opposite direction.

Richard L. Wilson

See also *Bolling v. Sharpe; Brown v. Board of Education; Plessy v. Ferguson.*

CUMMINGS V. MISSOURI

Court: U.S. Supreme Court
Citation: 71 U.S. 277
Date: March 20, 1867
Issues: Loyalty oaths

• The U.S. Supreme Court overturned statutes requiring loyalty oaths, viewing them as unconstitutional ex post facto laws and bills of atainder.

Justice Stephen J. Field wrote the opinions for both *Cummings* and its companion case, *Ex parte Garland,* which were decided by 5-4 votes with Justice Samuel F. Miller dissenting. *Cummings* involved a Missouri law that retroactively imposed loyalty oaths requiring people in various jobs to swear that they had not aided or sympathized with the southern cause during the Civil War. *Garland* dealt with a federal law requiring attorneys practicing in federal court to swear that they had not supported the Confederacy.

Field noted that, although these statutes did not impose fines or imprisonment, they were punitive because they banned those who could not take oaths honestly from practicing their professions. Sections 9 and 10 of Article I of the U.S. Constitution ban bills of attainder and ex post facto laws at the state and federal level. Field found the statutes in *Cummings* and *Garland* to be ex post facto retroactive legislation (laws that criminalized acts considered legal when committed) and bills of attainder because they imposed punishment without trial to a designated group of individuals. Miller, in dissent, argued that the statutes were not imposing punishment and therefore could not be either bills of attainder or ex post facto laws. This decision, never repudiated by the Supreme Court, was used in *United States v. Brown* (1965) to void a federal law that banned former communists from serving as labor union officials.

Richard L. Wilson

See also *Dennis v. United States; Scales v. United States; Yates v. United States.*

CURTISS-WRIGHT EXPORT CORP., UNITED STATES V. *See* UNITED STATES V. CURTISS-WRIGHT EXPORT CORP.

DAMES AND MOORE V. REGAN

Court: U.S. Supreme Court
Citation: 453 U.S. 654
Date: July 2, 1981
Issues: Presidential powers

• The U.S. Supreme Court upheld actions taken by President Jimmy Carter during the Iran hostage crisis, expanding the U.S. president's broad power to act in foreign affairs.

U.S. embassy personnel in Iran were taken captive in 1979 and held hostage by Iranians. To resolve the crisis before leaving office in January, 1981, President Jimmy Carter signed several executive orders implementing certain actions that met a number of Iranian conditions in return for release of the hostages. The actions included ending legal actions of U.S. citizens and nationals against Iran, voiding attachments against Iranian property in U.S. courts to satisfy judgments against Iran, and transfer of such claims to a new arbitration panel. The Supreme Court upheld these actions even when it was impossible to show that they were authorized by law. Some actions were covered by the International Emergency Economic Powers Act, but others lacked statutory authority. However, the Court relied on past congressional practice and court decisions granting broad executive authority in foreign affairs. The decision was criticized for granting the executive branch extremely broad powers in foreign affairs.

Richard L. Wilson

See also *Goldwater v. Carter; Humphrey's Executor v. United States; McCulloch v. Maryland; Martin v. Mott; Mississippi v. Johnson; Myers v. United States; United States v. Curtiss-Wright Export Corp.*

DANDRIDGE V. WILLIAMS

Court: U.S. Supreme Court
Citation: 397 U.S. 471
Date: April 6, 1970
Issues: Children's rights; Equal protection of the law;
Welfare rights

- In this case, the U.S. Supreme Court held that legislation involving social and economic matters such as the distribution of welfare benefits would be accorded deferential review and would not generally be found to violate the equal protection requirement of the Fourteenth Amendment.

The state of Maryland's Aid to Families with Dependent Children (AFDC) program made most of its grants on the basis of a computed standard of need. The program, however, imposed a maximum monthly grant of $250 per month regardless of a family's size or computed need. Plaintiffs with large families challenged the program, claiming that it violated the equal protection clause of the Fourteenth Amendment and the provisions of the federal Social Security Act. A majority of the Supreme Court rejected both claims.

Justice Potter Stewart delivered the Court's opinion. He emphasized that the case did not involve any of the rights guaranteed by the Bill of Rights. Instead, it was a form of social or economic legislation that the Court resolved should be accorded substantial deference. Justice Stewart argued that the benefit cap served valid purposes. It encouraged employment and avoided discrimination between welfare families and the families of the "working poor." It was enough, he said, that the statute was rationally based and free from "invidious discrimination."

Justices Thurgood Marshall, William Brennan, and William O. Douglas dissented—Douglas because he believed that Maryland's program violated federal law, and Marshall and Brennan because they believed the program violated both federal law and the equal protection clause of the Fourteenth Amendment. The latter argued that Maryland's program discriminated between small and large families by giving small families enough to survive but withholding the same benefit from large families. For Marshall and Brennan, the case was about children having enough to eat. Viewing the matter in this light, they argued that the state should have had to do more to justify its discrimination.

During the 1960's the Supreme Court protected a variety of rights through the equal protection clause of the Fourteenth Amendment and the equal protection component of the Fifth Amendment's due process clause. In *Dandridge v. Williams*, however, the Court refused to recognize a fundamental right to welfare benefits and signaled instead that the steady proliferation of rights guarded by the equal protection doctrine was ending. Especially in the area of social and economic legislation, such as the distribution of welfare benefits and other governmental benefits, *Dandridge* established a pattern of deferential review that usually upheld such legislation against constitutional challenge. This pattern would be reinforced within a few years when the Court held in *San Antonio Independent School District v. Rodriguez* (1973) that the Constitution did not guarantee a fundamental right to a public education.

Timothy L. Hall

See also *Goldberg v. Kelly*; *Gomez v. Perez*; *Graham v. Richardson*; *San Antonio Independent School District v. Rodriguez*; *Shapiro v. Thompson*.

DARBY LUMBER CO., UNITED STATES V. *See* UNITED STATES V. DARBY LUMBER CO.

DARTMOUTH COLLEGE V. WOODWARD

Court: U.S. Supreme Court
Citation: 4 Wheat. (17 U.S.) 518
Date: February 2, 1819
Issues: Freedom of contract; Property rights

- By deciding that a state charter of a private institution was protected by the contracts clause of the Constitution, the U.S. Supreme Court enhanced protection of corporate property from interference by the states.

Early in the nineteenth century, many Republicans wanted the states to exercise more controls over a new form of economic concentration—the corporation. Forces favorable to business usually desired fewer controls. Although privately owned and managed, corporations were created by legislative charters. In 1816 the Republican-dominated legislature of New Hampshire enacted three laws that changed the colonial charter of Dartmouth College and imposed a number of public controls. The Federalist-dominated trustees of the school appealed to the Supreme Court.

By a 5-1 majority, the Court declared the New Hampshire laws void because they were an unconstitutional impairment on the obligations of a contract. Writing for the Court, Chief Justice John Marshall found that the college was a private corporation and that the colonial charter was a contract. The states were required to respect such vested rights of private property. In a concurring opinion, Justice Joseph Story suggested that legislatures might retain some degree of control by writing "reservations" into charters, allowing for their modification in the future.

The *Dartmouth College* decision promoted the expansion of business interests when they were vulnerable to attack from state legislatures. In effect, the ruling allowed the contract clause to provide most Fifth Amendment protections for private property, which at that time did not apply to the states. The legislatures, however, managed to diminish the impact of *Dartmouth College* by including reservation clauses, as suggested by Justice Story. Also, in *Charles River Bridge v. Warren Bridge* in 1837, the Court took a more limited view of contracts.

Thomas Tandy Lewis

See also *Charles River Bridge v. Warren Bridge; Fletcher v. Peck.*

Davis v. Bandemer

Court: U.S. Supreme Court
Citation: 478 U.S. 109
Date: June 30, 1986
Issues: Equal protection of the law; Reapportionment
and redistricting

• The U.S. Supreme Court held that a gerrymandering scheme that benefits the dominant political party may be examined by the judiciary, serving notice to legislatures that an extreme partisan use of apportionment powers might be judged unconstitutional by the federal courts.

Indiana Democrats contended that the Republicans, who were in the majority, had sought and obtained partisan advantage in a 1981 reapportionment plan for the election of the state legislature. Irwin Bandemer and other Democrats filed suit, claiming that the scheme violated the equal protection rights of Democratic voters. By a 6-3 vote, the Supreme Court decided that the political question doctrine does not prevent a political party from making an equal protection challenge of partisan gerrymandering. By a 7-2 vote, however, the Court found that the degree of gerrymandering was not extreme enough to constitute a violation of the constitutional rights of the Democrats. Justice Byron R. White's plurality opinion declared that an apportionment scheme that disadvantaged a political party does not necessarily violate the equal protection clause, but that plaintiffs must show evidence that the will of the majority of voters is continually frustrated. It is important to note that the plaintiffs in *Bandemer* did not make any allegations of discrimination against an identifiable racial or ethnic group.

Thomas Tandy Lewis

See also *Gomillion v. Lightfoot; Reynolds v. Sims; Shaw v. Hunt.*

DAVIS V. BEASON

Court: U.S. Supreme Court
Citation: 133 U.S. 333
Date: February 3, 1890
Issues: Freedom of religion; Voting rights

• The U.S. Supreme Court allowed a territory to deny the vote to members of a religious sect that advocated an illegal practice.

In the landmark 1879 case, *Reynolds v. United States*, the Supreme Court upheld a federal ban on polygamy, a religious practice of members of the Church of Jesus Christ of Latter-day Saints (Mormons) at the time. Idaho subsequently enacted a territorial statute that denied the right to vote to anyone who practiced polygamy or who belonged to an organization that advocated polygamy. Samuel Davis and other nonpolygamous Mormons sued after they were not allowed to vote in the election of 1888.

By a 9-0 vote, the Court upheld the statute. Taking a very narrow view of both religion and the free exercise clause, Justice Stephen J. Field construed the statute as simply excluding the privilege of voting from those who encouraged and approved of the commission of "odious" crimes. Although persons could not be punished for their beliefs, membership in a church was considered a conduct; therefore membership itself was not protected by the First Amendment. Few people would defend *Davis* a century later. In *Romer v. Evans* (1996), Justice Anthony M. Kennedy observed that *Davis* was no longer good law to the extent that it held that advocacy of a certain practice could be the basis for denying a person the right to vote.

Thomas Tandy Lewis

See also *Employment Division, Department of Human Resources of Oregon v. Smith; Reynolds v. United States; Romer v. Evans; Yates v. United States.*

Debs, In re. *See* In re Debs

DeJonge v. Oregon

Court: U.S. Supreme Court
Citation: 299 U.S. 353
Date: January 4, 1937
Issues: Freedom of assembly and association

• The U.S. Supreme Court, in overturning a conviction under a state criminal syndicalism law, incorporated the right of freedom of peaceable assembly and association to the states through the Fourteenth Amendment.

Chief Justice Charles Evans Hughes wrote the Supreme Court's unanimous opinion (Justice Harlan Fiske Stone did not participate) overturning the conviction of Dirk DeJonge under Oregon's criminal syndicalism law. DeJonge had helped run a meeting sponsored by the Communist Party to protest actions taken by police against workers. Although DeJonge, some of the other leaders, and about 15 percent of attendees were affiliated with communists, the meeting was entirely orderly. Minor Communist Party activities may have taken place, but no one advocated violence or criminal syndicalism. The prosecution relied heavily on party literature not used in the meeting but found elsewhere that tangentially associated the Communist Party with syndicalism.

The Oregon supreme court upheld DeJonge's conviction on grounds that merely participating in a totally peaceful meeting called by the Communist Party could still violate the law. The Court reversed the decision, saying lawful discussion in a peaceful assembly is not a crime. This decision first applied the freedom of association to the states under the Fourteenth Amendment's due process clause.

Richard L. Wilson

See also *Aptheker v. Secretary of State; Communist Party v. Subversive Activities Control Board; Dennis v. United States; Scales v. United States; Schenck v. United States; Whitney v. California; Yates v. United States.*

DENNIS V. UNITED STATES

Court: U.S. Supreme Court
Citation: 341 U.S. 494
Date: June 4, 1951
Issues: Freedom of assembly and association; Freedom of the press

• The U.S. Supreme Court upheld the convictions of Communist Party members under the 1940 Smith Act, which led to more vigorous prosecution of alleged communists in the 1950's.

Chief Justice Fred M. Vinson wrote the 6-2 majority decision (Justice Tom C. Clark did not participate) in which the Supreme Court upheld the convictions of eleven Communist Party leaders for violating the 1940 Smith Act by teaching or advocating the "violent overthrow of the U.S. government." Although the Smith Act had always been aimed at communists, the U.S. government had avoided confrontation with the Soviet Union, a World War II ally. As the Cold War began, Republicans and Democrats began to compete with each other to prove their anticommunist fervor. A seriously flawed trial led to the conviction of the eleven party members. The circuit court of appeals upheld their conviction, and the Court agreed to hear the case solely on the question of the Smith Act's constitutionality, thereby eliminating many grounds for reversal. However, the tenor of the times and recent changes in the composition of the Court largely appointed by Franklin D. Roosevelt made it likely that the anticommunist legislation would have been upheld in any case.

Vinson significantly modified the clear and present danger test so that much less serious threats to public safety could be banned by creating a grave and probable danger standard. This view never actually achieved the status of a legal standard because only a plurality of Vinson and three others subscribed to it. Justice Robert H. Jackson rejected the modification of the clear and present danger rule but would have convicted the communists for conspiracy anyway. Justice Felix Frankfurter disliked the Smith Act but was constrained by his view of judicial self-restraint.

Justices Hugo L. Black and William O. Douglas wrote strong dissents attacking the majority for seriously misreading the clear and present danger test and damaging freedom of speech in the United States. Because one of the activities for which the convictions were upheld was the defendants' plan to publish a newspaper, these dissents also alleged that freedom of the press was endangered. Freed from the constraints of previous interpretations, the government began a vigorous prosecution of the Communist Party that continued until the Court's decision in *Yates v. United States* (1957) blunted the attack. However, *Yates* did not overturn *Dennis* or invalidate the Smith Act. The holding in *Dennis* is at variance with more recent decisions, but the Court never completely repudiated its grave and probable danger rule.

Richard L. Wilson

See also *Communist Party v. Subversive Activities Control Board; Elfbrandt v. Russell; Gitlow v. New York; Scales v. United States; Schenck v. United States; Yates v. United States.*

DeShaney v. Winnebago County Department of Social Services

Court: U.S. Supreme Court
Citation: 489 U.S. 189
Date: February 22, 1989
Issues: Due process of law

- The U.S. Supreme Court held that a state was not liable if its social workers failed to remove a child from the custody of the father even after reports of serious child abuse.

The Winnebago County Department of Social Services received numerous complaints of serious beatings administered to Joshua DeShaney by his father, Randy DeShaney, who was given custody of the boy in a divorce proceeding. Despite repeated reports from family members, physicians, case workers, and emergency medical personnel that the child had suffered from several beatings to the head, the social workers did not remove the boy from the home. Finally, the boy was beaten so badly that he suffered permanent brain damage. By a 6-3 vote, the Supreme Court ruled that a state had no constitutional obligation to protect a child from his father even though the state's social service workers had received multiple reports of serious child abuse. In his opinion for the Court, Chief Justice William H. Rehnquist found that the Fourteenth Amendment's due process clause was negatively worded and created no affirmative obligation for the state to act, even in cases when the state had notice and the child was very young. Justices William J. Brennan, Jr., Thurgood Marshall, and Harry A. Blackmun dissented vigorously, and Blackmun filed a separate dissent.

Richard L. Wilson

See also *Gomez v. Perez*; *In re Baby M*; *In re Gault*.

DIAMOND V. CHAKRABARTY

Court: U.S. Supreme Court
Citation: 447 U.S. 303
Date: June 16, 1980
Issues: Environmental issues and animal rights; Regulation of commerce

- The U.S. Supreme Court announced its 5-4 decision that a live, human-made microorganism is patentable. The decision allowed emerging biotechnology companies to acquire patent protection for their living products and to capitalize on the revolution in genetic engineering.

On March 17, 1980, the case of *Diamond v. Chakrabarty* was argued before the U.S. Supreme Court. Lawrence G. Wallace represented Diamond, and Edward F. McKie, Jr., represented Ananda M. Chakrabarty. Diamond asked the Supreme Court to overturn a decision by the Court of Customs and Patent Appeals that gave Chakrabarty a patent for his "invention" of a genetically engineered bacterium that was able to break down crude oil. On June 16, 1980, the Supreme Court announced that Chakrabarty's organism was a "new and useful manufacture or composition of matter" under patent rules. The Court upheld the patent for a live, human-made microorganism by a 5-4 majority. This decision allowed emerging biotechnology companies to acquire patent protection for their living products and to capitalize on the revolution in genetic engineering.

Thomas Jefferson's patent act of 1793 called for protection of "any new and useful art, machine, manufacture, or composition of matter, or any new or useful improvements [thereof]." Jefferson's goal was to reward and protect ingenuity. Living organisms were not patented. The 1930 Plant Variety Protection Act and the 1977 Plant Variety Protection Act authorized patents for some plants. Plant breeders working "in aid of nature" could also patent their work. The 1977 act, however, specifically excluded bacteria from its protection.

In 1972, Ananda M. Chakrabarty tried to patent his invention of a human-made, genetically engineered bacterium that could break down crude oil. Chakrabarty was a microbiologist working at the General Electric Research and Development Center in Schenectady, New York. He claimed to have discovered how to put four different plasmids—small circles of deoxyribonucleic acid (DNA) that give microbes properties such as antibiotic resistance—into a single organism. The organism was a common soil bacterium called *Pseudomonas*. Without the plasmids, the *Pseudomonas* was unable to break down oil. With the four plasmids, the *Pseudomonas* could break down compounds in oil such as camphor and octane. The combination of four plasmids was unique, and no other bacteria in nature had this combination. General Electric believed that Chakrabarty's invention could be valuable in treating oil spills, and the company sought to acquire a patent for it.

Chakrabarty registered three types of patent claims: for the method of developing the bacterium, for the method of combining materials for distributing the bacterium, and for the bacterium itself. The patent examiner accepted the first two claims but turned down the third. The examiner's reason was that microbes were products of nature, and living things were not patentable.

The Issue

Chakrabarty appealed to the Patent Office Board of Appeals, which also rejected Chakrabarty's claim. The board of appeals used the 1930 Plant Variety Protection Act to support its ruling. It said that this act was not intended to cover living things. Chakrabarty then appealed to the Court of Customs and Patent Appeals. This court, by a divided vote, reversed the ruling by the Patent Office Board of Appeals. It concluded that, for the purposes of patent rules, it was not important whether microorganisms were alive. In *Diamond v. Bergy*, the Court of Customs and Patent Appeals had already ruled that a microbe could be patented. (Bergy had applied for a patent for a pure culture of a bacterium called *Streptomyces vellosus*, which helped produce an antibiotic called lincomycin.)

On October 29, 1979, Lutrelle F. Parker, the acting commissioner of patents and trademarks, obtained a writ of *certiorari* (an appeal to reexamine the decision) to the U.S. Court of Customs and Patent Appeals. The case then went to the Supreme Court and was presented on March 17, 1980.

Justices Harry A. Blackmun, William H. Rehnquist, John Paul Stevens, Potter Stewart, and Chief Justice Warren E. Burger formed the majority opinion. This opinion stated that in the patent statutes, natural laws, physical phenomena, and abstract ideas were not patentable. New minerals found in the earth were not patentable. New plants found in the wild were not patentable. The patent statute, however, gave a patent to any person who invented or discovered "any" new and useful "manufacture" or "composition of matter."

The Supreme Court declared that the genetically engineered microbe was Chakrabarty's handiwork. It was "manufactured," and represented his own, not nature's, work. It was "new" because the bacterium, as Chakrabarty had constructed it, did not occur in nature. It was "useful": A human-made, genetically engineered bacterium able to break down multiple components of crude oil had obvious industrial use. Thus, the organism fell within the meaning of the patent statute. It was a product of human ingenuity with a distinctive name, character, and use.

The fact that Congress did not predict genetic engineering when it made the patent statutes did not necessarily exclude genetically engineered bacteria from the statutes until Congress specifically gave these bacteria patent protection. The Plant Variety Protection Acts of 1930 and 1977 excluded bacteria from patent protection. The Court's majority opinion was based on the belief that Congress did not intend to exclude living things that were "manufactures or compositions of matter." Congress could change the patent rules to specifically exclude bacteria made by genetic engineering from patent protection. It was up to Congress, not the courts, to decide what a patent protected.

Justices William J. Brennan, Thurgood Marshall, Lewis F. Powell, Jr., and Byron White formed the minority opinion against granting Chakrabarty a patent. In their opinion, most people believed that living things were not patentable. In the minority opinion, when Congress excluded bacteria from the 1977 Plant Variety Protection Act, it clearly meant to exclude all bacteria. Microbes should not be patented until Congress expressly permitted it. It was important, the minority opinion concluded, not to extend patent protection further than Congress intended.

The Court's opinion was to grant *certiorari* to determine whether a live human-made microorganism was patentable subject matter. In other words, the decision of the U.S. Court of Customs and Patent Appeals was reexamined and ruled to be fair. This decision meant that a patent could, and should, be granted to Chakrabarty and General Electric.

Significance

The legal ruling in *Diamond v. Chakrabarty* was actually a narrow interpretation of patent law. Did Chakrabarty's microbe constitute a "manufacture or composition of matter" within the meaning of the patent rules? Did Congress intend the patent rules to be liberal enough to include genetically engineered bacteria or conservative enough to completely exclude bacteria as the 1977 Plant Variety Protection Act implied?

Facts of nature, including physical laws such as Albert Einstein's theory of relativity and Isaac Newton's law of gravity, were not patentable. They were considered to be "free to all and reserved exclusively to none." Naturally occurring living organisms were also not patentable. In *Funk Brothers Seed Co. v. Kalo Inoculant Co.* (1948), the Supreme Court had ruled that simply finding useful bacteria in nature and producing an inoculum from them was not patentable. Chakrabarty's microbe, however, was genetically engineered. An individual bacterium might have some of the properties found in his microbe, but no single bacterium had all of the properties in his microbe. This made Chakrabarty's living organism unique.

The Supreme Court knew the impact that its decision would have on biotechnology; however, it rejected arguments against patenting the organism based on the potential hazards of genetic research. These were congressional and executive, but not judicial, concerns. As far as the Supreme Court was concerned, "whether [Chakrabarty's] claims were patentable might have determined whether research efforts were accelerated by the hope of reward or slowed by want of incentives but that was all." It was not up to the courts to debate the potential ecological damage of releasing or creating genetically engineered organisms. As it turned out, the debate over the potential ecological damage of releasing or creating genetically engineered organisms became a greater burden to the use of biotechnology than to the patenting of biotechnology products.

Scientists themselves considered the possibility that genetic engineering presented biological and ecological hazards. During the Asilomar Conference in California in 1975, scientists composed a set of self-imposed rules for doing research. The National Institutes of Health (NIH) approved a less restrictive set of rules for the performance of research in genetic engineering in 1979. Genentech, a biotechnology company, made Wall Street history in 1980 when its stock rose from thirty-five dollars to ninety-five dollars per share after trading for only thirty minutes. The new age of biotechnology looked as if it had arrived. Its promise, however, was not realized in the 1980's.

Genetically engineered or patented organisms had to be released before they could be marketed. Legal action by activists such as Jeremy Rifkin in the United States and the ecologically oriented Green Party in Germany effectively stopped scientists from releasing genetically engineered organisms until the close of the 1980's. Environmental activists often vandalized experiments with genetically engineered organisms. In 1987, Earth First! activists damaged research plants in Northern California treated with genetically engineered bacteria that reduced frost damage. In 1989, activists destroyed a plot of genetically engineered potatoes in the Netherlands.

In 1985, the federal courts ruled that private companies did not require NIH approval to field-test genetically engineered organisms. Biotechnology companies, however, still needed approval from the Environmental Protection Agency (EPA), which treated the release of genetically engineered organisms in the same manner as the release of other substances. Consequently, the regulatory steps that the EPA established to ensure safe release became expensive obstacles for biotechnology companies.

Genetically engineered products eventually appeared in the world market. Nogall, a genetically engineered bacterium used as a pesticide, went on sale in Australia in 1989. Several plant and animal products containing genetically engineered material were available to the public by the mid-1990's, including milk from cattle that had been treated with recombinant bovine somatotropin (rBST), a hormone that enhances milk production; plants that contained genetic information for a natural toxin (from the *Bacillus thuringiensis* bacterium) that made the plants resistant to caterpillar damage; tobacco plants infected with a virus that gave the plants greater resistance to further viral infection; and the Flavr Savr tomato, produced by Calgene, Incorporated, of Davis, California, which remained firm while ripening on the vine because it had recombinant genetic material inhibiting the enzyme that causes tomatoes to soften.

Patenting Chakrabarty's original organism was easier than using it in the natural environment. Many people believed that opportunities to use even naturally occurring oil-degrading microorganisms were so limited that the time and expense required to make a genetically engineered microbe to carry out the same tasks were not worth the effort and were unnecessary. Chakrabarty's patented bacterium proved no more effective than simple mixtures of organisms used to break down oil and was never field-tested. The effects of major oil spills at sea, such as those of the *Amoco Cadiz* in 1978 and the *Exxon Valdez* in 1989, were treated through the inoculation of the oil with mixtures of oil-degrading organisms and the addition of fertilizer to enhance the growth of naturally occurring organisms.

Mark S. Coyne

Further Reading

Dayan, Anthony, Peter Campbell, and Thomas Jukes, eds. *Hazards of Biotechnology: Real or Imaginary.* New York: Elsevier Applied Science, 1988. The scientists' perspective: advanced and technical. The first chapter is in favor of biotechnology. The second chapter presents a more balanced approach to the ecological consequences of biotechnology. The remaining chapters deal with specific cases.

Gibbs, Jeffrey, Iver Cooper, and Bruce Mackler. *Biotechnology and the Environment: International Regulation.* New York: Stockton Press, 1987. Regulatory aspects of biotechnology from around the world are useful for understanding some of the restrictions that inhibit the development of biotechnology.

Lappé, Marc. *Broken Code: The Exploitation of DNA.* San Francisco: Sierra Club Books, 1984. Takes a restrained approach to the uses of biotechnology. Somewhat more balanced than Rifkin's book.

Rifkin, Jeremy. *Algeny.* New York: Viking Press, 1983. Conversational, philosophical, and totally opposed to the idea of biotechnology. A good contrast to the other reference selections.

U.S. Congress. Office of Technology Assessment. *Bioremediation for Marine Oil Spills.* Washington, D.C.: U.S. Government Printing Office, 1991. Offers a nontechnical description of bioremediation and its use in environmental cleanup. Focus on the *Exxon Valdez* oil spill is particularly relevant.

Wade, Nicholas. *The Ultimate Experiment: Man-Made Evolution.* New York: Walker, 1977. Very good source of information about the early days of biotechnology. Deals in a nontechnical manner with the restrictions imposed on scientists (and imposed by scientists themselves) when the first genetic engineering experiments were run. Reveals the decisiveness with which the science community first approached genetic engineering and biotechnology.

Winston, Mark L. *Travels in the Genetically Modified Zone.* Cambridge, Mass.: Harvard University Press, 2002. Balanced work based on the author's discussions about genetically modified organisms with government officials, farmers, and activists in Canada, the United States, and Europe.

Witt, Steven. *Biotechnology, Microbes, and the Environment.* San Francisco: Center for Science Information, 1990. Short, balanced primer on biotechnology and microorganisms. Presents the process and problems of biotechnology in easily understood terms.

See also *Alcoa v. Federal Trade Commission.*

DILLON V. GLOSS

Court: U.S. Supreme Court
Citation: 256 U.S. 368
Date: May 16, 1921
Issues: Constitutionalism

• The U.S. Supreme Court upheld the conviction of a man accused of illegally transporting liquors, approving time limits for ratification of amendments and determining that their effective date would be based on ratification.

Justice Willis Van Devanter wrote the unanimous decision for the Supreme Court upholding the conviction of defendant Dillon for transporting liquors in violation of the Eighteenth Amendment. The defendant had challenged

Justice
Willis Van Devanter.
(Library of Congress)

his conviction on grounds that Congress had—for the first time—added a time limit for ratification of the proposed amendment and that the law under which he had been arrested was not yet in force as his arrest occurred less than one year after the Eighteenth Amendment was proclaimed by the secretary of state (although more than one year after its ratification). The Court concluded the deadline for ratification was reasonably contemporaneous and that the adoption of the amendment and not its announcement was the critical issue in the effective starting date of the provision. Subsequent proposed amendments all carried deadlines for ratification. The proposed Equal Rights Amendment contained a deadline that Congress extended in a manner that aroused controversy.

Richard L. Wilson

See also *Carroll v. United States; Coleman v. Miller; 44 Liquormart, Inc. v. Rhode Island; Kidd v. Pearson; License Cases; Marshall v. Barlow's; Moose Lodge v. Irvis; Olmstead v. United States; Rotary International v. Duarte.*

DISTRICT OF COLUMBIA V. HELLER

Court: U.S. Supreme Court
Citation: 554 U.S. ____
Date: June 26, 2008
Issues: Right to bear arms

- In this landmark decision, the U.S. Supreme Court interpreted the Second Amendment as guaranteeing an individual right to own and use firearms—a right not dependent on service in a militia. The Court also recognized a constitutional right to possess firearms for the purpose of self-defense.

The ambiguous wording of the U.S. Constitution's Second Amendment has long generated a great deal of controversy:

A well regulated Militia, being necessary to the security of a free State, the right of the people to keep and bear Arms, shall not be infringed.

Proponents of strict limits on the possession of guns have typically argued that the intent of the amendment is strictly to protect the collective right of the individual states to maintain armed militias. Persons who take gun ownership seriously, however, almost always contend that the purpose of the amendment is to protect an individual right. During the nineteenth century, several Supreme Court justices hinted about the meaning of the amendment, but the Court as a whole failed to issue a definite ruling on the issue. In an important 1939 ruling, *United States v. Miller*, the Court approved a federal law that made it illegal to possess unregulated sawed-off shotguns, with the justification that the Second Amendment was not intended to protect the right to own weapons not ordinarily used in militias.

In 1975, the city council of the District of Columbia passed one of the nation's strictest gun laws. In practice, the law had the effect of making it impossible for citizens to obtain permits to possess handguns in private homes. Although the law allowed home possession of rifles and shotguns, it required that they be stored unloaded and be either trigger locked or disassembled. Supporters of the law claimed that it saved lives and reduced violence in the city. Critics argued that the law did not stop criminals from obtaining firearms illegally, but that it actually encouraged criminal activity because it prevented law-abiding citizens from being able to protect themselves and their homes. Both sides could point to statistics as proof for their assertions.

In 2003, a private security officer named Dick Heller, who carried a handgun when on duty, applied for a permit to keep a handgun at home for self-protection. After his application was denied, Heller joined with five other city residents to file a lawsuit in federal court, arguing that the D.C. law violated their constitutional right to keep and bear arms. They lost in the district court, but the Court of Appeals for the D.C. Circuit ruled in their favor by a 2-1 margin. The opinion for the majority articulated an expansive "individual-right" interpretation of the amendment. The D.C. government responded by petitioning the U.S. Supreme Court for a writ of *certiorari*, which was granted. The case attracted national attention and attracted a total of sixty-seven *amicus curiae* (friend of the court) briefs.

The Court's Ruling

After reviewing the case, the Supreme Court ruled, by a 5-4 margin, to uphold the judgment of the Court of Appeals, recognizing the right to keep and use weapons for traditional uses, particularly self-defense. Speaking for the majority, Justice Antonin Scalia observed that when the phrase "right of the people" appears elsewhere in the Bill of Rights, it refers to a personal right. He therefore reasoned that the second clause is the controlling clause in the amendment, referring to a preexisting common-law right to carry weapons for self-defense. According to this interpretation, the prefatory clause supports but does not detract from the controlling clause. For support, Scalia pointed to historical materials, including state constitutions. Assessing the D.C. law, he asserted that the total ban on all private ownership of handguns (an entire class of weapons) was unconstitutional because a significant percentage of persons wish to own handguns, believing them to be the weapon of choice for self-defense. The D.C. law's requirements for the storage of rifles and shotguns, moreover, were also unconstitutional, because they rendered the weapons inoperative in emergencies. Scalia went on to write, however, that the amendment, like other parts of the Constitution, did not protect an absolute or unlimited right, and he explicitly endorsed almost all traditional restrictions, including "laws imposing conditions and qualifications on the commercial sale of arms."

Two of the four justices in the minority wrote dissenting opinions, arguing that the D.C. law was reasonable and entirely constitutional. Although conceding that the Second Amendment protected an individual right, they nevertheless argued that this right was only relevant to activities relevant to the operation of a well-regulated militia. They especially took issue with the view that the amendment guaranteed a right to use firearms in self-defense. Justice John Paul Stevens found that the framers of the amendment would not have inserted a preamble focusing on the need for a militia if they had intended to guarantee a right of self-defense. He found no justification, therefore, for departing from the *Miller* precedent.

Justice Stephen Breyer argued that cities with rampant gun violence needed broad authority to restrict guns and pointed to historical evidence that American cities of the late eighteenth century had ordinances restricting the use of guns in the interest of public safety. Accusing the majority of demonstrating "a lack of respect" for the Court's well-settled precedents, Breyer insisted that the Second Amendment did not guarantee any right of persons "to keep loaded handguns in the house in crime-ridden urban areas."

Significance

Constitutional scholar Cass Sunstein called the *Heller* decision a "Second Amendment revolution." However, the implications of the decision for future gun regulations seemed likely to remain limited. Few regulations in the country put severe restricting on the right of individuals to keep weapons in private homes for self-defense. Unquestionably the ruling encouraged the National Rifle Association (NRA) to aggressively challenge some of the more aggressive gun regulations. In 2009, for example, the NRA and the San Francisco Housing Authority reached an out-of-court settlement that eliminated a ban on guns in residential units.

Scalia's majority opinion in *Heller* left two important questions unanswered. First, the opinion did not specify whether the right to keep and bear arms is a fundamental right that requires all restrictions to be assessed according to the demanding standard of "strict scrutiny." If not a fundamental right, regulations would then be judged by the more lenient standard of "reasonableness." Also, the opinion did not consider whether the Second Amendment was binding on the states as a result of incorporation into the Fourteenth Amendment, although most observers expected that the Court would likely conclude that it does if an appropriate case were to reach the Court.

Thomas Tandy Lewis

Further Reading

Bogus, Carl, and Michael Bellesiles, eds. *The Second Amendment in Law and History: Historians and Constitutional Scholars on the Right to Bear Arms.* New York: New Press, 2001. Collection of essays by recognized scholars expressing a diversity of views on how the amendment should be interpreted.

Charles, Patrick J. *The Second Amendment: The Intent and Its Interpretation by the States and the Supreme Court.* Jefferson, N.C.: McFarland, 2009. Interesting analysis of the Second Amendment, agreeing with the *Heller* decision on an individual right but questioning whether the amendment's intent was to allow citizens to protect their homes.

Cornell, Saul. *A Well Regulated Militia: The Founding Fathers and the Origins of Gun Control in America.* New York: Oxford University Press, 2006. Although written before *Heller*, this is probably the most informed and balanced account of the Second Amendment's shifting interpretations.

Doherty, Brian. *Gun Control on Trial: Inside the Supreme Court Battle Over the Second Amendment.* Washington, D.C.: Cato Institute, 2009. The compelling story of the *Heller* decision, including the efforts of the plaintiffs, city officials, lawyers on both sides, and the justices on the Supreme Court.

Levy, Robert. "Second Amendment Redux: Scrutiny, Incorporation, and the Heller Paradox." *Harvard Journal of Law and Public Policy* 33 (Winter, 2010): 203-216. Excellent legal analysis of the *Heller* decision, emphasizing that the decision did not decide the level of scrutiny or whether the amendment applies to state laws.

Savage, David. *The Supreme Court and Individual Rights.* Washington, D.C.: CQ Press, 2009. Highly recommended for anyone who wants a quick, dependable summary of Heller and other major decisions on the Second Amendment.

See also *Powell v. McCormick; Presser v. Illinois; United States v. Lopez.*

DOBBINS V. ERIE COUNTY

Court: U.S. Supreme Court
Citation: 41 U.S. 435
Date: March 4, 1842
Issues: Taxation

- In this important example of the nineteenth century view of federalism, the U.S. Supreme Court ruled that a state could not tax a person's federal income.

A U.S. ship captain on duty in Pennsylvania challenged the validity of that state's tax on his federal income. The state supreme court upheld the tax, but the Supreme Court unanimously reversed its decision, holding that such a tax would infringe on the taxing power of the national government.

Dobbins is historically significant as an example of the nineteenth century view of federalism. It followed Chief Justice John Marshall's landmark decision in *McCulloch v. Maryland* (1819) by interpreting the parallel immunities of both the federal and state governments broadly so that neither could tax the other. It remained valid until indirectly overturned in *Graves v. New York ex rel. O'Keefe* (1939) and is no longer a valid legal principle.

Richard L. Wilson

See also *Collector v. Day; Graves v. New York ex rel. O'Keefe; Helvering v. Davis; McCulloch v. Maryland.*

DODGE V. WOOLSEY

Court: U.S. Supreme Court
Citation: 59 U.S. 331
Date: February 6, 1856
Issues: Freedom of contract; Taxation

- The U.S. Supreme Court's ruling that the state of Ohio's attempt to collect a tax from a bank chartered in its state constituted a breach of contract exemplifies the nineteenth century view of contracts and federalism.

Justice James M. Wayne wrote this 6-3 decision upholding an injunction against the collection of a tax by the state of Ohio on one of the banks chartered in the state. This bank was chartered under an Ohio statute pursuant to the state constitution that allowed it to pay 6 percent of its profits instead of paying taxes. That constitution and law were replaced in 1851 by a new law levying a higher tax than the old percentage of the profits, and John Woolsey, a bank shareholder, sued to enjoin collection of the tax on grounds that the original charter represented a contract that was being infringed by Ohio. The Court upheld this view of the contract and the injunction, although the Court later ruled that such a contractual provision had to be specific to a contract and not just a part of a general statute. However, *Dodge* was never overturned.

Richard L. Wilson

See also *Bank of Augusta v. Earle; Briscoe v. Bank of the Commonwealth of Kentucky; Providence Bank v. Billings; Veazie Bank v. Fenno.*

Justice James M. Wayne.
(Handy Studios/
Collection of the
Supreme Court of
the United States)

DOE V. BOLTON

Court: U.S. Supreme Court
Citation: 410 U.S. 179
Date: January 22, 1973
Issues: Reproductive rights; Right to privacy; Women's issues

• A companion case to *Roe v. Wade*, it established a woman's legal right to abortion and helped to define the limits of that right by limiting state requirements which make access difficult.

This case, brought by a pregnant Georgia woman, challenged the constitutionality of a Georgia law which prohibited all but medically necessary abortions. Additionally, the Georgia law included strict procedural requirements for obtaining even medically necessary abortions. A second doctor was required to approve the abortion, abortions could be performed only in state-certified hospitals, and a committee from that hospital had to review the case and give its approval. Finally, the law restricted medically necessary abortions to state residents.

"Mary Doe" challenged the law in a district court on the grounds that it infringed on her right to privacy and that the procedural requirements violated constitutional guarantees of due process of law and equal protection of the law. The district court did rule that the restriction of abortion only to cases in which the mother's life or health was threatened, in which there was serious risk of severe fetal abnormality, or in which pregnancy was a result of rape was an infringement on a woman's constitutional "right to privacy." The district court, however, upheld the procedural requirements on the grounds that the state has a proper interest in protecting the health and life of a potential person, the fetus.

The case was appealed to the U.S. Supreme Court, where it was heard as a companion case to *Roe v. Wade*. The Court affirmed a woman's right to abortion without restriction during the first trimester of pregnancy. Using guidelines established in *Roe v. Wade*, it held invalid the requirement that abortion could be performed only in state-accredited hospitals. The court argued that clinics and other facilities could provide trained personnel and equipment for performing abortions. To limit where abortions could be performed during the first trimester infringed on a woman's right to abortion. It also held that requiring approval by a second physician and a hospital committee was unacceptable, infringing unnecessarily on a woman's rights and imposing requirements that were not applied to other surgical procedures. Requiring a second physician's approval was also viewed as infringing on a doctor's freedom to practice medicine. Finally, the Court ruled that restricting abortion to state residents was not allowed because a state is required to provide services for all persons who enter a state and need or seek medical services.

Coupled with *Roe v. Wade*, the decision strongly affirmed a woman's right to abortion and firmly established a doctrine of trimesters in which no restrictions on abortion are allowed during the first trimester of pregnancy (the first three months) and only restrictions pertaining to the safety of the mother during the second. It prohibited states from enacting requirements that would make abortion unduly difficult to obtain during this time period.

Charles L. Kammer

See also *Akron v. Akron Center for Reproductive Health*; *Bigelow v. Virginia*; *Harris v. McRae*; *Maher v. Roe*; *Planned Parenthood of Central Missouri v. Danforth*; *Roe v. Wade*; *Rust v. Sullivan*; *Thornburgh v. American College of Obstetricians and Gynecologists*; *Webster v. Reproductive Health Services*.

DOLAN V. CITY OF TIGARD

Court: U.S. Supreme Court
Citation: 512 U.S. 374
Date: June 24, 1994
Issues: Land law; Takings clause

• The U.S. Supreme Court held that the government may not attach conditions to building permits that result in the taking of private property without just compensation, in violation of the Fifth and Fourteenth Amendments.

Florence Dolan applied for a building permit to expand her plumbing and electrical supply store in Tigard, Oregon. As part of a land-management program, the city refused to issue the permit unless she dedicated 10 percent of her land for two purposes: a public greenway for flood control and a pedestrian/bicycle pathway to relieve traffic congestion in the city. Dolan claimed that this requirement of dedicating land for a permit constituted a taking of private property without compensation. The state's high court rejected her claim.

By a 5-4 vote, the Supreme Court remanded the case for reconsideration. Speaking for the majority, Chief Justice William H. Rehnquist concluded that in the circumstances, the city had the burden to show a "rough proportionality" between the building permit requirements and the individualized problems associated with the building project. Judging from the record, Rehnquist did not think the city had demonstrated a reasonable relationship between the project and the need for the greenway space and the pathway. If the city simply wanted some of Dolan's land for drainage and recreation purposes, it would be required to pay her just compensation. In a dissent, Justice John Paul Stevens criticized the majority for imposing a "novel burden of proof" on a city implementing a valid land-use plan.

Thomas Tandy Lewis

See also *First English Evangelical Lutheran Church of Glendale v. County of Los Angeles; Hawaii Housing Authority v. Midkiff; Kelo v. City of New London; Nollan v. California Coastal Commission.*

DOMBROWSKI V. PFISTER

Court: U.S. Supreme Court
Citation: 380 U.S. 499
Date: April 26, 1965
Issues: Antigovernment subversion; Federal supremacy

• The U.S. Supreme Court held that a federal court may enjoin the enforcement of an excessively vague state statute when there is evidence of bad faith and harassment in the enforcement of the statute.

According to the doctrine of abstention, federal courts normally do not intervene in state court proceedings until after they are finalized. James Dombrowski, leader of a civil rights organization in Louisiana, alleged that state officials were using broad antisubversion statutes as an excuse to harass and intimidate members of his organization. Citing the abstention doctrine, a federal court refused Dombrowski's request for an injunction. By a 5-2 vote, however, the Supreme Court reversed the judgment. Justice William J. Brennan, Jr.'s opinion for the majority argued that the intervention was justified because the statutes were "overly broad and vague regulations of expressions" and because the harassment and bad faith of state officials produced a "chilling effect" on free speech. In dissent, Justice John M. Harlan II argued that the Court's departure from the traditional abstention doctrine was contrary to principles of federalism and comity.

At first the *Dombrowski* decision led to a large number of lawsuits, but a narrow interpretation of the decision in *Younger v. Harris* (1971) greatly limited the scope of federal intervention.

Thomas Tandy Lewis

See also *Ableman v. Booth*; *Ex parte Young*; *In re Neagle*; *South Dakota v. Dole*; *United States v. California*; *Ware v. Hylton*; *Younger v. Harris*.

DRED SCOTT V. SANDFORD. *See* SCOTT V. SANDFORD

DRONENBURG V. ZECH

Court: U.S. Court of Appeals for the District of Columbia
Citation: 741 F.2d 1388
Date: August 17, 1984
Issues: Gay and lesbian rights; Military law

• A long-standing policy of forbidding homosexuality in the U.S. military and discharging those found guilty of homosexual acts was upheld in the *Dronenburg* case. The Navy and the courts often applied disparate and inconsistent reasons for the ban.

On March 10, 1778, George Washington presided over the court-martial of a soldier accused of sodomy. The man who would become the nation's first president found the accused guilty and ordered that he be drummed and fifed out of camp and forbidden ever to return. Two centuries later, the U.S. military maintained an equally uncompromising attitude toward homosexuality.

Department of Defense Directive 1332.14, enclosure 3, part 1, section H, defined military policy on homosexuality in terms of theory, definitions, and procedures. Each branch in turn had its own regulations. The Navy was guided by SECNAVINST (Secretary of the Navy Instructions) 1910.4A, which stated:

> Homosexuality is incompatible with naval service. The presence in the naval environment of persons who engage in homosexual conduct or who, by their statements, demonstrate a propensity to engage in homosexual conduct seriously impairs the accomplishment of the naval mission. The presence of such members adversely affects the ability of the Department of the Navy to maintain discipline, good order, and morale; foster mutual trust and confidence among service members; ensure the integrity of the system of rank and command; facilitate assignment and world-wide deployment of service members who frequently must live and work under close conditions affording minimal privacy; recruit and retain members of the Department of the Navy; maintain the public acceptability of the Department of the Navy; and prevent breaches of security.

Although such intolerance dates back to the American Revolution, it was during World War II that efforts were intensified to identify and discharge offenders. The concern over homosexuality was exacerbated by the fear of communism and the House Committee on Un-American Activities: Communists and homosexuals were equated and sought out with equal fervor. In the military, homosexuality was tried as a crime in a court-martial. Autonomy of military courts allowed rampant abuse and the neglect of due process. In 1951, in an effort to ensure constitutional rights, Congress enacted the Uniform Code of Military Justice. The military responded by formulating an administrative procedure for "separation" of offenders from the services, thus bypassing the legal process and retaining its customary autonomy.

With the advent of administrative separations, personnel suspected of homosexuality were investigated and referred to military psychiatrists for medical diagnosis. Homosexual incidents or behavior were considered mental illness, in keeping with the social thinking of the period. Gay rights activist John D'Emilio estimated in 1983 that forty thousand to fifty thousand individuals were discharged from the military between 1950 and 1970 for homosexuality.

Navy Policy

The Navy reviewed its policy toward homosexuals in 1948, 1952, and 1957. The 1957 review was conducted by a five-member board chaired by Captain

S. H. Crittenden, Jr., which issued its massive report on March 15, 1957. The Crittenden Report stated that an estimated 37.5 percent of active service personnel had engaged in some form of homosexual activity, that homosexuals posed no greater security risk than heterosexuals, that those discharged for homosexuality were unfairly denied important rights and benefits, that sexual orientations and behaviors were better represented by a wide spectrum than by a simple polarity, and that "current Navy directives are too rigid and inflexible." For the next twenty years, the U.S. Navy systematically suppressed the Crittenden Report.

Most discharges for homosexuality were "other than honorable," depriving those discharged of veterans' benefits, eligibility for federal employment, and their good reputations. On January 21, 1978, the secretary of the Navy issued SECNAVINST 1900.9C, recommending honorable or general discharges for a majority of cases. The "other than honorable" discharge still applied in exceptional cases involving the use of force, underaged partners, abuse of rank, public exhibitionism, the exchange of money, or sexual activities in Navy locales. The revision also suggested possible criteria for the retention of accused personnel, such as the unlikelihood of recurrence or the individual's value to the Navy.

During the 1970's and early 1980's, a number of cases were appealed beyond the military justice system. Ensign Vernon Berg was a public affairs officer on the USS *Little Rock* in Italy in 1974. A Naval Academy graduate with a spotless performance record, Berg was in a monogamous homosexual relationship. The Naval Investigative Service initiated an investigation, and Berg was processed for discharge. His administrative hearing was held in Norfolk, Virginia, thousands of miles from his place of service. Berg's appointed Navy counsel and his private counsel from the American Civil Liberties Union were denied access to crucial witnesses and documents, and the five-member board and the base commander publicly voiced opposition to the retention of homosexuals in the Navy for any reason. Despite these irregularities, the district court denied Berg's request for a restraining order to discontinue the proceedings. Despite an impressive performance record and discreet private life, Berg received an other than honorable discharge.

During the 1970's and 1980's, various cases, including those of Miriam Ben-Shalom and James Woodward, were appealed as far as the Supreme Court but failed to compel any change in Navy policy. On December 12, 1983, *Newsweek* reported that 1,167 sailors had been discharged from the Navy for homosexual behavior in 1983. Most were discharged quickly and honorably. (That year, the Navy employed 565,000 personnel, which reflected a shortage of 22,000 from levels considered necessary to the Navy's operations.)

The *Newsweek* article focused on the first discharge of a commanding officer. Gerald Vanderwier was a nineteen-year veteran who had received a Bronze Star for his service in Vietnam. After allegations of fraternization with an enlisted man and four days of often graphic testimony in military court, Vanderwier was convicted of three counts of sodomy and relieved of command of the USS *Edward McDonnell.* His dismissal brought a $1,200 fine and the loss of veterans' benefits worth approximately $500,000. His wife and four children stood by him through his trial.

The period from 1981 to 1984 saw heightened activity on the issue. In 1982 and 1983, multiple investigations of enlisted personnel were held on the USS *Norton Sound* in Long Beach, California, and the USS *Dixon* in San Diego. The *Dixon* case involved allegations against twelve women and seventeen men and was compared to seventeenth century witch hunts. Airman Apprentice William Bruce Pearson was investigated and charged twice for the same alleged homosexual act, violating the Constitution's safeguard against double jeopardy. Cynthia Patrick, a twenty-eight-year-old commissioned reserve officer, was processed for discharge on the basis of a brief, solitary homosexual encounter that had transpired eight years before she joined the Navy. Given this atmosphere, the National Organization for Women, the National Lawyers Guild, and the Lambda Legal Defense Fund, in addition to the American Civil Liberties Union, actively fought to retain or reinstate discharged personnel.

Dronenburg's Case

The case of James L. Dronenburg, who was discharged on April 21, 1981, lasted three years and resulted in a major articulation of U.S. court policy. Dronenburg's appeal claimed that his discharge violated his constitutional rights to privacy and equal protection under the law. Hearing the case in the U.S. Court of Appeals for the District of Columbia were Robert H. Bork, who was later rejected by Congress for appointment to the U.S. Supreme Court, and Antonin Scalia, who was successfully appointed to the Supreme Court by President Ronald Reagan in 1986. The court decided against Dronenburg on August 17, 1984, and he was denied a rehearing that November.

In the published opinion, Bork acknowledged an evolving right to privacy in American jurisprudence but said that that right did not encompass homosexuality. He expressed an attitude of judicial restraint toward the potential for new interpretation of the Fifth Amendment's due process clause and asserted that democratic principles validate the majoritarian disapproval of homosexual behavior. In conclusion, Bork echoed military policy: "The effects of homosexual conduct within a naval or military unit are almost certain to be harmful to morale and discipline. The Navy is not required to produce social science data or the results of controlled experiments to prove what common sense and common experience demonstrate."

Significance

The Navy's ban on homosexuality and the affirmation of the court of appeals in *Dronenburg v. Zech* had complex and far-reaching effects on the personnel involved and on society's continuing opposition to homosexuality. In spite of the plethora of directives and regulations, the Navy's rationale and procedure were ambiguous and susceptible to selective and subjective application. The definitions and interpretations of homosexuality, homosexual acts, military morale, security risks, and the basic tenet of "incompatibility" were often unclear.

The Navy and the courts often applied disparate and inconsistent reasons for the ban. It was believed that homosexuality conflicted with the type of socialization necessary for naval functioning, and that the Navy presented an extreme case given long periods of isolation at sea. It was further believed that homosexuals posed security risks, being vulnerable to subversion or blackmail because of their secret lives; that sexual politics would create conflicts of interest; that homosexuals were effeminate and not suitable to Navy duty; and that ostracization would render them ineffectual. Some of these reasons derived from the Navy ban itself, whereas others were potentially true but falsely inferred.

The practical impact was loss of livelihood, benefits, and respect for thousands of otherwise qualified and even exemplary personnel. The Navy effectively deprived itself of the skills and contributions of these individuals. In addition, millions of dollars were devoted to the investigation, prosecution, and discharge of alleged homosexuals. Publicity resulted in incidents of abuse and vandalism against those discharged.

The ban and its validation by the court of appeals also reinforced societal prejudices. Heterosexual personnel seeking discharge falsely confessed to homosexuality and, to prove their claims, adopted "homosexual" behaviors that derived from and contributed to false stereotypes. Such individuals would also bait known homosexuals into incriminating contact, resulting in discharges for both. In addition, the Navy's fear of false claims bred skepticism of true homosexual confessions; some homosexuals who could no longer bear concealment were denied discharge on the grounds that they were lying, and even explicit proofs were denied. Its policies allowed the Navy to discharge homosexuals who wished to serve while maintaining others who wished to leave. The Navy also prolonged discharge procedures without explanation, incurring despondency and poor evaluations that in turn justified degraded discharges and supported contentions that homosexuals made poor sailors.

Many of those discharged for homosexuality were, like Vanderwier, happily married or, like Patrick, had limited homosexual experience; they were in fact bisexuals or adventurous heterosexuals. People in their late teens and early twenties often engage in sexual experimentation that does not determine permanent sexual orientation; Navy discharges falsely labeled and stigmatized such individuals. Moreover, the secrecy that the ban necessitated prevented the Navy or American society at large from learning how many homosexuals were actually in the service, the quality of their performance, and their true "compatibility" with military life.

Related Issues

As the number of women in the military grew, the ban on homosexuality became an instrument for sexist manipulation. The Crittenden Report stated in 1957 that homosexuality was more frequent among female personnel for a variety of reasons. Thus, male commanders who opposed the presence of women in the military could target lesbians for discharge.

In the 1980's and 1990's, the spread of acquired immunodeficiency syndrome (AIDS) further complicated the issues involved in the Navy ban. Initially, the Navy simply discharged AIDS patients among its ranks and was slow to develop counseling of any sort. One Army base in West Germany, rather than acknowledge the prevalence of homosexuality, attributed its AIDS cases to German prostitutes, thereby reporting uniquely inflated statistics for female-to-male transmission of the human immunodeficiency virus (HIV) that causes AIDS. As AIDS cases were diagnosed, information conveyed in medical examinations regarding homosexual behavior was reported and used in discharge proceedings. On December 4, 1985, John Lehman, Jr., secretary of the Navy since 1981, issued SECNAVINST 5300.30 calling for the mandatory testing of Navy personnel and recruits for HIV.

All branches of the armed services revised their policies with the introduction in 1993 of President Bill Clinton's "don't ask, don't tell" policy as law. This policy continued to encourage secrecy but forbade military recruiters to screen out homosexuals from military service and forbade commanders to investigate personal sexual behavior of those in the military.

Barry Mann

Further Reading

Berube, Allan. *Coming Out Under Fire: The History of Gay Men and Women in World War Two.* New York: Free Press, 1990. A comprehensive and clearly developed history of military policy and procedure regarding homosexuality and its effect on the lives of individuals who served. Includes forty-five photographs and illustrations from the period, detailed notes, and an index.

Boggan, E. Carrington, Marilyn G. Haft, Charles Lister, and John P. Rupp. *The Rights of Gay People: American Civil Liberties Union Handbook.* New York: Avon Books, 1975. Written by ACLU attorneys involved in relevant court battles, this is a general guide and sourcebook on homosexuality and American law as of 1975. Extensive appendixes delineate state laws, statutory licensing provisions, support organizations, and model gay rights documents.

Gibson, Lawrence E. *Get Off My Ship: Ensign Berg vs. the U.S. Navy.* New York: Avon Books, 1978. As recounted by Berg's lover, this is the story of a respected Navy public affairs officer who unsuccessfully fought his discharge. The writing is sensitive, detailed, and fairly objective given the author's involvement in the case. Gibson paints a clear and fascinating picture of the Navy's investigation, discharge, and appeal procedures.

Humphrey, Mary Ann. *My Country, My Right to Serve: Experiences of Gay Men and Women in the Military, World War II to the Present.* New York: HarperCollins, 1990. Humphrey gathered forty-one first-person accounts on being gay in the military, including stories told by active personnel under pseudonyms. Appendixes provide policy documents and support organizations, and the bibliography includes extensive periodical references.

Koppelman, Andrew. *The Gay Rights Question in Contemporary American Law.* Chicago: University of Chicago Press, 2003. Critiques arguments on both sides of the gay rights issue, discussing whether discrimination against gays is legally or morally defensible. Also provides some history regarding court decisions concerning gay rights.

Pinello, Daniel R. *Gay Rights and American Law.* New York: Cambridge University Press, 2003. Examines the development of gay rights throughout the American legal system, including both the Supreme Court and appellate courts. Discusses nearly four hundred court decisions between 1980 and 2000.

Rimmerman, Craig A., ed. *Gay Rights, Military Wrongs: Political Perspectives on Lesbians and Gays in the Military.* New York: Routledge, 1996. Ten essays explore the various aspects of discrimination against gays and lesbians in the military.

Shilts, Randy. *Conduct Unbecoming: Gays and Lesbians in the U.S. Military.* New York: St. Martin's Press, 1993. Shilts's moving prose is based on numerous documents and hundreds of interviews with gays and lesbians in the military.

Sloan, Irving J. *Homosexual Conduct and the Law: The Legal Standing of Gays and Lesbians.* Dobbs Ferry, N.Y.: Oceana, 1986. This compact, 150-page book examines legal issues and discrimination in employment, immigration, AIDS policies, insurance, and family matters. A short chapter focuses on gays in the military.

See also *Boy Scouts of America v. Dale; Frontiero v. Richardson; Lawrence v. Texas; Personnel Administrator of Massachusetts v. Feeney; Romer v. Evans.*

DUNCAN V. KAHANAMOKU

Court: U.S. Supreme Court
Citation: 327 U.S. 304
Date: February 25, 1946
Issues: Habeas corpus; Military law

- The U.S. Supreme Court held that the establishment of military tribunals to try civilians in a U.S. territory was illegal because it was not authorized by an act of Congress.

In late 1941, shortly after the attack on Pearl Harbor, the governor of Hawaii suspended the writ of habeas corpus, placed the territory under martial law, suspended all functions of the civilian government, and delegated executive and judicial powers to the military authorities. General Walter Short proclaimed himself military governor of Hawaii and established military courts that were not subject to review by the regular courts. Military authorities claimed that the Hawaiian Organic Act of 1900 authorized the temporary military regime. Duncan and another person imprisoned by the regime petitioned for a habeas corpus review.

By a 6-2 vote, the Supreme Court ordered the two prisoners released. Justice Hugo L. Black's majority opinion found that the Hawaiian Organic Act had not authorized a declaration of martial law except under conditions of actual invasion or rebellion. He pointed out that the 1900 statute had extended all the rights of the Constitution to the territory, and therefore, the civilians in Hawaii were entitled to all the constitutional guarantees of a fair trial. Although Black referred to the principles of *Ex parte Milligan* (1866), he carefully avoided any consideration of the constitutional limitations of Congress in the territories during time of war.

Thomas Tandy Lewis

See also *Ex parte Milligan; Ex parte Quirin; Frank v. Mangum; Hamdan v. Rumsfeld; McCleskey v. Zant; Moore v. Dempsey; Stone v. Powell.*

DUNCAN V. LOUISIANA

Court: U.S. Supreme Court
Citation: 391 U.S. 145
Date: May 20, 1968
Issues: Juries

- Overruling several earlier decisions, the U.S. Supreme Court held that the due process clause of the Fourteenth Amendment required states to apply the Sixth Amendment right to a jury trial in a serious criminal case.

Gary Duncan, a nineteen-year-old African American, defended his younger cousins who were having an exchange with four white boys, and apparently Duncan slapped the arm of one of the boys. Duncan was arrested and tried on charges of assault and battery, with a possible maximum sentence of two years in prison. Duncan and his lawyer requested a trial by jury, but the request was denied, since Louisiana law mandated a jury only when capital punishment or imprisonment at hard labor might be imposed. Duncan was found guilty, fined $150, and sentenced to sixty days in prison. After the Louisiana Supreme Court upheld the sentence, Duncan appealed to the U.S. Supreme Court.

Originally the Bill of Rights had applied only to the federal government, but by 1968 many of those rights had been applied to the states ("incorporated") through the due process clause of the Fourteenth Amendment. The precedents of the Supreme Court, however, had endorsed the approach of *Palko v. Connecticut* (1937), which interpreted due process as referring to "fundamental fairness" and recognized that jury trials were not essential to fairness or to a "scheme of ordered liberty."

In *Duncan v. Louisiana*, nevertheless, the Court held by a 7-2 vote that the states must recognize a defendant's "fundamental" right to a trial by jury in every serious criminal case. In the majority opinion, Justice Byron R. White wrote that the question was not simply whether a procedure was consistent with fairness, but whether it was "necessary to an Anglo-American regime of ordered liberty." He conceded that petty offenses carrying maximum penalties of less than six months were not subject to the Sixth and Fourteenth Amendments, but he insisted that any crime carrying a *possible* prison term of two years was sufficiently serious to entitle a defendant to a trial by jury.

Justice Byron R. White.
(Joseph Bailey, National
Geographic Society/
Courtesy, Supreme Court
of the United States)

In the *Duncan* opinions, the justices defended different theoretical views concerning the relationship between the Bill of Rights and the Fourteenth Amendment. Justice White endorsed a variant of the "selective incorporation" approach. Justice Hugo Black, in his concurring opinion, defended the "total incorporation" doctrine of applying all of the first eight amendments to the states. Finally, Justice John M. Harlan's dissent argued that the Fourteenth Amendment was not designed to incorporate, or to be limited to, the specific guarantees of those amendments and insisted that states should have the discretion to adopt alternative practices consistent with fundamental fairness.

The immediate impact of *Duncan* was somewhat limited, because all the states were already using juries in almost all serious criminal cases. The decision was important, however, because it was one of the last in a series of "incorporation" cases which required the states to follow most principles in the Bill of Rights. Later decisions softened the impact of *Duncan* by not requiring states to imitate all the requirements of federal jury trials.

Thomas Tandy Lewis

See also *McKeiver v. Pennsylvania; Palko v. Connecticut.*

Dunn v. Blumstein

Court: U.S. Supreme Court
Citation: 405 U.S. 330
Date: March 21, 1972
Issues: Equal protection of the law; Right to travel;
Voting rights

• The U.S. Supreme Court limited the ability of the states to impose residency requirements on voters.

James Blumstein moved to Tennessee on June 12, 1970, and attempted to register to vote on July 1, 1970. The county registrar refused to register him because Tennessee law allowed people to register only if they had been residents of the state for at least one year and residents of the county for three months. On constitutional grounds, Blumstein challenged the Tennessee durational residency requirement before a three-judge federal court. The court held the Tennessee law unconstitutional because it interfered with the right to vote and penalized some residents for exercising their right to interstate travel.

The Supreme Court framed the issue as whether the equal protection clause of the Fourteenth Amendment to the Constitution allowed a state to discriminate among its citizens based on how long they have been citizens. Equal protection analysis begins by asking whether a law or regulation impinges on a fundamental right or freedom. If it does, then the state must show a substantial or compelling interest before it may impose the regulation. In addition, the state must show that it has used the least drastic means to further its interest. The Court found that the Tennessee residency requirement impinged on two fundamental rights: voting and interstate travel. As a result, Tennessee had to show a compelling interest for its residency requirement and had to demonstrate that the requirement was the least drastic means that could be used to further its purposes.

Tennessee alleged that a one-year residency requirement could protect against voter fraud and give some assurance that voters were knowledgeable. Rejecting both arguments, the Court found that voter fraud could be prevented by other, less drastic means such as criminal penalties, which Tennessee had already passed. Furthermore, the Court could find no evidence that living in Tennessee for one year made a person into a more informed voter.

The concept of an intelligent voter was found to be elusive and susceptible to abuse.

The importance of *Dunn v. Blumstein* lies in its assertion that states and other governmental agencies cannot impose more than minimal burdens on the right to vote and other similar rights. Subsequent Supreme Court cases have, however, accepted fifty-day residency requirements.

David E. Paas

See also *Breedlove v. Suttles; Harper v. Virginia State Board of Elections; Katzenbach v. Morgan; Oregon v. Mitchell; South Carolina v. Katzenbach; United States v. Reese.*

DUPLEX PRINTING CO. V. DEERING

Court: U.S. Supreme Court
Citation: 254 U.S. 443
Date: January 3, 1921
Issues: Congressional powers; Labor law

- An antilabor U.S. Supreme Court majority severely curtailed labor union activity by limiting the protections granted to these organizations by Congress.

Justice Mahlon Pitney wrote this 6-3 opinion for the Supreme Court ruling that the 1914 Clayton Act did not protect labor unions from conviction for illegal restraints of trade, such as secondary boycotts. Through passage of the act, Congress had attempted to stop antiunion judges from issuing injunctions against labor unions for using secondary boycotts as a part of collective bargaining efforts. However, antiunion sentiment was strong on the Court at the time, and it used antitrust legislation against the unions.

Justices Louis D. Brandeis, Oliver Wendell Holmes, and John H. Clarke dissented in *Duplex Printing*, arguing that the Court was ignoring a legitimate congressional power to enact legislation that stipulated that labor unions were not monopolies in the usual sense of the word. *Duplex Printing* was effective for more than a decade until the Great Depression dramatically changed public and legal opinion. The leading dissenters later saw their views become

Justice Mahlon H. Pitney in 1913. (Harris & Ewing Collection/Library of Congress)

the law of the land. When Congress adopted prounion legislation such as the 1932 Norris-La Guardia Act, the New Deal era Court upheld exempting labor unions from antitrust legislation.

Richard L. Wilson

See also *Gompers v. Buck's Stove and Range Co.; In re Debs; Local 28 of Sheet Metal Workers International Association v. Equal Employment Opportunity Commission; Thornhill v. Alabama.*

---

du Pont de Nemours and Co., United States v. *See* United States v. E. I. du Pont de Nemours and Co.

E. C. Knight Co., United States v. *See* United States v. E. C. Knight Co.

E. I. du Pont de Nemours and Co., United States v. *See* United States v. E. I. du Pont de Nemours and Co.

Edelman v. Jordan

Court: U.S. Supreme Court
Citation: 415 U.S. 651
Date: March 25, 1974
Issues: States' rights

• This U.S. Supreme Court decision, reached by a conservative majority, protected states from class-action suits by citizens alleging that these states were undermining federal legislation by granting them benefits too late.

John Jordan sued Illinois by suing various of its state and county officials, asserting they were paying out benefits later than federal law mandated and therefore violating the Fourteenth Amendment rights of the beneficiaries. A federal district court agreed and ordered retroactive payments to the class-action beneficiaries. Illinois appealed and lost in the court of appeals. However, the Supreme Court ruled in favor of Illinois. In the 5-4 majority decision written by Justice William H. Rehnquist, the Court ruled that Illinois did not waive its Eleventh Amendment rights by participating in the federal program and that the Eleventh Amendment prohibited—within limits—federal court lawsuits against a state without the state's consent brought by citizens of that state or of other states. The Court reasoned that although *Ex parte Young* (1908) allowed injunctions against states in matters affecting future policies, it did not permit suits for retroactive payments.

Justices William O. Douglas, William J. Brennan, Jr., and Thurgood Marshall wrote separate dissents, and Justice Harry A. Blackmun joined Marshall. These dissenting justices opposed the majority holdings on more than one front. Later decisions limited the impact of *Edelman* and allowed Congress to circumvent this state immunity issue.

Richard L. Wilson

See also *Chisholm v. Georgia; Cohens v. Virginia; Ex parte Young; Seminole Tribe v. Florida.*

Edgewood Independent School District v. Kirby

Court: Texas Supreme Court
Citation: 777 S.W. 2d 391
Date: October 2, 1989
Issues: Education; Equal protection of the law

- Large disparities in public school funding between rich and poor districts in Texas were ended by a Texas Supreme Court decision and subsequent legislative act.

For many years following the development of its public school system, Texas financed its schools largely through local property taxes. These taxes were raised at the local level and spent on the local school system. Substantial amounts of state aid provided a minimum level of funding for every school district, but local districts were free to supplement these funds from local property taxes. Even though the level of state funding increased over the years, schools remained heavily dependent on money raised through local property taxes. School districts could levy taxes and spend the tax money as they wished, limited only by broad parameters set by the state.

The result of this system was that property-rich districts had a much greater ability to fund their school systems than did property-poor districts. In 1989, the one hundred wealthiest Texas school districts had twenty times the property wealth of the one hundred poorest districts. These wealthy districts could either have much lower taxes than the poor districts or could spend much more on their schools. Typically, they did both. It was not unusual for a property-rich district to have both lower taxes and ten times more discretionary money per pupil than a property-poor district. This resulted in considerable disparities in the education provided to children within the state. In some poorer districts, schools lacked such ordinary aspects of a good education as science teachers and labs, gymnasiums, and cafeterias. The problem was compounded by the fact that spending on education in Texas was among the lowest in the nation. Although there were great differences within the state, even the wealthiest districts tended to fall below the national average in terms of per-pupil expenditures.

Texas's system of financing education was first challenged at the federal level in the early 1970's. In 1973, the case of *San Antonio Independent School District v. Rodriguez* reached the U.S. Supreme Court. In that case, the Edgewood Independent School District, a property-poor district in San Antonio predominantly composed of African Americans and Mexican Americans, argued that the funding system violated the equal protection clause of the Fourteenth Amendment to the U.S. Constitution. The Court rejected this argument, finding that the system did guarantee to all children a minimum level of education through state-supplied aid. The Court held that even if education could be considered a right (which it doubted), the Court did not have the authority to guarantee people levels of education beyond the minimum. The Court also found it difficult, using its traditional "equal protection" analysis, to determine a class of people who were the object of discrimination in the case. It pointed out that poor people often did not live in poor districts, and poor districts often contained rich people.

The heart of the Court's opinion, however, was a concern for local control of education. The Court praised the freedom that local school control facilitated for political participation, experimentation, innovation, and healthy competition. Centralized control of the money, the Court asserted, would inevitably mean centralized control of education and a consequent loss of local freedom.

The Texas Court Case

Having lost on the national level, the Edgewood District turned in the 1980's to the Texas state constitution for relief. Joining with other poor school districts, and represented by the Mexican American Legal Defense and Educational Fund (MALDEF), the district brought suit against the state of Texas in May, 1984. The suit alleged that the state's school financing system discriminated against students in poor districts in violation of the Texas constitution. Partly as a response to this suit, the state legislature passed a school reform law in June, 1984, that substantially increased state aid to poorer districts. The suit

was reconstituted and continued, however, on the grounds that large disparities still existed between rich and poor districts.

In January, 1987, a state district judge ruled that the financing system did
indeed violate the Texas constitution. This decision was overturned by the
Third Court of Appeals in Texas, but that decision was in turn appealed by
MALDEF to the Texas Supreme Court. On October 2, 1989, in the case of
Edgewood Independent School District v. Kirby, the three Republican and six Democratic judges on the Supreme Court of Texas reached unanimous agreement that the state's system of financing schools was unconstitutional. The
court ordered the legislature to design a new system in time for the 1990-1991
school year. Speaking through Chief Justice Oscar Mauzy, the court held that
the Texas constitution required that there be "substantially equal opportunity
to have access to educational funds." There must be equal educational opportunity for children "regardless of where they live." What had been lost on the
federal level was now won on the state level.

A fierce political battle then ensued in the Texas statehouse. Governor William Clements, a Republican, insisted that the funding problem posed by the
court should not be solved through an increase in state taxes. In addition, representatives from districts that stood to gain were pitted against those from
districts that stood to lose. The legislature met in four special sessions during
the spring of 1990 to hammer out a new system. After three of these sessions,
the legislature agreed to a bill, only to have it vetoed by the governor because
it raised taxes. After the governor's veto, a court-appointed master threatened
an alternative "Robin Hood plan" that would shift hundreds of millions of tax
dollars from wealthy to poor school districts. Under this threat, the governor
and the legislature reached a compromise that attempted to solve the problem by increasing state aid to education but left substantial discretion to local
districts to raise additional funds.

MALDEF and the poor school districts, however, challenged this solution
in court as not providing sufficient aid for the poor districts and failing to
make expenditures in all districts equal. In September, 1990, State District
Judge F. Scott McCown agreed, ruling that the new law was unconstitutional
because it did not give all schools "substantially equal" access to funds for a
similar tax effort. Rather than order a new plan, the judge gave the legislature
another year to come up with a plan that met this criterion.

In the Texas gubernatorial election in November, 1990, Ann Richards, the
Democratic candidate, recaptured the statehouse from the Republicans. Because the Democrats already possessed solid control of the legislature, party
conflict became less of a factor when the legislature reconsidered school finance in the spring of 1991. This did not prevent another fierce political battle over who would bear the burden of the reform, however. The new gover-

nor took a relatively small part in the legislative negotiations that led to the passage of a variation of the "Robin Hood plan" in early April. The plan established minimum and maximum taxing levels, designed to force increased spending on schools over a four-year period. It guaranteed similar funds for similar taxing efforts by a combination of transferring property tax revenue from wealthy districts in a county to poor districts, increasing state aid for poorer districts and decreasing it for wealthier ones, and placing spending limits on the wealthiest districts.

The end result of court and legislative action was a substantial change in the Texas educational system. Many suburban and city districts faced a loss of revenue; many rural and poorer districts near cities gained substantial increases in funding. Spending per pupil was now roughly equal across the state.

Significance

The long-term effects of the court-ordered change in Texas education have taken some time to work out. The hoped-for improvement in the education in poorer districts has depended on the translation of the increased dollars available into better education for children through such changes as the hiring of better teachers and the improvement of facilities—results that have by no means been guaranteed. The plan also faced court challenges from wealthier districts, which alleged that it violated the Texas constitution by requiring shifts in property tax revenues from the districts in which they were raised to other districts.

The immediate impacts of the plan were felt most strongly by those school districts that faced decreased state aid or transfer of their property taxes to other districts. These included middle- and upper-class suburbs and large cities. The Dallas area provides an indication of the scope of these shifts: Five suburban school districts around Dallas were required to shift property tax revenue to other districts, and two additional districts, including the city of Dallas, lost substantial amounts of state aid. The districts that lost revenues responded by laying off teachers and constricting their curricula. Typical cuts included foreign-language instruction, honors classes, and other elements of the curriculum that enabled students to advance beyond the "basics." It was clear that the "best" Texas schools would no longer be quite so outstanding.

Large cities faced particularly severe problems. The city of Dallas lost half its state aid because of its large property base. Ironically, the city's schools were simultaneously faced with the possible loss of accreditation because of inadequacies in the system, given that within the Dallas system were some of the poorest and most difficult neighborhoods for schooling in the state. In its insistence on equality, the court did not consider that the growing complexity of cities' problems would make it more expensive for them to provide the same quality of education delivered in rural districts.

The change also brought about a new level of bureaucracy in the state's school system. To equalize tax revenues among local school districts, new countywide taxing districts were created to supplement the local districts. These required boards to decide how to levy and distribute taxes as well as staff to administer the boards' decisions. Increases in administrative costs and regulation were the inevitable results.

The 1989 decision of the Texas Supreme Court thus led to mixed results. On one hand, there was a prospect of improved education for children in poor districts. On the other, the best schools were hurt, local initiative was diminished, hard-pressed cities were left with decreased funds, and an already large educational bureaucracy was expanded. There was a strong possibility that the education of some would be improved, but only at the cost of dragging others down, achieving universal mediocrity.

School financing remained a controversial subject in Texas. In November, 2005, the Texas Supreme Court declared unconstitutional the state's $1.50 cap per $100 in property value on statewide property taxes collected by local districts. The same ruling observed ongoing disparities between rich and poor districts. The court did not view these disparities as unconstitutional at the time of the ruling, but it observed that they might soon become so and cautioned that the legislature needed to act promptly to prevent this. In a special legislative session in May, 2006, Texas lawmakers approved reforms to meet the court's ruling and deadlines, allowing local discretion in setting tax rates. This led to a decrease in local property taxes, but other reforms dedicated state surpluses to cover local shortfalls in tax revenue, dedication of new taxes to buy down future local revenue shortfalls, and new minimal business taxes. These reforms allowed the state to extend teacher pay raises. The ability of these reforms to sustain quality education over the long term, however, remained an open question.

Glen E. Thurow

Further Reading

Areen, Judith, and Leonard Ross. *The Supreme Court Review* 1973, 33-35. Offers an interesting analysis of the problems of wealth and equal protection, focusing on the national case involving Texas school finance.

Coons, John E., William H. Clune, III, and Stephen D. Sugarman. *Private Wealth and Public Education.* Cambridge, Mass.: Harvard University Press, 1970. The seminal work advancing the view that school districts should receive a fixed amount of revenue per pupil for any particular level of tax effort regardless of the level of the property tax base.

Pritchett, C. Herman. "The New Due Process: Equal Protection." In *Constitutional Civil Liberties*. Englewood Cliffs, N.J.: Prentice Hall, 1984. Provides a good summary of the legal thinking about equality that lay behind the Texas Supreme Court decision about school financing, including a succinct discussion of the treatment of wealth by the U.S. Supreme Court.

Richards, David A. J. "Equal Opportunity and School Financing." *University of Chicago Law Review* 32 (1973): 41. Presents a thorough discussion of the legal and constitutional issues that can be raised about the financing of schools through the local property tax.

See also *Lemon v. Kurtzman*; *San Antonio Independent School District v. Rodriguez*; *Swann v. Charlotte-Mecklenburg Board of Education*; *Wisconsin v. Yoder.*

EDMONSON V. LEESVILLE CONCRETE CO.

Court: U.S. Supreme Court
Citation: 500 U.S. 614
Date: June 3, 1991
Issues: Juries

• The U.S. Supreme Court extended its ruling that potential jurors could not be peremptorily excluded on the basis of race from criminal trials to include civil trials.

In *Batson v. Kentucky* (1986), the Supreme Court ruled that litigants in criminal trials could not use peremptory challenges to exclude federal court jurors on the basis of race because such exclusions violated the excluded person's Fifth Amendment rights. In this 6-3 decision, it extended its decision to civil as well as criminal trials. In his opinion for the Court, Anthony M. Kennedy argued that even if the litigants' private attorneys, not the state, make the exclusion, state action is involved because the attorneys are using the public court forum. Private parties must follow the same rules the state does when it uses the courts. Justice Sandra Day O'Connor was joined in a forceful dissent by Justices William H. Rehnquist and Antonin Scalia, who argued that the attorneys' challenges of jurors were essentially private choices. The dissenters rejected the idea that state action was inherent in all court proceedings.

Richard L. Wilson

See also *Batson v. Kentucky; Strauder v. West Virginia; Williams v. Mississippi.*

===

EDWARDS V. AGUILLARD

Court: U.S. Supreme Court
Citation: 482 U.S. 578
Date: June 19, 1987
Issues: Education; Establishment of religion

- In this case the U.S. Supreme Court dealt a major blow to proponents of "creation science" by finding that a Louisiana statute forbidding public school instruction in evolution without corresponding instruction in "creation science" violated the establishment clause.

Edwards v. Aguillard involved a Louisiana statute called the Balanced Treatment for Creation-Science and Evolution-Science in Public School Instruction Act, which prohibited public schools from teaching only the theory of evolution, requiring them—if they taught about evolution—to teach also scientific evidence in support of creation as it is described in the Bible. A group of parents, teachers, and religious leaders subsequently challenged the act, claiming that it violated the establishment clause (the clause in the First Amendment stating that Congress shall "make no law respecting an establishment of religion"). The Supreme Court, in a 6-2 decision, agreed.

Applying the three-part test of *Lemon v. Kurtzman* (1971), which required a statute to have a secular purpose, a predominantly secular effect, and no excessive entanglement between government and religion to survive an establishment clause challenge, the Court in *Edwards* determined that Louisiana's act violated this test because it lacked a secular purpose. Although the act stated that its purpose was to protect academic freedom, the Court, in an opinion by Justice William Brennan, found this purpose a sham. The act, according to the majority opinion, gave teachers no more freedom than they already possessed to discuss varying theories of the world's origins. Furthermore, the act unfairly forced creation science in several ways—for example, by providing for the development of curriculum guides and the provision of resource materials for creation science but not for instruction concerning evolution.

The Court sensed a religious purpose at the heart of the Louisiana act and, having done so, declared it an unconstitutional establishment of religion. Justice Antonin Scalia, in an opinion joined by Chief Justice William H. Rehnquist, disagreed with the majority on precisely this point. He argued that the majority had misconstrued the act's purposes. According to Scalia, that purpose was simply to protect students from being indoctrinated with respect to the theory of evolution without exposure to other theories concerning the world's origin. This purpose, he believed, was a permissible one and should have satisfied the demands of the establishment clause.

The decision in *Edwards v. Aguillard* is significant for reaffirming the Court's vigilant watchfulness over the public schools against what it views as attempts to smuggle religious teaching into the classrooms. For the majority in the case, Louisiana's "Balanced Treatment Act" was in some ways a rerun of the famous Scopes "monkey" trial that pitted Clarence Darrow against William Jennings Bryan in a debate between the Bible and evolution. The Supreme Court had previously ruled in *Epperson v. Arkansas* (1968) that the establishment clause barred state attempts to forbid the teaching of evolution. Here the Court went a step further and prohibited Louisiana from attempting to stage a debate between creationism and evolution.

Timothy L. Hall

See also *Epperson v. Arkansas; Lemon v. Kurtzman.*

EDWARDS V. CALIFORNIA

Court: U.S. Supreme Court
Citation: 314 U.S. 160
Date: November 24, 1941
Issues: Right to travel

• The U.S. Supreme Court, in striking down a law barring indigents from entering California, strengthened the constitutional right to travel, especially for poor citizens.

Justice James F. Byrnes.
(Library of Congress)

The Supreme Court unanimously ruled that California's Great Depression era "Okie Law" was unconstitutional in its attempt to bar any person from bringing an indigent person into California. Justice James F. Byrnes, in his opinion for the Court, relied on Article I, section 8 of the Constitution (the commerce clause) and viewed the issue as the transportation of people as if they were property in interstate commerce. In his concurrence, Justice Robert H. Jackson agreed with the result but attacked the reasoning. He objected to equating people with property to give them constitutional rights as U.S. citizens. Jackson argued that the Fourteenth Amendment's privileges and immunities clause should be used to grant people the right to travel across state lines, which he saw as a basic feature of U.S. citizenship. Jackson's view would strengthen the privileges and immunities clause, which is not frequently cited by the Court.

Richard L. Wilson

See also *Aptheker v. Secretary of State; Dunn v. Blumstein; Kent v. Dulles; United States v. Guest.*

EDWARDS V. SOUTH CAROLINA

Court: U.S. Supreme Court
Citation: 372 U.S. 229
Date: February 5, 1963
Issues: Civil rights and liberties; Freedom of assembly and association

- In this incorporation case, the U.S. Supreme Court held that local officials could not block an otherwise lawful demonstration because they disliked the demonstrators' political views.

About two hundred African American students marched peacefully in small groups from a church to the South Carolina state capitol, an obviously public forum, to protest the state's racially discriminatory laws. A few dozen police officers initially told them they could march peacefully but about an hour later ordered them to disperse under threat of arrest. A crowd had gathered to watch the demonstrators but did not seem threatening, and the police presence was ample. The demonstrators responded by singing patriotic and religious songs until some two hundred demonstrators were arrested and convicted of breach of the peace. Their conviction was upheld by the South Carolina Supreme Court.

The Supreme Court, by an 8-1 vote, reversed the convictions of the civil rights demonstrators. Justice Potter Stewart, in the majority opinion, applied the First Amendment right to freedom of assembly to the states, refusing to let the states bar demonstrations of unpopular views in traditional forums. In line with other time, place, and manner decisions, the Court used the Fourteenth Amendment's due process clause to incorporate the peaceable assembly portion of the First Amendment and to apply it to the states. Justice Tom C. Clark dissented, defending the state's action.

Richard L. Wilson

See also *Adderley v. Florida; DeJonge v. Oregon; Hague v. Congress of Industrial Organizations; Klopfer v. North Carolina; Village of Skokie v. National Socialist Party of America.*

Eichman, United States v. *See* United States v. Eichman

Eisenstadt v. Baird

Court: U.S. Supreme Court
Citation: 405 U.S. 438
Date: March 22, 1972
Issues: Equal protection of the law; Reproductive rights; Right to privacy

- Overturning a state ban on the distribution of contraceptives to unmarried persons, the Court employed a broad right to privacy and insisted that classifications of persons be rationally related to legitimate objectives.

While concluding a lecture on contraception at Boston University, William Baird exhibited contraceptive articles and gave a young woman a package of vaginal foam. Based on a ninety-year-old Massachusetts statute making it a felony to dispense contraceptives to unmarried persons, Baird was tried and convicted at a bench trial in the Massachusetts Superior Court. After his conviction was upheld by the Massachusetts Supreme Judicial Court, he was successful in his petition for a writ of habeas corpus in the federal court of appeals. The sheriff of Suffolk County, Thomas Eisenstadt, appealed the case to the U.S. Supreme Court.

A few years earlier, in *Griswold v. Connecticut* (1965), the Court had recognized a "right of privacy" which included the liberty for married persons to acquire contraceptives and contraceptive information. Based on the reading of this case, it was not clear how the Court would decide regarding the Massachusetts law.

The Court voted six to one that Massachusetts could not outlaw the distribution of contraceptives to single persons when they were legally available to married persons. Delivering the opinion for the Court, Justice William Brennan interpreted *Griswold* to mean that procreational decisions were constitutionally protected under the right to privacy, and he added the idea that the right to privacy inheres in the individual rather than the marital couple. All fundamental freedoms, moreover, were under the umbrella of the equal protection clause of the Fourteenth Amendment. This clause did not prohibit states from treating different classes of persons in different ways, but the amendment did mean that all classifications must be reasonable and bear a substantial relation to a legitimate concern of the state. Brennan could find no legislative purpose that would justify limiting contraceptives to married persons.

The *Eisenstadt* decision was important for three reasons. First, the Court presented a broad conception of procreational freedom as an element of the right to privacy, with the latter reaffirmed as a fundamental right. Second, the Court explicitly recognized that the right to privacy inheres in the individual rather than in a more narrow relationship or place. Third, by attaching the right to privacy with the application of the equal protection clause to distinctions between the married and the unmarried, the Court was clearly extending the strict scrutiny test to broader issues and categories. One year after *Eisenstadt*, the implications of the decision would become apparent in the famous case of *Roe v. Wade* (1972).

Thomas Tandy Lewis

See also *Adamson v. California; Doe v. Bolton; Griswold v. Connecticut; Roe v. Wade.*

ELFBRANDT V. RUSSELL

Court: U.S. Supreme Court
Citation: 384 U.S. 11
Date: April 18, 1966
Issues: Loyalty oaths

- The U.S. Supreme Court invalidated an Arizona statute and its accompanying statutory gloss, which together required employees to take an oath to support the federal and state constitutions, threatening prosecution for perjury and immediate discharge of an employee belonging to any organization committed to overthrowing the government.

Barbara Elfbrandt, a teacher and a Quaker, refused to take the oath and sued on the grounds that the legislature had not adequately explained the meaning of the statute and its accompanying gloss. Her lawyers referred to *Baggett v. Bullitt* (1964) and other cases in which the Supreme Court had struck down loyalty oaths that had restricted individual rights to free expression of ideas and political association.

Speaking for a 5-4 majority, Justice William O. Douglas argued that the legislative gloss interfered with the freedom of association guaranteed by the First and Fourteenth Amendments. He referred to several precedents in which the Court had held that a blanket prohibition of association with groups having both legal and illegal purposes interfered with the freedom of political expression and association.

Elfbrandt was typical of a half dozen cases in which the Court overturned loyalty oaths on grounds of vagueness or overbreadth. However, in *Cole v. Richardson* (1972), the Court upheld a requirement that state employees take an oath or affirmation similar to the one in Article VI of the U.S. Constitution.

Thomas Tandy Lewis

See also *Cummings v. Missouri; Dennis v. United States; Keyishian v. Board of Regents; Lovell v. City of Griffin; Noto v. United States; Scales v. United States; Slochower v. Board of Education of New York City; Whitney v. California; Yates v. United States.*

ELROD V. BURNS

Court: U.S. Supreme Court
Citation: 427 U.S. 347
Date: June 28, 1976
Issues: Labor law

• In this case, the U.S. Supreme Court acted to protect government employees from being fired simply because they were not affiliated with the same political party as a newly elected local official.

In December 1970, Richard Elrod, a Democrat, replaced a Republican predecessor and became sheriff of Cook County, Illinois. John Burns, the chief deputy of the Process Division in the sheriff's office, and other Republican employees were discharged because they were not political supporters of the new Democratic leaders who had gained control of the sheriff's office. The termination of their employment was consistent with established practices in Cook County, where employees who were not part of the civil service system were routinely replaced if they did not belong to the same political party as newly elected leaders.

Burns and the other discharged Republican employees challenged their terminations, however, on the grounds that the firings violated their First Amendment right to free association. They believed that they should be free to act on their beliefs by joining and supporting the Republican Party without placing their jobs at risk when Democrats gained control of local governmental offices.

Five justices on the Supreme Court agreed with Burns that the firings violated his constitutional rights. Justice William J. Brennan's opinion concluded that "patronage dismissals severely restrict political belief and association." The dissenting justices asserted that patronage hiring and firing were essential to maintaining the stability and accountability of political parties in the American democratic system.

The five justices who found fault with Burns's firing could not agree about how far their decision should go toward limiting traditional political patronage employment practices in local government. They all agreed, however, that politically motivated firings of nonpolicymaking personnel were improper. The Supreme Court distinguished between policymaking personnel, who could be replaced because they needed to make discretionary decisions in accordance with the wishes of new governmental leaders, and nonpolicymaking personnel, who simply follow orders in processing forms and administering the programs initiated by leaders.

The *Elrod* decision was especially important because it laid the groundwork for the Supreme Court's subsequent examinations of patronage employment practices in government. In subsequent decisions in *Branti v. Finkel et al.* (1980) and *Rutan v. Republican Party of Illinois* (1990), the Court further limited the ability of newly elected officials to make employment decisions based on employees' political party affiliations. Eventually the justices placed limitations on the firings of some kinds of policymaking personnel as well as on the use of political party affiliation in hiring decisions.

Although the Supreme Court's decisions did not eliminate the use of political considerations in governmental employment decisions, they limited the decision-making power enjoyed by newly elected political officials. By permitting lower-level government employees to win lawsuits, the justices made government officials more cautious about explicitly applying political criteria in hiring and firing any but the highest-level employees.

Christopher E. Smith

See also *Davis v. Bandemer; Greer v. Spock; Rutan v. Republican Party of Illinois; United Public Workers v. Mitchell.*

EMPLOYMENT DIVISION, DEPARTMENT OF HUMAN RESOURCES OF OREGON V. SMITH

Court: U.S. Supreme Court
Citation: 494 U.S. 872
Date: April 17, 1990
Issues: Freedom of religion; Illegal drugs; Native American sovereignty

• Narrowly interpreting the free exercise clause, the U.S. Supreme Court allowed Oregon to apply its drug laws to prohibit Native Americans from using peyote in religious ceremonies.

Alfred Smith and Galen Black, two members of the Native American Church, were fired from their jobs in a drug rehabilitation clinic after their employer discovered that they used the hallucinogenic drug peyote during religious rituals. They applied for unemployment compensation, but Oregon's Department of Human Resources denied their claims based on a state law that disqualified employees who were discharged for work-related "misconduct."

A state appellate court and the Oregon Supreme Court ruled that the denial of benefits was a violation of the free exercise clause of the First Amendment. Oregon appealed to the U.S. Supreme Court, contending that Smith's free exercise of religion had to be balanced by the state's interest in preventing the use of harmful drugs. The Supreme Court's first judgment was to remand the case to the Oregon Supreme Court to decide whether state law made an exception for the religious use of peyote. Oregon's court responded that state law provided no exception and that the only issue was the religious freedom of the First Amendment. The Supreme Court accepted the case for a second time.

The Supreme Court's major precedent, *Sherbert v. Verner* (1963), suggested that Oregon could prevail only if it could defend its policy with the "compelling state interest" test combined with the "least restrictive alternative" test. From this perspective, it appeared difficult for Oregon to justify the refusal of unemployment benefits to Smith and Black. The Court had upheld the *Sherbert* tests in at least seven cases since 1963.

In the *Smith* case, however, the Court voted six to three that Oregon had no constitutional obligation to make a religious exception for illegal drugs, provided that the law was reasonable, neutral, and generally applicable to all persons. Writing for the majority, Justice Antonin Scalia argued that in enforcing valid criminal laws not specifically directed at religious acts, government had no obligation to make a religious exemption. Such matters were generally left to the legislature's discretion, even if an "unfortunate consequence" was an incidental burden on unpopular religious practices.

In a concurring opinion, Justice Sandra Day O'Connor insisted that the Oregon policy could and should be justified according to *Sherbert*'s compelling interest test. The three dissenters agreed with O'Connor concerning the appropriate test, but they maintained that Oregon had not shown a compelling state interest to refuse to allow peyote for religious usage.

The *Smith* decision appeared to limit the extent to which religious minorities might claim constitutional protection for unpopular practices. Religious leaders and civil libertarians were outraged at the ruling, and Congress responded to the anti-*Smith* movement by passing the Religious Freedom Restoration Act (RFRA) of 1993. The RFRA was designed to restore both the compelling state interest test and the least restrictive means test against any incidental burden on religious practice.

Thomas Tandy Lewis

See also *California v. Cabazon Band of Mission Indians; Cherokee Cases; Ex parte Crow Dog; Johnson and Graham's Lessee v. McIntosh; Lone Wolf v. Hitchcock; Sherbert v. Verner; Talton v. Mayes; Worcester v. Georgia.*

ENGEL V. VITALE

Court: U.S. Supreme Court
Citation: 370 U.S. 421
Date: June 25, 1962
Issues: Children's rights; Education; Establishment of religion; Parental rights

• In this controversial ruling, the U.S. Supreme Court found that the reading of a nondenominational prayer in public school classrooms violates the establishment clause of the First Amendment, as applied to the states through the Fourteenth Amendment.

In 1958, the New York State Board of Regents composed a twenty-two-word nondenominational prayer, for adoption by local school districts. The prayer, which was to be recited at the beginning of the school day, read as follows: "Almighty God, we acknowledge our dependence upon Thee, and we beg Thy blessings upon us, our parents, our teachers, and our country."

The Board of Education of Union Free School District #9 adopted the prayer as part of the opening activities of schools in the district. Lawrence Roth, a parent in the district, believed that the Regents' Prayer violated the rights of those children who would otherwise choose not to take part. Even though the prayer was not compulsory, Roth believed that young children would feel pressured to participate and that the school district, as a state agency, had no right to impose religious perspectives on students. Roth was joined in a class action suit by nine other parents, including Steven Engel, whose name (alphabetically first) became a part of the case's title.

The case was brought before the New York Supreme Court (a trial court in New York), which ruled in favor of the school district. The trial court pointed out that the prayer was not compulsory. Parents opposing the prayer argued that the practice of reciting the school prayer, authorized by the school district and state Board of Regents, violated the establishment clause of the First Amendment. The establishment clause states that "Congress shall make no

After the Supreme Court banned school prayer, school teachers found other ways to start the day. Here, an elementary school teacher in Pittsburgh reads from a book called The School Day Begins. *(Library of Congress)*

law respecting an establishment of religion." The New York State appellate division and New York State Court of Appeals both upheld the practice of reciting the prayer. The U.S. Supreme Court reversed the decision.

The Court's Ruling

In a 7-1 decision written by Justice Hugo L. Black, the majority declared that encouraging recitation of the prayer was "wholly inconsistent" with constitutional dictates. Black wrote that "neither the fact that the prayer may be denominationally neutral, nor the fact that its observance on the part of the students is voluntary can serve to free it from the limitations of the Establishment Clause." Black argued that the Court's decision was not hostile to religion. Historically, he pointed out, the Constitution's Framers supported separation of church and state because they knew "that one of the greatest dangers to the freedom of the individual to worship in his own way lay in the Government's placing its official stamp of approval upon one particular kind of prayer or one particular form of religious services."

The sole dissenter, Justice Potter Stewart, disagreed with the reasoning and conclusions of his colleagues: "I cannot see how an 'official religion' is established by letting those who want to say a prayer say it." He further asserted that to deny the wishes of schoolchildren to recite the prayer "is to deny them the opportunity of sharing in the spiritual heritage of our Nation." Stewart pointed out that many governmental bodies make reference to God, for example, in the opening of Supreme Court sessions, daily congressional sessions, and in the swearing in of the president of the United States.

Reaction to *Engel v. Vitale* was vociferous and often angry. The Supreme Court justices received thousands of telegrams. While some public officials, such as President John F. Kennedy, supported the Court's decision, many others spoke out against it. Numerous constitutional amendments were introduced in Congress in attempts to overturn the decision. One such amendment, the Becker Amendment, passed in the House but could not muster the two-thirds vote necessary for a constitutional amendment in the Senate. While prayer in the schools became less common as a result of the ruling in *Engel v. Vitale*, many school districts at first refused to comply with the decision and prayer continued. By 1965, protests over the decision had waned.

Mary A. Hendrickson

Further Reading

Gold, Susan Dudley. *Engel v. Vitale: Prayer in the Schools.* Tarrytown, N.Y.: Marshall Cavendish Benchmark, 2006. Part of its publisher's Supreme Court Milestones series designed for young-adult readers, this volume offers an accessible history and analysis of *Engel v. Vitale* that examines opposing

sides in the case, the people involved, and the case's lasting impact. Includes bibliography and index.

Haas, Carol. *Engel v. Vitale: Separation of Church and State.* Berkeley Heights,
N.J.: Enslow, 1994. Designed for young-adult readers, this volume examines the issues leading up to *Engel v. Vitale,* people involved in the case, the
legal development of the case, and the historical impact of the ruling. Includes chapter notes, further reading list, and index.

See also *Abington School District v. Schempp; Edwards v. Aguillard; Epperson v. Arkansas; Lee v. Weisman; Wallace v. Jaffree.*

EPPERSON V. ARKANSAS

Court: U.S. Supreme Court
Citation: 393 U.S. 97
Date: November 12, 1968
Issues: Establishment of religion

- The U.S. Supreme Court found laws banning the teaching of evolution to be an unconstitutional establishment of religion.

The Supreme Court unanimously overturned an Arkansas supreme court
ruling that upheld Arkansas "Monkey Law" statutes banning the teaching of
evolution in public elementary schools, secondary schools, and universities.
The Court held that Arkansas violated the freedom of religion mandate of
the First Amendment as applied to the states by the Fourteenth Amendment
under the incorporation doctrine. Justice Abe Fortas wrote the majority
opinion, with Justices John M. Harlan II and Hugo L. Black concurring. In
1982 Arkansas responded by passing a new law that required all public
schools to "balance" any teaching of evolution with the teaching of creation
by a "supreme power." This was declared unconstitutional in a federal district
court in *McLean v. Arkansas Board of Education* (1982). This case was very similar to one covering a Louisiana policy later declared unconstitutional by the
Court in a 7-2 decision in *Edwards v. Aguillard* (1987).

Richard L. Wilson

See also *Edwards v. Aguillard; Engel v. Vitale; Illinois ex rel. McCollum v. Board of
Education; Lee v. Weisman; Wallace v. Jaffree.*

Erie Railroad Co. v. Tompkins

Court: U.S. Supreme Court
Citation: 304 U.S. 64
Date: April 25, 1938
Issues: Common law; Diversity jurisdiction

- In ruling that under the Rules of Decision Act, federal courts were to proceed if multistate lawsuits occurred, the U.S. Supreme Court not only overturned one of its previous decisions but also declared it to have been unconstitutional.

The Supreme Court decided *Erie* by an 8-0 vote (Benjamin N. Cardozo did not participate), but the three separate concurrences by Justices Pierce Butler, James C. McReynolds, and Stanley F. Reed weakened the impact of this decision. The issue in this case is complicated and still partially unresolved. The Court has diversity jurisdiction if it is faced by lawsuits in which the parties are citizens of different states and often subject to different laws. Because it would be unfair to choose one state's law over another arbitrarily, the Judiciary Act of 1789 provided that "the laws of the several states . . . shall be regarded as rules of decision in trials at common law" in federal courts. This provision, known as the Rules of Decision Act in contemporary law, indicates that federal courts should follow state "substantive" law in cases where diversity jurisdiction occurs but does not establish clearly the appropriate sources of state law.

Erie is one of a number of attempts to resolve the matter, which remains the subject of some confusion. An earlier attempt can be found in Justice Joseph Story's opinion in *Swift v. Tyson* (1842), in which he held that the federal courts should use the various statutes and real property laws but should rely on general doctrines or principles of commercial law for contracts and commercial transactions. This in effect created a federal common law, but this was problematic. After the middle of the nineteenth century, this common law expanded dramatically as did the power of the federal courts. When coupled with substantive due process and freedom of contract, the *Swift* decision was often used to nullify federal and state attempts to regulate corporations.

In this politically and economically charged atmosphere, Justice Louis D. Brandeis asserted in his opinion for the Court that there was no "federal general common law," thereby declaring the *Swift* ruling unconstitutional. However, this did not end the matter, as even Brandeis found it necessary to recognize the necessity of some types of specialized federal common law. Several attempts to establish guidelines have failed to fully resolve this matter.

Richard L. Wilson

See also *Bank of the United States v. Deveaux; Louisville, Cincinnati, and Charleston Railroad Co. v. Letson; Pennoyer v. Neff; Strawbridge v. Curtiss; Swift v. Tyson.*

ERZNOZNIK V. JACKSONVILLE

Court: U.S. Supreme Court
Citation: 422 U.S. 205
Date: June 23, 1975
Issues: Censorship; Pornography and obscenity

• This decision, holding unconstitutional an ordinance prohibiting drive-in theaters with screens visible from public areas from showing films containing nudity, denied that government could shield citizens from all exposure to nudity in film.

This case involved a challenge to the constitutionality of a Jacksonville, Florida, ordinance prohibiting drive-in theaters with screens visible from public streets or other places from exhibiting films containing nudity. After a state trial court upheld the ordinance against a First Amendment challenge, a state appeals court affirmed its ruling. When Florida's supreme court declined to overturn these lower court decisions, the U.S. Supreme Court accepted the case for review. It ultimately held, in a 6-3 decision, that Jacksonville's ordinance violated freedom of speech.

In an opinion written by Justice Lewis Powell, a majority of the Court found that the ordinance discriminated against films solely on the basis of their content—that is, whether they contained nudity. He noted that content-based discriminations are generally disfavored under the First Amendment.

During the course of these legal proceedings, the city conceded that not all films containing nudity are obscene and that its ordinance therefore restricted some speech which was not obscene and therefore protected by the First Amendment. However, the city urged that it was entitled to suppress nudity visible from a public place as a nuisance because of the offense some citizens might experience upon exposure to nude film images, to protect children from exposure to such images, and to enhance traffic safety by eliminating possible distractions to passing motorists.

The Supreme Court found each of these asserted justifications insufficient to warrant the city's restriction of protected speech. Citizens, the Court observed, must sometimes endure offense as the price of freedom, especially citizens who—offended by nudity glimpsed on a drive-in theater's screen—can readily avert their eyes. Furthermore, the Court continued, the ordinance could not be justified as protecting children from what might be obscene to their eyes, since not all nudity could be characterized as obscene, even to children. Finally, the Court declined to uphold the ordinance as a means of securing traffic safety, since the city had excluded only nudity in films, not other kinds of images which might also be distracting to passing motorists.

Chief Justice Warren Burger, together with justices William H. Rehnquist and Byron White, dissented. The chief justice, joined by Rehnquist, chided the Court's majority for suggesting that bystanders could simply avert their eyes from a huge projection screen. In addition, he and the other dissenters pointed out that the city certainly had authority to protect the public from actual physical nudity in public places. Consequently, these justices argued, the city should be able to preserve the public from unsolicited glimpses of nudity on a drive-in theater's screen just as they could protect citizens from physical displays of nudity in a public park.

Timothy L. Hall

See also *American Booksellers Association, Inc. v. Hudnut; Ashcroft v. Free Speech Coalition; Freedman v. Maryland; Miller et al. v. Civil City of South Bend; Miller v. California; New York v. Ferber; Osborne v. Ohio; Roth v. United States; Times Film Corp. v. City of Chicago.*

ESCOBEDO V. ILLINOIS

Court: U.S. Supreme Court
Citation: 378 U.S. 478
Date: June 22, 1964
Issues: Confessions; Right to counsel

- The U.S. Supreme Court barred the use of confessions in criminal cases when they are obtained after the police have refused a suspect's request for an attorney and have failed to warn the suspect that any admissions can be used against him or her.

Viewed historically, *Escobedo v. Illinois* was a transition case, bridging the right-to-counsel rulings in *Gideon v. Wainwright* (1963) and the capstone case of *Miranda v. Arizona* (1966).

In *Gideon*, the Supreme Court ruled that a criminal defendant is entitled to an attorney in his or her trial. *Gideon* thus definitely answered the question of the applicability of the Sixth Amendment's right-to-counsel guarantee to state action which had been pending since the 1932 case of *Powell v. Alabama*, in which a coincidence of factors had prompted the Supreme Court to set aside a guilty verdict on the grounds that the defendants had not enjoyed adequate counsel. In *Miranda*, decided two years after *Escobedo*, the Supreme Court wove together several threads of developing judicial thought to rule that a person also has a right to counsel during pretrial questioning once the process moves to the (accusatory) stage of eliciting evidence to be used to convict the suspect being questioned. In between, *Escobedo v. Illinois* suggested the need to move the right to counsel from the courtroom to the precinct house because of the constitutionally objectionable nature of the questioning techniques used to elicit Escobedo's confession.

In a nutshell, Danny Escobedo was tricked into confession (he was falsely informed that his co-accused had fingered him for the crime) after requesting an attorney. Indeed, accounts of Escobedo's interrogation indicated that his lawyer was, at the time of Escobedo's confession, in an adjacent room being physically restrained by the police from seeing his client. This image was too much for the Supreme Court majority. In a 5-4 opinion, the Court ruled that the state's unwillingness to grant Escobedo's request for counsel rendered his confession inadmissible.

Escobedo v. Illinois is thus analogous to such cases as *Rochin v. California* (1952) in the Fourth Amendment area involving the admissibility of illegally seized evidence. In *Wolf v. Colorado* (1949), the Supreme Court absorbed the Fourth Amendment's protection against illegal searches and seizures into the due process clause of the Fourteenth Amendment, but it did not go so far as to exclude illegally seized evidence from being admitted in court. In a number of cases that followed, the zeal of the police to obtain conviction with minimal attention to a suspect's rights (as in *Rochin*, where the accused's stomach was illegally and involuntarily pumped to obtain damning evidence) prompted the Supreme Court to apply to state actors the exclusionary rule which already precluded federal law-enforcement agencies from introducing illegally obtained evidence (*Mapp v. Ohio*, 1961).

So it was with the *Escobedo* case. The case achieved instant notoriety; Danny Escobedo's face even graced the cover of one week's edition of *Time* magazine. In constitutional law, however, *Miranda v. Arizona* remains the major case involving both the pretrial right to an attorney and the admissibility of evidence and confessions obtained in pretrial interrogations.

Joseph R. Rudolph, Jr.

See also *Gideon v. Wainwright; Mapp v. Ohio; Massiah v. United States; Miranda v. Arizona; Powell v. Alabama; Rochin v. California; Wolf v. Colorado.*

EUCLID V. AMBLER REALTY CO.

Court: U.S. Supreme Court
Citation: 272 U.S. 365
Date: October 12, 1926
Issues: Land law; Takings clause; Zoning

- The U.S. Supreme Court, in a landmark decision, established the constitutionality of zoning ordinances by concluding they were a legitimate form of police power.

When comprehensive zoning ordinances began to be adopted in the first two decades of the twentieth century, many legal scholars and courts doubted their constitutionality on a number of grounds. Ambler Realty owned a large tract of land it was holding for industrial development, but it found the value of its property significantly reduced as the result of the city of Euclid's decision to adopt a zoning ordinance. Ambler sued on multiple grounds including the takings clause, due process, and equal protection. The lower court ruled that Ambler had suffered a taking without just compensation, but the Supreme Court reversed its decision, upholding Euclid's zoning law—and by analogy—most other zoning laws. Although criticism of many zoning laws continues, the Court does not appear ready to change its decision. Justice George Sutherland wrote for a 6-3 majority, facing dissents by Justices Willis Van Devanter, James C. McReynolds, and Pierce Butler.

Richard L. Wilson

See also *Belle Terre v. Boraas; City of Renton v. Playtime Theaters; First English Evangelical Lutheran Church of Glendale v. County of Los Angeles; Moore v. City of East Cleveland; Penn Central Transportation Co. v. City of New York; Young v. American Mini Theatres.*

EVANS V. ABNEY

Court: U.S. Supreme Court
Citation: 396 U.S. 435
Date: January 29, 1970
Issues: Housing discrimination; Land law

- The U.S. Supreme Court imposed a racially neutral principle to decide a question of the legitimacy of race-based restrictions on park land donated to a municipality.

Justice Hugo L. Black wrote the 6-2 majority opinion upholding a decision of a Georgia court that a park built on land donated to the city of Macon explicitly for use as a whites-only park had to be closed and the property returned to the heirs of the person donating the land. Previous decisions made it clear that Macon was barred on equal protection grounds from operating the park on a racially restrictive basis. Because the benefactor had been explicit in his instructions, the Court decided the only proper course of action was to return the land to the heirs. Although African Americans were still denied access to the park, so were whites, thus preserving racial neutrality. Justices William O. Douglas and William J. Brennan, Jr., dissented, and Thurgood Marshall did not participate.

Richard L. Wilson

See also *Buchanan v. Warley; Corrigan v. Buckley; Reitman v. Mulkey; Shelley v. Kraemer; Spallone v. United States.*

EVERSON V. BOARD OF EDUCATION OF EWING TOWNSHIP

Court: U.S. Supreme Court
Citation: 330 U.S. 1
Date: February 10, 1947
Issues: Education; Establishment of religion; Parental rights

• The U.S. Supreme Court for the first time held that the Fourteenth Amendment incorporated the establishment clause of the First Amendment.

A New Jersey statute provided for local school districts to reimburse parents for transportation of their children to and from schools, both public and private. The board of education of the Township of Ewing authorized such reimbursement. Arch R. Everson, a taxpayer, challenged the statute on the grounds that such aid to parents of parochial school students was subsidizing religion, thereby violating the First Amendment prohibition against the establishment of religion.

Writing for the 5-4 majority opinion, Justice Hugo L. Black stated that Everson contended that the state statute and the board of education's authorization violated the federal Constitution in two aspects. First, they authorized the state to take by taxation the private property of some and bestow it upon others, to be used for their own private purposes. This, Black said, allegedly violated the due process clause of the Fourteenth Amendment. Citing two earlier cases, *Cochran v. Louisiana State Board of Education* (1930) and *Interstate Railway v. Massachusetts* (1907), Black said that the Court had allowed parents to send their children to a religious rather than a public school if the school meets with secular educational requirements of the state. The New Jersey parochial schools, he stated, met the requirements.

In the second aspect of the violation of the Constitution, the New Jersey statute, wrote Black, was challenged as a "law respecting an establishment of religion." He emphasized that the First Amendment was made applicable to the states by the Fourteenth Amendment and therefore commanded that a state "shall make no law respecting an establishment of religion, or prohibiting the free exercise thereof." While the First Amendment prohibits states from consistently contributing to religious schools, he said, the same amendment prohibits states from hampering their citizens in the free exercise of their own religion. It cannot exclude individual Roman Catholics, Lutherans, Jews, or members of other groups, or either believers or nonbelievers, from receiving the benefits of public welfare legislation.

Such legislation could include the requirement that a local transit company provide reduced fares to schoolchildren, including those attending parochial schools. If general government services as police and fire protection, and public highways and sidewalks, were cut off from church schools, it would make it difficult for them to operate. This was not the purpose of the First Amendment. State power cannot be used to favor or to handicap religions. In describing state power as being neutral in its relation with religious believers and nonbelievers, Black quoted Thomas Jefferson, who said that "a wall of separation [exists] between church and state."

The importance of *Everson v. Board of Education of Ewing Township* is twofold. On the one hand, it prohibits state-supported churches, while on the other hand it does not prohibit a state from extending state benefits to all its citizens without regard to their religious belief.

Bill Manikas

See also *Abington School District v. Schempp; Illinois ex rel. McCollum v. Board of Education; Lemon v. Kurtzman; Tilton v. Richardson.*

EX PARTE CROW DOG

Court: U.S. Supreme Court
Citation: 109 U.S. 557
Date: December 17, 1883
Issues: Native American sovereignty; Treaties

• The U.S. Supreme Court held that federal law does not preempt tribal authority unless Congress clearly expressed its intent to do so.

Crow Dog, a Brule Sioux, was convicted and sentenced to death in a Dakota territorial court for the murder of another Sioux. Under tribal law, Crow Dog would not have received a sentence of death but would have been required to support the victim's family. He sought a writ of habeas corpus, contending that the federal government had no criminal jurisdiction over disputes among Native Americans in Indian territory. The U.S. government asserted that the Treaty of 1868 implicitly provided for federal jurisdiction over criminal prosecutions.

By a 9-0 vote, the Supreme Court ruled in favor of Crow Dog's claim. In his opinion, Justice Stanley Matthews wrote that although Congress possessed the constitutional authority to determine the scope of Indian self-government, it had not clearly expressed its intent to limit tribal authority in Dakota territory. Unless the legislation was explicit, the Indian tribes retained exclusive jurisdiction over Indian affairs on the reservations. Reacting to the decision, Congress in 1885 passed the Major Crimes Act, which provided federal jurisdiction over seven felonies committed on Indian lands.

The *Crow Dog* precedent, which remains good law, requires that treaties and statutes are normally interpreted in favor of retained Indian sovereignty and treaty rights. This principle is especially important in regard to nineteenth century documents that tend to contain many ambiguities. In areas such as the retained rights to hunt and fish, for example, the *Crow Dog* decision often helped Native American lawyers prevail in court.

Thomas Tandy Lewis

See also *California v. Cabazon Band of Mission Indians; Cherokee Cases; Employment Division, Department of Human Resources of Oregon v. Smith; Johnson and Graham's Lessee v. McIntosh; Lone Wolf v. Hitchcock; Santa Clara Pueblo v. Martinez.*

EX PARTE MCCARDLE

Court: U.S. Supreme Court
Citation: 74 U.S. 506
Date: April 12, 1869
Issues: Congressional powers; Separation of powers

- The U.S. Supreme Court acquiesced to a congressional withdrawal of appellate jurisdiction in a case that threatened to bring down the Republican Party's Reconstruction program.

Article III of the U.S. Constitution authorizes Congress to make exceptions and regulations concerning the Court's appellate jurisdiction. *Ex parte Mc-*

Justice Salmon P. Chase.
(Library of Congress)

Cardle led to the Supreme Court's most important decision involving this congressional power.

Following the Civil War (1861-1865), Congress enacted the Reconstruction Act of 1867, which imposed military rule over most of the Southern states. Under the statute, military tribunals were authorized to try civilians if they interfered with the Reconstruction governments. William McCardle, editor of the *Vicksburg Times*, was arrested and charged with publishing "incendiary and libelous articles." Based on the Habeas Corpus Act of 1863, which had extended federal jurisdiction to anyone "restrained in violation of the Constitution," McCardle appealed to the Supreme Court. He asserted that it was unconstitutional to try civilians in military tribunals when the civil courts were open and referred to *Ex parte Milligan* (1866).

Shortly after the Court heard arguments in the *McCardle* case, Congress repealed the provision in the Habeas Corpus Act that had allowed McCardle's appeal. Speaking for the Court, Chief Justice Salmon P. Chase acknowledged Congress's authority under Article III, and the case was therefore dismissed for lack of jurisdiction. Chase wrote that it was unnecessary to inquire whether, absent the 1867 law, the Court might have exercised appellate jurisdiction according to other statutes, especially the Judiciary Act of 1789. By acquiescing, the Court avoided a direct constitutional confrontation. However, Chase interpreted the congressional repeal of 1868 very narrowly, which meant that it did not place significant limits on the Court's future jurisdiction. Several months later, in *Ex parte Yerger* (1869), the Court agreed to hear another challenge to military trials, this time under the 1789 statute.

The *McCardle* precedent, which the Court never repudiated, left many unanswered questions about the potential power of Congress under Article III. Some experts believe that a determined Congress could remove the Court's jurisdiction over controversial issues such as prayers in school. Others argue that congressional powers could never extend to limiting jurisdiction in cases involving fundamental constitutional rights. In *United States v. Klein* (1872), the Court rejected a congressional attempt to restrict the Court's jurisdiction in a case involving the president's pardoning power.

Thomas Tandy Lewis

See also *Civil Rights Cases; Ex parte Milligan; Hall v. DeCuir; Korematsu v. United States; Mississippi v. Johnson; Texas v. White.*

EX PARTE MERRYMAN

Court: U.S. Circuit Court, Baltimore
Citation: 17 F. Cas. 144
Date: May 28, 1861
Issues: Civil rights and liberties; Habeas corpus; Military law; Warfare and terrorism

• President Abraham Lincoln's suspension of the writ of habeas corpus as an executive emergency act at the outbreak of the Civil War provoked a clash with the chief justice of the United States and became the first of several celebrated wartime civil liberties cases.

For centuries, wherever Anglo-American law prevails, a citizen's right to a writ of habeas corpus—that is, the right not to be arrested and held by government authorities without being charged—has been regarded a basic civil liberty. As secession continued and fighting that signaled the opening of the Civil War erupted, President Lincoln authorized Union military commanders to suspend the privilege of habeas corpus. Article I, section 9 of the U.S. Constitution stipulates that this privilege "shall not be suspended" unless "in cases of rebellion or invasion the public safety may require it."

Of particular concern to Lincoln were the border states which teetered on the brink of secession. Maryland, adjoining Washington, D.C., was one of these states and, indeed, hostile actions against Union forces were already under way there. John Merryman was a wealthy and well-born Maryland landowner—in fact, a descendant of Francis Scott Key, who had written the national anthem. Merryman was also a lieutenant in a secessionist cavalry unit that had destroyed bridges and telegraph lines during April, 1861. Along with other suspected traitors, Merryman's arrest was ordered by a Union general, William H. Keim. Merryman's lawyer promptly petitioned a federal circuit court in Baltimore for a writ of habeas corpus. Merryman, meantime, was imprisoned at Fort McHenry.

In 1861, justices of the U.S. Supreme Court still were assigned individually to preside over one of nine federal circuit courts. In this instance, Chief Justice Roger B. Taney, a Marylander, was presiding over the federal court in Baltimore when Merryman's petition reached him. Taney denied the president's right to suspend the writ. The chief justice reasoned that the Constitution placed the right of suspension in the Congress and that Congress had not exercised that power. Further, Taney argued that the Constitution neither sanctioned the arrest of civilians by army officers without prior authorization by civil courts nor allowed citizens to be imprisoned indefinitely without trial. Lincoln refused to obey Taney's ruling, declaring before a special session of Congress on July 4, 1861, that suspension was necessary in order to quell the rebellion and preserve the nation.

Opinions concerning both Lincoln's action and Taney's ruling were divided. As had been true of earlier clashes between presidents and the U.S. Supreme Court, the president could enforce his view, and without his acquiescence the Court could not. Nevertheless, in a few weeks Merryman was released. Although he was indicted by a U.S. circuit court, he was never brought to trial. Passage of the Habeas Corpus Act of 1863 represented an effort to respect authority of the courts while not seriously restricting executive and military decisions.

Clifton K. Yearley

See also *Ableman v. Booth; Boumediene v. Bush; Brecht v. Abrahamson; Duncan v. Kahanamoku; Fay v. Noia; Frank v. Mangum; McCleskey v. Zant; Moore v. Dempsey; Stone v. Powell.*

Ex parte Milligan

Court: U.S. Supreme Court
Citation: 71 U.S. 2
Date: April 3, 1866
Issues: Constitutionalism; Habeas corpus; Military law;
Warfare and terrorism

• In this case, which began during the Civil War, the U.S. Supreme Court for the first time limited the authority of military courts acting under presidential authority to try civilians for acts subverting a war effort.

In October, 1864, Union military authorities in Indiana arrested Lambdin P. Milligan, a civilian, and several other Confederate sympathizers for conspiring to attack federal arsenals and free Confederate prisoners. The military acted under authority of President Abraham Lincoln's order stipulating that military courts could try and punish persons "guilty of any disloyal practice

Lambdin P. Milligan.
(Indiana Historical
Society)

affording aid and comfort to the rebels." After a military commission found Milligan and two others guilty and sentenced them to be hanged, Milligan disputed the commission's jurisdiction and sought a writ of habeas corpus asserting his constitutional right to a trial by jury.

In 1866 the U.S. Supreme Court ruled unanimously in Milligan's favor and ordered that he be released. Though unanimous in its holding, the Court split, five to four, in its reasoning. The majority opinion, written by Justice David Davis, held that "it is the birthright of every American citizen, when charged with crime, to be tried and punished according to law." Military authority could thus not lawfully supersede civilian authority "where the courts are open and their process unobstructed"—as was the case in Indiana. In what became a famous statement of a fundamental principle of American constitutionalism, Davis wrote: "The Constitution of the United States is a law for rulers and people, equally in war and peace, and covers with the shield of its protection all classes of men, at all times, and under all circumstances. No doctrine, involving more pernicious consequences, was ever intended by the wit of man than that any of its provisions can be suspended during any of the great exigencies of government."

While such sweeping language appears to deny martial law any trace of legitimacy, Davis argued in the same opinion that if "courts are actually closed" because of foreign invasion or civil war, then within a "theater of active military operations" the military may "govern by martial law until the laws can have their free course." Four justices differed from the majority in maintaining that the military's actions in the Milligan case would have been legal had Congress expressly authorized them; however, the majority held that even Congress lacks power to establish a system of military rule where civil courts are open and functioning.

The importance of *Ex parte Milligan* is twofold. While it establishes the legitimacy of martial law when invasion or rebellion makes normal law enforcement impossible, it also prohibits such martial law if the civil courts are functioning, even during wartime. *Milligan* has stood as a landmark for more than a century. Although the Court has never expressly repudiated it, some commentators believe that its principles were violated by the internment of Japanese Americans in World War II—an action that the Supreme Court upheld in *Korematsu v. United States* (1944).

Joseph M. Bessette

See also *Boumediene v. Bush; Ex parte Quirin; Frank v. Mangum; Korematsu v. United States; McCleskey v. Zant; Moore v. Dempsey; Stone v. Powell.*

Ex parte Quirin

Court: U.S. Supreme Court
Citation: 317 U.S. 1
Date: July 31, 1942
Issues: Habeas corpus; International law; Military law;
Warfare and terrorism

- Upholding the secret trials of enemy spies in military tribunals, the U.S. Supreme Court held that the right to trial in regular federal courts, as well as the protections of the Fifth and Sixth Amendments, did not extend to aliens accused of crimes of war.

During World War II, four German saboteurs landed on Long Island, New York, and another four landed at Ponte Verdra Beach, Florida. Agents of the Federal Bureau of Investigation (FBI) captured the eight Germans and turned them over to the military, which quickly tried them on charges of violating the international laws of war. The defendants tried to stop the proceedings with habeas corpus petitions, claiming that the military tribunal had no jurisdiction because regular criminal courts were available. As a precedent, they pointed to precedent in *Ex parte Milligan* (1866). In addition, they objected to the fact that military tribunals utilized juries and did not follow many of the procedures required by the Fifth and Sixth Amendments.

At a special session in July, the Supreme Court unanimously rejected the petition, thus allowing the execution of six of the saboteurs about a week later. Chief Justice Harlan Fiske Stone's opinion for the Court declared that the *Milligan* precedent only applied to U.S. citizens who were not in the armed services. Stone further held that the use of a military tribunal was justified by a combination of the president's powers as commander in chief and a congressional statute, Article of War 15, authorizing military trials for those committing crimes of war. He also pointed to precedents for such tribunals, going back to the trial of John Andre, a British spy, during the Revolutionary War. The justices demonstrated a great deal of deference toward the executive branch's policies in fighting a popular war. They had no desire to make a critical assessment of the principles of due process in the trials, and they ignored the fact that one of the saboteurs had earlier become a naturalized American citizen before returning to Germany. In a similar case involving a Japanese general, *In re Yamashita* (1946), two dissenting justices would argue that the

Justice Harlan Fiske Stone. (Harris & Ewing/ Collection of the Supreme Court of the United States)

Court was not following the due process requirements of the Fifth Amendment.

In 2001, following the terrorist attacks on the World Trade Center and the Pentagon building, President George W. Bush issued an executive order authorizing military commissions to conduct trials of aliens charged with terrorist acts. In defending the policy, Bush's lawyers quoted from the *Quirin* and *Yamashita* decisions. In the case of *Hamdan v. Rumsfeld* (2006), however, based on the later Uniform Code of Military Justice (UCMJ) as well as the Geneva Convention of 1949, the Court decided that Bush had no authority to set up such commissions.

Thomas Tandy Lewis

See also *Boumediene v. Bush; Ex parte Milligan; Frank v. Mangum; Hamdan v. Rumsfeld; McCleskey v. Zant; Moore v. Dempsey; Stone v. Powell.*

Ex parte Siebold

Court: U.S. Supreme Court
Citation: 100 U.S. 371
Date: March 8, 1880
Issues: Voting rights

• The U.S. Supreme Court broadly read the federal government's power when it determined that the federal government could punish a state official for mixed federal-state duties.

Justice Joseph P. Bradley wrote the opinion for the 7-2 majority, upholding the conviction of a Baltimore election official under the 1870 Enforcement Act for stuffing ballot boxes. The act made it illegal for state officials to fail to perform their duties under state or federal law in a federal election. The official argued that he could not be convicted for federal offenses because he was a state official on whom a federal duty could not be imposed. However, noting that this election was for a federal congressional seat, the Supreme Court held that a violation of a mixed federal-state duty was an offense against the federal government for which he could be punished. The Court limited the scope of the 1870 act to federal elections only. Justices Stephen J. Field and Nathan Clifford dissented, but it was Justice Field who asserted that the federal government did not have the right to mandate duties for a state official.

Richard L. Wilson

See also *Ableman v. Booth; Graves v. New York ex rel. O'Keefe; Massachusetts v. Mellon; Osborn v. Bank of the United States.*

Ex parte Yarbrough

Court: U.S. Supreme Court
Citation: 110 U.S. 651
Date: March 3, 1884
Issues: Private discrimination; Voting rights

• This 1884 decision is the only nineteenth century case in which the U.S. Supreme Court allowed the federal government to enforce the Fifteenth Amendment by punishing private individuals for obstructing a citizen's right to vote.

In *Ex parte Yarbrough*, also known as the *Ku Klux Klan* case, Jasper Yarbrough and his fellow Klansmen were convicted in federal court of using violence against an African American, Berry Saunders, to prevent him from voting in a federal election. The Supreme Court unanimously upheld the conviction. Justice Samuel F. Miller broadly interpreted the Fifteenth Amendment as a guarantee that a citizen must not be prevented from voting in federal elections because of his race. In *James v. Bowman* (1903), however, the Court ignored *Yarbrough* and held that congressional enforcement of the Fifteenth Amendment was limited to state action.

Thomas Tandy Lewis

See also *Breedlove v. Suttles; Gray v. Sanders; Guinn v. United States; Harper v. Virginia State Board of Elections; South Carolina v. Katzenbach; United States v. Reese.*

Ex parte Young

Court: U.S. Supreme Court
Citation: 209 U.S. 123
Date: March 23, 1908
Issues: Federal supremacy

• Although federal courts had not been allowed to intervene in pending state court proceedings, the U.S. Supreme Court held that in extraordinary circumstances, a federal court may issue an injunction ordering state officials not to enforce a state statute until its validity has been decided in court.

A 1907 Minnesota law reduced railroad rates and imposed severe day-to-day penalties for violations. In addition to challenging the reduced rates, the railroads asserted that the day-to-day fines were ruinous, which violated the due process requirements of the Fourteenth Amendment. Therefore, the railroads went to the federal district court to seek a temporary injunction to stop state officials from imposing the fine while the case was being adjudicated. A federal district court issued such an injunction to Edward Young, Minnesota's attorney general. When Young was jailed for ignoring the order, he petitioned the Supreme Court for a writ of habeas corpus.

By an 8-1 vote, the Court upheld the injunction. Justice Rufus W. Peckham's opinion for the majority justified the federal court's action by creating a legal fiction. If the officer was enforcing an unconstitutional statute, the officer was not acting in his official capacity but was a private individual misusing the state's authority for his own purposes. The lone dissenter, Justice John Marshall Harlan argued that the majority's ruling would "practically obliterate the Eleventh Amendment." Ironically, the Court subsequently deter-

Justice Rufus W. Peckham.
(Library of Congress)

mined, in *Simpson v. Shepard* (1913), that the 1907 law was constitutional, which meant that Young had not been acting illegally after all.

At the time, the *Young* decision was very unpopular. In 1910 Congress established special three-judge federal courts to handle suits for injunctions against state officers. The Johnson Act of 1934 prohibited most federal injunctions against state regulations of rates. After World War II, federal courts applied the *Young* doctrine when enjoining state officials from depriving persons of civil rights and civil liberties.

Thomas Tandy Lewis

See also *Ableman v. Booth; Dombrowski v. Pfister; Edelman v. Jordan; Martin v. Hunter's Lessee; Murdock v. Memphis; South Dakota v. Dole; United States v. California; Ware v. Hylton; Younger v. Harris.*

FAIRFAX'S DEVISEE V. HUNTER'S LESSEE

Court: U.S. Supreme Court
Citation: 11 U.S. 203
Date: March 15, 1813
Issues: Federal supremacy; Treaties

- In this case and one in 1816, the U.S. Supreme Court engaged in a constitutional power struggle with the Virginia supreme court over seized Loyalist property and the state's treaty obligations.

Justice Joseph Story wrote the opinion for himself and only two other justices because three others, Chief Justice John Marshall and Justices Bushrod Washington and Thomas Todd, were not present. Justice William Johnson dissented. The most obvious issue was whether Virginia could pass a law upholding the seizure of property from Tory Loyalists during the Revolutionary War and whether Virginia had to fulfill its obligations under the controversial 1794 Jay Treaty. The Virginia supreme court of appeals upheld the state's seizure of property from British Loyalists and Virginia's position on its treaty obligations. Story ruled in favor of the Loyalist claim, but the authority of the Supreme Court was under attack partly because of the narrowness of the

Court's majority. Virginia refused to accept the Court's authority and declared section 25 of the 1789 Judiciary Act to be unconstitutional. The case returned to the Court as *Martin v. Hunter's Lessee* in 1816.

Richard L. Wilson

See also *Holmes v. Jennison; Martin v. Hunter's Lessee; Ware v. Hylton.*

Faretta v. California

Court: U.S. Supreme Court
Citation: 422 U.S. 806
Date: June 30, 1975
Issues: Right to counsel

- In this case, the U.S. Supreme Court ruled that the Sixth Amendment guarantees criminal defendants the right to conduct their own defense.

Charged with grand theft, Anthony Faretta was appointed a public defender at his arraignment. Worried that the public defender's heavy caseload would prevent him from giving his case adequate attention, Faretta asked to represent himself. He had previously represented himself in a case, but his trial judge in this case was hesitant to grant his request. Nevertheless, after cautioning Faretta of the ramifications of waiving counsel, the judge accepted his request. Before the trial began, the judge reviewed Faretta's ability to represent himself by questioning him on jury selection and on the hearsay rule. Not satisfied with Faretta's responses, the judge revoked his earlier decision and appointed a public defender for Faretta.

Faretta was tried and found guilty. Afterward, he appealed his conviction on the basis that he had been denied the right to conduct his own defense. An appellate court upheld the lower court's decision, noting that Faretta had no constitutional right to represent himself, and the Supreme Court of California refused to review the case. Faretta then appealed his case to the U.S. Supreme Court.

The Court decided in Faretta's favor, ruling that the Sixth Amendment's phrase "assistance of counsel" means that defendants are primarily responsible for their own defense. The Court added that counsel must be available to provide aid to receptive defendants. In essence, therefore, the Sixth Amendment confers a right to self-representation. The Court also noted that when defendants "knowingly and intelligently" give up right to counsel after being apprised of the dangers of self-representation, their choices should be noted in the court records. Therefore, in forcing Faretta to accept a state-appointed public defender against his will, the California court deprived him of his constitutional right to conduct his own defense.

The right to counsel is guaranteed in the Sixth Amendment to the U.S. Constitution. Criminal defendants are always reminded of this right when the Miranda warning is read to them. A corollary to this right to counsel, however, is that counsel must be effective. To be certain that lay persons unfamiliar with the intricacies of the law do not jeopardize their cases, even when they are innocent, defendants are encouraged to use the knowledge and skills of professional counsel. Nevertheless, defendants may waive the assistance of counsel and represent themselves in court.

Judges have the responsibility to determine if defendants are capable of acting as their attorneys. They consider several matters in making this determination: Can the defendants communicate effectively in English? Have they enough basic legal knowledge to conduct their defenses without unnecessary interruptions, delays, or the possibility of mistrials or appeals? Defendants who choose to defend themselves cannot afterward complain that they lacked effective counsel.

Victoria M. Time

Further Reading

Acker, J. R., and D. C. Brody. *Criminal Procedure: A Contemporary Perspective.* 2d ed. Sudbury, Mass.: Jones and Bartlett, 2004.

Roberson, C. *Criminal Procedure Today: Issues and Cases.* 2d ed. Upper Saddle River, N.J.: Prentice-Hall, 2003.

Stuckey, G. B., C. Roberson, and H. Wallace. *Procedures in the Justice System.* 7th ed. Upper Saddle River, N.J.: Prentice-Hall, 2004.

Zalman, M. *Criminal Procedure: Constitution and Society.* 3d ed. Upper Saddle River, N.J.: Prentice-Hall, 2002.

See also *Argersinger v. Hamlin; Betts v. Brady; Escobedo v. Illinois; Gideon v. Wainwright; Johnson v. Zerbst; Minnick v. Mississippi; Powell v. Alabama.*

Fay v. Noia

Court: U.S. Supreme Court
Citation: 372 U.S. 391
Date: March 18, 1963
Issues: Due process of law; Habeas corpus

- The U.S. Supreme Court upheld the right of those convicted of state offenses to use habeas corpus petitions in federal courts, notwithstanding minor time limitations in state law.

Justice William J. Brennan, Jr., wrote for the 6-3 majority, upholding the right of state prisoners to use habeas corpus petitions in federal courts even if they have failed to comply strictly with state statute-of-limitation provisions. Basically, the Supreme Court abandoned its earlier ruling that the exhaustion of state remedies had to include a petition to be heard by the Court (*certiorari*). Because so few *certiorari* petitions are granted and the process is so time-consuming, it is a burdensome requirement. In this case, defendant Noia had been convicted of murder with the use of a coerced confession in a state court despite the Court's prior prohibition on the use of coerced confessions. The state admitted this and relied solely on Noia's failure to file a timely appeal from the state appellate court, a technicality that the Court did not find compelling under the circumstances, although it did satisfy the dissenting justices: Tom C. Clark, John M. Harlan II, and Potter Stewart.

Richard L. Wilson

See also *Ableman v. Booth; Betts v. Brady; Boumediene v. Bush; Brecht v. Abrahamson; Ex parte Merryman; Frank v. Mangum; McCleskey v. Zant; Moore v. Dempsey; Stone v. Powell.*

FEDERAL TRADE COMMISSION V. PROCTER & GAMBLE CO.

Court: U.S. Supreme Court
Citation: 386 U.S. 568
Date: April 11, 1967
Issues: Antitrust law; Regulation of commerce

- The U.S. Supreme Court ruled that Procter & Gamble could not merge with Clorox under the terms of the Celler-Kefauver Act. This ruling established that the act could be used to prevent mergers between conglomerates that would hinder competition by other companies, even if the merging conglomerates were not themselves in direct competition with each other.

On August 1, 1957, Procter & Gamble Company acquired the Clorox Chemical Company. Clorox was the leading producer of liquid laundry bleach and controlled 48.8 percent of the market. Its nearest rival, Purex, had a 15.7 percent market share. The balance of the liquid bleach market was shared by about two hundred small producers.

Procter & Gamble was the nation's largest producer of soaps, detergents, cleansers, and toothpastes. Household bleach was a logical extension of its product line. As the nation's largest advertiser, Procter & Gamble spent more than $80 million in 1957, together with an additional $47 million on sales promotion. This prodigious merchandising muscle raised the concern of other bleach producers and the Federal Trade Commission (FTC). Within two months following the merger, a complaint was filed by the FTC to require divestiture (that is, the separation of the two companies) on the grounds that the merger violated section 7 of the Clayton Antitrust Act, as amended by the Celler-Kefauver Act of 1950. This section provided that no corporation could acquire another company if the effect of such an acquisition was substantially to lessen competition or to tend to create a monopoly.

Antitrust Law

The Clayton Antitrust Act, passed in 1914, was directed at mergers that substantially lessened competition or tended to create a monopoly. It provided that no commercial corporation could acquire or share the stock or capital of any other corporation if doing so would substantially lessen competition between the two corporations. There were two fatal defects in the law, however. The first was that it covered only mergers effected through the acquisition of stock. Accordingly, the law could be circumvented if the acquiring company purchased only the assets of the acquired company. Second, the law applied only if the merger would substantially lessen competition between the two merging companies. This limited application of the act to horizontal mergers, that is, mergers involving companies that produced or sold the same product.

The law did not apply to vertical mergers, mergers between firms at different stages of the production or distribution process. Such mergers occur, for example, when a manufacturer acquires a chain of retail outlets to market its product. Vertical integration had, however, been successfully prosecuted under the Sherman Antitrust Act in *United States v. Paramount Pictures, Inc.* (1948), when the major motion picture studios were ordered to divest themselves of the theater chains they owned. More important, the Clayton Act could not be utilized to prevent conglomerate mergers that substantially threatened and lessened competition. A conglomerate merger is a merger between two companies that neither compete with one another nor stand in the vertical relationship of supplier and customer.

Because of these limitations, only fifteen mergers had been ordered dissolved as a result of antitrust actions between 1914 and 1950, and only five of these had been the results of Clayton Act proceedings. The courts interpreted the antimerger provision of the Clayton Act by imposing standards that were used in determining whether a monopoly existed under the Sherman Antitrust Act of 1890: A merger would have to create a market share of monopolistic proportions before it could be struck down.

To remedy these defects in the Clayton Act, Congress in 1950 had enacted the Celler-Kefauver Act. This amendment to the Clayton Act made asset acquisition as well as share acquisition subject to the law. It also made all mergers that would substantially lessen competition subject to the act, not only those that would lessen competition between the acquired company and the acquiring company.

The Issue
Thus, at the time of the Procter & Gamble case, the Clayton Act had been utilized primarily against horizontal mergers. Such mergers directly and obviously tended to extinguish competition. The Procter & Gamble merger with Clorox, however, was a conglomerate merger. The issue before the FTC was whether this conglomerate merger could be prevented under the amended Clayton Act. An examiner was charged to investigate the situation.

The FTC examiner, Everett F. Haycraft, held that the deal tended to create a monopoly in the bleach business despite the fact that Procter & Gamble had not been in the industry before the acquisition. That, he said, was because of the tremendous economic power that could be brought to bear by Procter & Gamble even in businesses that it did not dominate. As part of Procter & Gamble, Clorox could enhance its position in the bleach field, because it would be backed by Procter & Gamble's power, promotion experience, consumer acceptance, and control of retail shelf space. None of these advantages could be matched by other bleach manufacturers. Haycraft also noted the decreased market share of other bleach producers following the merger, evidence that Clorox had increased its market power.

Haycraft's findings were upheld by the Federal Trade Commission. In an opinion written by Commissioner Philip Elman, it was noted that this was not a true conglomerate merger (one that combines two companies with entirely different product lines) but instead what Elman termed a "product extension merger." Elman considered laundry bleach to be a product extension of laundry detergent, in which Procter & Gamble already controlled the largest market share. The products were virtually indistinguishable when it came to marketing and advertising techniques. Because Procter & Gamble was not in the bleach business prior to the merger, Elman could not rely on the usual test of increased market share to establish a violation. Elman instead devised a new concept of "potential competition" that would make the merger illegal under the Clayton Act.

Elman reasoned that because Procter & Gamble was a potential entrant into the bleach business prior to the merger, it prevented Clorox, the leading producer, from profiting unduly. At any time, Procter & Gamble could have entered the bleach market and gained a sizable market share at the expense of Clorox. The merger removed this potential source of competition and thus rendered the bleach market less competitive. Furthermore, the merger would discourage new companies from entering the bleach market and would adversely affect the existing producers. Procter & Gamble could use its economic clout to get more supermarket shelf space for its bleach, outspend any competitor in advertising, and engage in predatory pricing financed out of its profits from other lines to stifle existing and nascent competition.

Procter & Gamble appealed the FTC's decision, and the appellate court reversed that decision. The court stated that the findings of the FTC were based on treacherous conjecture. The case was then appealed to the U.S. Supreme Court. The Court, in a unanimous decision issued on April 11, 1967, reversed the court of appeals and upheld the FTC decision ordering divestiture.

Justice William O. Douglas wrote the opinion of the Court. According to Douglas, Procter & Gamble reduced competition by acquiring Clorox and not entering the bleach industry on its own. Smaller firms would become more cautious in competing as a result of their fear of retaliation by Procter & Gamble with its extensive resources and advertising budget, twenty times that of Clorox before the merger. Furthermore, newcomers could not be expected to enter the market under such circumstances. Finally, when Procter & Gamble was on the sidelines of the bleach industry, it was one of the few companies that could have entered on its own with the temerity to challenge a firm as solidly entrenched as Clorox.

Justice John Marshall Harlan II filed a concurring opinion. He criticized the majority opinion for not laying down clearer legal guidelines and thereby leaving the FTC, lawyers, and businesspeople in doubt as to what would be expected of them in future cases. A major source of disagreement between Justices Harlan and Douglas was the use of business efficiency as a defense for a merger. Harlan stated that true business efficiency achieved by a merger should be allowed as a defense. Harlan, however, did not accept the claim of Procter & Gamble that savings in advertising costs represented a legitimate efficiency defense.

Significance

Federal Trade Commission v. Procter & Gamble Co. added a new dimension to antitrust law. The meaning of the Celler-Kefauver Amendment to section 7 of the Clayton Act was first tested in *Brown Shoe Co. v. United States* (1962). Brown Shoe Company, the nation's fourth largest shoe company, merged with the G. R. Kinney Company, which operated the nation's largest chain of retail shoe stores. The companies did not compete against each other. One was a manufacturer, the other a retailer. Nevertheless, the Supreme Court found that this vertical merger was in violation of the amended Clayton Act. The Court reasoned that the merger substantially lessened competition, since other shoe manufacturers had been steadily foreclosed from marketing their shoes in the retail outlets acquired by the Brown Shoe Company.

It was thus clear that the Supreme Court would apply the Clayton Act as amended to vertical mergers as well as horizontal mergers. What was not readily apparent, and what became the complex issue of law in the Procter & Gamble case, was how the Celler-Kefauver Act would be applied to a conglomerate merger. The decision of the Supreme Court in *Federal Trade Commission v. Procter & Gamble Co.* was thus destined to be a landmark case in antitrust law.

In its decision, the Supreme Court adopted and refined the rationale of the Federal Trade Commission. Competition in the bleach industry would be substantially lessened because of the elimination of potential competition and the creation of new barriers to entrants. Procter & Gamble, instead of forming its own bleach company, acquired Clorox. This eliminated potential competition and, under the circumstances, was interpreted to be illegal under the Clayton Act. The presence of Procter & Gamble in the bleach market was so formidable that it would create an insurmountable barrier to any new company that was considering entering the market.

This was a new approach. The decision meant that illegal lessening of competition under antitrust law could flow from the structure of a conglomerate rather than from the makeup of the market in which the conglomerate operates. The rationale for this decision was that a conglomerate's structure could allow it to cross-subsidize an operation in one area with earnings from another area. Such cross-subsidization would give a conglomerate a tremendous advantage over traditional firms that specialized in one area or product. Thus, Procter & Gamble's entry into the bleach market through the acquisition of Clorox was destructive of competition, since no other company had the resources to compete with Procter & Gamble.

The Court's decision in *Federal Trade Commission v. Procter & Gamble Co.* had a chilling effect on the merger mania that was sweeping the United States in the 1960's. Between 1962 and 1968, 110 of the companies on the Fortune 500 list had disappeared as a result of mergers. It was now established law that companies involved in a merger would not be exempt from antitrust action simply because they were not competitors.

Gilbert T. Cave

Further Reading

Areeda, Phillip, Louis Kaplow, and Aaron Edlin. *Antitrust Analysis: Problems, Text, Cases.* 6th ed. New York: Aspen, 2004. Textbook containing case studies of the major antitrust cases in American history. Bibliographic references and index.

Einhorn, Henry Adler, and William Paul Smith. *Economic Aspects of Antitrust.* New York: Random House, 1968. A collection of readings and cases involving antitrust law. Good for someone seeking basic knowledge. Recommended for understanding the development of antitrust law.

Green, Mark J., with Beverly C. Moore, Jr., and Bruce Wasserstein. *The Closed Enterprise System.* New York: Grossman, 1972. The introduction, written by Ralph Nader, sets forth the views that find support in this book. A well-documented, detailed, and critical survey of antitrust enforcement from a consumerist's point of view. Easy to read and interesting.

Hylton, Keith N. *Antitrust Law: Economic Theory and Common Law Evolution.* New York: Cambridge University Press, 2003. Comprehensive text on economic principles behind antitrust and the development of American antitrust law over more than one hundred years of litigation. Includes a chapter on the Alcoa case. Bibliographic references and index.

Narver, John C. *Conglomerate Mergers and Market Competition*. Berkeley: University of California Press, 1967. Traces the development of conglomerate mergers. Small, but one of the most comprehensive books on conglomerate mergers.

Singer, Eugene M. *Antitrust Economics: Selected Legal Cases and Economic Models*. Englewood Cliffs, N.J.: Prentice-Hall, 1968. Classic antitrust cases are examined and analyzed with scholarly thoroughness in both law and economics. Graphs, charts, and economic formulas accompany the analysis. Recommended for advanced students and antitrust lawyers.

See also *Northern Securities Co. v. United States*; *Standard Oil v. United States*; *United States v. American Tobacco Co.*; *United States v. E. I. du Pont de Nemours and Co.*; *United States v. Paramount Pictures, Inc.*; *United States v. United States Steel Corp.*

FEDORENKO V. UNITED STATES

Court: U.S. Supreme Court
Citation: 449 U.S. 490
Date: January 21, 1981
Issues: Citizenship; Immigration

- The Fedorenko decision established that the citizenship of a naturalized citizen may be revoked in cases when individuals intentionally provided false information to enter the country or to obtain materialization.

Following World War II, Feodor Fedorenko, who was born in Ukraine, obtained a visa to enter the United States under the Displaced Persons Act of 1948 (DPA), which did not apply to anyone who had voluntarily assisted the enemy or had participated in persecuting civilians. Fedorenko became a naturalized citizen in 1970. A decade later, witnesses testified that he had concealed his service as an armed guard at Treblinka, a Nazi extermination camp, and that he had committed atrocities against inmates. Fedorenko claimed that the German army had forced him to serve in the camp, although he admitted that he had never tried to escape. The government brought denaturalization action under the Immigration and Nationality Act of 1952, which requires revocation of citizenship that was procured by "willful misrepresentation." Ruling in favor of Fedorenko, the district court held that because his service in the camp had been involuntary, his misrepresentation was not material to his admission.

Reversing the ruling by a 7-2 margin, the U.S. Supreme Court ordered Fedorenko's denaturalization based on the fact that the language of the DPA made him ineligible to receive a visa. Speaking for the majority, Justice Thurgood Marshall criticized the district court for ignoring the clear and explicit wording of the DPA. Once the district court determined that either immigration or naturalization had resulted from willful misrepresentation, it had no discretion to excuse Fedorenko's conduct. The DPA, moreover, referred to the objective fact of persecuting others, so that even if he had acted under duress, the DPA would not have allowed him to enter the country. In 1984, Fedorenko was deported to the Soviet Union, where he was executed by a firing squad two years later.

Thomas Tandy Lewis

See also *Afroyim v. Rusk; Ozawa v. United States; Trop v. Dulles; United States v. Wong Kim Ark.*

FEINER V. NEW YORK

Court: U.S. Supreme Court
Citation: 340 U.S. 315
Date: January 15, 1951
Issues: Freedom of speech

- In this street oratory case, the U.S. Supreme Court tolerated a level of government control of speech that is no longer acceptable.

Chief Justice Fred M. Vinson wrote the opinion for the 6-3 majority over strong dissents from Justices Hugo L. Black, William O. Douglas, and Sherman Minton. Irving Feiner, a college student, stood on a box making a speech to a racially and politically mixed audience of more than seventy people who had a strongly mixed reaction to the speech and seemed to become unruly. Feiner refused to stop even after requested to do so by a police officer and was arrested for violating a New York law making it a "breach of the peace" to use intentionally "abusive language." Despite Feiner's assertion of

First Amendment protection, the Supreme Court upheld his conviction as necessary to stop a "clear and present danger to public safety." Black's strong dissent argued that Feiner was being punished for unpopular political views. Similar speech was judged to be under First Amendment protection in *Brandenburg v. Ohio* (1969).

Richard L. Wilson

See also *Brandenburg v. Ohio; Hazelwood School District v. Kuhlmeier; Terminiello v. Chicago; Tinker v. Des Moines Independent Community School District.*

Feist Publications v. Rural Telephone Service Co.

Court: U.S. Supreme Court
Citation: 499 U.S. 340
Date: March 27, 1991
Issues: Regulation of commerce

- The U.S. Supreme Court rejected the notion that copyrights should be granted to those whose only claim to copyright is that they gathered information.

Rural Telephone Service Company published a directory containing information that Feist Publications used in preparing its own somewhat different but overlapping directory. Rural sued, alleging copyright infringement and arguing that the effort they made to collect even public domain data was entitled to copyright protection. The Supreme Court did not accept Rural's view, asserting the more traditional view that quality or creativity was entitled to copyright protection but not the simple compilation of material. Justice Sandra Day O'Connor wrote the unanimous opinion of the Supreme Court; Justice Harry A. Blackmun concurred. This case amplified the Court's position set forth in *Harper and Row Publishers v. Nation Enterprises* (1985).

Richard L. Wilson

See also *Katzenbach v. McClung; Wabash, St. Louis, and Pacific Railway Co. v. Illinois; Wickard v. Filburn.*

FERGUSON V. CITY OF CHARLESTON

Court: U.S. Supreme Court
Citation: 532 U.S. 67
Date: March 21, 2001
Issues: Right to privacy; Search and seizure; Women's issues

• The U.S. Supreme Court held that the Fourth Amendment prohibits hospitals from testing pregnant women for illegal drugs without their consent if the purpose is to notify the police of illegal behavior.

A public hospital of Charleston, South Carolina, reacting to the growing number of "crack babies," instituted a program of automatically testing maternity patients for cocaine and other illegal drugs, and then alerting the police when the test results were positive. The police used the threat of prosecution to coerce the women into substance abuse treatment. A small number of noncooperative women were prosecuted. In a suit against the city, Crystal Ferguson and nine other plaintiffs alleged that the tests were unconstitutional in the absence of either a warrant or informed consent. The city argued that the program was justified by the "special need" of preventing pregnant women from endangering their fetuses.

By a 6-3 vote, the U.S. Supreme Court agreed with the plaintiffs. Writing for the majority, Justice John Paul Stevens explained that the "special needs" exception to the Fourth Amendment, which the Court had allowed to protect the public safety in special circumstances, did not apply to programs which were so directly connected to law enforcement. While the ultimate goal of the program might have been to coerce the women into treatment, the immediate objective of the searches was to obtain evidence of wrongdoing that would be admissible in criminal prosecutions. The question of whether any of the ten plaintiffs had voluntarily consented to the tests was left to the lower courts to decide.

Thomas Tandy Lewis

See also *National Treasury Employees Union v. Von Raab; Skinner v. Railway Labor Executives' Association; Vernonia School District 47J v. Acton.*

FERGUSON V. SKRUPA

Court: U.S. Supreme Court
Citation: 372 U.S. 726
Date: April 22, 1963
Issues: Regulation of business

• In upholding a state regulation, the U.S. Supreme Court declared that the concept of substantive due process had been repudiated.

This case involved a Kansas statute that prohibited anyone except lawyers from engaging in the business of debt adjustment. By a 9-0 vote, the Supreme Court upheld the constitutionality of the Kansas law. Writing the majority opinion, Justice Hugo L. Black took the opportunity to express his strong animosity to the earlier practice of overturning such regulations with the doctrine of substantive due process. Without inquiring whether there was any rational justification for the law, Black declared that it was entirely up to the state legislature to decide on the "wisdom and utility" of economic regulations. Justice John M. Harlan II, concurring in the result, wrote that the law had a rational relation to a constitutionally permissible objective. It was clear that Black and Harlan disagreed about substantive due process, but their differences would become much more pronounced in the landmark case of *Griswold v. Connecticut* (1965).

Thomas Tandy Lewis

See also *BMW of North America v. Gore*; *Chicago, Burlington, and Quincy Railroad Co. v. Chicago*; *Griswold v. Connecticut*; *Kansas v. Hendricks*; *Meyer v. Nebraska*; *Moore v. City of East Cleveland*; *O'Gorman and Young v. Hartford Fire Insurance Co.*

FIREFIGHTERS LOCAL UNION NO. 1784 V. STOTTS ET AL.

Court: U.S. Supreme Court
Citation: 467 U.S. 561
Date: June 12, 1984
Issues: Affirmative action; Civil rights and liberties; Employment discrimination; Labor law

• The U.S. Supreme Court ruled that labor agreements could use seniority as a criterion for layoffs even when that use would oppose the goals of affirmative action programs.

Reflecting broad public concerns and controversies about a gamut of civil liberties, a combination of liberals and conservatives in Congress, goaded by President Lyndon B. Johnson, fought for passage of the 1964 Civil Rights Act. Title VII of the act delineated a series of formal and informal remedial procedures designed to end employment discrimination based on race, color, religion, sex, or national origin. The objective of Title VII was to pave the way for equal employment opportunity for all Americans.

Ultimately, the constitutionality of the act's major sections would be tested by the U.S. Supreme Court as litigation relating to the act reached the Court on appeal or came to the justices for review. While Earl Warren was chief justice of the United States (1953-1969), the Court's interpretations of a wide range of civil liberties were expansive. The Court's decisions in these cases, as was frequently noted, often amounted to additional "legislation." In regard to labor law, decisions of the Warren Court were characterized by their focus on intergovernmental relationships. The Court found few occasions to define the rights of individuals in the workplace and no occasions to strike down employment discrimination based on sex.

The Burger Court

Beginning in 1969, those two tasks were undertaken by the Court under Earl Warren's successor, Warren E. Burger, despite pundits' predictions that Burger would lead a conservative reaction in the field of civil rights. On the contrary, the Burger Court broke new ground in labor law by delineating the rights of individuals in the workplace, often in the light of provisions of the 1964 Civil Rights Act.

It was in this context that the case of *Firefighters Local Union No. 1784 v. Stotts et al.* came to argument before the Court on December 6, 1983. The case questioned the legality of using job seniority as a criterion for layoffs. As legal scholars noted, along with issues associated with affirmative action and so-called reverse discrimination, seniority problems were among the most sensitive and bitterly contested in the realm of antidiscrimination legislation embodied in provisions of Title VII of the 1964 Civil Rights Act. Moreover, the AFL-CIO, which had played a major role in mustering political support for passage of the 1964 act, had battled consistently to preserve the integrity of seniority systems. Black workers, notoriously among those "last hired and first fired," however, perceived established seniority systems as additional road-blocks to their advancement and job security.

Carl Stotts, a black captain in the Memphis, Tennessee, fire department, joined others in a class-action lawsuit invoking Title VII of the 1964 Civil Rights Act. Participants in the suit alleged that Memphis city officials displayed a pattern of racial discrimination in their hiring and promotion practices in the fire department. Entering a consent decree with the courts, the city accordingly evinced its willingness to reform the department's hiring and promotion policies, but broader considerations intervened. Fiscal difficulties soon thereafter required a budget reduction that, in turn, meant employee layoffs. At this juncture, a district court prohibited the city from following its seniority system in effecting the layoffs on grounds that proposed reductions would have a racially discriminatory effect. Modifications in the city's system thereafter resulted in the layoffs of white employees who had more seniority than black employees who were retained, in compliance with the district court's wishes.

Seniority Systems

The district court was following what it believed to be the direction confirmed by many lower court rulings, namely, that established seniority systems must be struck down if they perpetuated the effects of past discrimination, regardless of whether these systems had been designed to discriminate intentionally. This line of ruling obviously contradicted the intent of Congress. In enacting the 1964 Civil Rights Act, Congress, under pressure from the AFL-CIO and other organizations, had made every effort to ensure that Title VII would in no way upset established seniority plans. Nevertheless, grudgingly and at considerable expense, unions and management thereafter were forced to comply with court rulings or face costly litigation.

In 1977, this situation was reversed by the U.S. Supreme Court's decision, drafted by Justice Potter Stewart, in *Teamsters v. United States.* The decision, returning to what the majority of the Court believed to be the intent of Congress, declared that bona fide seniority plans, even if discriminatory in their past or present effects, were immunized by provisions of Title VII, specifically its section 703(h).

Such was the situation when Justice Byron White delivered the heart of the *Firefighters* decision, namely, that the district court had erred in mandating that white employees be laid off by the city of Memphis when otherwise the established seniority system would have called for the layoff of black employees with less seniority. Justice White, noting the earlier *Teamsters* ruling, declared that section 703(h) permitted "the routine application of a seniority system absent proof of an intention to discriminate." Memphis had, in the Court's estimation, a bona fide seniority system before the district court ruled and the consent decree causing modification in the city's plan went into effect. White stated that section 703(h) seemed clear enough in declaring it legal employment practice for an employer "to apply different standards of compensation, or different terms, conditions, or privileges of employment" in establishing or maintaining a "bona fide seniority or merit system," provided these differences were not the result of intentional discrimination based on race, color, sex, religion, or national origin.

Seniority systems have been cherished by labor because they provide objective standards for what otherwise might be arbitrariness or favoritism on the part of management or unions in respect to job security. The *Firefighters* decision reinforced seniority systems even if such systems resulted in adverse consequences for members of minority groups.

Significance

The so-called White rule, announced by Justice Byron White on June 12, 1984, in practice meant that a bona fide seniority plan could not cause white workers to be laid off ahead of black workers with less seniority. This left Memphis's new affirmative action employees, all black, at the same risk of layoffs as all other workers. Affirmative action plans thus could prevent some whites from being hired, but they could not cause them to be fired. From the perspectives of black leaders and black workers, the rule perpetuated workplace policies that had placed them in the position of being the last hired and the first fired. It mattered little that such was not the intent of Justice White.

In 1986, although the specifics of the litigation differed from those in *Firefighters,* White cast a deciding vote reinforcing his views in *Wygant v. Jackson Board of Education.* A Jackson, Mississippi, school board and the Jackson Teachers Union had signed an agreement designed to prevent minority teachers hired under affirmative action plans from being laid off. The agreement stipulated that the minority teachers were to be protected even if tenured white teachers had to be laid off. White's ruling treated the results of the Jackson affirmative action plan as reverse discrimination. White teachers were being fired because of their race, and in his view no affirmative action scheme justified that result.

The decisions handed down by White and the Court's majority in conflicts arising between seniority plans and affirmative action policies from 1977 through 1986 represented an effort to reflect more accurately the intent of Congress in its enactment of the 1964 Civil Rights Act and the drafting of Title VII. Without directly overruling the Court's earlier decision in *Griggs v. Duke Power Company* (1971), a landmark "adverse impact" case that prohibited even unintentional discrimination, the Court narrowed its interpretations of what constituted discrimination.

During the quarter century after passage of the 1964 Civil Rights Act, a number of important changes occurred in the business world, in organized labor, and in congressional attitudes. For example, caught between officially divergent interpretations of what constituted discrimination—that is, determinations of the will of Congress on one hand and Supreme Court decisions on the other—many of the nation's leading business interests and institutions receiving federal or state funds had begun implementing voluntary affirmative action plans. In some instances, these voluntary plans were structured around implicit "quotas" to be used in guiding minority hiring. Moreover, businesses' incentive to comply with nondiscriminatory practices was inspired less by fear of traditional collective bargaining with trade unions than it was by threats posed by potential suits filed by the Equal Employment Opportunity Commission (EEOC), by feminist groups, by civil rights organizations, by consumers' groups, and by the alleged victims of discrimination.

The New Unionism

In addition, trade unionism of the traditional kind, which had fought for and won great gains for manufacturing and assembly-line workers from the 1930's until the early 1950's, was being supplanted by a new unionism. Because of rapid technological change and the diminishing importance of manufacturing in the American economy, the new unionism was heavily influenced by new breeds of workers. Among them were semiprofessional and white-collar workers, who by 1980 accounted for more than half of the labor force, as well as rapidly expanding contingents of service workers. In addition, at the close of the 1980's more than half of all employees were women, most of whom were keenly aware of previous and present sex discrimination. Most semiprofessional and white-collar workers were inclined to downplay the significance of seniority systems in regard to hiring, pay, promotions, retirement, and layoffs. Instead, in regard to these matters they favored the application of merit principles.

Structural and attitudinal changes such as these that developed through the 1970's and 1980's, as well as the direction taken by the Supreme Court between the *Griggs* decision and the ruling in *Firefighters*, led Congress to enact the Civil Rights Act of 1991. This new act followed the Court's ruling in *Wards Cove Packing Co. v. Atonio* in 1989. The decision basically overruled *Griggs*, rejecting "business necessity" as the sole criterion justifying the maintenance of practices that had disparate impacts—that is, that were discriminatory. The Court lamented the fact that any employer with a racially imbalanced workforce was likely to be hauled into court and forced to engage in costly and time-consuming defense of employment methods. Further, the Court recognized that the sole option available to employers was the adoption of racial quotas. In the spirit of the *Firefighters* decision, the Court held that constraining employers to move to this option was never intended by Congress in Title VII of the 1964 Civil Rights Act.

By 1991, congressional majorities viewed matters differently. Although the 1991 Civil Rights Act made no mention of quotas, it did nothing to curtail employer incentives to engage in race-conscious hiring; in fact, it encouraged the adoption of implicit quotas. The act of 1991 expanded the antidiscrimination interpretations of *Griggs* and broadened the scope of compensatory damages that could be collected by proven victims of discrimination. Employers could defend themselves against charges of discrimination by proving that their practices rested on "business necessity." Complainants bore the burden of proving that each particular challenged practice caused a disparate impact. The act likewise weakened the *Firefighters* decision by expanding rights to challenge discriminatory seniority systems. As Congress and the Supreme Court pursued different and often confusing paths in seeking to end discrimination with justice to all, some civil libertarians opined that civil rights acts had become the major threat to civil rights, while others denounced the legislation for having achieved too little.

Clifton K. Yearley

Further Reading

Epstein, Richard A. *Forbidden Grounds: The Case Against Employment Discrimination Laws.* Cambridge, Mass.: Harvard University Press, 1992. Scholarly evaluation of the substance and consequences of modern civil rights legislation and court decisions by a civil rights expert. Among the best critical surveys available. Includes informative page notes, table of cases, and extensive index.

Gould, William B., IV. *Agenda for Reform: The Future of Employment Relationships and the Law.* Cambridge, Mass.: MIT Press, 1993. Excellent, clearly written, and scholarly work discusses many aspects of employment law. Chapter 3 deals with the history of job security and seniority, and chapter 8 presents a fine discussion of the 1991 Civil Rights Act, race, and discrimination.

Hacker, Andrew. *Two Nations: Black and White, Separate, Hostile, Unequal.* Rev. ed. New York: Charles Scribner's Sons, 2003. Reflective, substantive analysis of the subject of race in the United States, including conflicts in the workplace over seniority and many other issues involved in discrimination. Maintains critical balance, but overall offers a depressing picture.

Heckscher, Charles C. *The New Unionism: Employee Involvement in the Changing Corporation.* New York: Basic Books, 1988. Extremely interesting discussion of changes over time in American employees' values, rights, organization, and relations with corporate employers.

McWhirter, Darien A. *Your Rights at Work.* New York: John Wiley & Sons, 1989. A crisp, reasonably accurate guide to civil rights as related to the workplace. Heavily based on court decisions. Well presented and informative.

Player, Mark. *Federal Law of Employment Discrimination in a Nutshell.* 6th ed. St. Paul, Minn.: West Law School, 2009. Reference guide to employment discrimination law lays out the highlights in a brief, orderly fashion. Includes table of cases and index.

Rutherglen, George. *Employment Discrimination: Law and Theory.* New York: Foundation Press, 2009. Huge volume that includes a detailed analysis of laws and principles concerning disparate impact.

Zimmer, Michael, Charles Sullivan, and Rebecca White. *Cases and Materials on Employment Discrimination.* 7th ed. Austin, Tex.: Wolters Kluwer, 2008. Comprehensive text dealing with both legislation and case law.

See also *Griggs v. Duke Power Co.*; *Johnson v. Santa Clara County*; *Martin v. Wilks*; *Regents of the University of California v. Bakke*; *United Jewish Organizations of Williamsburgh v. Carey*; *United Steelworkers of America v. Weber*; *Wards Cove Packing Co. v. Atonio.*

First English Evangelical Lutheran Church of Glendale v. County of Los Angeles

Court: U.S. Supreme Court
Citation: 482 U.S. 304
Date: June 9, 1987
Issues: Local government; Takings clause; Zoning

- In this case involving buildings in a flood plain, the U.S. Supreme Court first ruled that a zoning ordinance could result in a taking, thus requiring just compensation under the Fifth Amendment.

A flood destroyed buildings that belonged to the First English Evangelical Lutheran Church in Southern California. The church found it could not rebuild because the buildings had been constructed on a flood plain, and a county ordinance banned building in such areas. The church challenged the ordinance, and California courts found the church could recover only if the ordinance was ruled an unlawful taking and the county refused to withdraw the ordinance. The Supreme Court found that the rescinding of an invalid ordinance was not an adequate remedy and the county must pay for excessive interference during the time the ordinance was in effect. The Court did not determine exactly when the taking actually occurred and how the damages might be calculated but did say that small delays that are a normal part of the process are not a taking. Justice John Paul Stevens expressed his concern, in his dissent, that this ruling would have a chilling effect on land-use planning because local governments might worry about potential liability. The case was returned to the lower courts, which found that the ordinance was not a taking.

Richard L. Wilson

See also *Dolan v. City of Tigard; Euclid v. Ambler Realty Co.; Hawaii Housing Authority v. Midkiff; Kelo v. City of New London; Penn Central Transportation Co. v. City of New York.*

FIRST NATIONAL BANK OF BOSTON V. BELLOTTI

Court: U.S. Supreme Court
Citation: 435 U.S. 765
Date: April 26, 1978
Issues: Political campaigning

• This decision extended the impact of *Buckley v. Valeo* to referendum campaigns.

The U.S. Supreme Court, by a 5-4 vote, struck down a clause in Massachusetts law restricting the amount of money corporations could contribute to support or oppose referenda. Justice Lewis F. Powell, Jr., wrote the 5-4 majority opinion, which extended the *Buckley v. Valeo* (1976) distinction between contributions to campaigns to influence opinion and those to candidates. Although corporations could contribute freely to referenda, unlike individuals, they could be prohibited from spending money directly on a candidate or outside a candidate's campaign to benefit his or her efforts. Justices Byron R. White and William H. Rehnquist dissented strongly, asserting that states should be able to limit corporate campaign expenditures.

Richard L. Wilson

See also *Buckley v. Valeo; Luther v. Borden; Pacific States Telephone and Telegraph Co. v. Oregon.*

FLAST V. COHEN

Court: U.S. Supreme Court
Citation: 392 U.S. 83
Date: June 10, 1968
Issues: Establishment of religion; Standing

- For the first time since the 1920's, the U.S. Supreme Court ruled that a taxpayer could sue the government for the misuse of government money but carefully limited the right of suit.

By an 8-1 vote, the Supreme Court ruled that a group of taxpayers could sue to stop federal funds from being spent on teaching secular subjects in parochial schools. After *Frothingham v. Mellon* (1923), federal taxpayers lacked standing and were unable to sue on the constitutionality of federal expenditures. However, in *Flast v. Cohen*, the Court allowed such suits if taxpayers could demonstrate that a logical link existed between their status and the type of enactment attacked and show that the challenged enactment exceeded specific constitutional limitations. Chief Justice Earl Warren wrote the majority opinion and was supported by concurrences from Justices William O. Douglas, Abe Fortas, and Potter Stewart. Justice John M. Harlan II dissented, fearing a large increase in inappropriate taxpayer challenges to the government. Subsequently, more conservative justices were named to the Court and the Harlan view increased in importance. In particular, the Court indicated that it would not expand the *Flast* ruling in *United States v. Richardson* (1974).

Richard L. Wilson

See also *Agostini v. Felton; Everson v. Board of Education of Ewing Township; Frothingham v. Mellon; Lemon v. Kurtzman; Mueller v. Allen; Pierce v. Society of Sisters; United States v. Richardson; Zelman v. Simmons-Harris.*

FLETCHER V. PECK

Court: U.S. Supreme Court
Citation: 6 Cranch (10 U.S.) 8
Date: March 16, 1810
Issues: Freedom of contract; Judicial review; Property rights

- In this ruling, the U.S. Supreme Court's broad construction of the Constitution's contracts clause enhanced protection from legislative interference for vested rights in private property. For the first time, moreover, the Court declared that a state law was unconstitutional and therefore invalid.

Although it is almost axiomatic that many cases from which great constitutional principles are derived have sordid backgrounds, few can match the comic-opera corruption behind the U.S. Supreme Court's March 16, 1810, *Fletcher v. Peck* decision, a case that began fifteen years earlier.

On January 7, 1795, the Georgia legislature passed a bill permitting the sale of some thirty-five million acres of fertile, well-watered land for $500,000, payable over a five-year period. The purchasers were four land companies that had been formed to speculate in western lands. The fact that the state of Georgia itself did not have clear title to the lands apparently did not bother the state's legislature because, with one exception, every member of the legislature had been bribed. The problem of unclear title also did not trouble Georgia's governor, who signed the legislation into law.

To be sure, the legislature's action was not without some benefits to Georgia. The state needed the money, and the problem of wresting the title to the land from the Native American tribes through action by the federal government now became the concern of the speculators. The state had sold a slightly smaller tract to other speculators six years earlier with a similarly clouded title and on inferior terms, and the electorate of state had not been disturbed. In the interval, however, Eli Whitney had invented the cotton gin, which revolutionized the cotton industry. Now, the same lands would be in great demand for the production of cotton, assuming that their Native American residents could be removed.

The gross dishonesty of the whole transaction upset many conscientious citizens. As a consequence, in 1796, a new legislature was elected in which every member pledged to vote for the repeal of the act of sale. On February 13, the state passed the Rescinding Act. So strong was the feeling in the state that a formal ceremony was held on the steps of the state house, during which a copy of the initial bill was formally burned. The fraud became known as the Yazoo affair.

However, as quick as Georgia's efforts to undo the fraudulent deal had been, they did not come in time to prevent the sale of certain of the lands to presumably innocent third parties. It was over these titles that the legal and political battles took place. The land companies involved in the transactions did not consider the Rescinding Act to be valid, and they continued to sell the land. Most of the purchasers lived in the Middle Atlantic and New England states, and they were greatly concerned as to the validity of their purchases. To defend their purchases, the New England-Mississippi Company was formed to protect the rights of investors. The company sought an opinion from Secretary of the Treasury Alexander Hamilton concerning the legality of the land claims. Hamilton did not attempt to investigate the question of Georgia's title to the land but, in a pamphlet published in 1796, stated that if the titles were valid, the Rescinding Act was void and in his opinion, the courts would so rule. Armed with an opinion from one of the country's most distinguished public servants, the company continued to offer its lands to both prospective settlers and speculators.

Federal Government Proposal

At the same time that the New England-Mississippi Company was selling its lands, a proposal was made to the U.S. Congress, with the full backing of the Jefferson administration, that the United States should enter into an arrangement whereby Georgia would cede its claims to the lands in question to the federal government in return for compensation. In addition, the federal government would handle the claims to the area of the several Native American tribes and the Spanish government. This proposal became law. The report of the commissioners whom Jefferson appointed to study the problem proposed that five million acres of the lands be retained and the proceeds from their sale be used to indemnify the Yazoo land purchasers. Although the claims of the speculators, in the commissioners' opinion, could not be supported, they proposed the indemnity for them to ensure "the tranquility of those who may hereafter inhabit the territory," and argued that the federal government should enter into a compromise on reasonable terms.

The federal action caused a political fight of major proportions. When the commissioners' proposal reached the floor of the House of Representatives, it was attacked by a wildly indignant Congressman John Randolph, who was determined to defeat it by any means possible. Randolph's motives were partly ideological and partly emotional. He had been in Georgia when the Rescinding Act had been passed and had been present at the burning ceremony. He apparently believed that he understood the depths of the popular opposition to the grant in Georgia. He contended that Georgia had no initial right to make the sale, that the sale was firmly rooted in fraud and corruption so as to make it invalid, and that it was legally impossible to sell a third purchaser a better title.

Randolph was opposed in the House by Gideon Granger, the postmaster general, who was lobbying with his considerable ability in favor of the measure. After four days of intensive debate, Randolph's eloquence won and the measure was defeated. Afterward, supporters of the legislation brought up the measure annually for several years, only to be defeated each time. Eventually, the purchasers followed the implicit advice given earlier by Alexander Hamilton by seeking relief through the courts.

The "friendly" suit of *Fletcher v. Peck* originated in the sale made by John Peck of Massachusetts to Robert Fletcher of New Hampshire of fifteen thousand acres of Yazoo lands. It was Fletcher's intention to test the legality of his purchase. Because the litigants lived in different states, the case was heard in the federal courts. After Justice William Cushing of the Supreme Court, acting in his capacity as a circuit judge, found for Peck in October, 1807, the case was appealed to the Supreme Court.

Supreme Court justice William Johnson later said in a concurring opinion that the controversy had the appearance of a feigned case, but that his admiration for the attorneys involved in the case had induced him "to abandon [his] scruples, in the belief that they would never consent to impose a mere feigned case upon this Court." Luther Martin, Peck's attorney, contended that the several states were free, sovereign, and independent entities, and that "the sovereignty of each, not of the whole, was the principle of the Revolution." Consequently, Martin argued, the federal courts had no jurisdiction in the matter. John Quincy Adams, who was later replaced by Joseph Story, the future Supreme Court justice, based his own case on Hamilton's old opinion that the grant was a contract, and under Article I, section 10 of the U.S. Constitution, it could not be rescinded.

Justice William Cushing.
(Library of Congress)

Public Welfare vs. Public Confidence

The issue in *Fletcher v. Peck* was essentially a question of public welfare versus public confidence in the sanctity of land grants. To refuse to allow the states the authority to repeal the land grant, especially in the context of an obvious fraud, would undermine the public welfare and invite land speculators to corrupt state legislatures. At the same time, to give the state legislature the right to revoke the land grant would jeopardize public confidence in all public grants, and in turn would discourage investment and the exploitation of land.

"That corruption," John Marshall wrote at the beginning of his opinion in *Fletcher v. Peck*, "should find its way into the governments of our infant republics and contaminate the very source of legislation . . . [is a circumstance] deeply to be deplored." Despite this, the Rescinding Act of the Georgia legislature was still void.

Marshall did not clearly establish the reasons that the repeal of the land grant was constitutionally infirm. At one point in his opinion, he argued that the 1796 act of the Georgia legislature impaired the obligation of a contract in violation of Article I, section 10 of the Constitution; elsewhere, he suggested that the Georgia act was a violation of the ex post facto clause of the same article and section. "The rescinding act," he wrote, "would have the effect of an ex post facto decision. It forfeits the estate of Fletcher for a crime not committed by himself, but from those from who he purchased." This argument had the defect of ignoring the fact that the ex post facto clause had been held applicable only to criminal cases in *Calder v. Bull* in 1798, and the law in *Fletcher* dealt solely with a civil subject.

Elsewhere in the opinion, following one of the arguments of Alexander Hamilton, Marshall intimated that the Rescinding Act was invalid because it conflicted with the nature of society and government. At the conclusion of his opinion, Marshall said that "the state of Georgia was restrained by general principles which are common to our free institutions or by the particular provisions of the Constitution."

Significance

Despite the ambiguity and shortcomings of Marshall's opinion, *Fletcher v. Peck* was the first clear precedent for the assertion by the Supreme Court of a power to declare state laws unconstitutional. Its immediate practical effect was negligible; Georgia no longer owned the Yazoo lands, as they had been ceded to the federal government. However, *Fletcher* did lay the foundations for using the contract clause of the Constitution to protect private property interests against the vagaries of state legislatures. As such, it is a reflection of the overall strategy of the Marshall Court to facilitate investment and energize the U.S. economy.

Although the speculators had won in the Supreme Court, they were not to secure a congressional, or monetary, victory until 1814, when Congress, after John Randolph's failure to win reelection, passed an appropriation of five million dollars to buy up their now untarnished titles.

Gustav L. Seligman, updated by David L. Sterling

Further Reading

Beveridge, Albert J. *Conflict and Construction, 1800-1815.* Vol. 4 in *The Life of John Marshall.* Boston: Houghton Mifflin, 1919. This classic biography of Marshall devotes almost sixty pages to a discussion of *Fletcher v. Peck.*

Haines, Charles G. *The Role of the Supreme Court in American Government and Politics, 1789-1835.* Berkeley: University of California Press, 1944. A study of the Supreme Court in its formative period. Gives adequate coverage to *Fletcher v. Peck* and places it in the framework of the Court's development.

Hunting, Warren B. *The Obligation of Contracts Clause of the United States Constitution.* Baltimore: Johns Hopkins University Press, 1919. Contains a technical discussion of an important phase of U.S. constitutional history. Detailed coverage of *Fletcher v. Peck.*

Lewis, Thomas T., and Richard L. Wilson, eds. *Encyclopedia of the U.S. Supreme Court.* 3 vols. Pasadena, Calif.: Salem Press, 2001. Comprehensive reference work on the Supreme Court that contains substantial discussions of *Fletcher v. Peck,* contracts, John Marshall, Joseph Story, and many related subjects.

Newmyer, R. Kent. *John Marshall and the Heroic Age of the Supreme Court.* Baton Rouge: Louisiana State University Press, 2001. Examination of Chief Justice Marshall's legal philosophy, as it was expressed in his Court decisions, that places his beliefs in historical context.

_____. *Supreme Court Justice Joseph Story: Statesman of the Old Republic.* Chapel Hill: University of North Carolina Press, 1985. A comprehensive, analytical biography of Story, one of the lawyers in *Fletcher v. Peck* and a future associate of John Marshall.

White, G. Edward. *The Marshall Court and Cultural Change, 1815-1835.* Abridged ed. New York: Oxford University Press, 1991. Although abridged, this study of the record of the Marshall Court contains almost eight hundred pages of text and almost eighty pages on the contract clause cases.

Wright, Benjamin F., Jr. *The Contract Clause of the Constitution.* Cambridge, Mass.: Harvard University Press, 1938. A more detailed study of the contract clause than Hunting's and broader in scope.

See also *Budd v. New York; Calder v. Bull; Chicago, Milwaukee, and St. Paul Railway Co. v. Minnesota; Hayburn's Case; Hylton v. United States; Marbury v. Madison; Stuart v. Laird; Yakus v. United States.*

FLORIDA V. BOSTICK

Court: U.S. Supreme Court
Citation: 501 U.S. 429
Date: June 18, 1991
Issues: Search and seizure

- The U.S. Supreme Court held that the Fourth Amendment allows the controversial police practice of randomly approaching individuals in public places and asking them for permission to search their belongings, as long as the request is not coercive in nature.

It is an elementary principle of law that persons may waive their constitutional rights. In *Schneckloth v. Bustamonte* (1973), the Court held that, when a suspect is not in custody, the evidence obtained in a consensual search may be used in a criminal trial even when the suspect did not know that he could refuse to agree to the search. Encouraged by this ruling, some police officers routinely boarded buses or trains and asked individual passengers for permission to search their luggage. Using this technique, two officers found cocaine in a bag belonging to Terrance Bostick. The police claimed that they advised Bostick of his right to refuse the search, but he denied that he gave his permission. After the trial court denied Bostick's motion to suppress the evidence, the Florida supreme court held that Bostick had been unconstitutionally seized because a "reasonable person" would not have felt free to leave the bus to avoid police questioning.

By a 6-3 vote, the Supreme Court reversed the judgment. Justice Sandra Day O'Connor's majority opinion quoted earlier decisions holding that the police did not need reasonable suspicion in order to ask questions of a person in a public place and that such questioning did not constitute a seizure. Because there were many circumstances preventing Bostick from leaving the bus, O'Connor concluded that the legal issue was not whether a reasonable person would have felt free to leave but rather whether a reasonable person would have felt free to refuse to submit to the search. The "reasonable person test," moreover, presupposes "an innocent person." Thus, the Court remanded the case to the state courts for a reexamination of "all the circumstances" of the search in order to decide whether Bostick had given his consent voluntarily.

Expanding upon *Bostick* in *Ohio v. Robinette* (1996), the Court ruled that the police are not required to inform motorists who are stopped for other reasons that they are "free to go" before their consent will be recognized as voluntary.

Thomas Tandy Lewis

See also *California v. Acevedo; California v. Greenwood; Carroll v. United States; Chimel v. California; Knowles v. Iowa; New York v. Belton.*

===

FORD V. WAINWRIGHT

Court: U.S. Supreme Court
Citation: 477 U.S. 399
Date: June 26, 1986
Issues: Capital punishment; Medical ethics

• This case forced the criminal justice system to examine controversies surrounding mental illness and the death penalty, in particular what types of mental conditions should spare condemned prisoners from execution.

On July 19, 1974, Alvin Bernard Ford was convicted of first-degree murder after shooting a Fort Lauderdale police officer in a robbery attempt. Ford was sentenced to death by electric chair in the Florida court system. During his trial and sentencing, Ford appeared to be mentally competent. After his first year of prison, Ford received only one disciplinary report for his behavior. In 1982, his mental condition gradually began to decline, and he started having delusions. For example, Ford thought that his family was being held hostage at the prison and that the Ku Klux Klan had made him a target of conspiracy. Ford's communication skills deteriorated; his writing and speaking became incoherent.

Florida law stipulated that if the governor is informed that a death row inmate may be insane, a commission of psychiatrists must be appointed to examine the person. The examiners must determine whether the person understands the consequences of the death penalty and why it is being imposed. After a thirty-minute interview, two of the three psychiatrists diagnosed Ford as psychotic, yet all three determined that Ford was competent enough to be executed. Relevant testimony of two psychiatrists who had worked with Ford over time, however, was not included in the fact-finding process. They concluded that Ford was severely psychotic and not competent to be executed. No opportunity was given to other knowledgeable experts to dispute the findings of the state-appointed commission. Based on the commission's results, the governor found Ford to be competent and issued a death warrant for his execution.

Florida's Eleventh Circuit Court of Appeals stayed the execution to hear the issues. The court decided against Ford. The U.S. Supreme Court agreed to hear Ford's appeal. In a 5-4 decision, the Supreme Court overturned the decision of the Florida court and ordered that the case be remanded to federal district court for a full hearing. Justice Thurgood Marshall wrote the majority opinion of the Supreme Court. He concluded that the Eighth Amendment prohibits the states from imposing the death penalty on prisoners who are insane. The court found that Florida's process of evaluating condemned prisoners did not provide adequately for deciding whether Ford was competent to be executed.

Before the federal district court could determine Ford's competency, Alvin Ford died in prison. His death left issues unresolved, such as how competency is defined, what should be done in cases where the inmate wavers between stages of competency and incompetence, whether medication should be used to restore an inmate's mental health before execution, and whether mentally retarded inmates are competent for execution.

Michelle R. Royle

See also *Atkins v. Virginia; McCleskey v. Kemp; Penry v. Lynaugh.*

44 LIQUORMART, INC. V. RHODE ISLAND

Court: U.S. Supreme Court
Citation: 517 U.S. 484
Date: May 13, 1996
Issues: Freedom of speech; Regulation of business

- Rhode Island's efforts to ban all liquor-price advertising was held to be an unconstitutional abridgment of commercial speech.

In 1956 the state of Rhode Island enacted legislation that generally prohibited liquor stores licensed in the state and out-of-state manufacturers from advertising the prices of any alcoholic products that they sold within Rhode Island. The legislation also prohibited Rhode Island media from publishing or broadcasting any advertisements mentioning prices of any alcoholic beverages. In addition, a regulation of the Rhode Island liquor control administrator provided that no placard or sign visible from the exterior of a package store could make any reference to the price of any alcoholic beverage.

On May 13, 1996, the U.S. Supreme Court, in a seminal decision broadening constitutional protections of commercial speech, struck down the statutes and regulations. Although unable to agree on an opinion as to the proper standard for determining the validity of the liquor-price advertising ban, the members of the Court unanimously agreed that the statutes and the implementing regulations abridged speech in ways that violated the First Amendment.

Six justices held that the Twenty-first Amendment did not qualify the First Amendment's prohibition against laws abridging freedom of speech. Five justices held that Rhode Island had failed to carry the heavy burden of justifying, for First Amendment purposes, the complete ban on liquor-price advertising. Four justices expressed the view that regulations that entirely suppress commercial speech in order to pursue a policy not related to consumer protection must be reviewed with "special care," and that such blanket bans should not be approved unless the speech itself is deceptive or related to unlawful activity.

The justices also said that where a state entirely prohibits the dissemination of truthful, nonmisleading commercial messages for reasons related to the preservation of fair bargaining process, there is little reason to depart from the rigorous review that the First Amendment generally demands. Moreover, Rhode Island's advertising ban could not survive the applicable "special care" review standard, as it did not directly advance the state's substantial interest in promoting temperance, and it was more extensive than necessary to serve that interest. Finally, the Court ruled that various arguments in support of Rhode Island's claim that it had merely exercised appropriate "legislative judgment" in determining that a price advertising ban would best promote temperance would have to be rejected.

Stephen F. Rohde

See also *Bates v. State Bar of Arizona; Bigelow v. Virginia.*

FRANK V. MANGUM

Court: U.S. Supreme Court
Citation: 237 U.S. 309
Date: April 19, 1915
Issues: Due process of law; Habeas corpus; Trial by jury

- The U.S. Supreme Court refused federal relief for a defendant convicted of murder in state court under conditions of mob intimidation.

When Leo Frank, a Jewish capitalist, was tried in Georgia for the murder of a young woman, a large anti-Semitic mob intimidated the jury as it reached a guilty verdict. Almost all observers agreed that the trial did not conform to the due process requirements of the Fourteenth Amendment. Based on traditional notions of federalism, nevertheless, the federal district court rejected Frank's petition for a writ of habeas corpus. Speaking for the 7-2 majority, Justice Mahlon Pitney upheld and defended the lower court's hesitancy to intervene in a state criminal proceeding. Several years later, the Court in *Moore v. Dempsey* (1923) agreed to grant habeas corpus relief for defendants convicted in a similar mob-dominated trial. Justice Oliver Wendell Holmes dissented in *Frank* and wrote the majority opinion in *Moore*.

Thomas Tandy Lewis

See also *Arizona v. Fulminante; Brecht v. Abrahamson; Hoyt v. Florida; McCleskey v. Zant; Moore v. Dempsey; Stone v. Powell.*

FREEDMAN V. MARYLAND

Court: U.S. Supreme Court
Citation: 380 U.S. 51
Date: March 1, 1965
Issues: Censorship; Pornography and obscenity

• This U.S. Supreme Court decision established procedural safeguards that government must observe before it can bar exhibitions of films that it deems to be obscene.

In an effort to combat obscenity, the state of Maryland enacted legislation in the 1950's providing that no film could be publicly exhibited unless the State Board of Censors gave its approval. A film exhibitor named Ronald Freedman refused to submit his film *Revenge at Daybreak* to the board prior to exhibition—even though the film was not obscene—because of his objections to the censorship process. After being convicted of violating the Maryland statute, Freedman appealed his conviction on the ground that the statute requiring prior approval by the state before showing a film constituted a form of prior restraint that violated the First Amendment to the U.S. Constitution.

Four years earlier the U.S. Supreme Court had upheld, in a 5-4 decision, a Chicago municipal code provision requiring the submission of motion pictures to a censorship board in advance of exhibition in *Times Film Corporation v. Chicago* (1961). The petitioner in that case had argued that *any* prior restraint on the exhibition of a film was unconstitutional. The Court rejected that argument but did not address the issue of whether such a censorship system must comply with certain safeguards in order to pass constitutional muster.

In his own appeal to the Supreme Court, Freedman addressed the issue left unresolved in the *Times Film Corp.* case. He argued that Maryland's statute did not afford sufficient procedural safeguards to film exhibitors whose films were rejected by the board of censors. The Court unanimously agreed, holding that a state could require its board of censors to approve films prior to their exhibition only if the process observed certain procedural safeguards. The Court specified that a board of censors could not bar a film's exhibition without first securing a judicial order emanating from an adversary proceeding at which the board has borne the burden of establishing that the film is obscene. Because Maryland's law did not satisfy this criterion, the Court struck it down as an invalid prior restraint.

In several decisions following the Freedman case, the Supreme Court imposed procedural safeguards on censorship of other forms of communications. The Court has, for example, imposed procedural requirements in cases involving censorship of mail, parades, and distribution of flyers and leaflets. The Freedman decision led to the demise of municipal and state censor boards. In its place, the film industry adopted a rating system designating sexually explicit films X so that minors are not admitted to view them.

Davison M. Douglas

See also *Burstyn v. Wilson; Erznoznik v. Jacksonville; Miller v. California; Mutual Film Corp. v. Industrial Commission of Ohio; Times Film Corp. v. City of Chicago.*

FRONTIERO V. RICHARDSON

Court: U.S. Supreme Court
Citation: 411 U.S. 677
Date: May 14, 1973
Issues: Equal protection of the law; Military law; Sex discrimination; Women's issues

• In this case, the U.S. Supreme Court held that a female member of the armed services who was not entitled to the same dependent benefits as a male had been unconstitutionally discriminated against.

Under federal law, a male member of the armed services could automatically claim his spouse as a dependent and thus receive greater housing and medical benefits. A female member of the armed services, however, could only obtain such benefits if she demonstrated that her spouse was in fact dependent on her for more than half his support. After a servicewoman was denied benefits for failure to make the requisite showing concerning her spouse, she instituted a suit in federal court claiming that the law violated the equal protection component of the Fifth Amendment's due process clause. Although a majority of the Supreme Court could not agree on the precise standard by which to judge this claim, eight members of the Court agreed that the federal law at issue violated the Constitution.

Justice William J. Brennan wrote for four members of the Court and argued that legislative classifications based on gender are inherently suspect and should be accorded the same stringent review given laws that discriminate on the basis of race. Like race, Justice Brennan suggested, gender is an immutable characteristic. To disqualify an individual from some benefit purely on the basis of gender was, he claimed, inconsistent with the principles of justice that normally require legal burdens to bear some relation to individual responsibility. He concluded that the federal government could not justify its discrimination in this case and that the law therefore violated the equal protection requirements.

In a separate opinion representing the views of three justices, Justice Lewis

Powell thought the case could be resolved without deciding upon a particular standard of review for all sex-discrimination cases. He thought it best to declare the law unconstitutional without attempting to elaborate a general constitutional doctrine concerning gender discrimination. Since the proposed Equal Rights Amendment was still being debated by the states, he believed that it would be premature for the Court to venture far in this area until the people of the United States had themselves deliberated the matter of sex discrimination. A single member of the court, Justice William Rehnquist, dissented without writing an opinion.

In the years following this case, the Court ultimately agreed that gender discriminations should be accorded some special review, though not so stringent a scrutiny as the Court had applied to instances of racial discrimination. *Frontiero* was important because, along with the Court's decision in *Reed v. Reed* (1971) two years earlier, it demonstrated that gender discriminations based on outmoded stereotypes would no longer be viewed with benevolence by the Court.

Timothy L. Hall

See also *Personnel Administrator of Massachusetts v. Feeney; Reed v. Reed; Rostker v. Goldberg; United States v. Virginia.*

FROTHINGHAM V. MELLON

Court: U.S. Supreme Court
Citation: 262 U.S. 447
Date: June 4, 1923
Issues: Standing; Taxation

- The U.S. Supreme Court held that payment of taxes does not establish the standing to sue necessary to challenge the constitutionality of congressional spending statutes.

Harriet Frothingham filed suit as a federal taxpayer to prevent the secretary of the treasury from spending money under the Maternity Act of 1921, which provided grants to the states for programs designed to reduce maternal and infant mortality. She alleged that the statute violated the Tenth Amendment and that it also deprived taxpayers of property without due process of law.

By a 9-0 vote, the Supreme Court ruled that the suit was not a legitimate judicial controversy because Frothingham lacked standing to sue. Justice George Sutherland reasoned that the plaintiff in the case would have to show an immediate and direct personal injury from the enforcement of the statute and not merely a remote and uncertain interest shared with all taxpayers. Sutherland wrote that a taxpayer of a municipality would have the necessary standing to sue, but he did not mention possible taxpayer challenges to spending by the states. The Court substantially modified the rule against federal taxpayer standing in *Flast v. Cohen* (1968).

Thomas Tandy Lewis

See also *Flast v. Cohen*; *Massachusetts v. Mellon*; *United States v. Richardson*.

FULLILOVE V. KLUTZNICK

Court: U.S. Supreme Court
Citation: 448 U.S. 448
Date: July 2, 1980
Issues: Affirmative action

• The U.S. Supreme Court upheld a federal public works program that required a 10 percent set-aside of federal funds for minority-controlled businesses.

The Public Works Employment Act of 1977 was the first federal statute to include an explicitly race-conscious classification since the Freedman's Bureau Act of 1877. Nonminority contractors challenged the act as a violation of the equal protection component of the Fifth Amendment's due process clause.

The six justices voting to uphold the statute were divided into two plurality opinions, each supported by three justices. In one opinion, Chief Justice Warren E. Burger deferred to the special powers of Congress under the spending and commerce clauses as well as the enforcement clause of the Fourteenth Amendment. Applying the strict scrutiny test, moreover, Burger concluded that the set-asides were an appropriate means for the Congress to pursue its compelling interest "in redressing the discrimination that affects minority contractors." In the other plurality opinion, Justice William J. Brennan, Jr., insisted that whites as a class did not suffer from historical discrimination, and therefore, he argued that all affirmative action programs should be judged according to the standard of intermediate scrutiny.

The *Fullilove* decision encouraged the passage of numerous set-aside programs at the federal, state, and local levels. The Court, however, put stringent limits on such programs in *Richmond v. J. A. Croson Co.* (1989) and *Adarand Constructors v. Peña* (1995), holding that all racial classifications must be reviewed according to the strict scrutiny test.

Thomas Tandy Lewis

See also *Adarand Constructors v. Peña; Bolling v. Sharpe; Regents of the University of California v. Bakke; Richmond v. J. A. Croson Co.; United Steelworkers of America v. Weber.*

FURMAN V. GEORGIA

Court: U.S. Supreme Court
Citation: 408 U.S. 238
Date: June 29, 1972
Issues: Capital punishment; Cruel and unusual punishment

• In *Furman v. Georgia*, the U.S. Supreme Court decided that the death penalty as applied in 1972 constituted cruel and unusual punishment in violation of the U.S. Constitution.

Since ancient times and the injunction of "an eye for an eye," capital punishment has been an accepted practice. In the United States, there have been periods when efforts to abolish capital punishment have had some influence, balanced by periods during which the trend was to sanction its use. From the end of the eighteenth century until the U.S. Civil War (1861-1865), opponents of capital punishment worked to reduce the number of crimes punishable by death. With the Civil War came a period of acceptance of capital punishment. Another movement in the early twentieth century to abolish the death penalty ended with the beginning of World War I. After 1920, however, there was a gradual decline in the United States in interest in and use of the death penalty. In 1930, 155 persons were executed. In 1960, the death penalty was used only 56 times.

Around this time, in 1959, the American Law Institute (ALI), an organization of legal scholars that was little known to the public but widely respected among lawyers, recommended that if the death penalty were to be retained, there should be changes in the statutes allowing its use. The ALI recommended that when there was the possibility of the death penalty, the defendant should have a bifurcated trial: one trial to establish innocence or guilt and another trial to determine the penalty if guilty. The reason for this was to allow the defendant a chance to testify at the penalty phase while still retaining a constitutional right not to speak during the first trial. In addition, the ALI suggested that the death penalty could not be imposed unless the jury found that aggravating circumstances were present and mitigating circumstances were absent. The reason for this recommendation was to provide some guidelines for jurors when they imposed the death penalty.

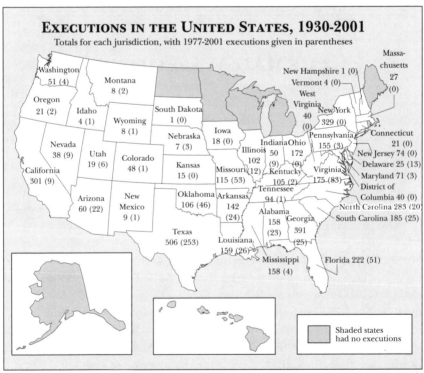

EXECUTIONS IN THE UNITED STATES, 1930-2001
Totals for each jurisdiction, with 1977-2001 executions given in parentheses

Washington 51 (4)
Montana 8 (2)
Oregon 21 (2)
Idaho 4 (1)
Wyoming 8 (1)
South Dakota 1 (0)
Nevada 38 (9)
Utah 19 (6)
Colorado 48 (1)
Nebraska 7 (3)
California 301 (9)
Arizona 60 (22)
New Mexico 9 (1)
Kansas 15 (0)
Texas 506 (253)
Iowa 18 (0)
Illinois 102
Missouri (12) 115 (53)
Oklahoma 106 (46)
Arkansas 142 (24)
Louisiana 159 (26)
Indiana 50 (9)
Ohio 172 (0)
Kentucky 105 (2)
Tennessee
Alabama 158 (23)
Mississippi 158 (4)
Georgia 391 (25)
New Hampshire 1 (0)
Vermont 4 (0)
West Virginia 40
New York 329 (0)
Pennsylvania 155 (3)
Virginia 175 (83)
Florida 222 (51)
Massachusetts 27 (0)
Connecticut 21 (0)
New Jersey 74 (0)
Delaware 25 (13)
Maryland 71 (3)
District of Columbia 40 (0)
North Carolina 283 (20)
South Carolina 185 (25)

Shaded states had no executions

Note: There were 4,291 total executions, 1930-1997, including 33 prisoners executed in the federal system. The total for 1977-1997 of 432 prisoners executed includes no federal executions.

Source: U.S. Department of Justice, Bureau of Justice Statistics, *Capital Punishment 1997* (December, 1998); *Understanding Constitutional Issues: Selections from the CQ Researcher* (Washington, D.C.: CQ Press, 2004).

Constitutionality of the Death Penalty

In 1963, in a case involving a rapist sentenced to death, Justice Arthur J. Goldberg of the Supreme Court disagreed with the majority of justices, who confirmed the rapist's sentence. Goldberg stated that it was the Supreme Court's task to determine whether the death penalty was constitutional. Lawyers in the Legal Defense Fund (LDF), a branch of the National Association for the Advancement of Colored People (NAACP), were encouraged by this statement. Fresh from battles to enforce desegregation, LDF lawyers saw that the death penalty, particularly as it was applied to black men convicted of raping white women, was an area in which they wanted to become involved. By 1967, the LDF had decided to undertake the representation of all inmates on death row. The organization brought several class-action suits on behalf of these inmates. From that date until after the *Furman* decision in 1972, there was a moratorium on all executions. In the cases brought by the LDF, the attorneys were determined that the Supreme Court eventually would have to answer the question that Goldberg had asked: Is the death penalty constitutional?

Regarding these cases, one commentator has said that the LDF lost every battle except the first and the last. The first battle came in *Witherspoon v. Illinois* in 1968. At issue in this case was whether a potential juror who expressed misgivings about the death penalty could be dismissed automatically from jury duty in a capital case. This was the common practice at the time, and the Supreme Court ruled that such a practice was improper. A number of death row inmates were thus entitled to new trials.

This case was the only success for several years. Anthony Amsterdam, a professor at the University of Pennsylvania Law School and later a professor at Stanford Law School, was the key strategist for the LDF in arguing the cases. Several times before *Furman*, Amsterdam argued in the Supreme Court that juries should have standards, such as aggravating or mitigating circumstances, before them when imposing the death penalty, just as the ALI had recommended. Amsterdam also argued for a bifurcated jury, again as the ALI had suggested. The Supreme Court rejected both arguments in 1971 in *McGautha v. California*. Following this defeat, the LDF's only remaining theory with which to challenge the death penalty was to declare that it was cruel and unusual punishment, which is prohibited by the Eighth Amendment to the U.S. Constitution. On June 28, 1971, the Supreme Court announced that it would answer this challenge to the death penalty in the case of *Furman v. Georgia*.

Furman v. Georgia consisted of four cases involving four African American defendants, all of whom had been sentenced to death. Two of the defendants were murderers and two were rapists. All of the victims were white. The man who gave his name to the case, William Henry Furman, had entered his victim's home to commit burglary. When his victim discovered him, Furman tried to run away. In the process, Furman's gun accidentally discharged, killing the victim. Although Furman was found competent to stand trial, it was discovered after the shooting that he was mentally subnormal and subject to psychotic episodes. Nevertheless, he was convicted and sentenced to death. The fate of more than six hundred death row prisoners depended on how the Supreme Court would decide his case.

Cruel and Unusual Punishment

Several times in the twentieth century, the Court had decided that a punishment meted out to a convicted criminal was cruel and unusual. In the most important case, *Trop v. Dulles* (1958), the Court decided that loss of citizenship for a defendant who had deserted the armed forces during war was cruel and unusual punishment. The Court stated that the Eighth Amendment prohibiting cruel and unusual punishment takes its meaning "from evolving standards of decency that mark the progress of a maturing society." Implicit in this statement was the sense that the meaning of cruel and unusual punishment could change over time. The justices in *Furman* were to decide if the "standards of decency" in 1972 had evolved to the point that capital punishment must be abolished.

Anthony Amsterdam argued on behalf of Furman before the Supreme Court in January, 1971. Before the Supreme Court delivered its opinion in June, 1972, the California Supreme Court decided in another case that Amsterdam had argued that the death penalty in California was unconstitutional. Tension mounted concerning what the U.S. Supreme Court would decide in *Furman.*

On June 29, 1972, a 5-4 majority of the justices found that as it was currently applied, the death penalty constituted cruel and unusual punishment in violation of the Constitution. Each of the nine justices wrote a separate opinion. Two of the justices in the majority, William J. Brennan and Thurgood Marshall, declared that the death penalty was unconstitutional under any circumstance. Justices William O. Douglas, Potter Stewart, and Byron White stated that the death penalty was cruel and unusual punishment because it was arbitrary and capricious in the way it was currently imposed. Some of the dissenters, although personally opposed to the death penalty, stated that it was not up to the Court but to state legislatures to decide the question. Thus, by the narrowest of margins, the Supreme Court in 1972 decided that the death penalty was not constitutional and allowed more than six hundred prisoners to leave death row.

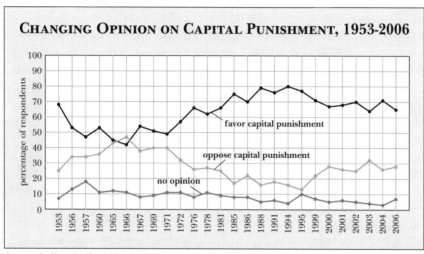

Changing Opinion on Capital Punishment, 1953-2006

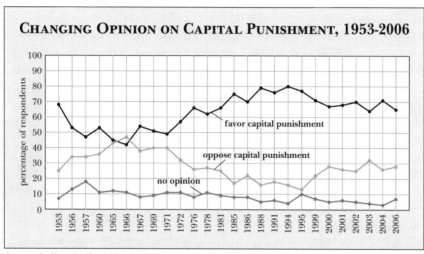

Source: Gallup Polls, 2004. Polls were not taken in all years. In years in which more than one poll was taken, data are entered from the latest polls. Data for 2006 are from a nationwide USA Today/Gallup Poll taken in May, 2006.

Significance

Although the United States briefly joined the rest of the Western world when it abolished capital punishment in *Furman v. Georgia* in 1972, there were indications in the decision that under certain circumstances the death penalty might be constitutional. One immediate reaction to the decision was that states started rewriting their death penalty statutes. Two years after *Furman*, twenty-eight states had new statutes. By 1976, thirty-five states had rewritten their death penalty laws. By that time, there were 450 inmates on death row.

In 1976, the Supreme Court agreed to hear the case of *Gregg v. Georgia* in order to decide whether one of these new statutes was constitutional. The defendant had been convicted of murder and sentenced to death under a new statute. This statute required a bifurcated jury, with separate trials to determine guilt and punishment. It also required that the jury find aggravating circumstances to condemn and consider mitigating circumstances to reprieve, and that there be an automatic appeal of any death sentence imposed, to the highest court in the state. The Supreme Court found that this statute was constitutional, and capital punishment was thus reinstated. In 1977, Gary Gilmore became the first man to be executed since the moratorium on executions was established in 1967.

Since that time, there have been continuing challenges to various aspects of the death penalty. In 1977, the Supreme Court decided that the death penalty was a disproportionate punishment for the crime of rape. In 1987, the Court decided that studies showing that blacks received the death penalty more frequently than whites did not necessarily mean that any racial bias was involved, so the death penalty was not unconstitutional on grounds of discrimination. In 1989, the Court upheld the imposition of the death penalty for a convicted murderer who was mildly to moderately retarded as well as deciding that the death penalty could be imposed on those who were minors at the time of their crime. In June, 1991, the Court decided that victim impact statements are permissible at the sentencing of the defendant. The euphoria that accompanied the *Furman* decision had long since abated. By the early years of the twenty-first century, there were no indications that the Supreme Court was moving toward ruling against the death penalty.

Jennifer Eastman

Further Reading

Banner, Stuart. *The Death Penalty: An American History.* Cambridge, Mass.: Harvard University Press, 2002. Presents a well-researched, comprehensive examination of the history of the death penalty in the United States.

Bedau, Hugo Adam. *The Courts, the Constitution, and Capital Punishment.* Lexington, Mass.: Lexington Books, 1977. Provides clear analysis of the cases appearing before the Supreme Court in the period surrounding the *Furman* decision. Gives all possible constitutional theories against the death penalty and how they have been used, successfully or not. The author is an ardent abolitionist but presents balanced, well-reasoned arguments both for and against the death penalty.

Bedau, Hugo Adam, and Chester M. Pierce, eds. *Capital Punishment in the United States.* New York: AMS Press, 1975. Comprehensive survey of capital punishment after the *Furman* decision. These essays were collected because the *Furman* decision left open the constitutionality of the death penalty. The aim was to get as many social scientists as possible to comment on it, particularly concerning its deterrent effects. Includes bibliography and index.

Berger, Raoul. *Death Penalties: The Supreme Court's Obstacle Course.* 1982. Reprint. Bridgewater, N.J.: Replica Books, 2000. Scholarly work argues that the Court exceeded its proper boundaries in deciding *Furman.* Posits that the cruel and unusual punishment clause should be interpreted as it was when the Constitution was written.

Friendly, Fred W., and Martha J. H. Elliott. "Willie Francis's Two Trips to the Chair: Punishment and the Death Penalty." In *The Constitution: That Delicate Balance.* New York: Random House, 1984. Presents a moving account of one of the times before the *Furman* decision when the Supreme Court considered the death penalty as cruel and unusual punishment. Francis did not die the first time he was electrocuted, and the Court ruled that it was not cruel and unusual punishment to electrocute him a second time. Francis was so worn down by the appeals process that he acquiesced to the second try and died.

Herda, D. J. *Furman v. Georgia: The Death Penalty Case.* Berkeley Heights, N.J.: Enslow, 1994. Designed for young-adult readers, this volume examines the issues leading up to the *Furman* case, people involved in the case, the legal development of the case, and the historical impact of the ruling. Includes chapter notes, further reading list, and index.

Latzer, Barry. *Death Penalty Cases: Leading U.S. Supreme Court Cases on Capital Punishment.* 2d ed. Burlington, Mass.: Butterworth-Heinemann, 2002. Contains excerpts from twenty-five court cases, including *Furman v. Georgia.* Designed as an introductory text.

_____. *Death Penalty in a Nutshell.* St. Paul, Minn.: Thomson/West, 2005. A clearly written overview of death penalty arguments and cases. Discusses special topics such as race and gender bias and execution of the innocent.

Meltser, Michael. *Cruel and Unusual: The Supreme Court and Capital Punishment.* New York: Random House, 1973. Provides complete coverage of the cases, individuals, legal issues, and social trends that led to *Furman.* Good analysis of cases preceding Furman and of the LDF's strategy.

Parrish, Michael E. *The Supreme Court and Capital Punishment: Judging Death.* Washington, D.C.: CQ Press, 2010. Comprehensive history of U.S. Supreme Court rulings on capital punishment issues. Particular attention is given to the role of race in death-penalty cases, the constitutionality of specific methods of execution, public opinion, and the execution of minors and mentally ill defendants.

Stefoff, Rebecca. *Furman v. Georgia: Debating the Death Penalty.* Tarrytown, N.Y.: Marshall Cavendish Benchmark, 2008. Part of its publisher's Supreme Court Milestones series designed for young-adult readers, this volume offers an accessible history and analysis of the *Furman* case that examines opposing sides in the case, the people involved, and the case's lasting impact. Includes bibliography and index.

See also *Gregg v. Georgia; Hudson v. Palmer; Louisiana ex rel. Francis v. Resweber; Rhodes v. Chapman; Rummel v. Estelle; Stanford v. Kentucky; Trop v. Dulles; Weems v. United States; Woodson v. North Carolina.*

GARCIA V. SAN ANTONIO METROPOLITAN TRANSIT AUTHORITY

Court: U.S. Supreme Court
Citation: 469 U.S. 528
Date: February 19, 1985
Issues: Congressional powers; Regulation of commerce

- Using the commerce clause, the U.S. Supreme Court removed almost all limitations on Congress's power to regulate the states.

In *Garcia*, the Supreme Court had to determine whether the hour and wage provisions of the Fair Labor Standards Act (1938) applied to a public transportation system owned and operated by the city of San Antonio. The Court's ruling in *National League of Cities v. Usery* (1976) established four tests that Congress had to meet before it could regulate states under the commerce clause. These tests were unclear, and nearly ten years later they remained unclear, although the Court had made numerous rulings. By a 5-4 vote, the Court reversed *Usery* and removed almost all limitations on congressional power to regulate the states.

Justice Harry A. Blackmun, in the opinion for the Court, opted to abandon the four tests and *Usery*. He argued that the states had representatives in Congress and that these members could be counted on to defend the states' interests, pointing out the special protection states received in the Senate where every state has two senators no matter how small. This controversial decision was accompanied by a number of dissents expressing the hope that *Garcia* would be overturned. Lewis F. Powell, Jr., asserted that representation in Congress is an inadequate defense for the states because members of Congress, though elected from the states, become members of the federal government when they enter Congress.

Richard L. Wilson

See also *Katzenbach v. McClung; National League of Cities v. Usery; United States v. Lopez; Wabash, St. Louis, and Pacific Railway Co. v. Illinois.*

GARRISON V. LOUISIANA

Court: U.S. Supreme Court
Citation: 379 U.S. 64
Date: November 23, 1964
Issues: Freedom of expression

• The U.S. Supreme Court made it clear that the government must show malice in order to obtain a constitutional criminal libel conviction.

Writing for the Supreme Court, Justice William J. Brennan, Jr., unanimously reversed the criminal libel conviction of Louisiana attorney general Jim Garrison, a critic of the theory that Lee Harvey Oswald acted alone in assassinating President John F. Kennedy. Garrison had criticized eight Louisiana judges who in turn won a criminal libel conviction against him. The Court held that such a conviction for criticism of elected officials would have required a showing of actual malice or a reckless disregard for the truth in order to have been valid. Justices Arthur J. Goldberg, Hugo L. Black, and William O. Douglas concurred.

Richard L. Wilson

See also *Gertz v. Robert Welch; Milkovich v. Lorain Journal Co.; New York Times Co. v. Sullivan; Time v. Hill.*

GAULT, IN RE. *See* IN RE GAULT

GEDULDIG V. AIELLO

Court: U.S. Supreme Court
Citation: 417 U.S. 484
Date: June 17, 1974
Issues: Equal protection of the law; Sex discrimination

• The U.S. Supreme Court upheld a California law denying disability benefits to pregnant women, but its ruling was later set aside by federal legislation.

Three state employees challenged California's disability benefits system, which denied medical benefits to pregnant women, charging that the plan violated the equal protection clause of the Fourteenth Amendment. Although the California law had been amended to include such benefits by the time the Supreme Court received the case, the Court held six to three that the plan was constitutional and did not discriminate against women because the benefit drew the line between women who were and were not pregnant. Justice William J. Brennan, Jr., dissented, arguing that policies based on differences in physical characteristics linked to sex did not provide equal protection. Congress passed the 1978 Pregnancy Discrimination Act to remedy the Court's decision.

Richard L. Wilson

See also *Automobile Workers v. Johnson Controls; Bowe v. Colgate-Palmolive; Frontiero v. Richardson; Hoyt v. Florida; Meritor Savings Bank v. Vinson; Phillips v. Martin Marietta Corp.; Stanton v. Stanton; Weeks v. Southern Bell.*

GELPCKE V. DUBUQUE

Court: U.S. Supreme Court
Citation: 68 U.S. 175
Date: January 11, 1864
Issues: Federalism

• The U.S. Supreme Court showed a lack of respect for state judiciaries in deciding that it would not be bound by state supreme court decisions.

Dubuque, Iowa, railroad promoters issued potentially questionable bonds exceeding the state's debt limit. Reformers on the new Iowa supreme court overturned earlier Iowa supreme court rulings that accepted the bond's validity. An 8-1 majority on the Supreme Court overturned the Iowa court and its own 1862 ruling that the Court should follow the state supreme court's most recent interpretation of the state constitution. The Court stated it could not be bound by the oscillations of state supreme courts. In dissent, Justice Samuel F. Miller argued that the state supreme court should be the final arbiter of its own state's constitution. In its lack of respect for state courts, the Court foreshadowed its later substantial due process interpretation.

Richard L. Wilson

See also *Ableman v. Booth; Dombrowski v. Pfister; Erie Railroad Co. v. Tompkins; Ex parte Young; Martin v. Hunter's Lessee; Swift v. Tyson; Younger v. Harris.*

GENERAL ELECTRIC V. GILBERT

Court: U.S. Supreme Court
Citation: 429 U.S. 125
Date: December 7, 1976
Issues: Reproductive rights; Women's issues

• This case found the U.S. Supreme Court allowing a company to treat pregnancy differently from other disabilities.

General Electric Company provided its employees with a disability plan that paid weekly nonoccupational sickness and accident benefits but excluded disabilities arising from pregnancy. The plan was challenged as a violation of Title VII of the Civil Rights Act of 1964, which prohibits discrimination in the workplace based on several factors, including sex.

Nevertheless, Justice William Rehnquist, in a 6-3 decision, upheld the plan, saying it was not gender-based discrimination because the selection of risks covered by the plan did not operate to discriminate against women. The plan was merely an insurance package that covered some risks but excluded others. It covered exactly the same categories of risk for both male and female employees, and there was no proof that the package was worth more to men than to women. Simply because it did not cover pregnancy disability did not mean that it was discriminatory. The plan did not have to be all-inclusive, and pregnancy related disabilities constituted an additional risk.

The impact of this case went even further than the initial decision. Two years later, Congress passed legislation requiring employers to treat pregnancy like any other physical condition. Thus, the dissenters in *General Electric v. Gilbert* were vindicated.

Robert W. Langran

See also *Automobile Workers v. Johnson Controls*; *Monell v. Department of Social Services*; *Phillips v. Martin Marietta Corp.*

GENESEE CHIEF V. FITZHUGH

Court: U.S. Supreme Court
Citation: 53 U.S. 443
Date: February 20, 1852
Issues: Admiralty law

- By upholding an 1845 federal law expanding internal navigation, the U.S. Supreme Court substantially increased federal control of inland waterways.

Chief Justice Roger Brooke Taney wrote the 8-1 majority opinion expanding federal admiralty authority over navigable inland freshwater rivers and lakes, thereby setting aside the earlier reliance on the British admiralty rule that the central government controlled only tidal waters. Taney found that a rule sufficient for an island was not adequate for a nation with the continental expanse of the United States. Specifically, the Supreme Court sustained an 1845 federal statute that sought to expand internal navigation in the new era of steam-powered boats. Justice Peter V. Daniel dissented, arguing that the English rule should govern because it was in effect at the time the Constitution was adopted, a view that would have restricted the development of commerce.

Richard L. Wilson

See also *Champion v. Ames*; *Cooley v. Board of Wardens of the Port of Philadelphia*; *Gibbons v. Ogden*; *New York v. Miln*.